Arata
THE LEGEND

14

We are Man, born of Heaven and Earth,
Moon and Sun and everything under them.

Eyes, Ears, Nose, Tongue, Body, Mind...

Purity will pierce evil and
open up the world of darkness.

All life will be reborn and invigorated.

Appear now.

STORY & ART BY
Yuu Watase

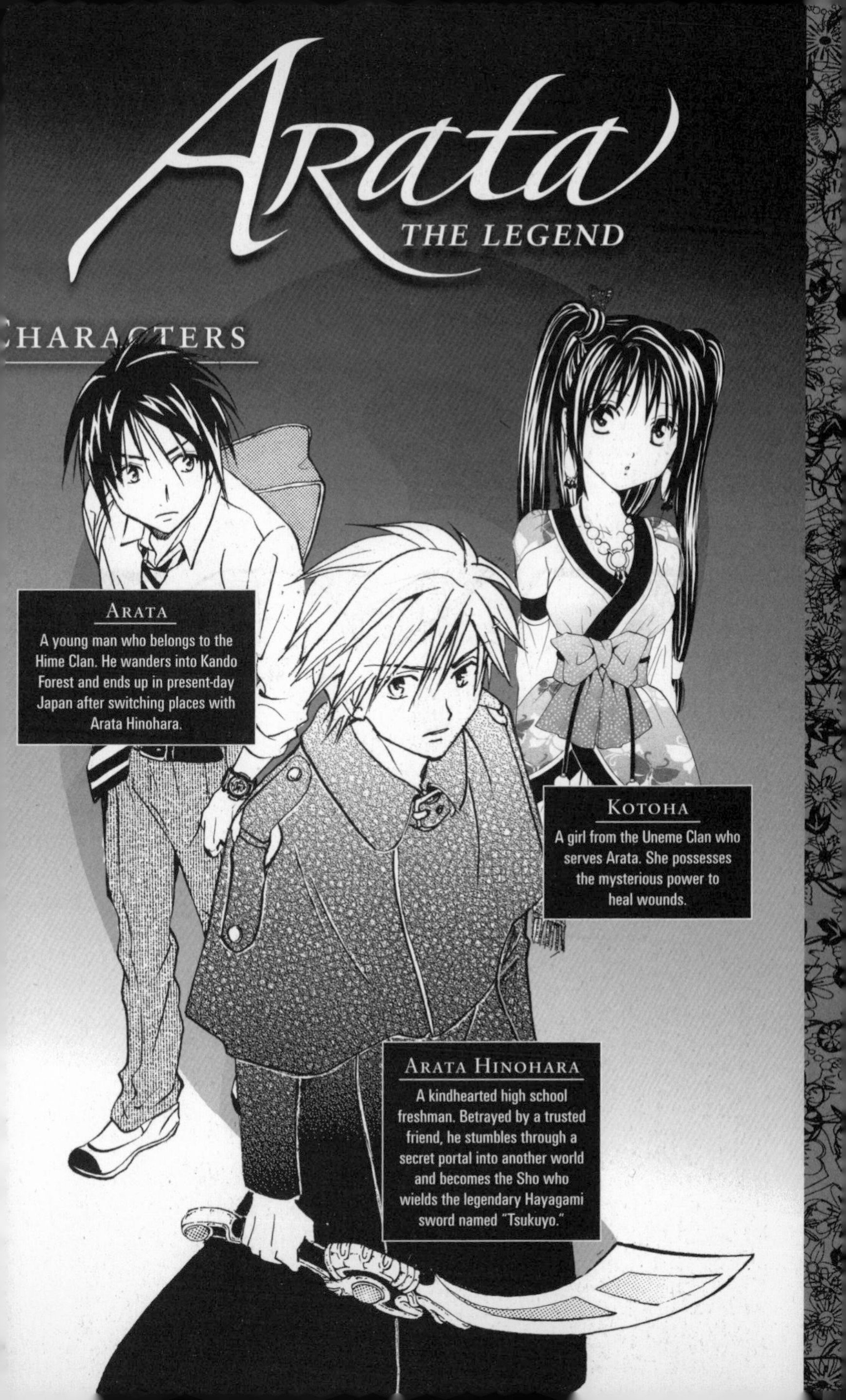
Arata
THE LEGEND
CHARACTERS
ARATA
A young man who belongs to the Hime Clan. He wanders into Kando Forest and ends up in present-day Japan after switching places with Arata Hinohara.
KOTOHA
A girl from the Uneme Clan who serves Arata. She possesses the mysterious power to heal wounds.
ARATA HINOHARA
A kindhearted high school freshman. Betrayed by a trusted friend, he stumbles through a secret portal into another world and becomes the Sho who wields the legendary Hayagami sword named "Tsukuyo."

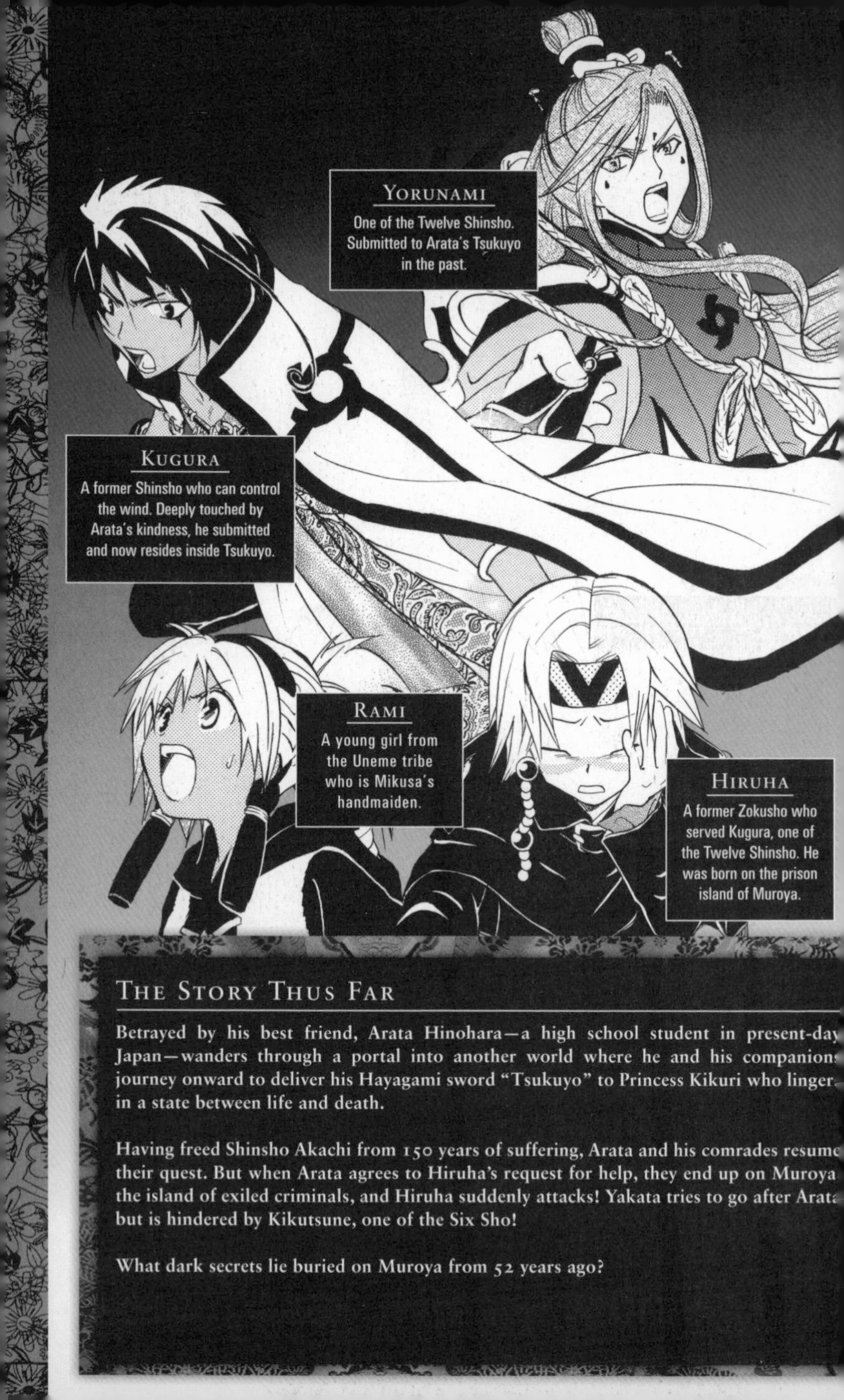
YORUNAMI
One of the Twelve Shinsho. Submitted to Arata's Tsukuyo in the past.
KUGURA
A former Shinsho who can control the wind. Deeply touched by Arata's kindness, he submitted and now resides inside Tsukuyo.
RAMI
A young girl from the Uneme tribe who is Mikusa's handmaiden.
HIRUHA
A former Zokusho who served Kugura, one of the Twelve Shinsho. He was born on the prison island of Muroya.

The Story Thus Far

Betrayed by his best friend, Arata Hinohara—a high school student in present-day Japan—wanders through a portal into another world where he and his companions journey onward to deliver his Hayagami sword "Tsukuyo" to Princess Kikuri who lingers in a state between life and death.

Having freed Shinsho Akachi from 150 years of suffering, Arata and his comrades resume their quest. But when Arata agrees to Hiruha's request for help, they end up on Muroya the island of exiled criminals, and Hiruha suddenly attacks! Yakata tries to go after Arata but is hindered by Kikutsune, one of the Six Sho!

What dark secrets lie buried on Muroya from 52 years ago?

14
Arata
THE LEGEND

CONTENTS

CHAPTER 128
THE INCIDENT OF 52 YEARS AGO

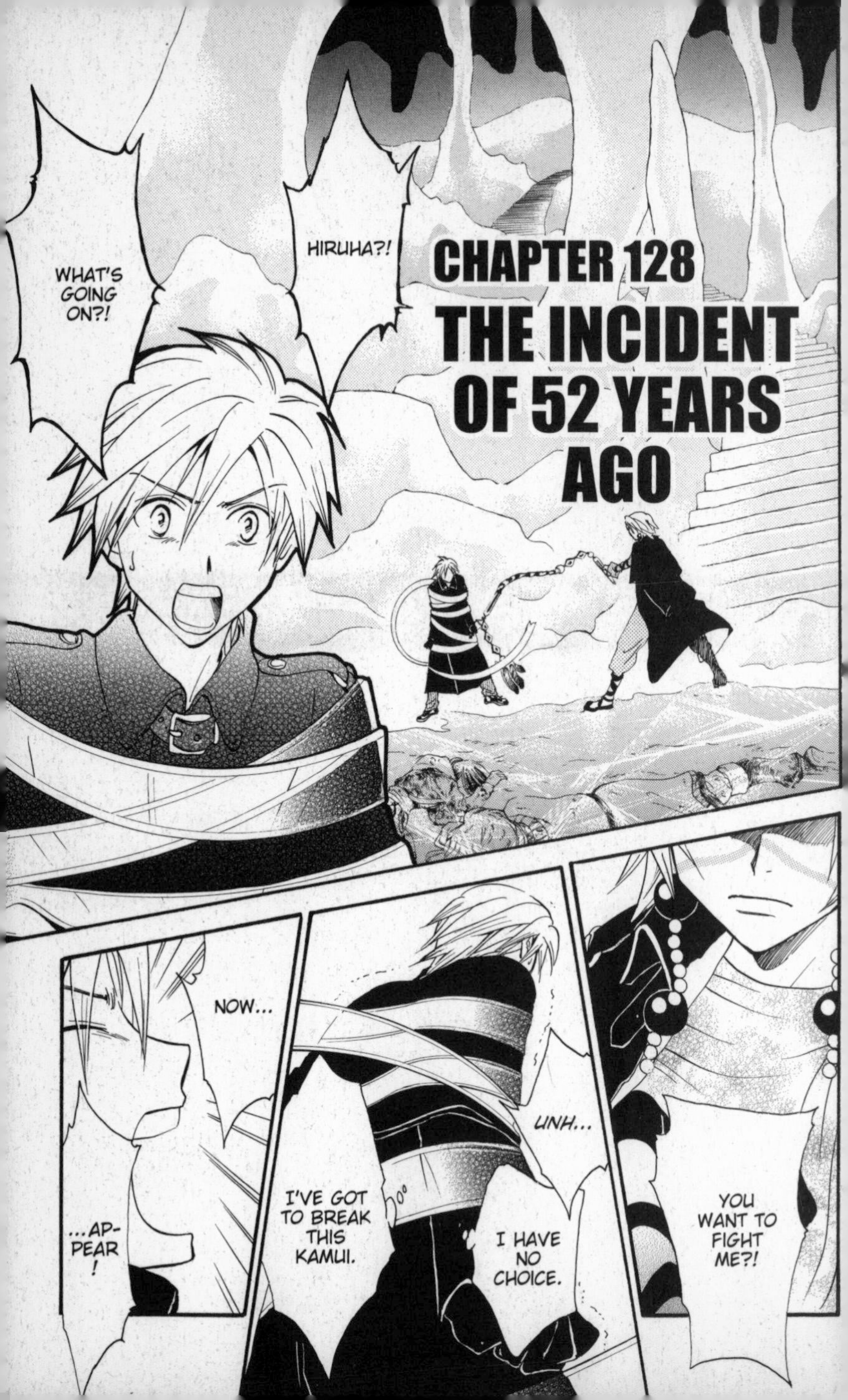
HIRUHA?!
WHAT'S GOING ON?!
YOU WANT TO FIGHT ME?!
UNH...
I HAVE NO CHOICE.
I'VE GOT TO BREAK THIS KAMUI.
NOW...
...AP-PEAR!

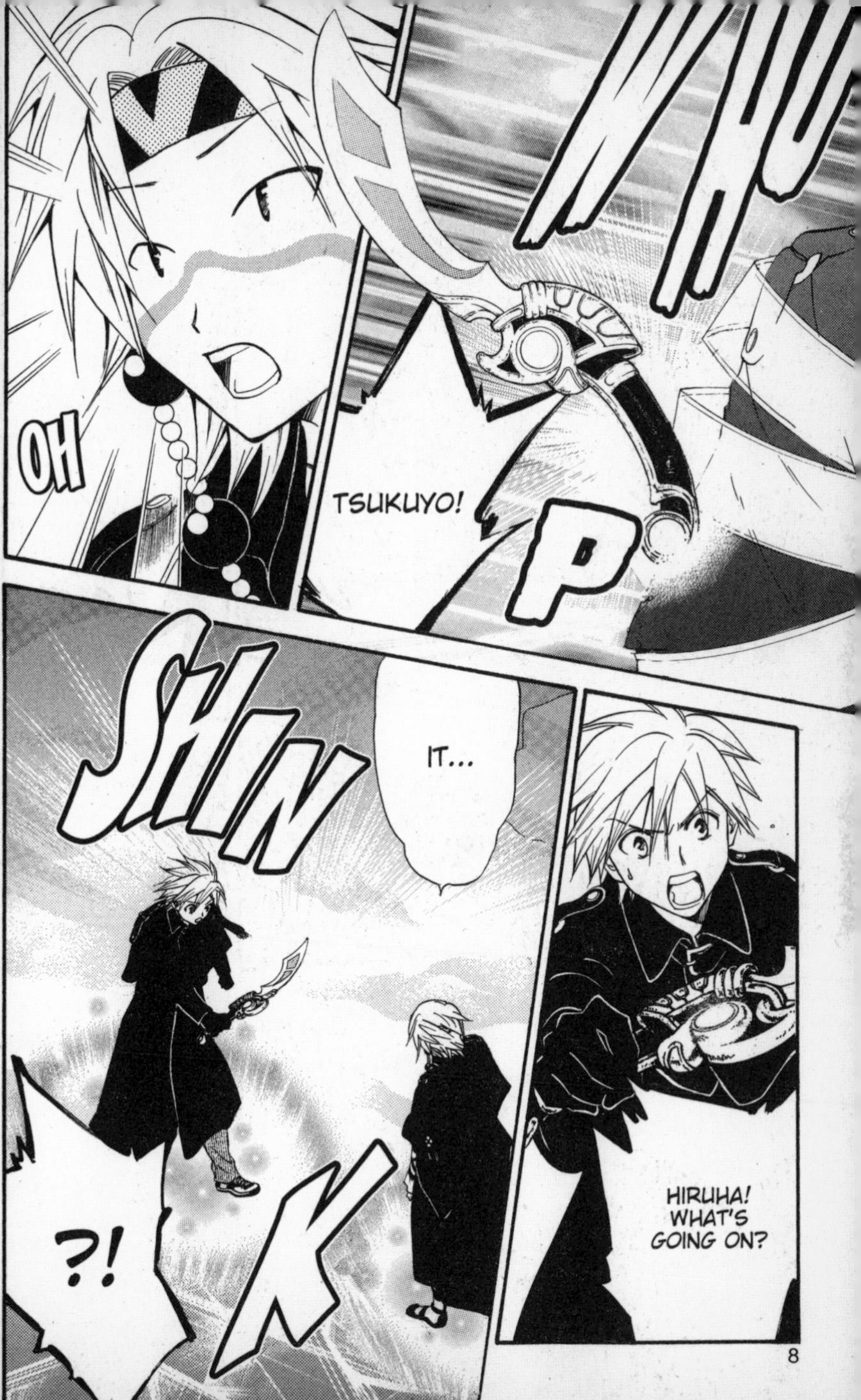
WHU
TSUKUYO!
P
OH
HIRUHA! WHAT'S GOING ON?
SHIN
IT...
K
?!

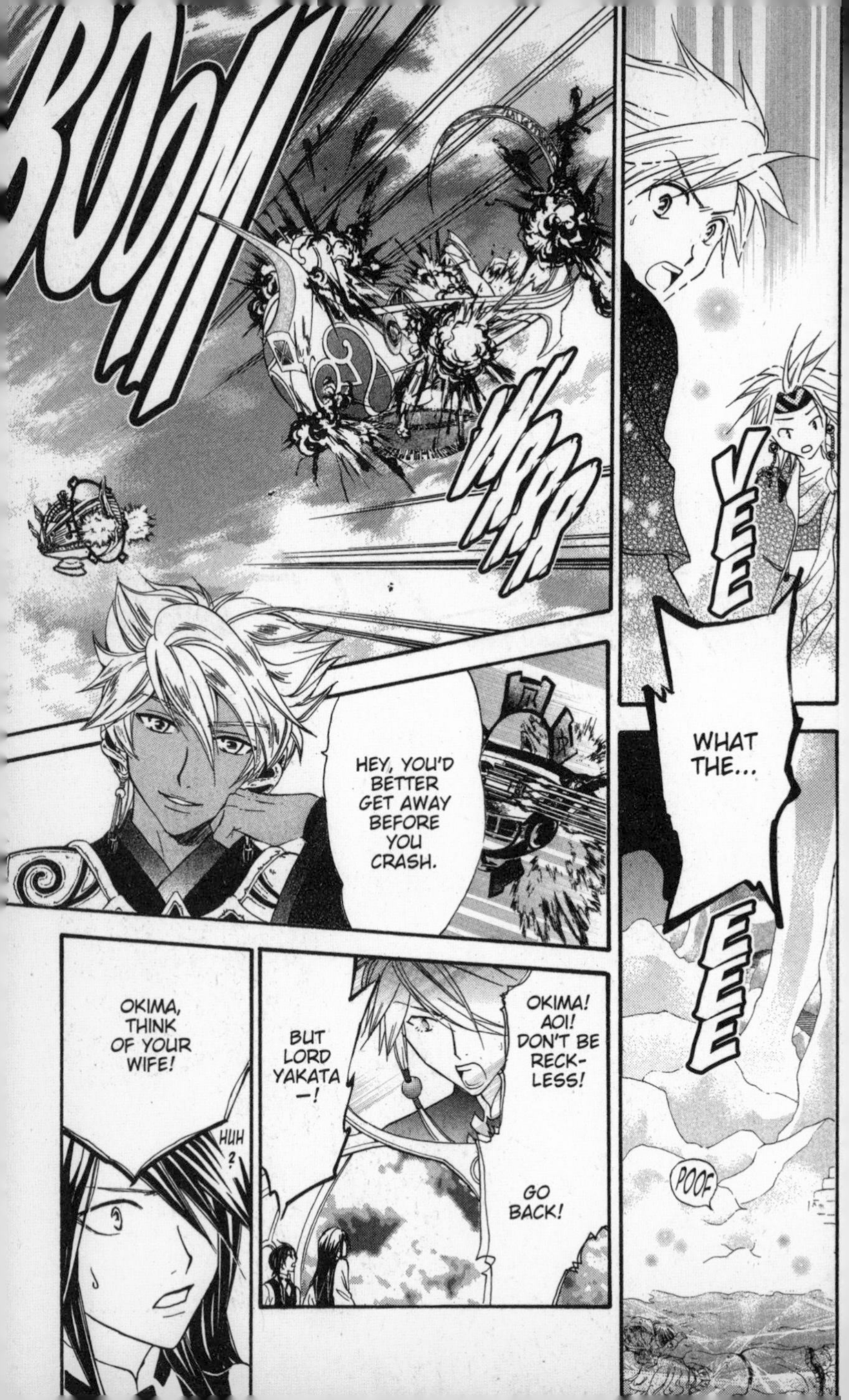
VEEE
WHAT THE...
EEEE
POOF
BOOM
HEY, YOU'D BETTER GET AWAY BEFORE YOU CRASH.
OKIMA! AOI! DON'T BE RECK-LESS!
BUT LORD YAKATA —!
GO BACK!
OKIMA, THINK OF YOUR WIFE!
HUH ?

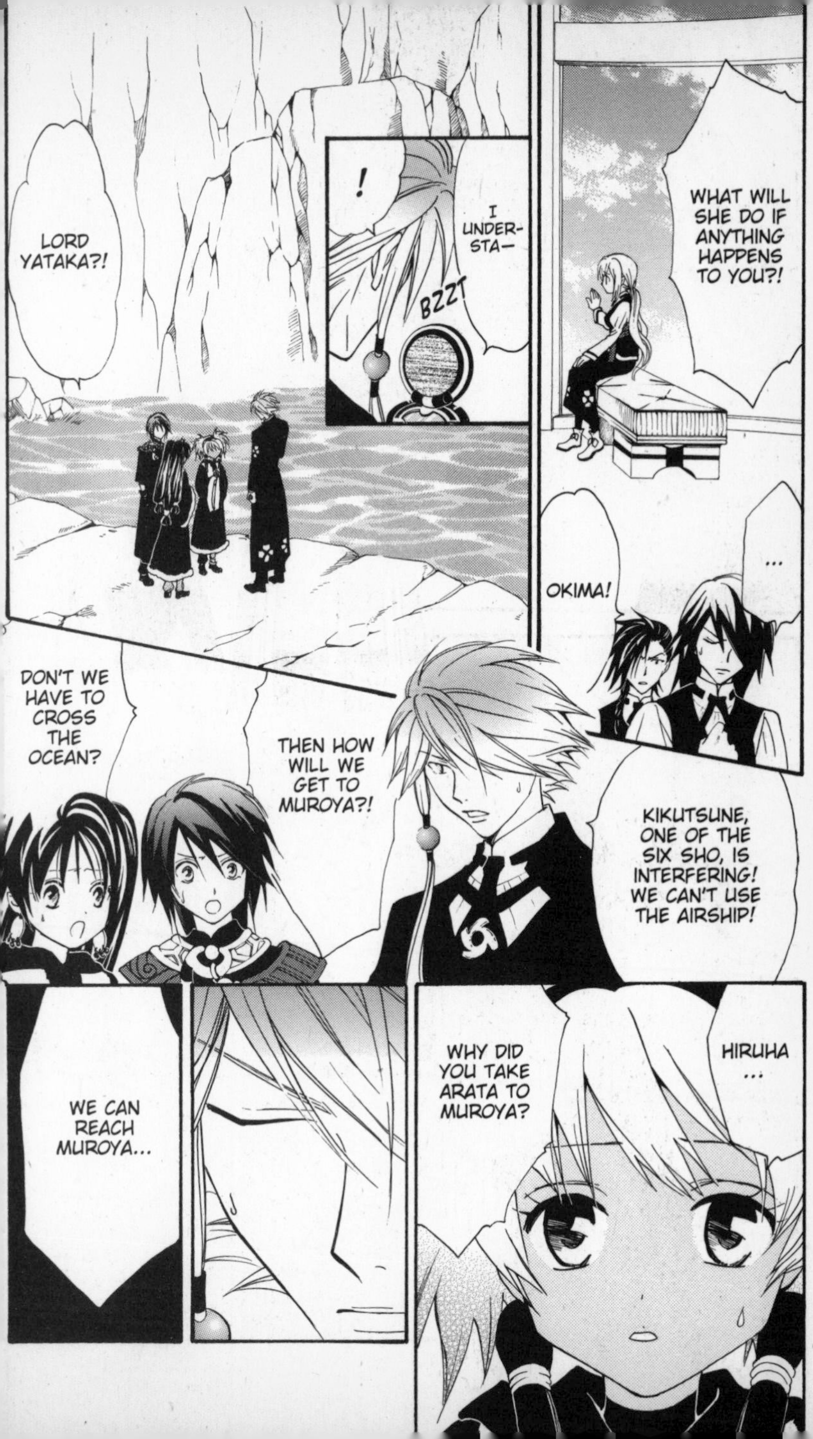

WHAT WILL SHE DO IF ANYTHING HAPPENS TO YOU?!
I UNDER-STA—
BZZT
!
LORD YATAKA?!
...
OKIMA!
KIKUTSUNE, ONE OF THE SIX SHO, IS INTERFERING! WE CAN'T USE THE AIRSHIP!
THEN HOW WILL WE GET TO MUROYA?!
DON'T WE HAVE TO CROSS THE OCEAN?
HIRUHA ...
WHY DID YOU TAKE ARATA TO MUROYA?
WE CAN REACH MUROYA...

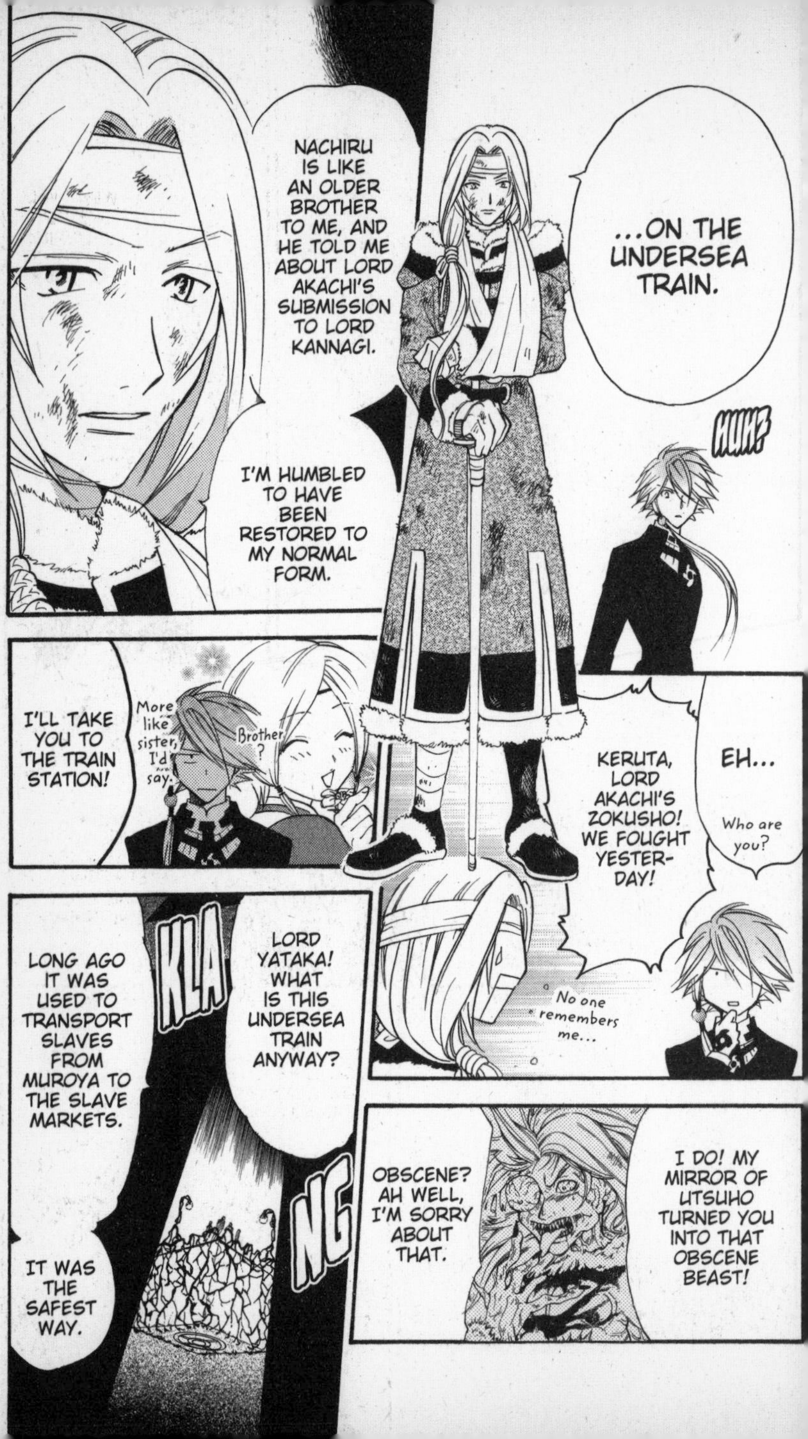

...ON THE UNDERSEA TRAIN.
HUH?
NACHIRU IS LIKE AN OLDER BROTHER TO ME, AND HE TOLD ME ABOUT LORD AKACHI'S SUBMISSION TO LORD KANNAGI.
I'M HUMBLED TO HAVE BEEN RESTORED TO MY NORMAL FORM.
EH...
Who are you?
KERUTA, LORD AKACHI'S ZOKUSHO! WE FOUGHT YESTER-DAY!
No one remembers me...
I'LL TAKE YOU TO THE TRAIN STATION!
Brother?
More like sister, I'd say.
I DO! MY MIRROR OF UTSUHO TURNED YOU INTO THAT OBSCENE BEAST!
OBSCENE? AH WELL, I'M SORRY ABOUT THAT.
LORD YATAKA! WHAT IS THIS UNDERSEA TRAIN ANYWAY?
KLANG
LONG AGO IT WAS USED TO TRANSPORT SLAVES FROM MUROYA TO THE SLAVE MARKETS.
IT WAS THE SAFEST WAY.

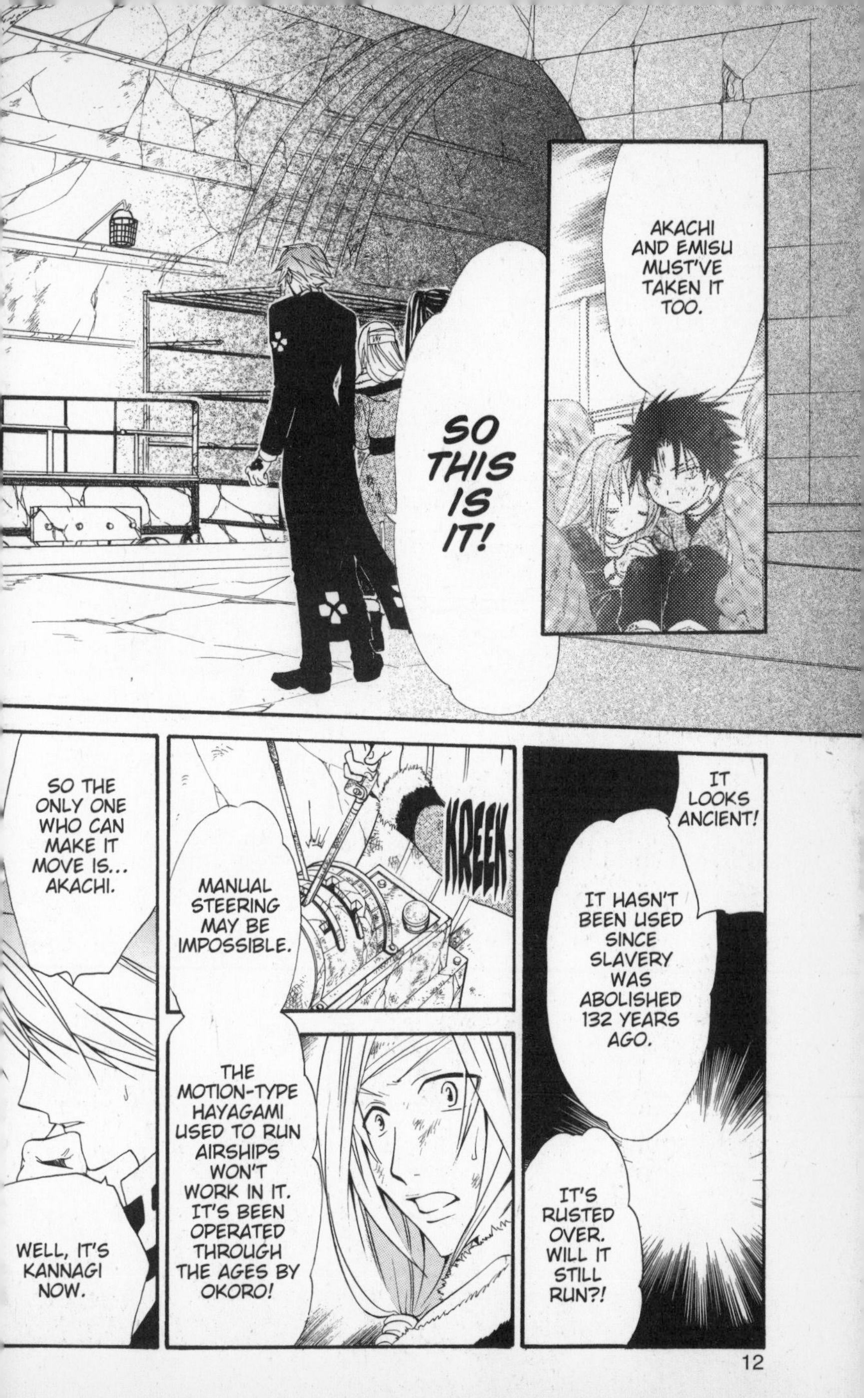
AKACHI AND EMISU MUST'VE TAKEN IT TOO.
SO THIS IS IT!
IT LOOKS ANCIENT!
IT HASN'T BEEN USED SINCE SLAVERY WAS ABOLISHED 132 YEARS AGO.
IT'S RUSTED OVER. WILL IT STILL RUN?!
KREEK
MANUAL STEERING MAY BE IMPOSSIBLE.
THE MOTION-TYPE HAYAGAMI USED TO RUN AIRSHIPS WON'T WORK IN IT. IT'S BEEN OPERATED THROUGH THE AGES BY OKORO!
SO THE ONLY ONE WHO CAN MAKE IT MOVE IS... AKACHI.
WELL, IT'S KANNAGI NOW.

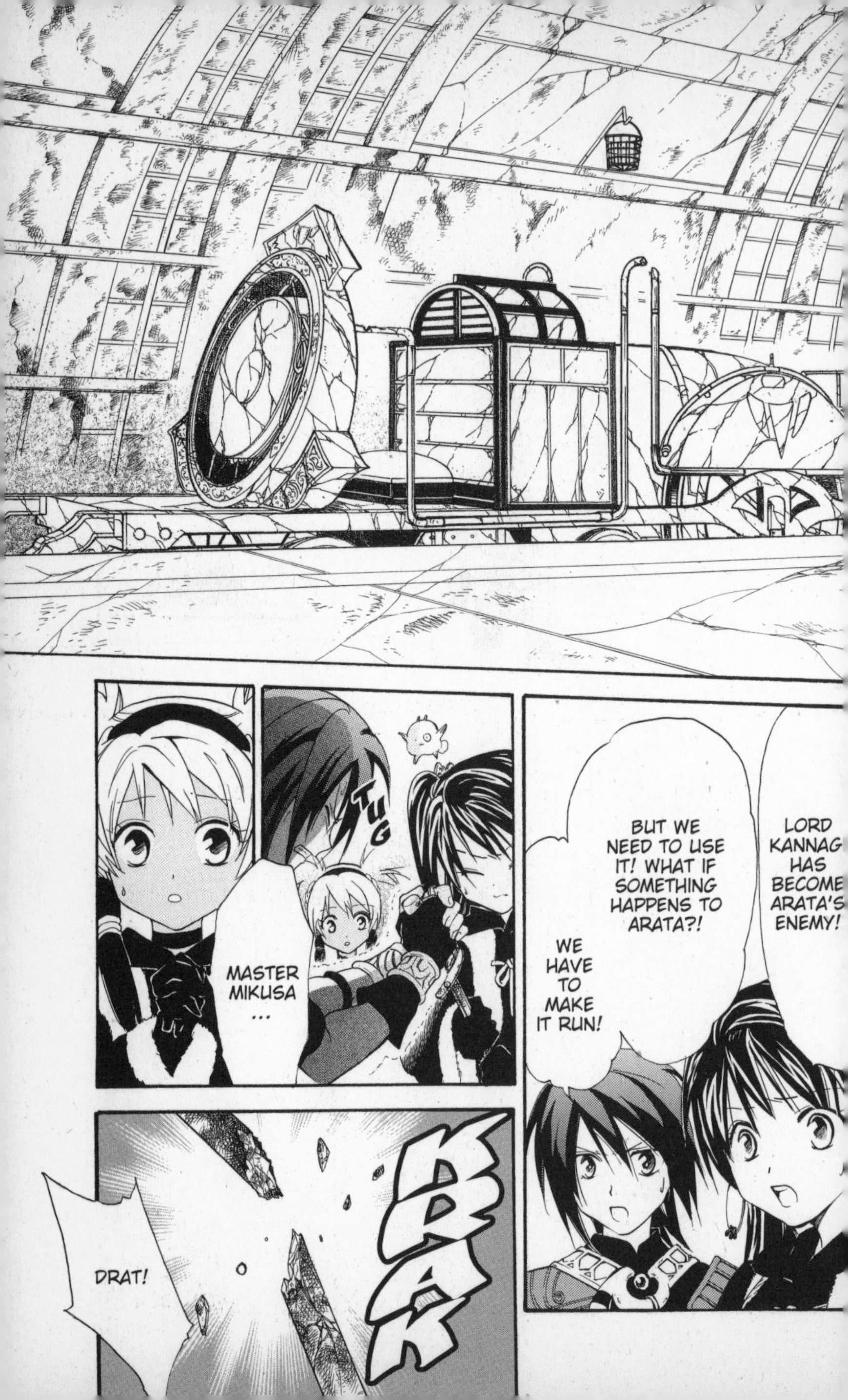
LORD KANNAG HAS BECOME ARATA'S ENEMY!
BUT WE NEED TO USE IT! WHAT IF SOMETHING HAPPENS TO ARATA?!
WE HAVE TO MAKE IT RUN!
TUG
MASTER MIKUSA ...
DRAT!

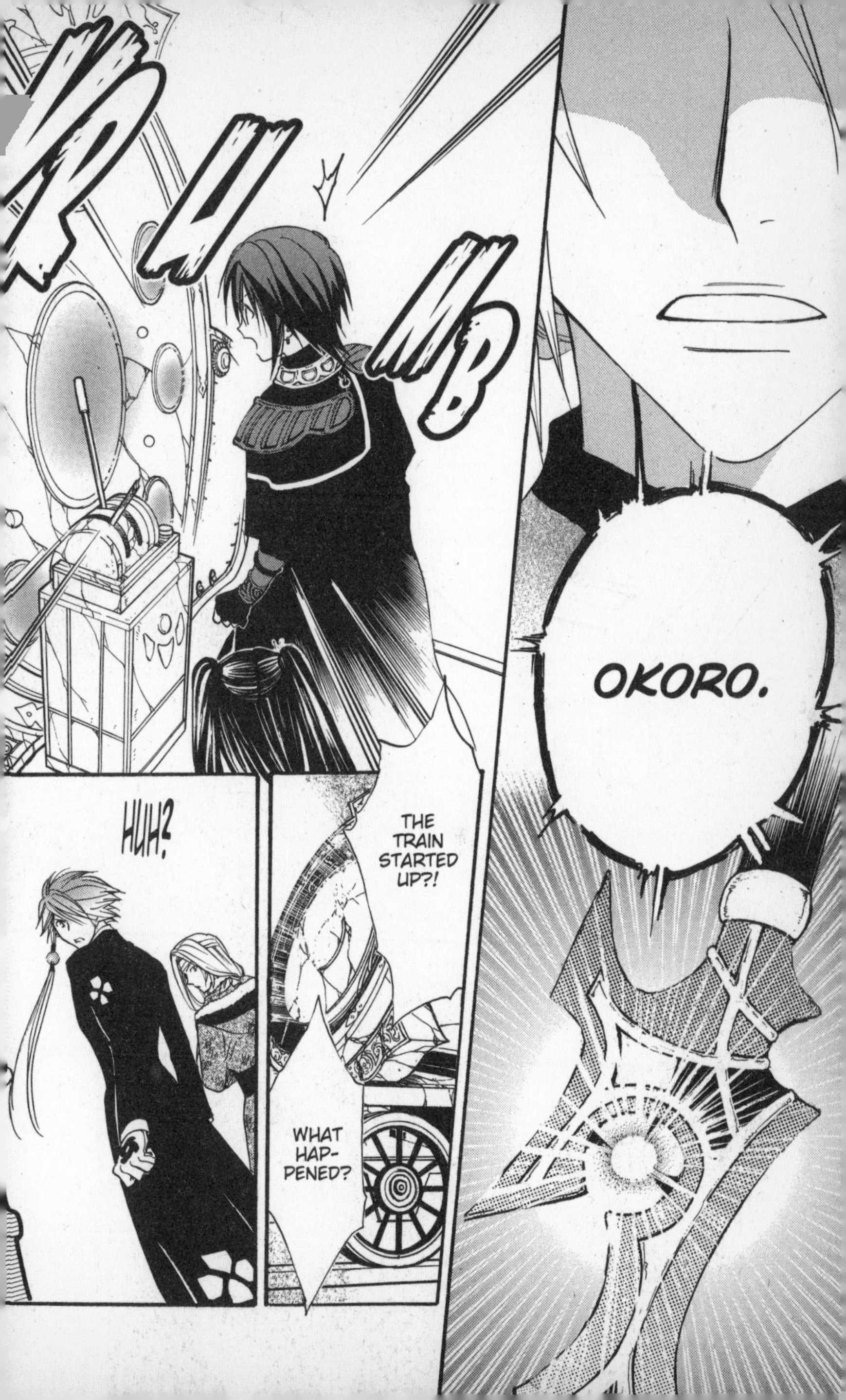
OKORO.
THE TRAIN STARTED UP?!
WHAT HAP-PENED?
HUH?

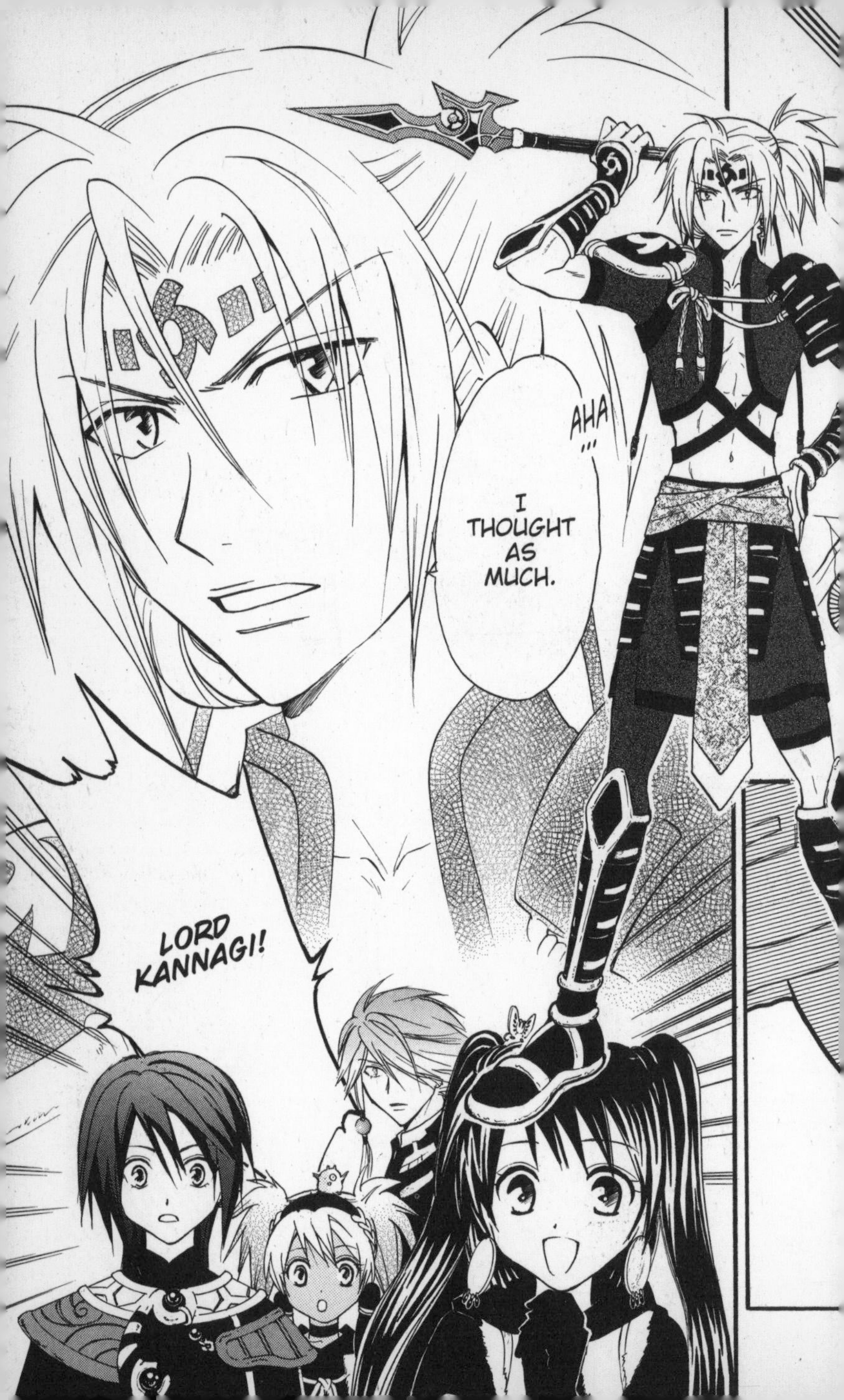
AHA ...
I THOUGHT AS MUCH.
LORD KANNAGI!

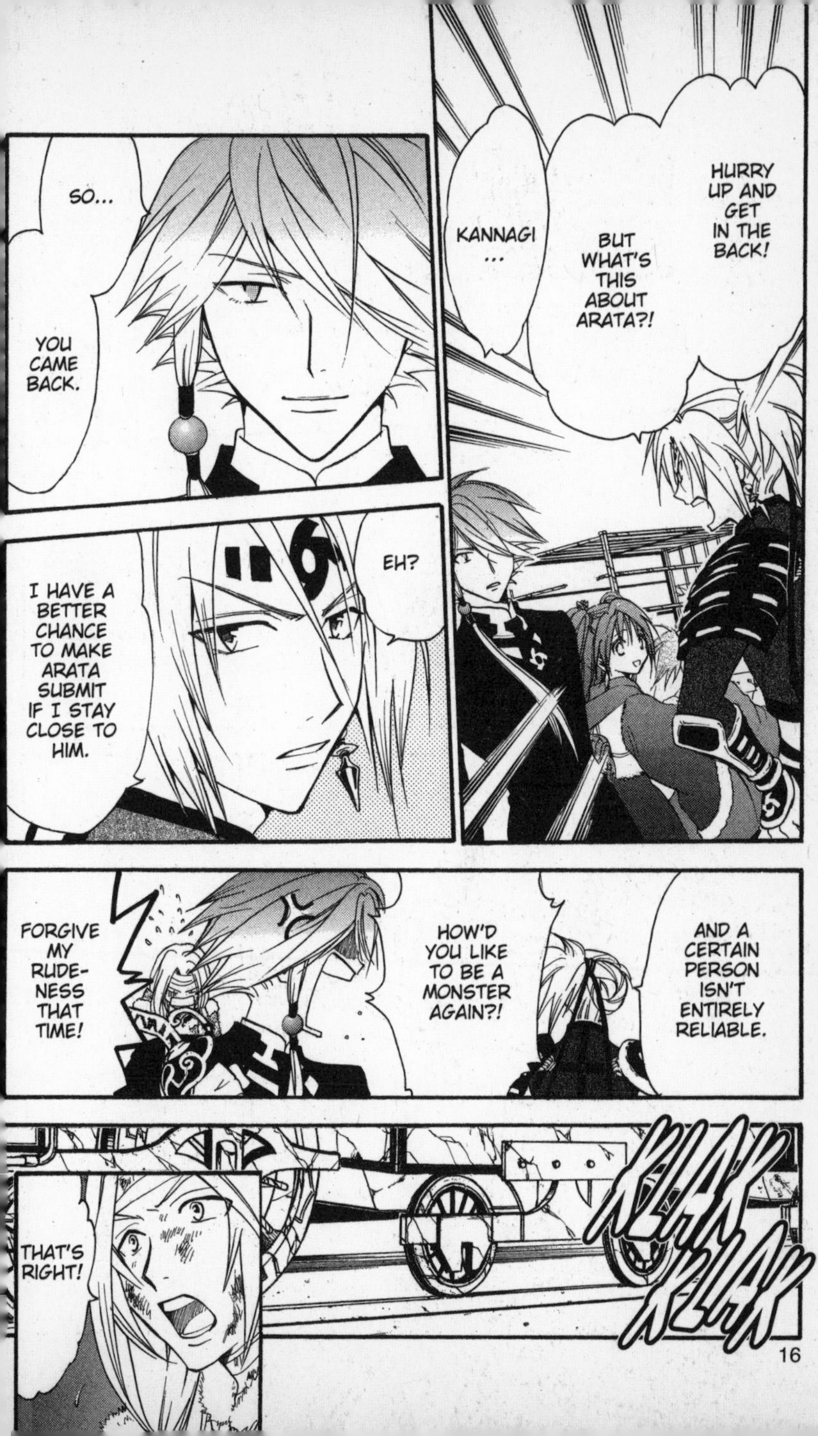
HURRY UP AND GET IN THE BACK!
BUT WHAT'S THIS ABOUT ARATA?!
KANNAGI ...
SO...
YOU CAME BACK.
EH?
I HAVE A BETTER CHANCE TO MAKE ARATA SUBMIT IF I STAY CLOSE TO HIM.
AND A CERTAIN PERSON ISN'T ENTIRELY RELIABLE.
HOW'D YOU LIKE TO BE A MONSTER AGAIN?!
FORGIVE MY RUDE-NESS THAT TIME!
KLAK KLAK
THAT'S RIGHT!

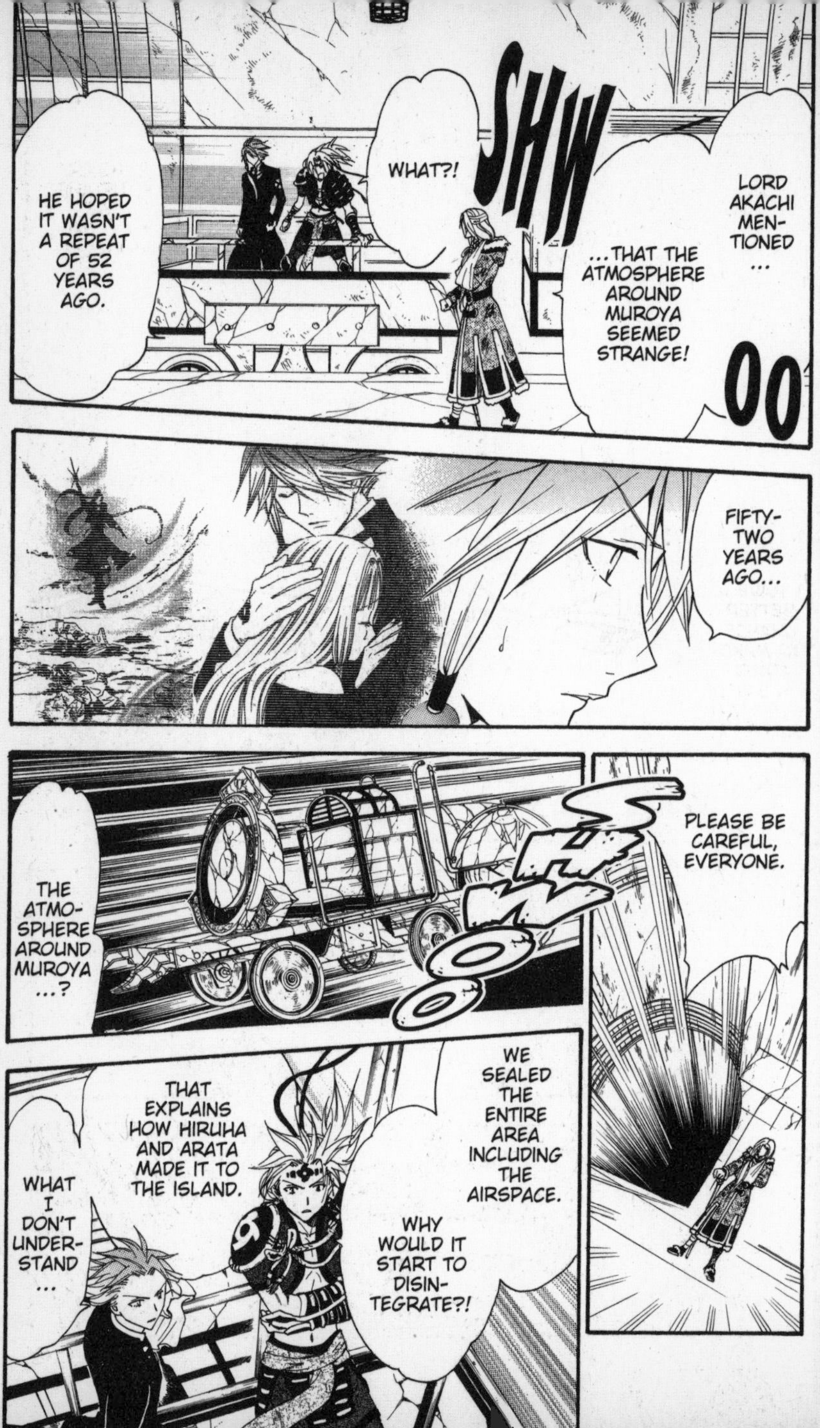
LORD AKACHI MENTIONED...
...THAT THE ATMOSPHERE AROUND MUROYA SEEMED STRANGE!
SHWOO
WHAT?!
HE HOPED IT WASN'T A REPEAT OF 52 YEARS AGO.
FIFTY-TWO YEARS AGO...
PLEASE BE CAREFUL, EVERYONE.
SHWOOO
THE ATMOSPHERE AROUND MUROYA...?
WE SEALED THE ENTIRE AREA INCLUDING THE AIRSPACE.
WHY WOULD IT START TO DISINTEGRATE?!
THAT EXPLAINS HOW HIRUHA AND ARATA MADE IT TO THE ISLAND.
WHAT I DON'T UNDERSTAND...

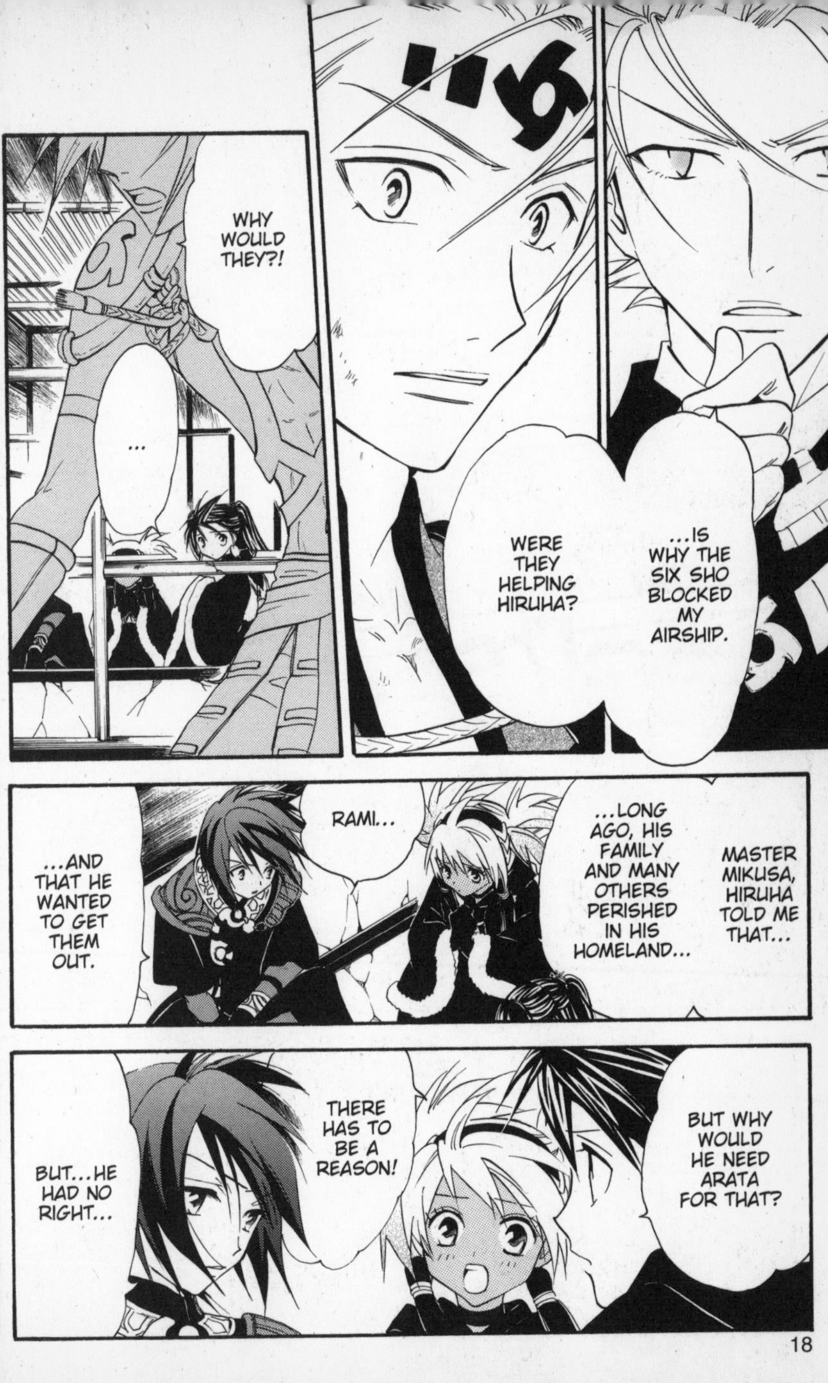

WERE THEY HELPING HIRUHA?
...IS WHY THE SIX SHO BLOCKED MY AIRSHIP.
WHY WOULD THEY?!
...
MASTER MIKUSA, HIRUHA TOLD ME THAT...
...LONG AGO, HIS FAMILY AND MANY OTHERS PERISHED IN HIS HOMELAND...
RAMI...
...AND THAT HE WANTED TO GET THEM OUT.
BUT WHY WOULD HE NEED ARATA FOR THAT?
THERE HAS TO BE A REASON!
BUT...HE HAD NO RIGHT...

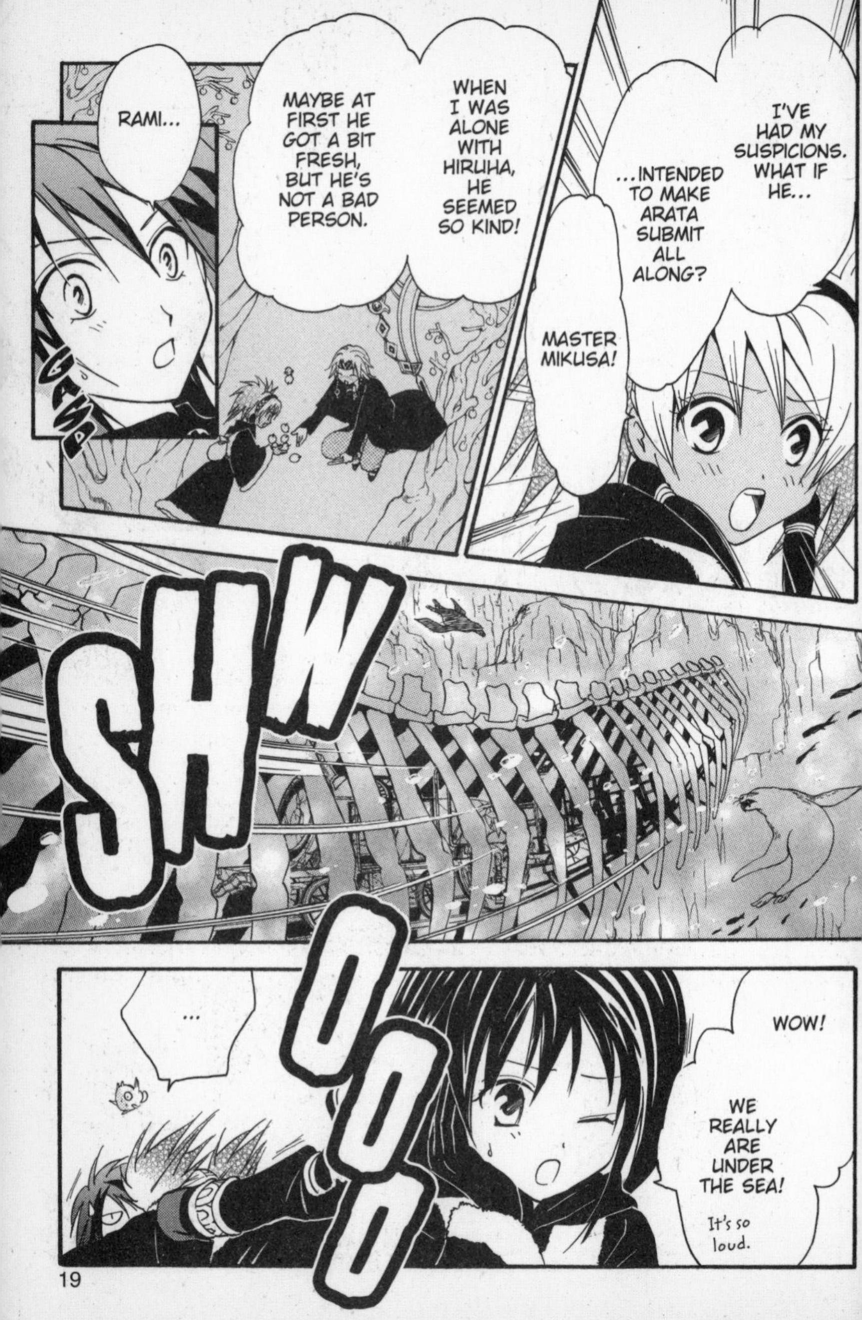
I'VE HAD MY SUSPICIONS. WHAT IF HE...
...INTENDED TO MAKE ARATA SUBMIT ALL ALONG?
MASTER MIKUSA!
WHEN I WAS ALONE WITH HIRUHA, HE SEEMED SO KIND!
MAYBE AT FIRST HE GOT A BIT FRESH, BUT HE'S NOT A BAD PERSON.
RAMI...
SHWOOOOO
WOW!
WE REALLY ARE UNDER THE SEA!
It's so loud.
...

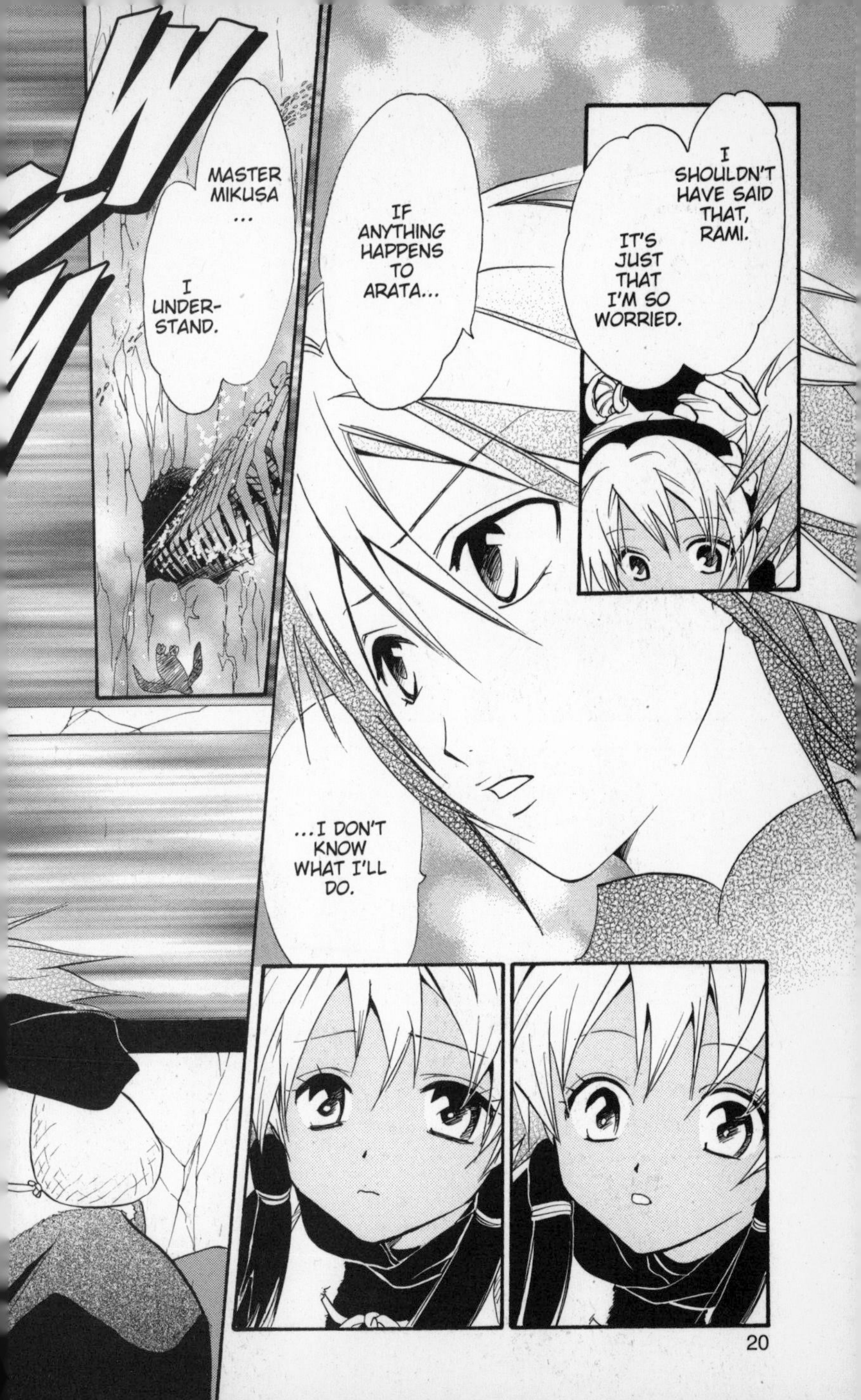
I SHOULDN'T HAVE SAID THAT, RAMI.
IT'S JUST THAT I'M SO WORRIED.
IF ANYTHING HAPPENS TO ARATA...
...I DON'T KNOW WHAT I'LL DO.
MASTER MIKUSA ...
I UNDER-STAND.

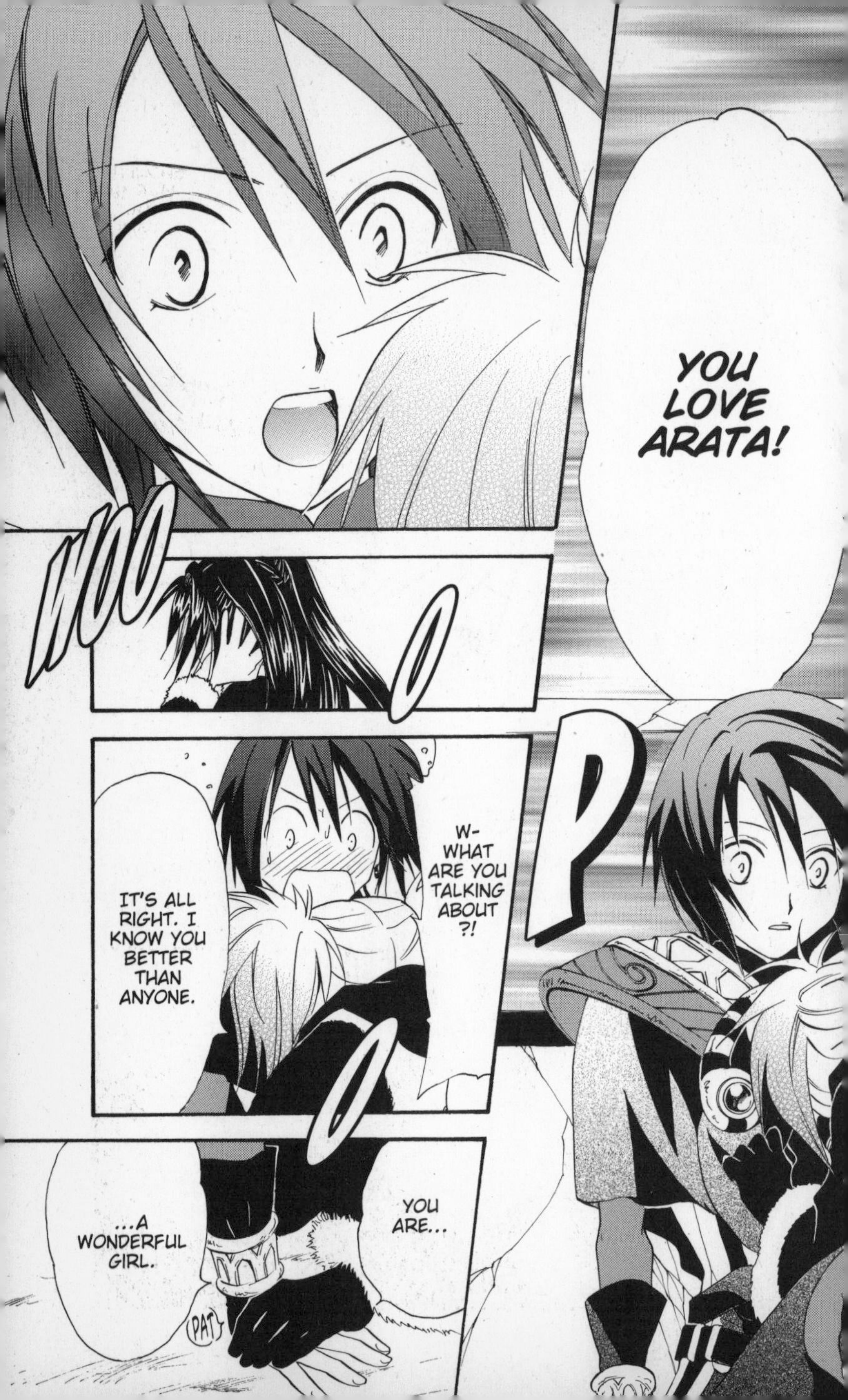
YOU LOVE ARATA!
W-WHAT ARE YOU TALKING ABOUT ?!
IT'S ALL RIGHT. I KNOW YOU BETTER THAN ANYONE.
YOU ARE...
...A WONDERFUL GIRL.
PAT

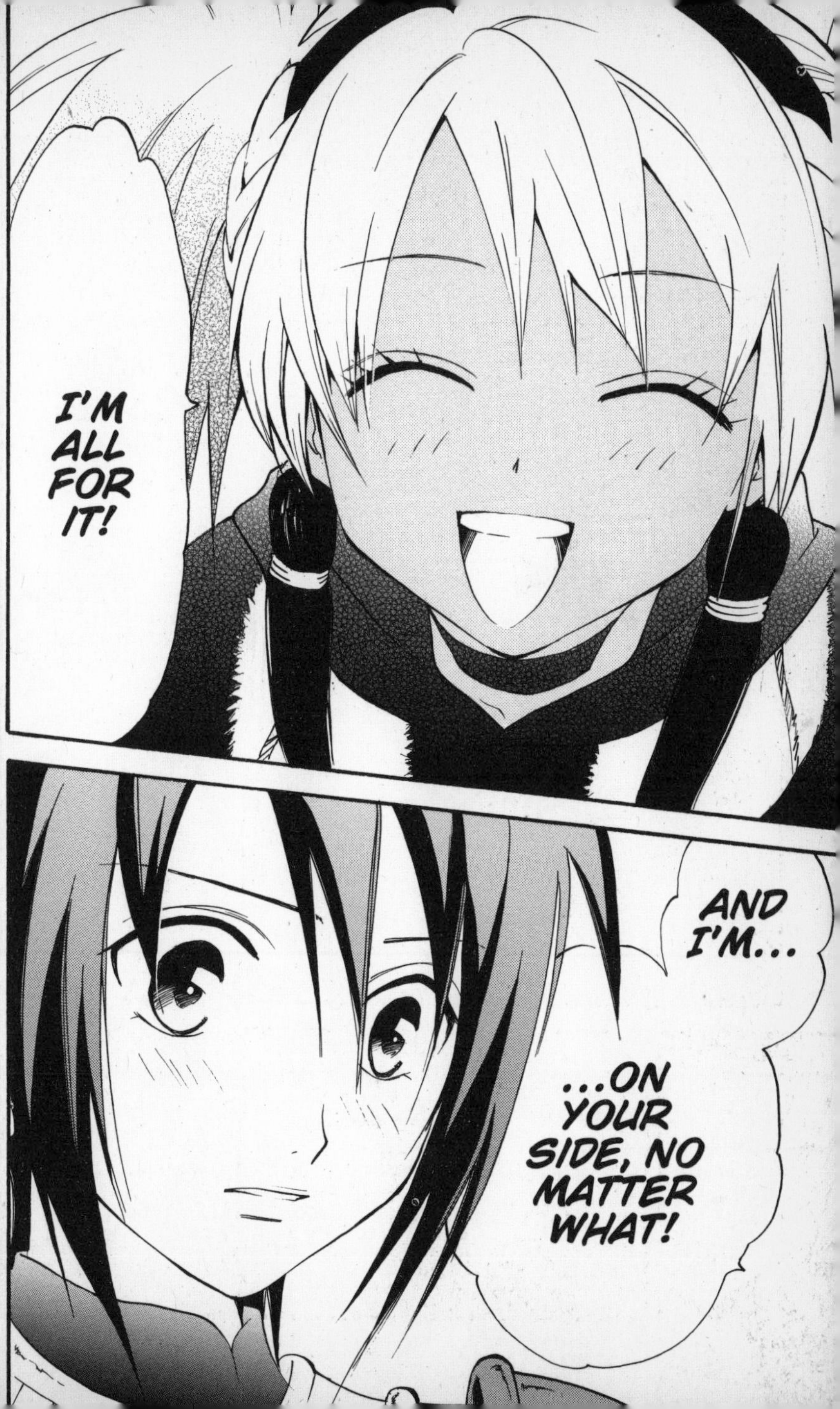
I'M ALL FOR IT!
AND I'M...
...ON YOUR SIDE, NO MATTER WHAT!

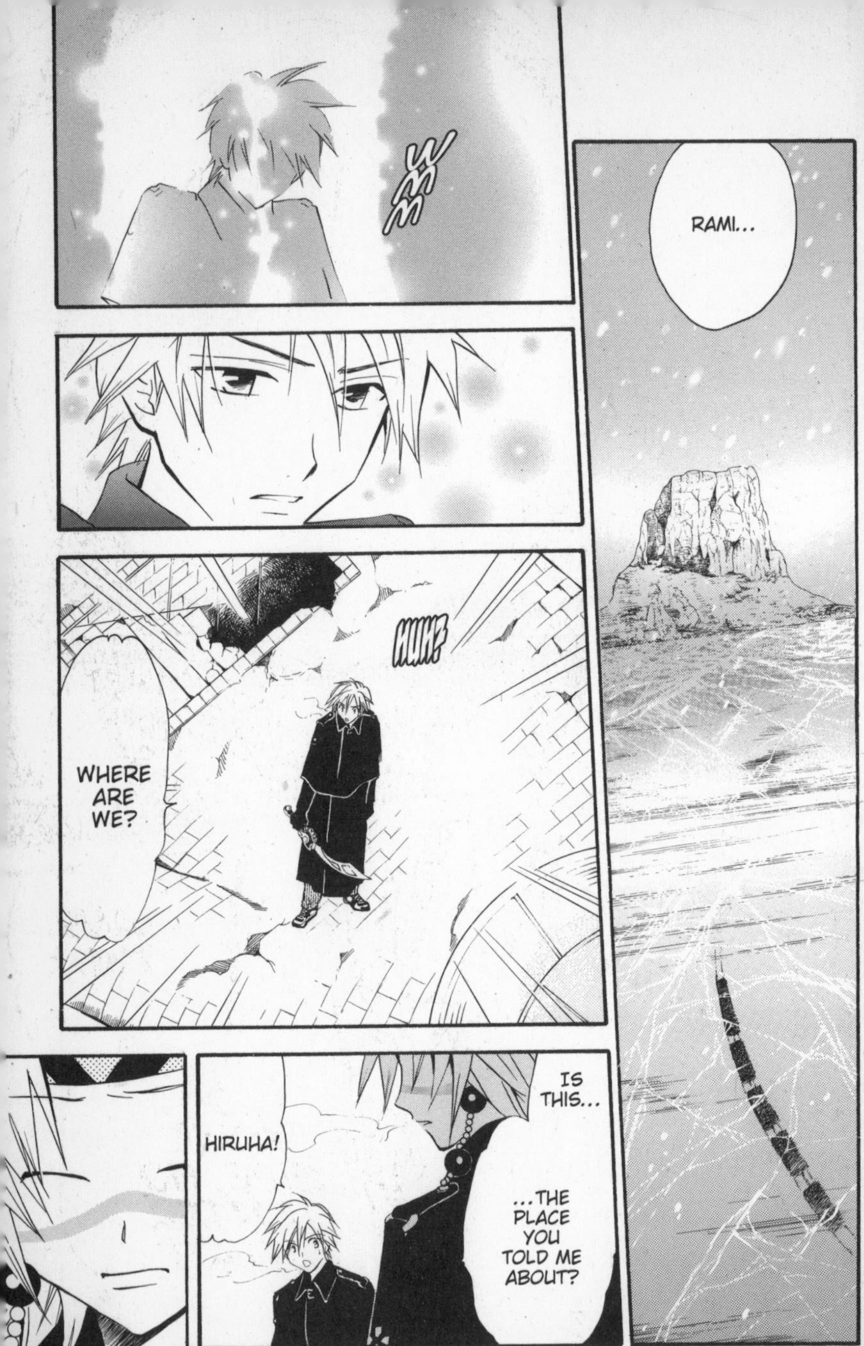
RAMI...
HUH?
WHERE ARE WE?
IS THIS...
HIRUHA!
...THE PLACE YOU TOLD ME ABOUT?

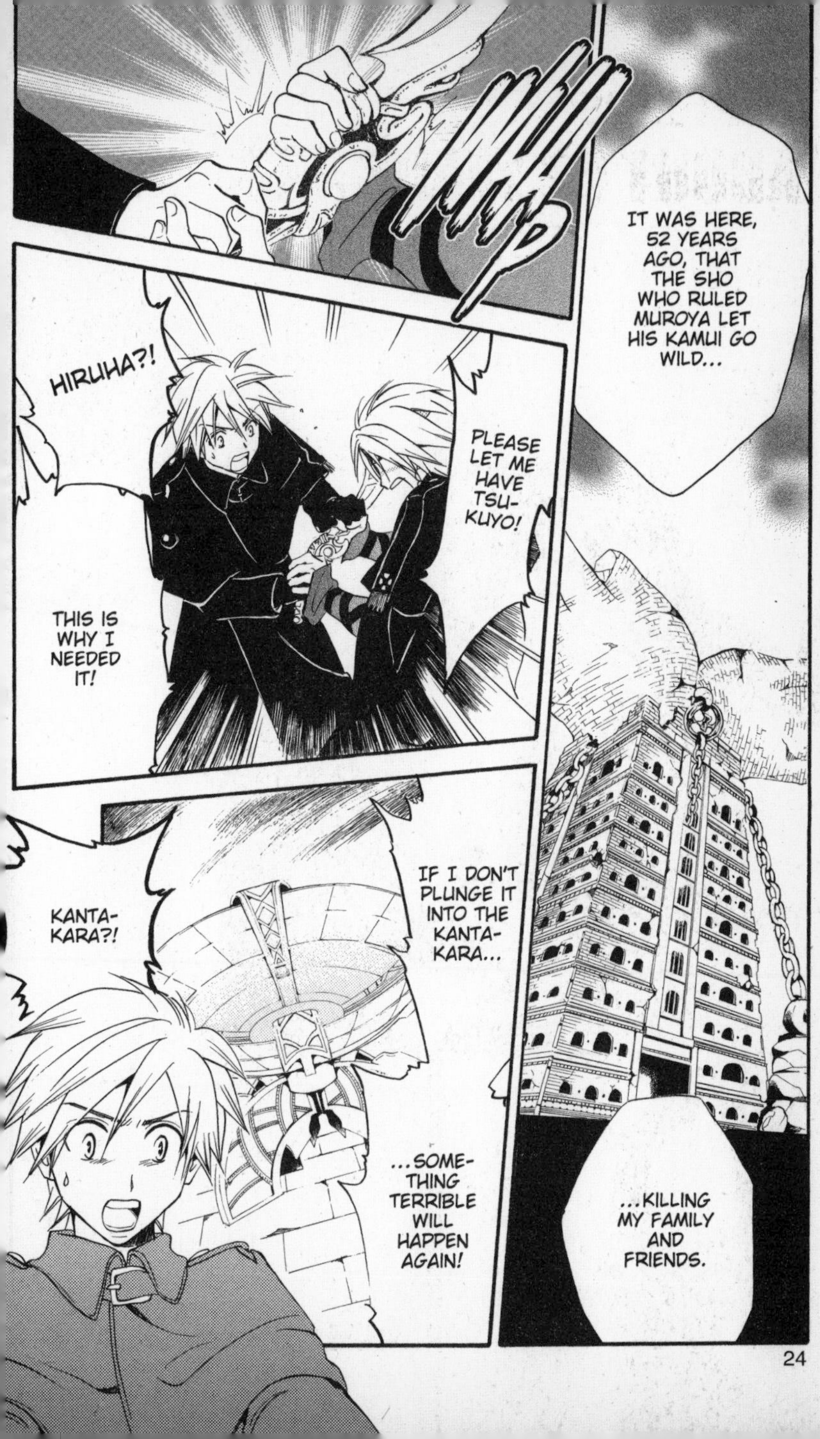
IT WAS HERE, 52 YEARS AGO, THAT THE SHO WHO RULED MUROYA LET HIS KAMUI GO WILD...
...KILLING MY FAMILY AND FRIENDS.
WHAP
HIRUHA?!
PLEASE LET ME HAVE TSU-KUYO!
THIS IS WHY I NEEDED IT!
IF I DON'T PLUNGE IT INTO THE KANTA-KARA...
KANTA-KARA?!
...SOME-THING TERRIBLE WILL HAPPEN AGAIN!

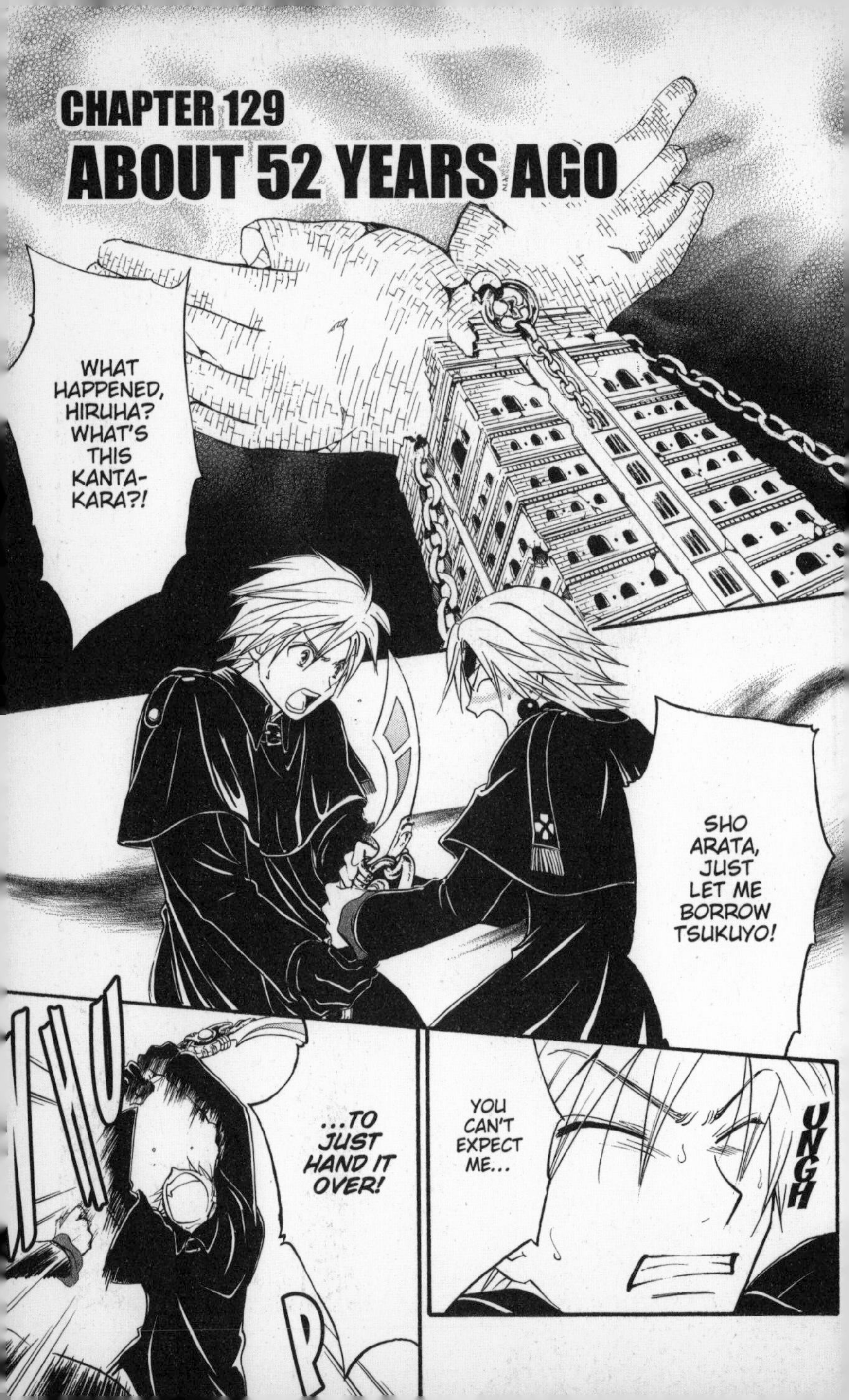
CHAPTER 129
ABOUT 52 YEARS AGO
WHAT HAPPENED, HIRUHA? WHAT'S THIS KANTA-KARA?!
SHO ARATA, JUST LET ME BORROW TSUKUYO!
UNGH
YOU CAN'T EXPECT ME...
...TO JUST HAND IT OVER!

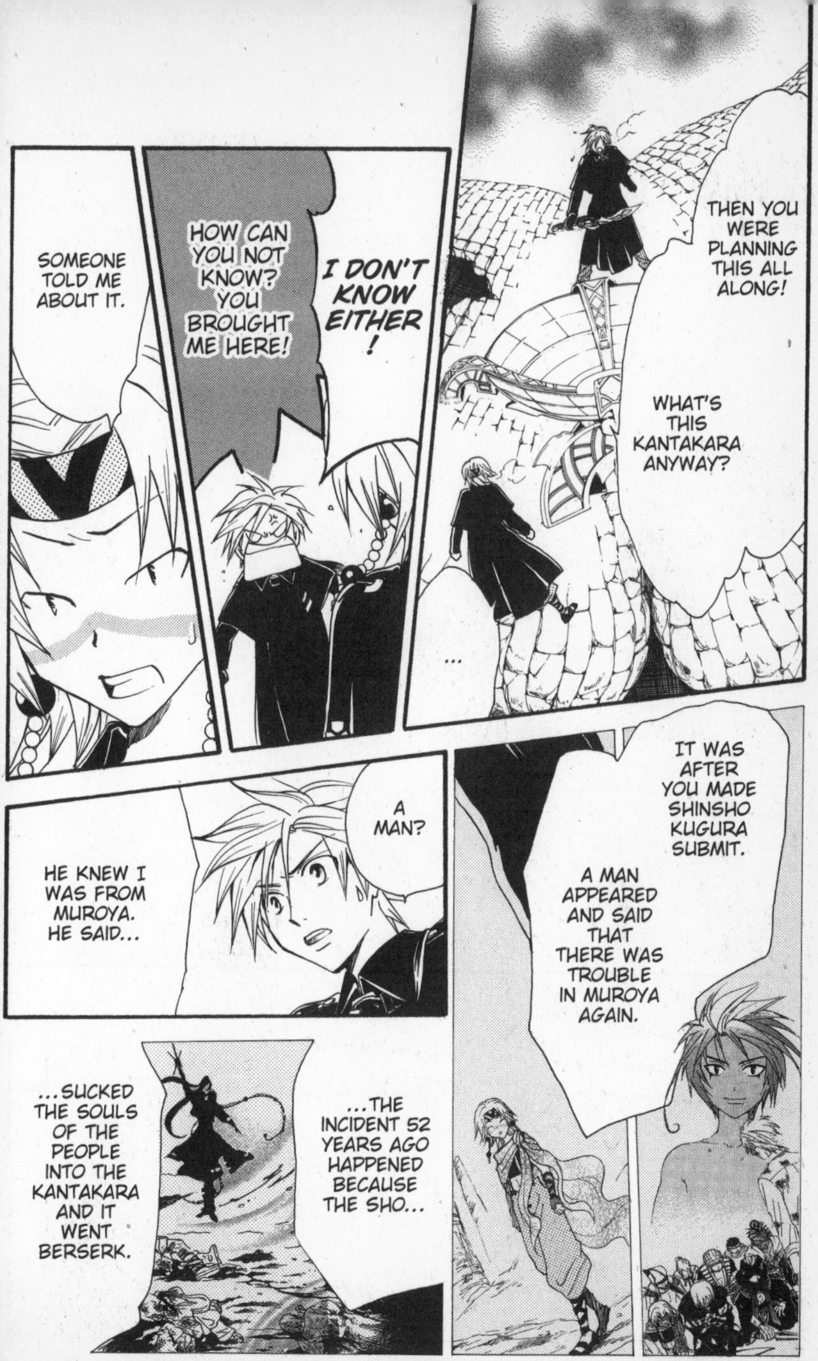
THEN YOU WERE PLANNING THIS ALL ALONG!
WHAT'S THIS KANTAKARA ANYWAY?
...
I DON'T KNOW EITHER!
HOW CAN YOU NOT KNOW? YOU BROUGHT ME HERE!
SOMEONE TOLD ME ABOUT IT.
IT WAS AFTER YOU MADE SHINSHO KUGURA SUBMIT.
A MAN APPEARED AND SAID THAT THERE WAS TROUBLE IN MUROYA AGAIN.
A MAN?
HE KNEW I WAS FROM MUROYA. HE SAID...
...THE INCIDENT 52 YEARS AGO HAPPENED BECAUSE THE SHO...
...SUCKED THE SOULS OF THE PEOPLE INTO THE KANTAKARA AND IT WENT BERSERK.

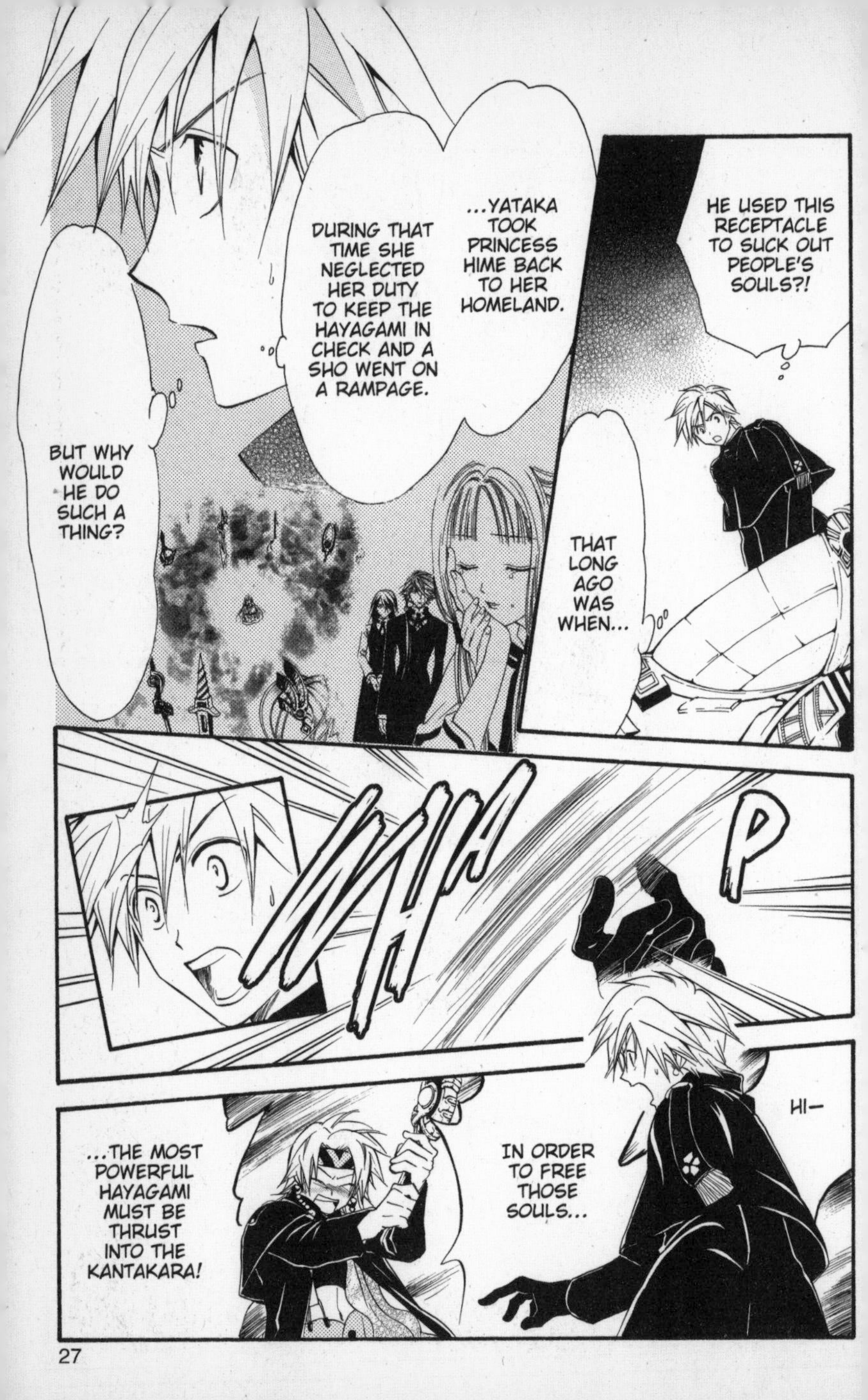
HE USED THIS RECEPTACLE TO SUCK OUT PEOPLE'S SOULS?!
THAT LONG AGO WAS WHEN...
...YATAKA TOOK PRINCESS HIME BACK TO HER HOMELAND.
DURING THAT TIME SHE NEGLECTED HER DUTY TO KEEP THE HAYAGAMI IN CHECK AND A SHO WENT ON A RAMPAGE.
BUT WHY WOULD HE DO SUCH A THING?
WHAP
HI—
IN ORDER TO FREE THOSE SOULS...
...THE MOST POWERFUL HAYAGAMI MUST BE THRUST INTO THE KANTAKARA!

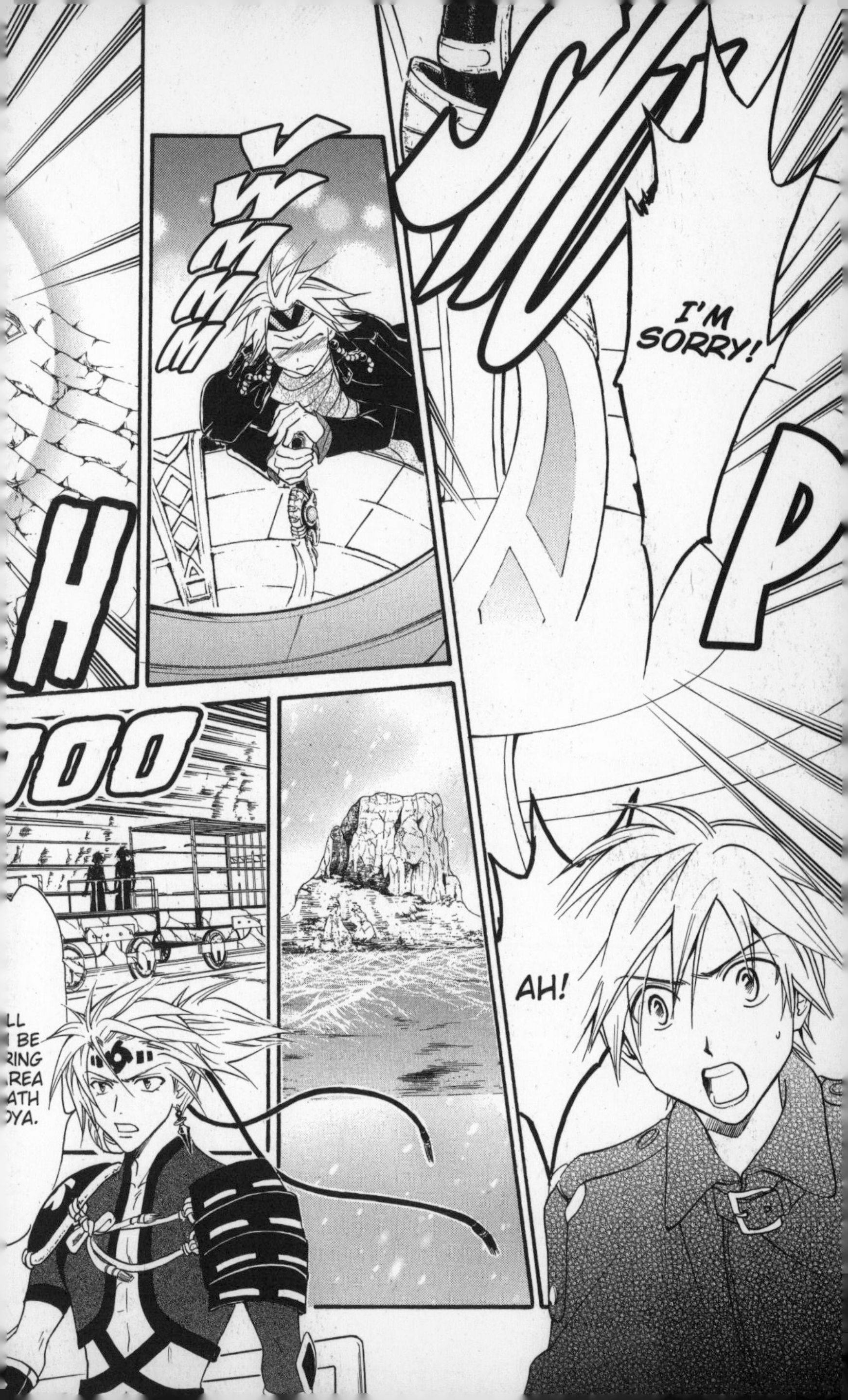
I'M SORRY!
AH!

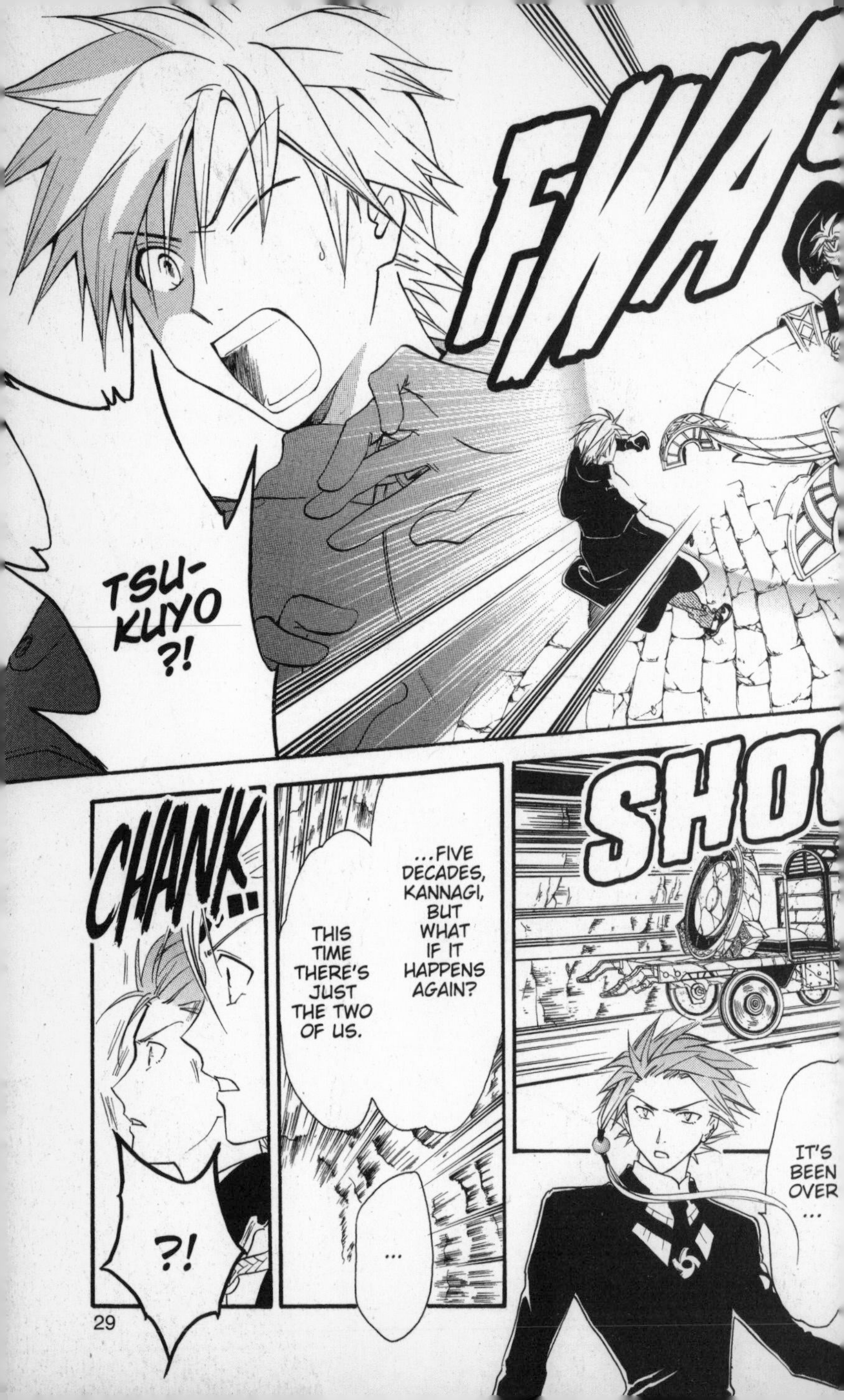
FWA
TSU-KUYO ?!
SHOO
IT'S BEEN OVER ...
...FIVE DECADES, KANNAGI, BUT WHAT IF IT HAPPENS AGAIN?
THIS TIME THERE'S JUST THE TWO OF US.
...
CHANK..
?!

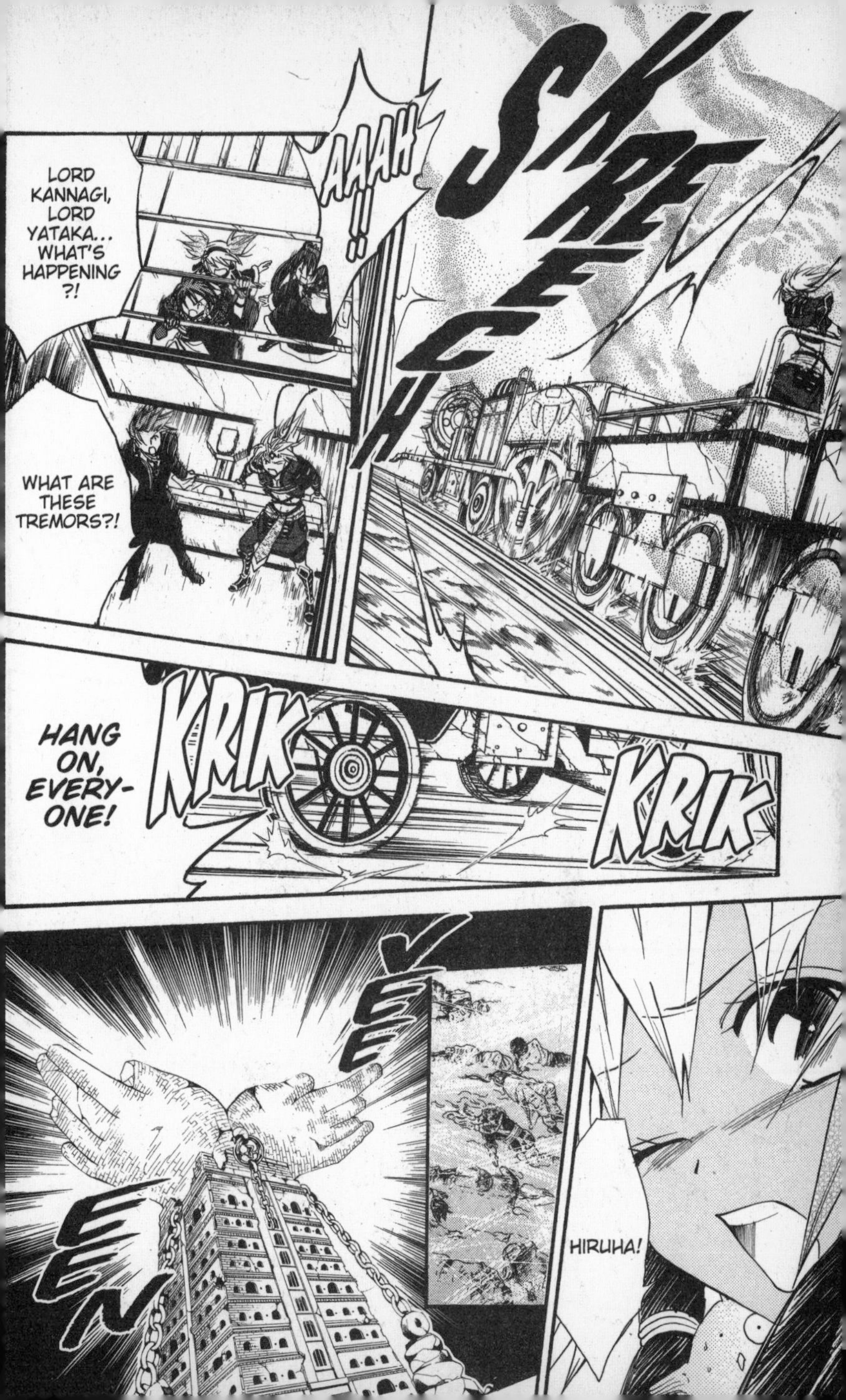
SHREECH
AAAH!!
LORD KANNAGI, LORD YATAKA... WHAT'S HAPPENING?!
WHAT ARE THESE TREMORS?!
KRIK
KRIK
HANG ON, EVERY-ONE!
HIRUHA!
VEEE
EEN

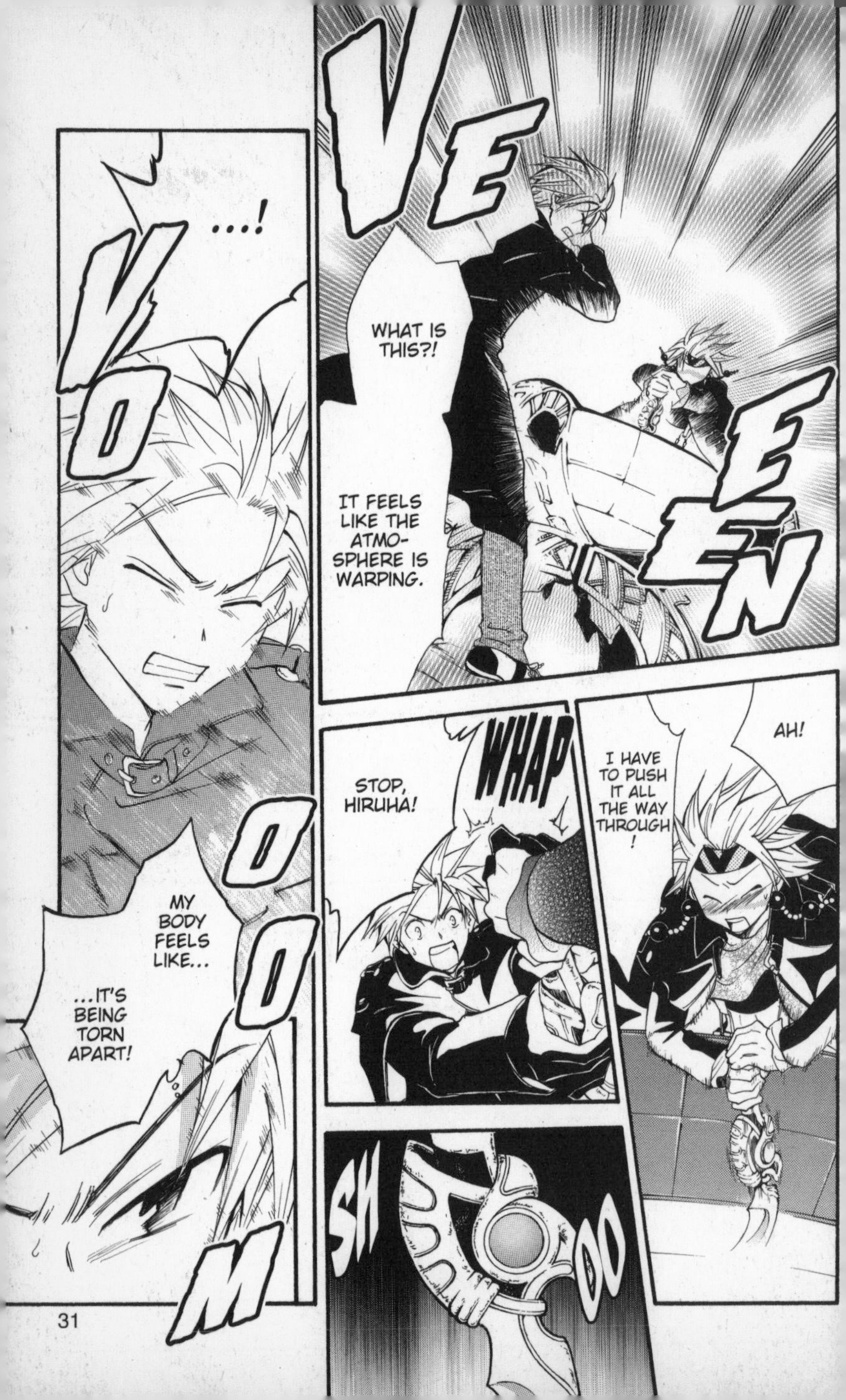
VEEEN
WHAT IS THIS?!
IT FEELS LIKE THE ATMO-SPHERE IS WARPING.
AH!
I HAVE TO PUSH IT ALL THE WAY THROUGH!
WHAP
STOP, HIRUHA!
SHOO
VOOOM
...!
MY BODY FEELS LIKE...
...IT'S BEING TORN APART!

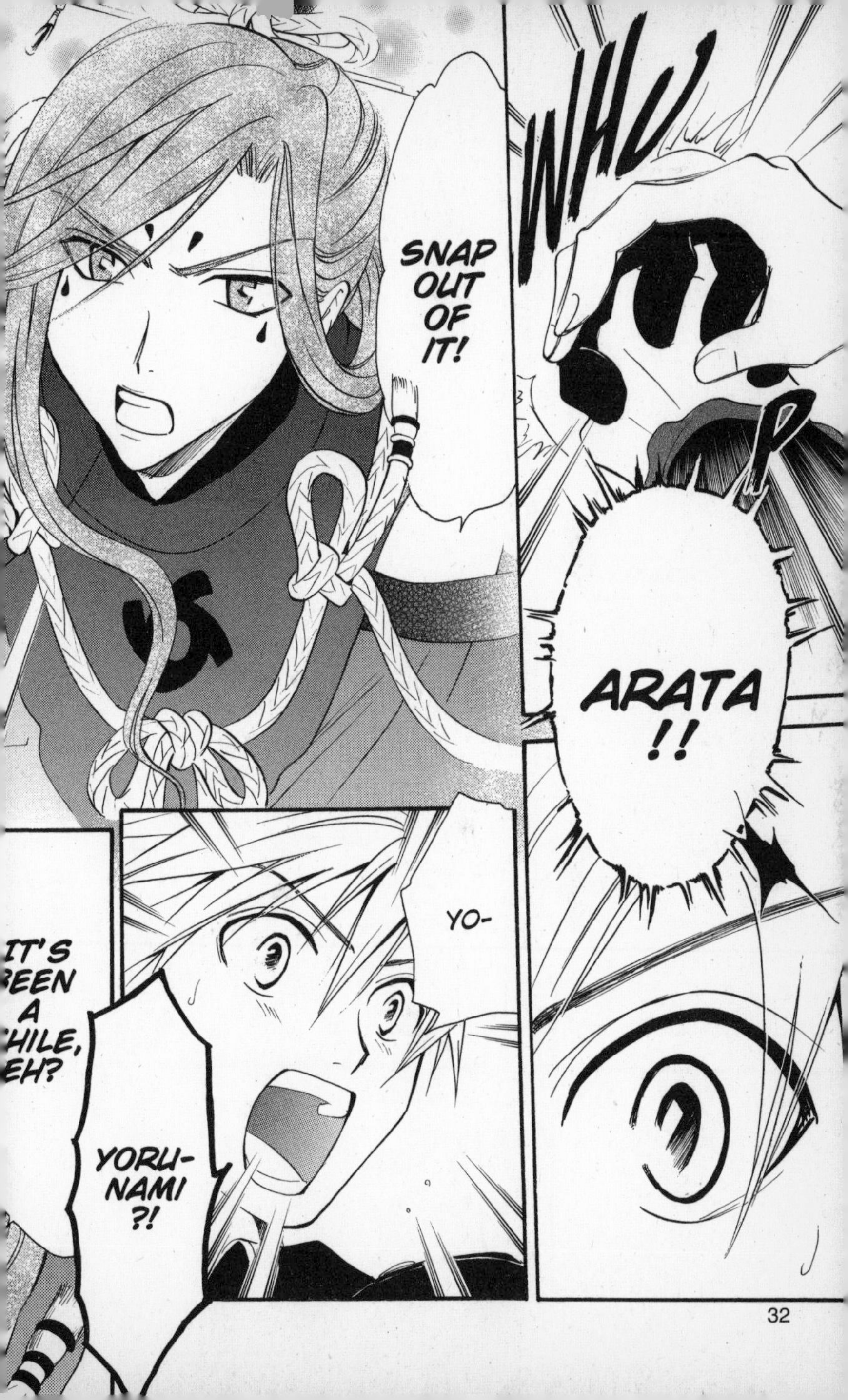
WHAP
SNAP OUT OF IT!
ARATA!!
YO-
YORU-NAMI?!
IT'S EEN A HILE, EH?

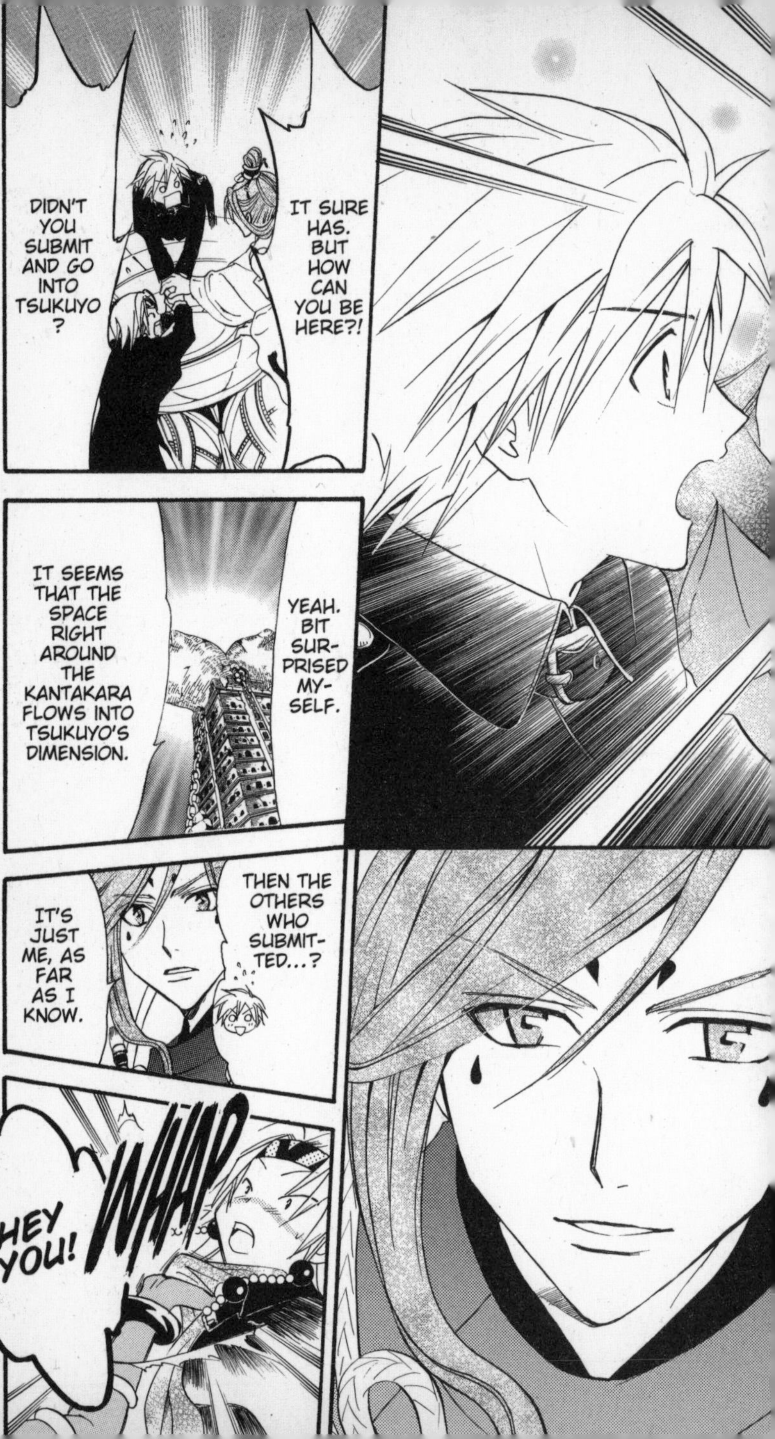
IT SURE HAS. BUT HOW CAN YOU BE HERE?!
DIDN'T YOU SUBMIT AND GO INTO TSUKUYO?
YEAH. BIT SUR-PRISED MY-SELF.
IT SEEMS THAT THE SPACE RIGHT AROUND THE KANTAKARA FLOWS INTO TSUKUYO'S DIMENSION.
THEN THE OTHERS WHO SUBMIT-TED...?
IT'S JUST ME, AS FAR AS I KNOW.
WHAP
HEY YOU!

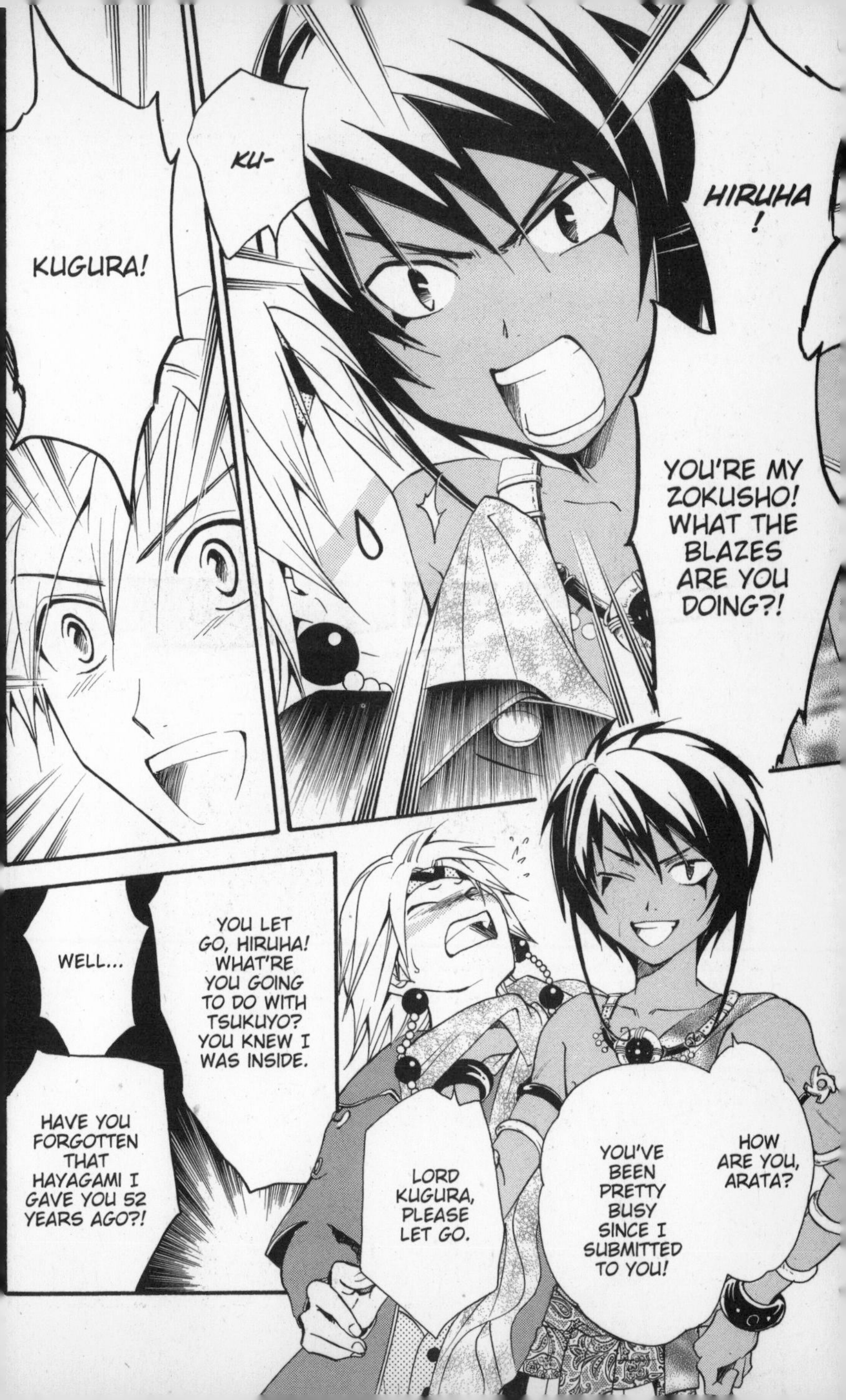
HIRUHA!
KU-
YOU'RE MY ZOKUSHO! WHAT THE BLAZES ARE YOU DOING?!
KUGURA!
HOW ARE YOU, ARATA?
YOU'VE BEEN PRETTY BUSY SINCE I SUBMITTED TO YOU!
LORD KUGURA, PLEASE LET GO.
YOU LET GO, HIRUHA! WHAT'RE YOU GOING TO DO WITH TSUKUYO? YOU KNEW I WAS INSIDE.
WELL...
HAVE YOU FORGOTTEN THAT HAYAGAMI I GAVE YOU 52 YEARS AGO?!

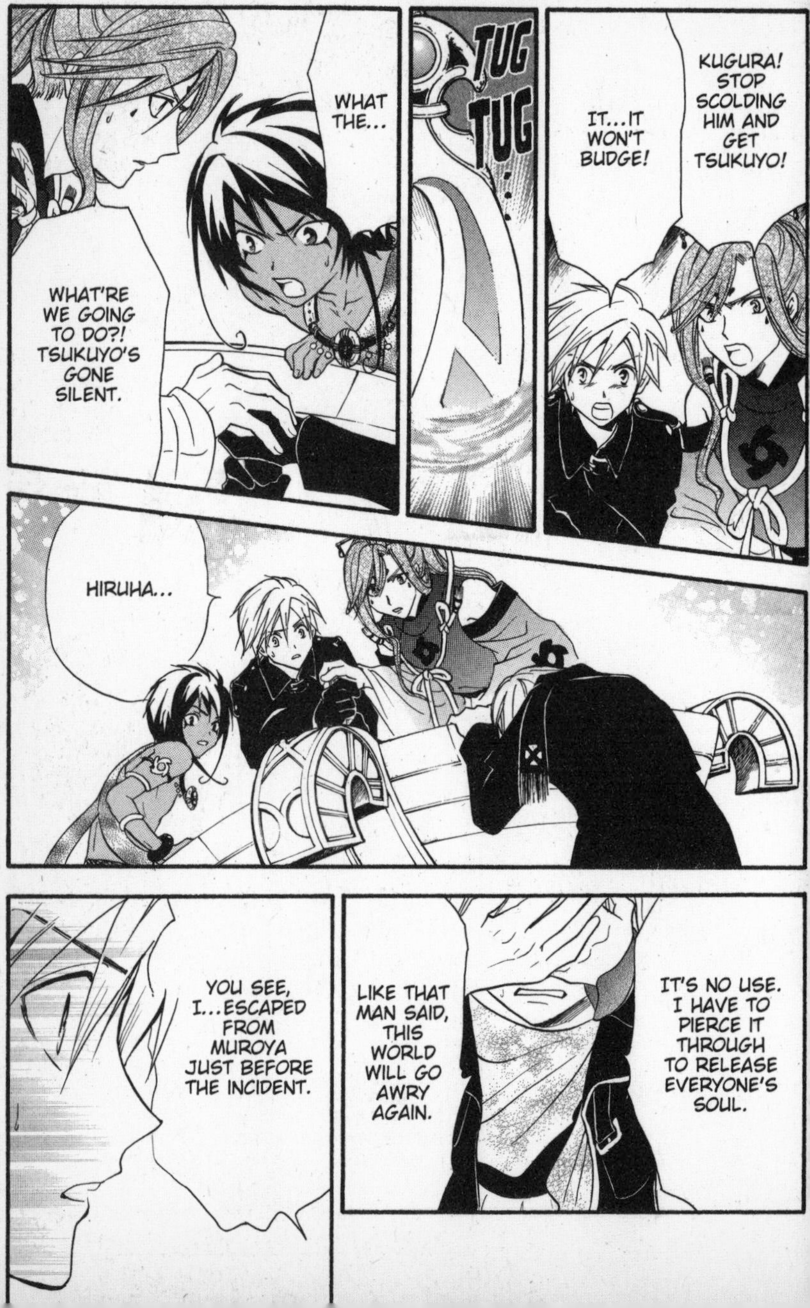
KUGURA! STOP SCOLDING HIM AND GET TSUKUYO!
IT...IT WON'T BUDGE!
TUG TUG
WHAT THE...
WHAT'RE WE GOING TO DO?! TSUKUYO'S GONE SILENT.
HIRUHA...
IT'S NO USE. I HAVE TO PIERCE IT THROUGH TO RELEASE EVERYONE'S SOUL.
LIKE THAT MAN SAID, THIS WORLD WILL GO AWRY AGAIN.
YOU SEE, I...ESCAPED FROM MUROYA JUST BEFORE THE INCIDENT.

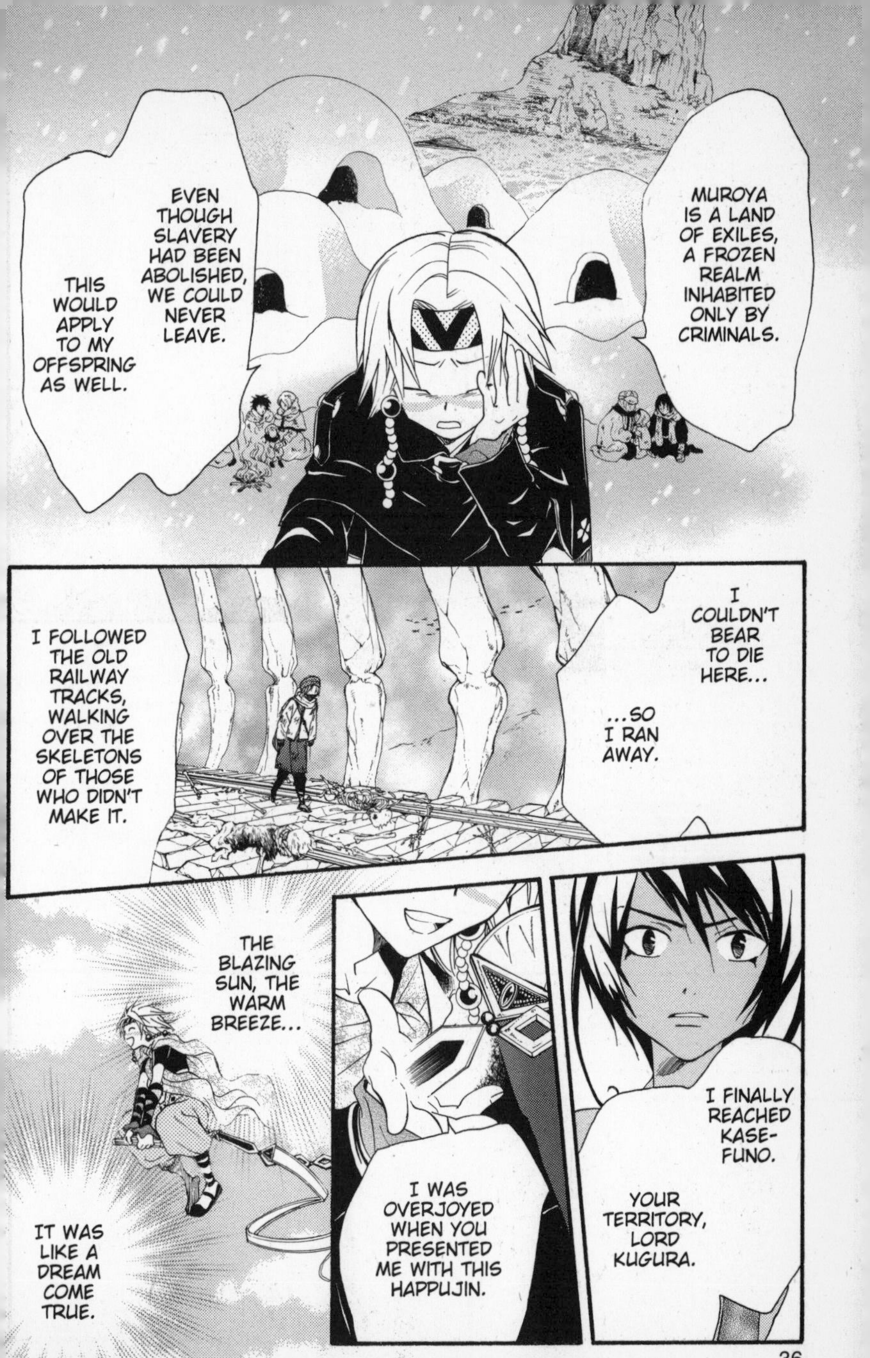
MUROYA IS A LAND OF EXILES, A FROZEN REALM INHABITED ONLY BY CRIMINALS.
EVEN THOUGH SLAVERY HAD BEEN ABOLISHED, WE COULD NEVER LEAVE.
THIS WOULD APPLY TO MY OFFSPRING AS WELL.
I COULDN'T BEAR TO DIE HERE...
...SO I RAN AWAY.
I FOLLOWED THE OLD RAILWAY TRACKS, WALKING OVER THE SKELETONS OF THOSE WHO DIDN'T MAKE IT.
I FINALLY REACHED KASE-FUNO.
YOUR TERRITORY, LORD KUGURA.
I WAS OVERJOYED WHEN YOU PRESENTED ME WITH THIS HAPPUJIN.
THE BLAZING SUN, THE WARM BREEZE...
IT WAS LIKE A DREAM COME TRUE.

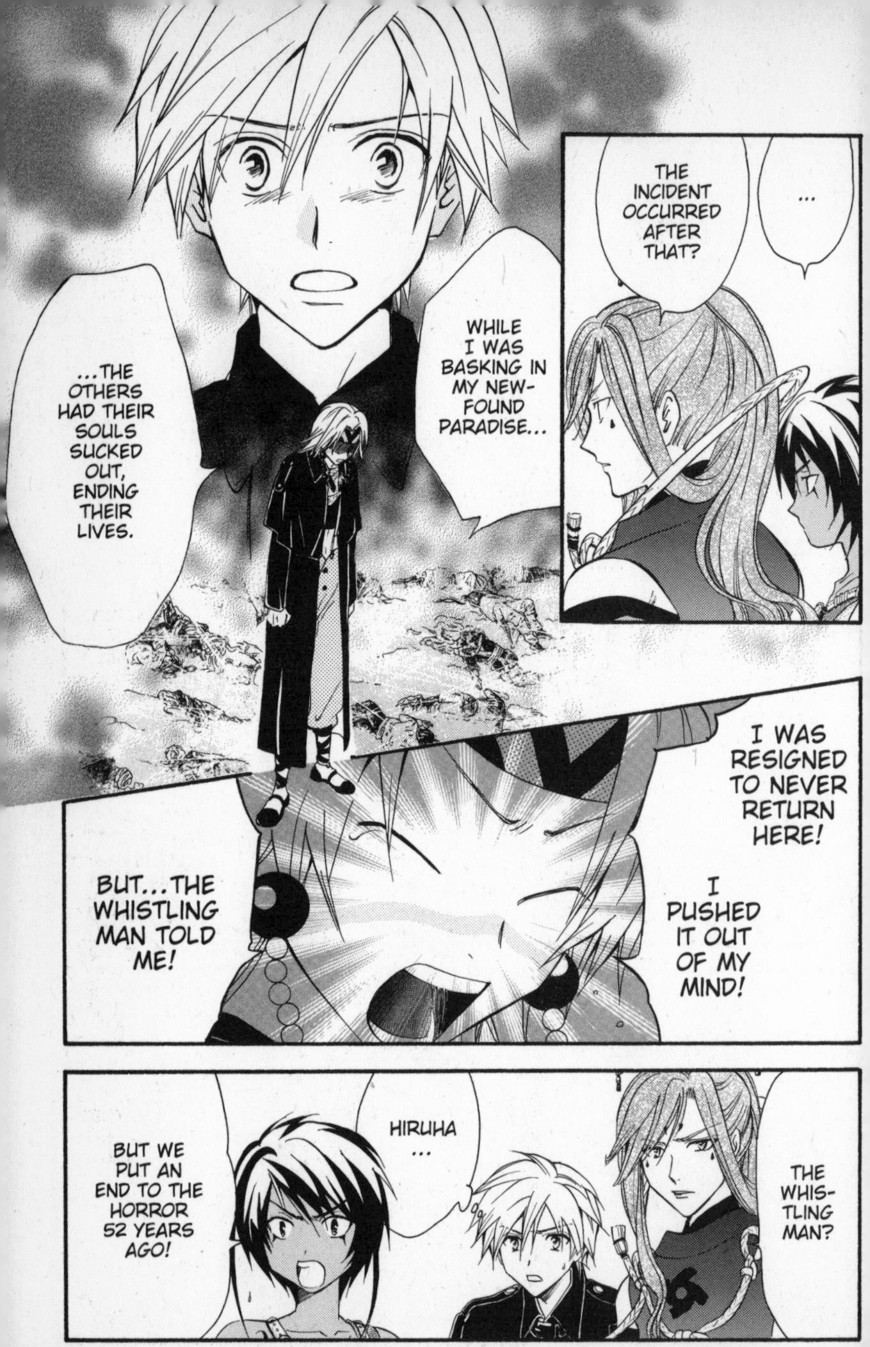
...
THE INCIDENT OCCURRED AFTER THAT?
WHILE I WAS BASKING IN MY NEW-FOUND PARADISE...
...THE OTHERS HAD THEIR SOULS SUCKED OUT, ENDING THEIR LIVES.
I WAS RESIGNED TO NEVER RETURN HERE!
I PUSHED IT OUT OF MY MIND!
BUT...THE WHISTLING MAN TOLD ME!
THE WHIS-TLING MAN?
HIRUHA...
BUT WE PUT AN END TO THE HORROR 52 YEARS AGO!

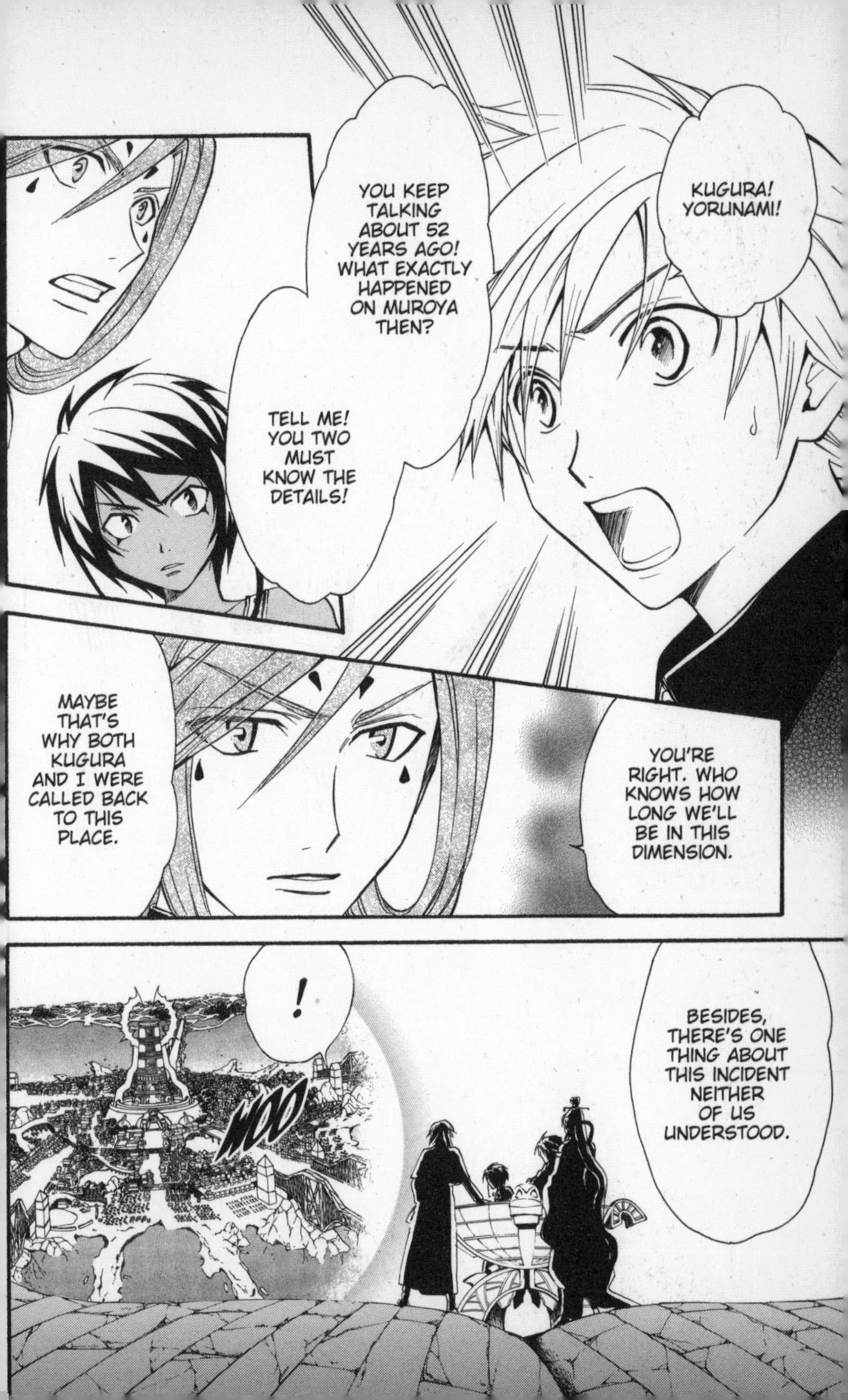
KUGURA! YORUNAMI!
YOU KEEP TALKING ABOUT 52 YEARS AGO! WHAT EXACTLY HAPPENED ON MUROYA THEN?
TELL ME! YOU TWO MUST KNOW THE DETAILS!
YOU'RE RIGHT. WHO KNOWS HOW LONG WE'LL BE IN THIS DIMENSION.
MAYBE THAT'S WHY BOTH KUGURA AND I WERE CALLED BACK TO THIS PLACE.
BESIDES, THERE'S ONE THING ABOUT THIS INCIDENT NEITHER OF US UNDERSTOOD.
!
WOO

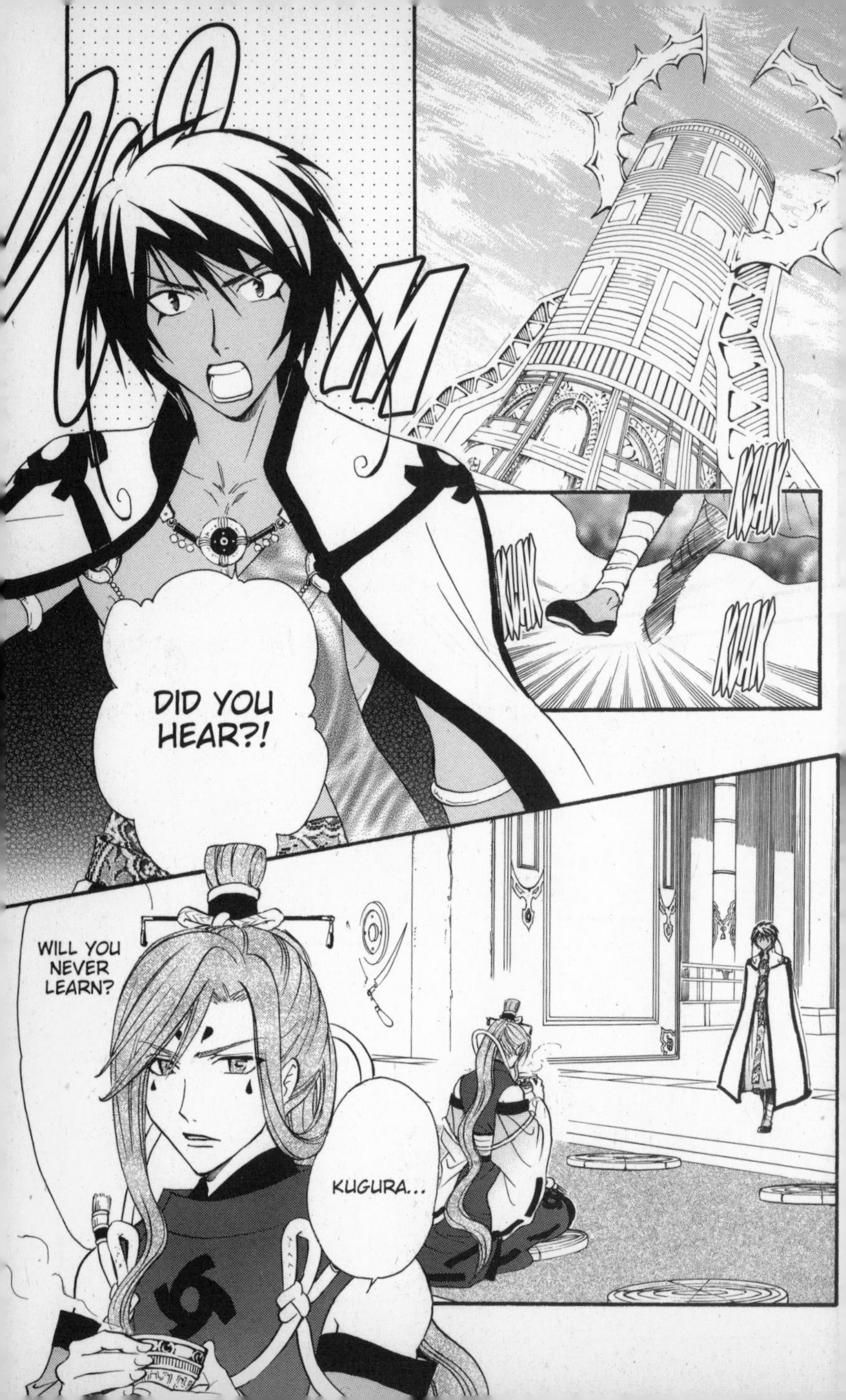
KRAK
KRAK
KRAK
DOOM
DID YOU HEAR?!
KUGURA...
WILL YOU NEVER LEARN?

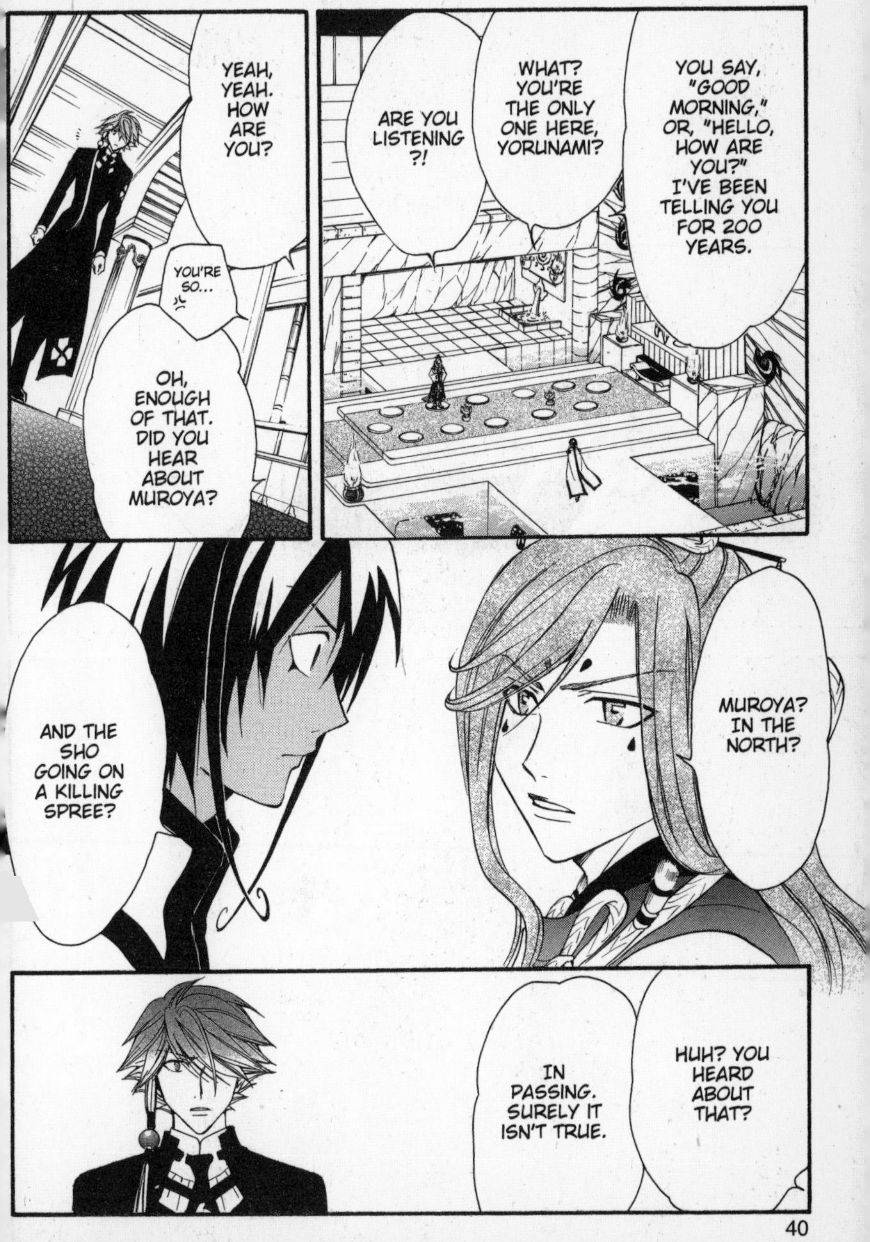
YOU SAY, "GOOD MORNING," OR, "HELLO, HOW ARE YOU?" I'VE BEEN TELLING YOU FOR 200 YEARS.
WHAT? YOU'RE THE ONLY ONE HERE, YORUNAMI?
ARE YOU LISTENING ?!
YEAH, YEAH. HOW ARE YOU?
YOU'RE SO...
OH, ENOUGH OF THAT. DID YOU HEAR ABOUT MUROYA?
MUROYA? IN THE NORTH?
AND THE SHO GOING ON A KILLING SPREE?
HUH? YOU HEARD ABOUT THAT?
IN PASSING. SURELY IT ISN'T TRUE.

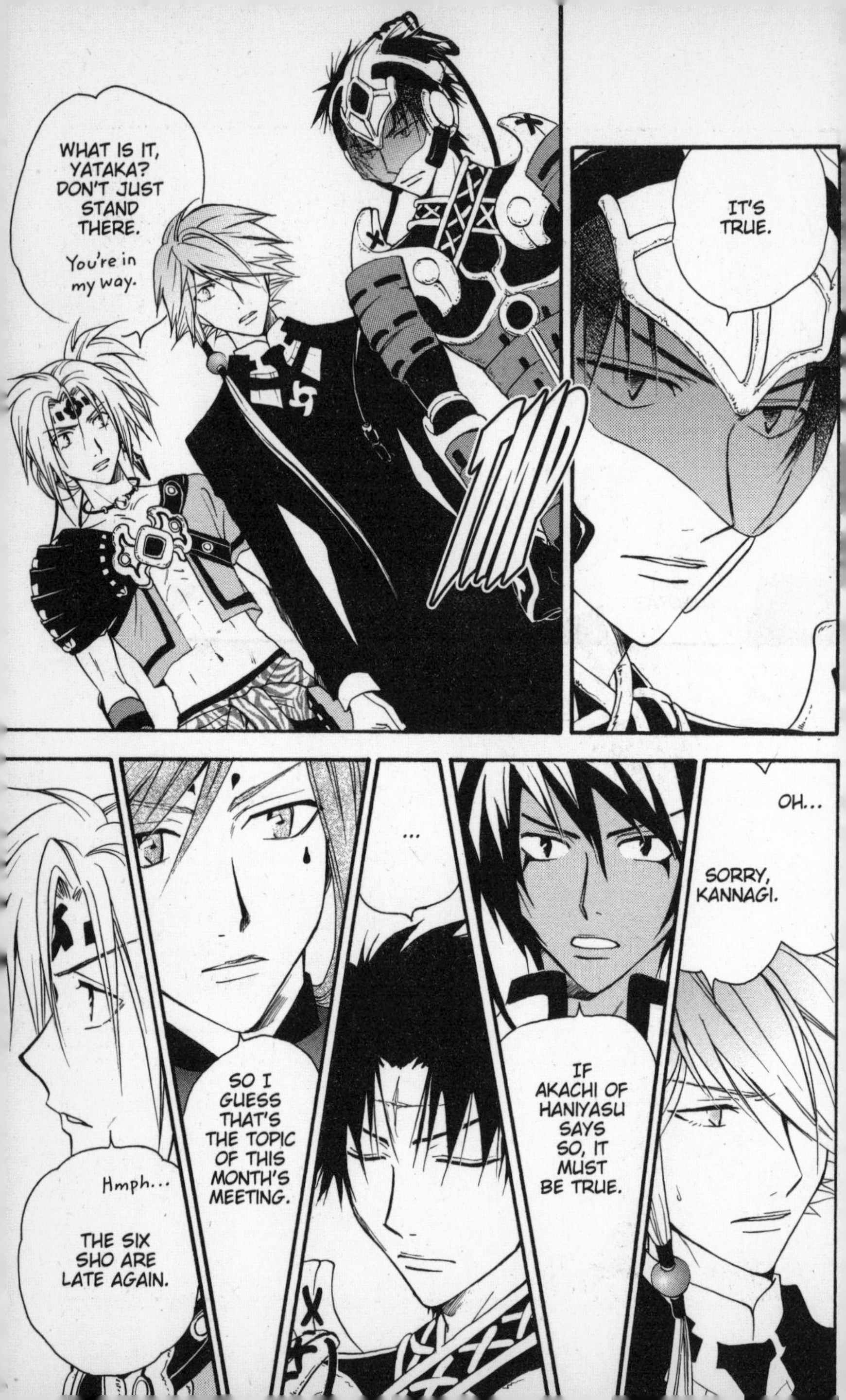
IT'S TRUE.
WHAT IS IT, YATAKA? DON'T JUST STAND THERE.
You're in my way.
OH...
SORRY, KANNAGI.
IF AKACHI OF HANIYASU SAYS SO, IT MUST BE TRUE.
...
SO I GUESS THAT'S THE TOPIC OF THIS MONTH'S MEETING.
Hmph...
THE SIX SHO ARE LATE AGAIN.

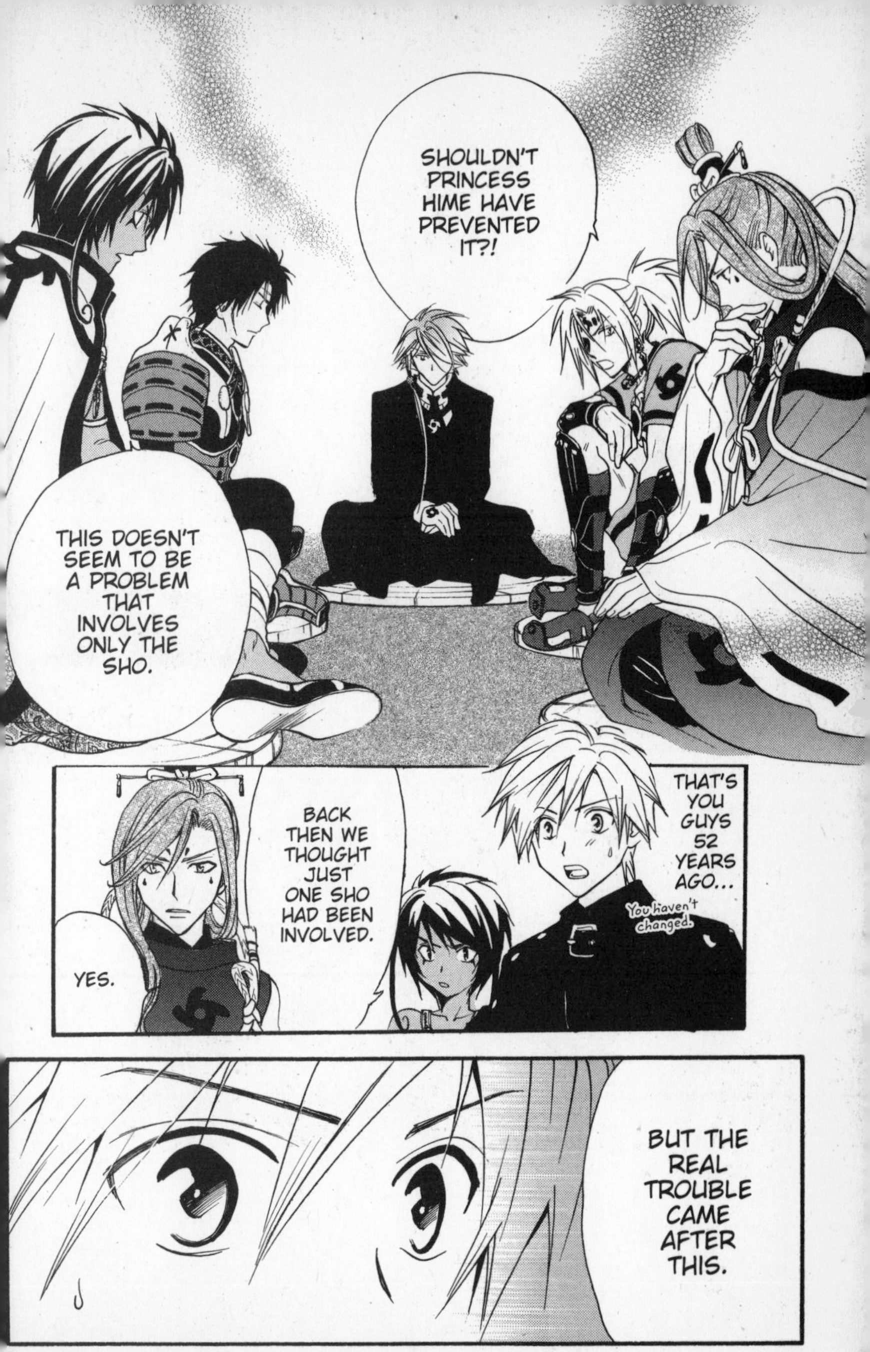
SHOULDN'T PRINCESS HIME HAVE PREVENTED IT?!
THIS DOESN'T SEEM TO BE A PROBLEM THAT INVOLVES ONLY THE SHO.
THAT'S YOU GUYS 52 YEARS AGO...
You haven't changed.
BACK THEN WE THOUGHT JUST ONE SHO HAD BEEN INVOLVED.
YES.
BUT THE REAL TROUBLE CAME AFTER THIS.

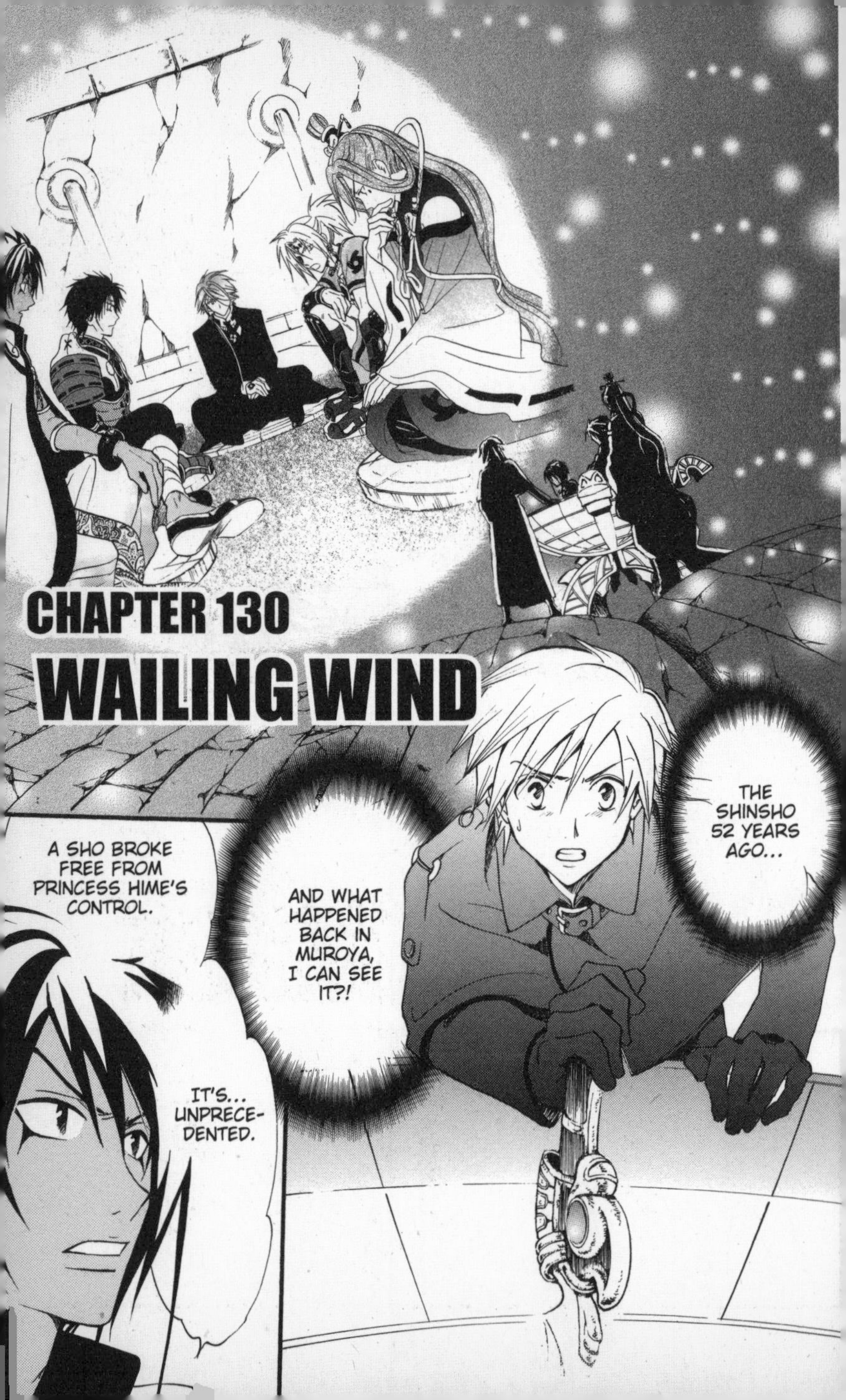
CHAPTER 130
WAILING WIND
THE SHINSHO 52 YEARS AGO...
AND WHAT HAPPENED BACK IN MUROYA, I CAN SEE IT?!
A SHO BROKE FREE FROM PRINCESS HIME'S CONTROL.
IT'S... UNPRECE-DENTED.

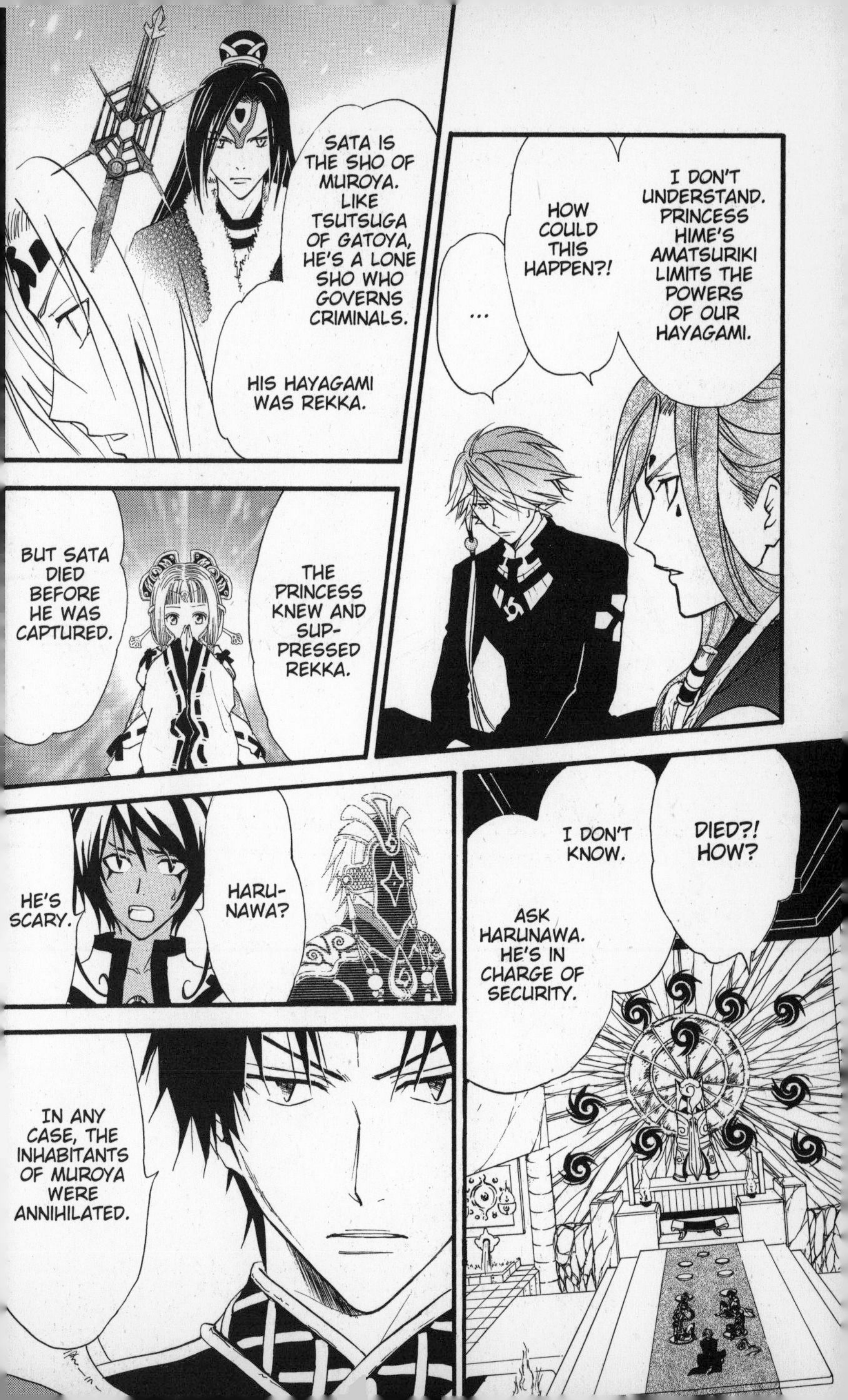

SATA IS THE SHO OF MUROYA. LIKE TSUTSUGA OF GATOYA, HE'S A LONE SHO WHO GOVERNS CRIMINALS.
HIS HAYAGAMI WAS REKKA.
I DON'T UNDERSTAND. PRINCESS HIME'S AMATSURIKI LIMITS THE POWERS OF OUR HAYAGAMI.
HOW COULD THIS HAPPEN?!
...
THE PRINCESS KNEW AND SUP-PRESSED REKKA.
BUT SATA DIED BEFORE HE WAS CAPTURED.
DIED?! HOW?
I DON'T KNOW.
ASK HARUNAWA. HE'S IN CHARGE OF SECURITY.
HARU-NAWA?
HE'S SCARY.
IN ANY CASE, THE INHABITANTS OF MUROYA WERE ANNIHILATED.

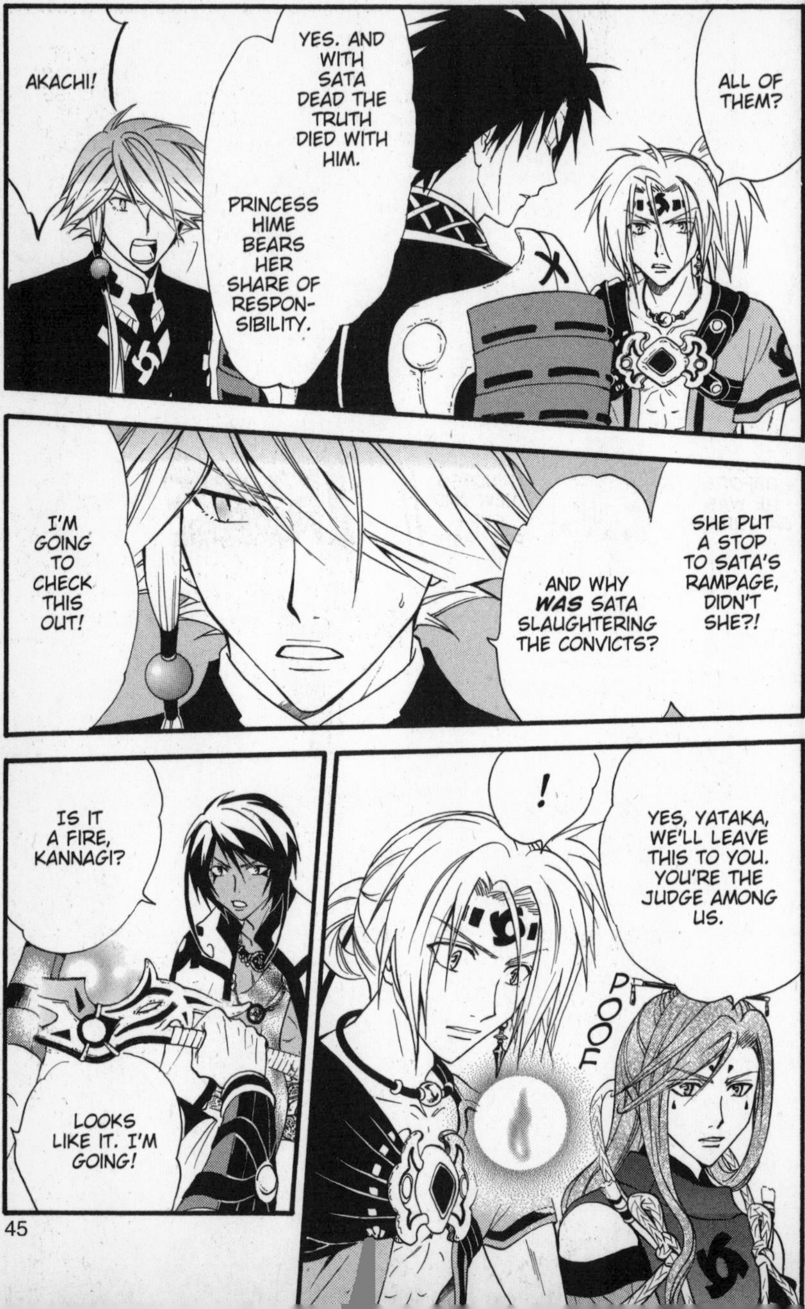
ALL OF THEM?
YES. AND WITH SATA DEAD THE TRUTH DIED WITH HIM.
PRINCESS HIME BEARS HER SHARE OF RESPON-SIBILITY.
AKACHI!
SHE PUT A STOP TO SATA'S RAMPAGE, DIDN'T SHE?!
AND WHY *WAS* SATA SLAUGHTERING THE CONVICTS?
I'M GOING TO CHECK THIS OUT!
YES, YATAKA, WE'LL LEAVE THIS TO YOU. YOU'RE THE JUDGE AMONG US.
!
POOF
IS IT A FIRE, KANNAGI?
LOOKS LIKE IT. I'M GOING!

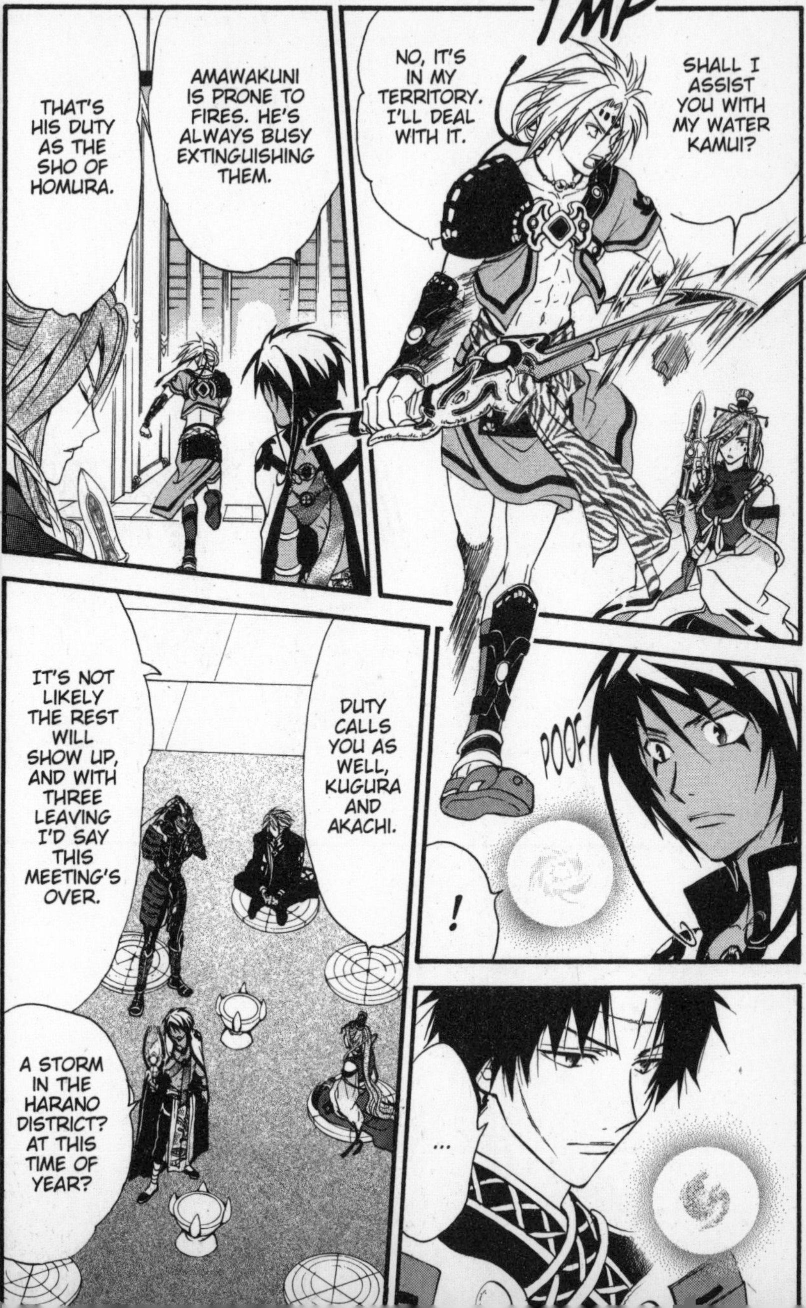
TMP
SHALL I ASSIST YOU WITH MY WATER KAMUI?
NO, IT'S IN MY TERRITORY. I'LL DEAL WITH IT.
AMAWAKUNI IS PRONE TO FIRES. HE'S ALWAYS BUSY EXTINGUISHING THEM.
THAT'S HIS DUTY AS THE SHO OF HOMURA.
POOF
!
...
DUTY CALLS YOU AS WELL, KUGURA AND AKACHI.
IT'S NOT LIKELY THE REST WILL SHOW UP, AND WITH THREE LEAVING I'D SAY THIS MEETING'S OVER.
A STORM IN THE HARANO DISTRICT? AT THIS TIME OF YEAR?

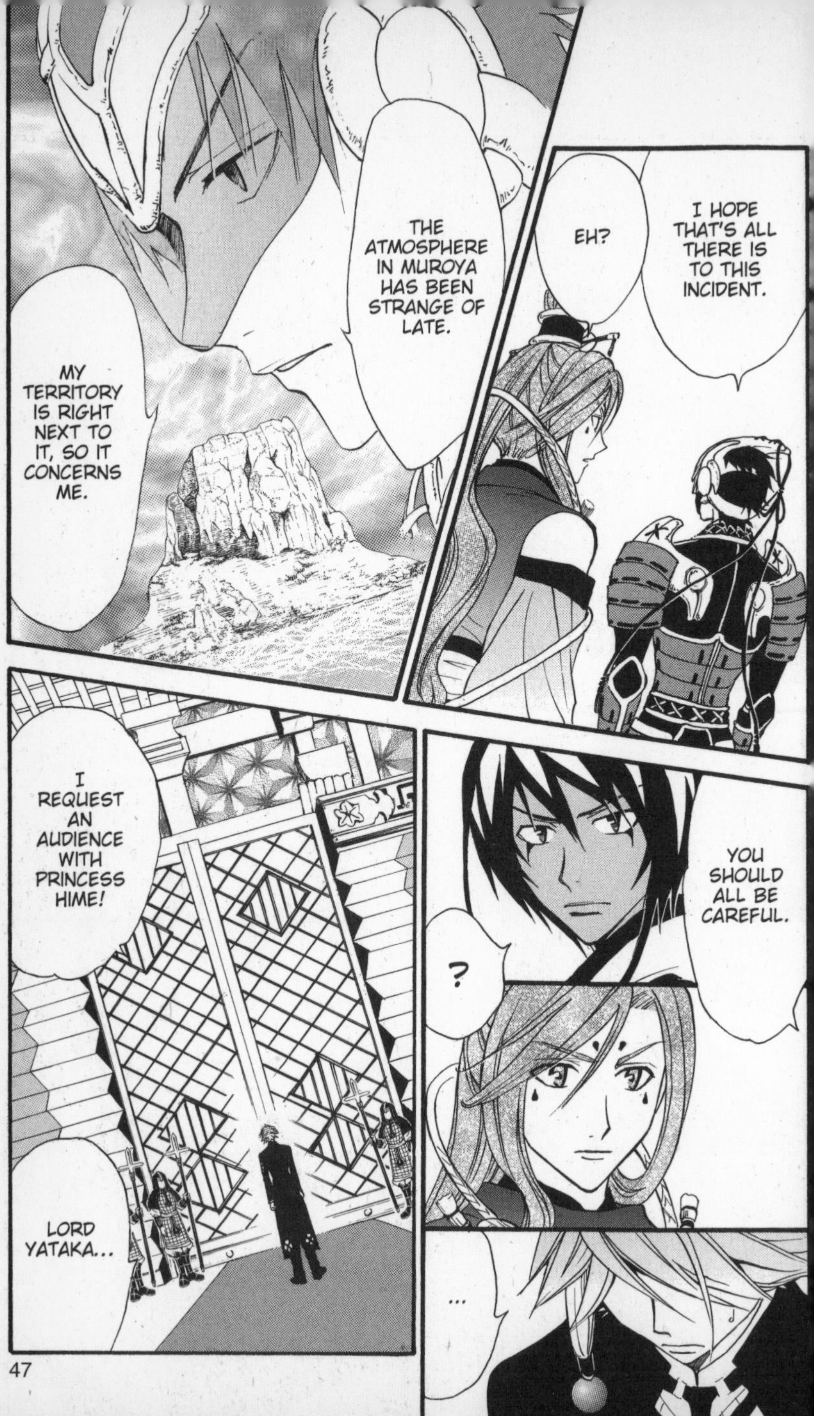
THE ATMOSPHERE IN MUROYA HAS BEEN STRANGE OF LATE.
MY TERRITORY IS RIGHT NEXT TO IT, SO IT CONCERNS ME.
I HOPE THAT'S ALL THERE IS TO THIS INCIDENT.
EH?
YOU SHOULD ALL BE CAREFUL.
?
...
I REQUEST AN AUDIENCE WITH PRINCESS HIME!
LORD YATAKA...

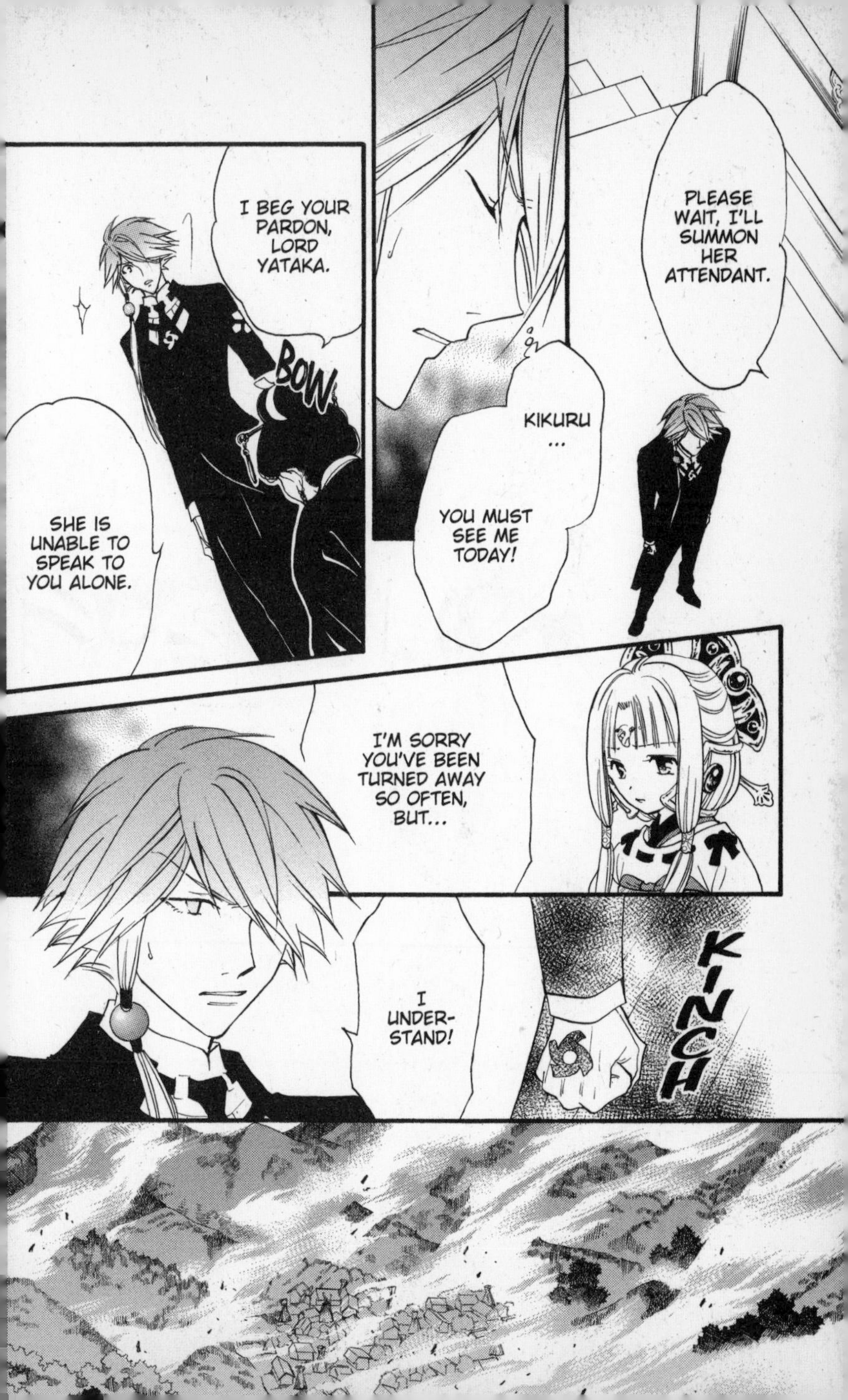
PLEASE WAIT, I'LL SUMMON HER ATTENDANT.
KIKURU ...
YOU MUST SEE ME TODAY!
I BEG YOUR PARDON, LORD YATAKA.
BOW
SHE IS UNABLE TO SPEAK TO YOU ALONE.
I'M SORRY YOU'VE BEEN TURNED AWAY SO OFTEN, BUT...
KINCH
I UNDER-STAND!

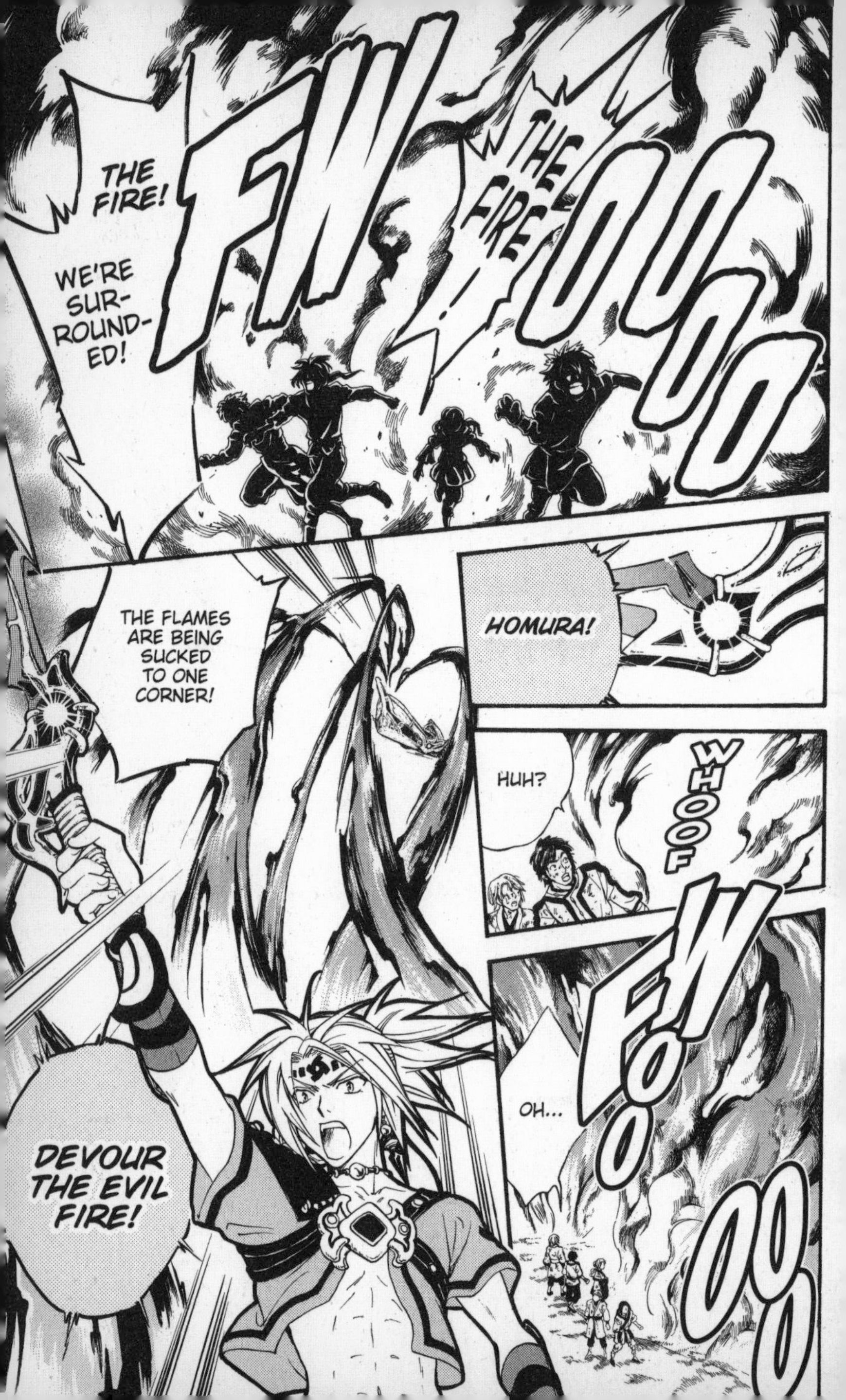

THE FIRE
FWOOOO
THE FIRE!
WE'RE SUR-ROUND-ED!
HOMURA!
HUH?
WHOOF
OH...
FWOOOOOOO
THE FLAMES ARE BEING SUCKED TO ONE CORNER!
DEVOUR THE EVIL FIRE!

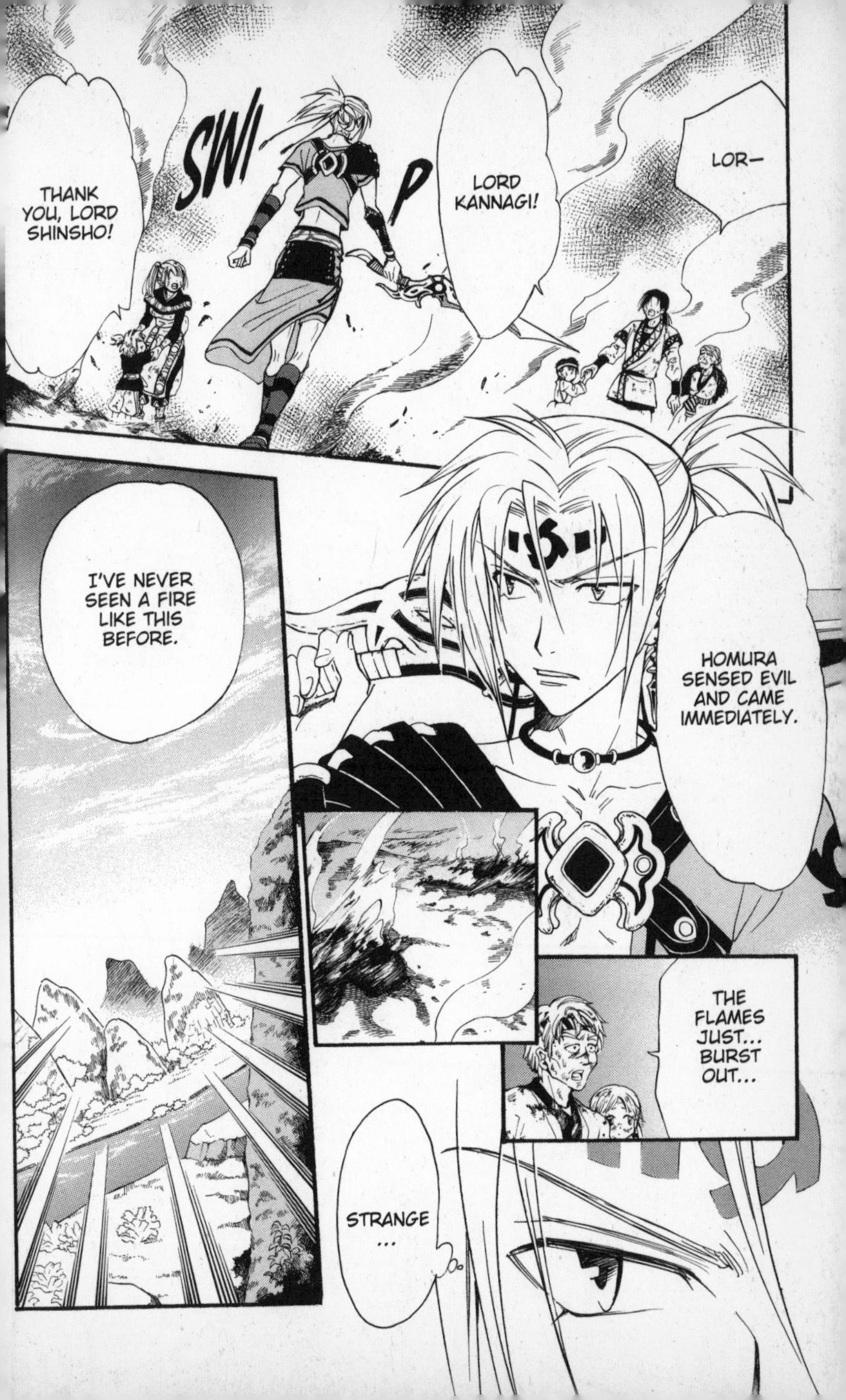
LOR—
LORD KANNAGI!
SWIP
THANK YOU, LORD SHINSHO!
HOMURA SENSED EVIL AND CAME IMMEDIATELY.
I'VE NEVER SEEN A FIRE LIKE THIS BEFORE.
THE FLAMES JUST... BURST OUT...
STRANGE...

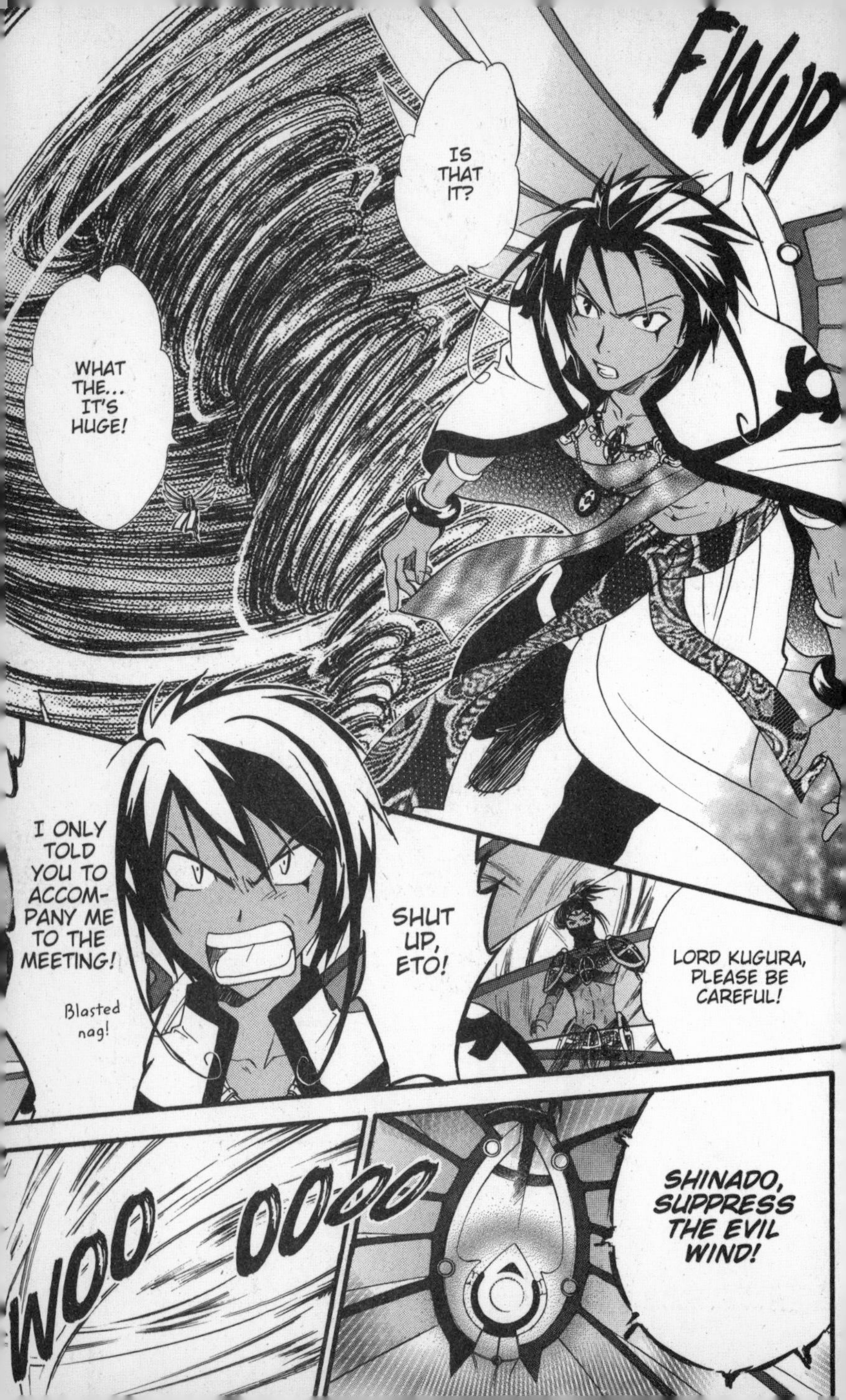
FWUP
IS THAT IT?
WHAT THE... IT'S HUGE!
LORD KUGURA, PLEASE BE CAREFUL!
SHUT UP, ETO!
I ONLY TOLD YOU TO ACCOMPANY ME TO THE MEETING!
Blasted nag!
SHINADO, SUPPRESS THE EVIL WIND!
WOO OOOO

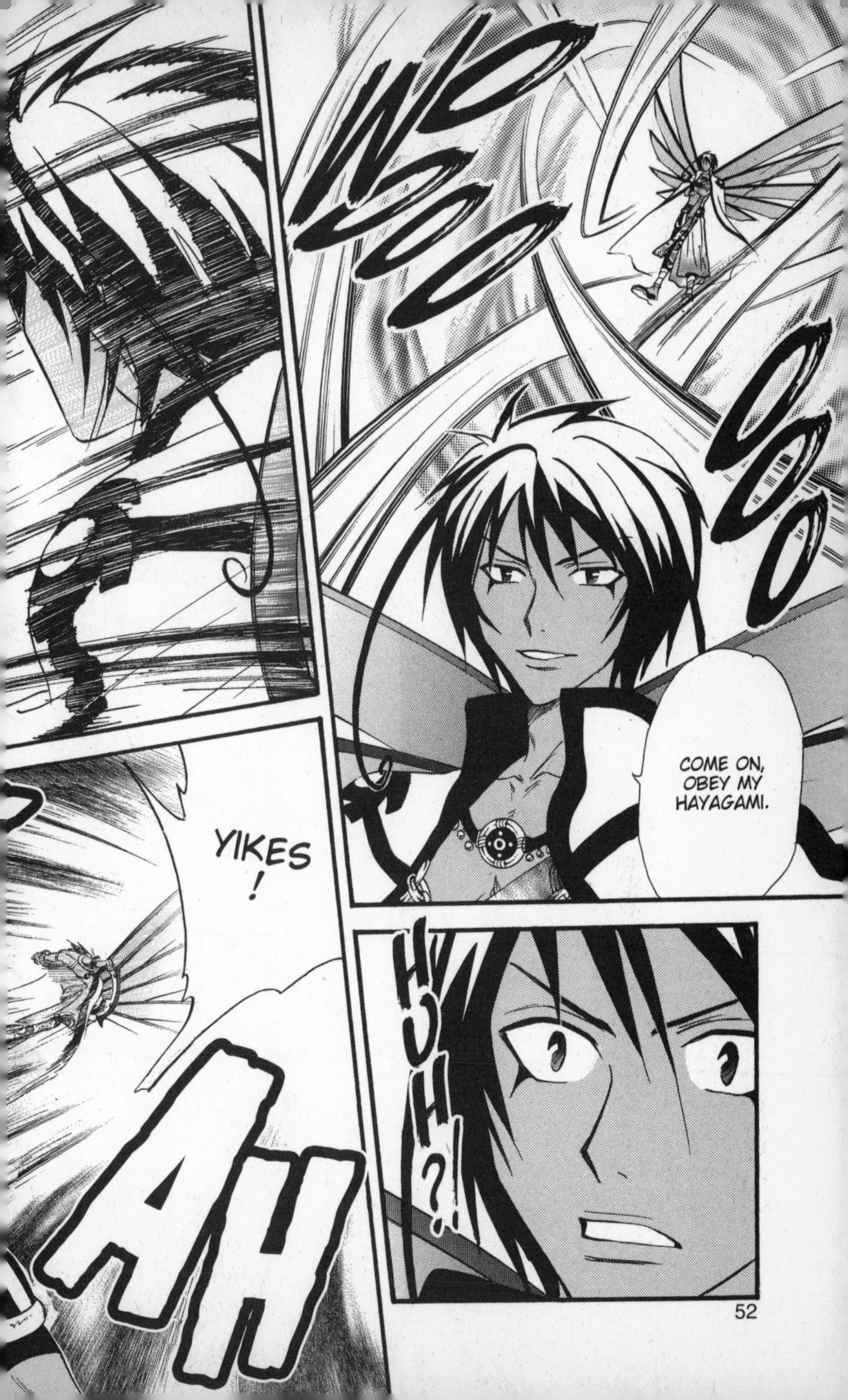
WOOOO
OOOO
COME ON, OBEY MY HAYAGAMI.
HUH?!
YIKES!
AH

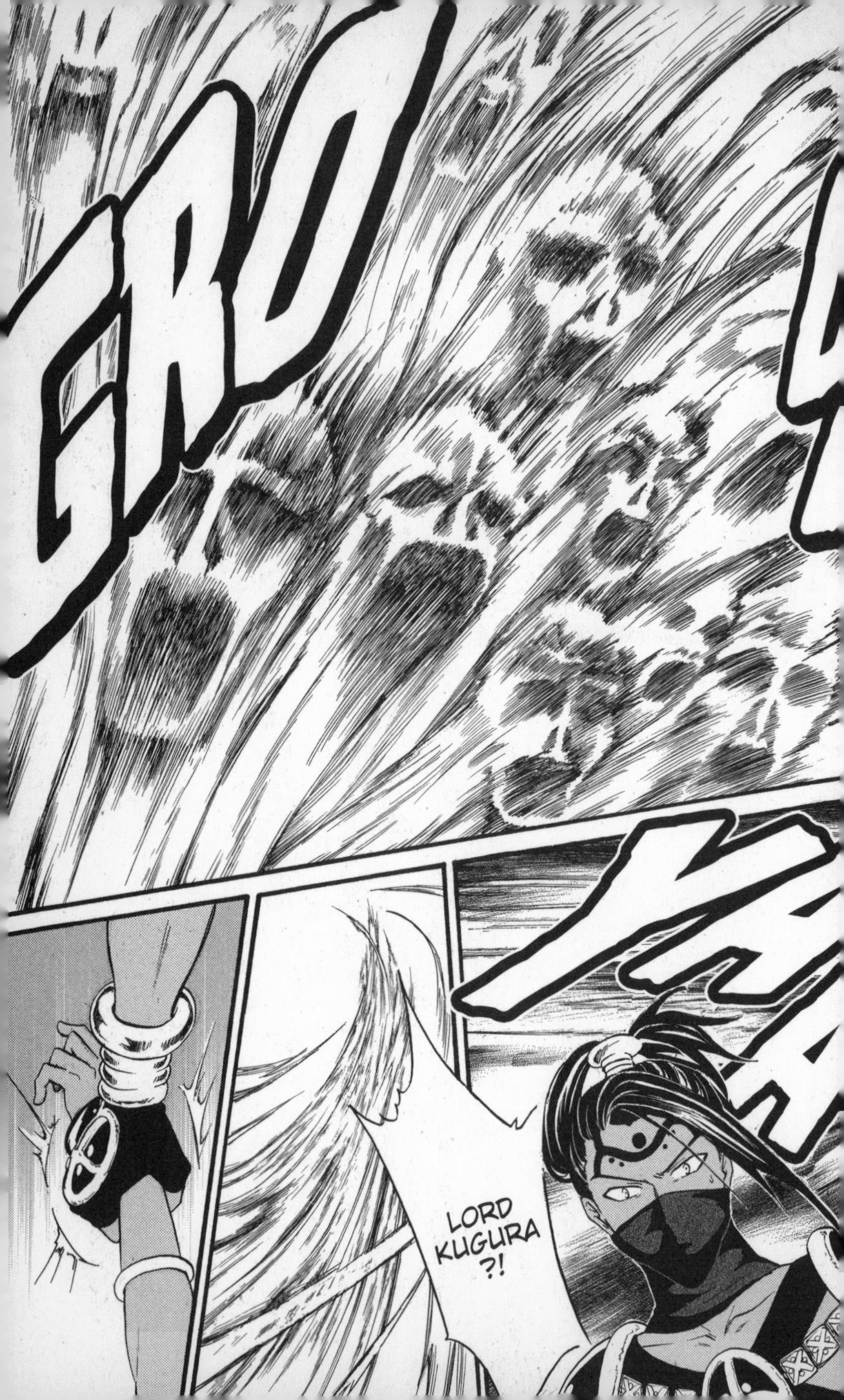
LORD KUGURA ?!

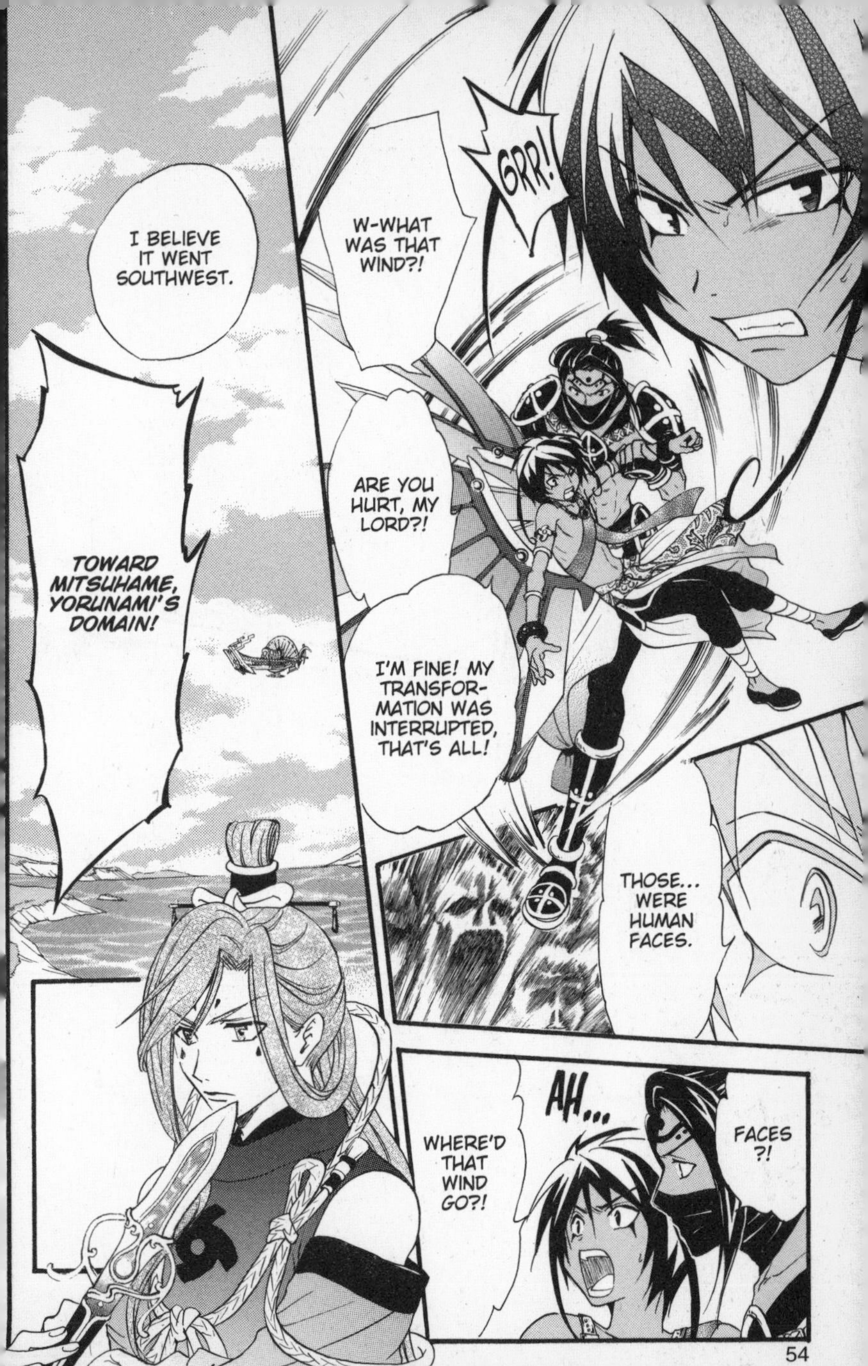
GRR!
W-WHAT WAS THAT WIND?!
ARE YOU HURT, MY LORD?!
I'M FINE! MY TRANSFOR-MATION WAS INTERRUPTED, THAT'S ALL!
THOSE... WERE HUMAN FACES.
FACES ?!
AH...
WHERE'D THAT WIND GO?!
I BELIEVE IT WENT SOUTHWEST.
TOWARD MITSUHAME, YORUNAMI'S DOMAIN!

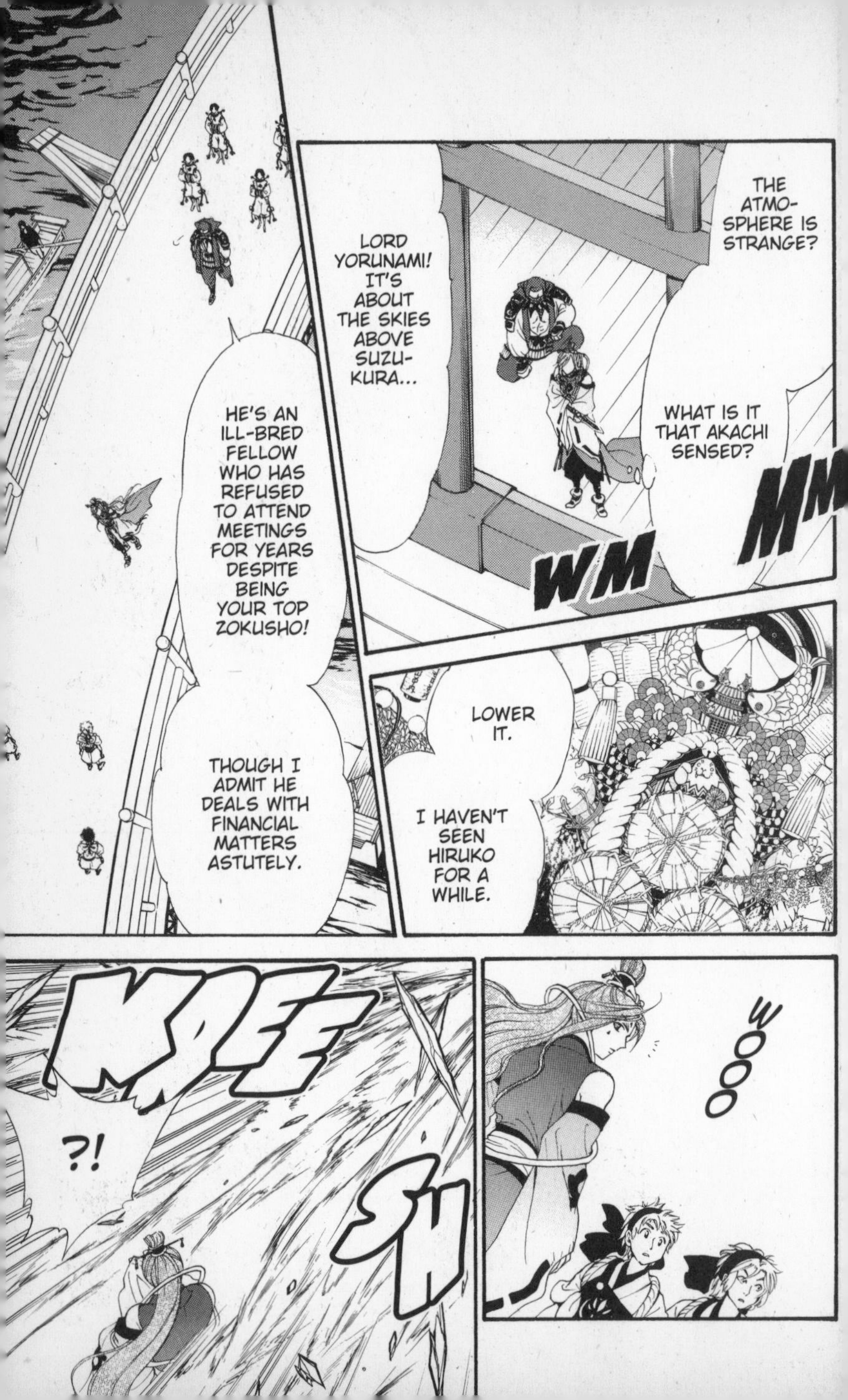
THE ATMOSPHERE IS STRANGE?
WHAT IS IT THAT AKACHI SENSED?
LORD YORUNAMI! IT'S ABOUT THE SKIES ABOVE SUZUKURA...
WM MM
LOWER IT.
I HAVEN'T SEEN HIRUKO FOR A WHILE.
HE'S AN ILL-BRED FELLOW WHO HAS REFUSED TO ATTEND MEETINGS FOR YEARS DESPITE BEING YOUR TOP ZOKUSHO!
THOUGH I ADMIT HE DEALS WITH FINANCIAL MATTERS ASTUTELY.
WOOOO
?!
SH

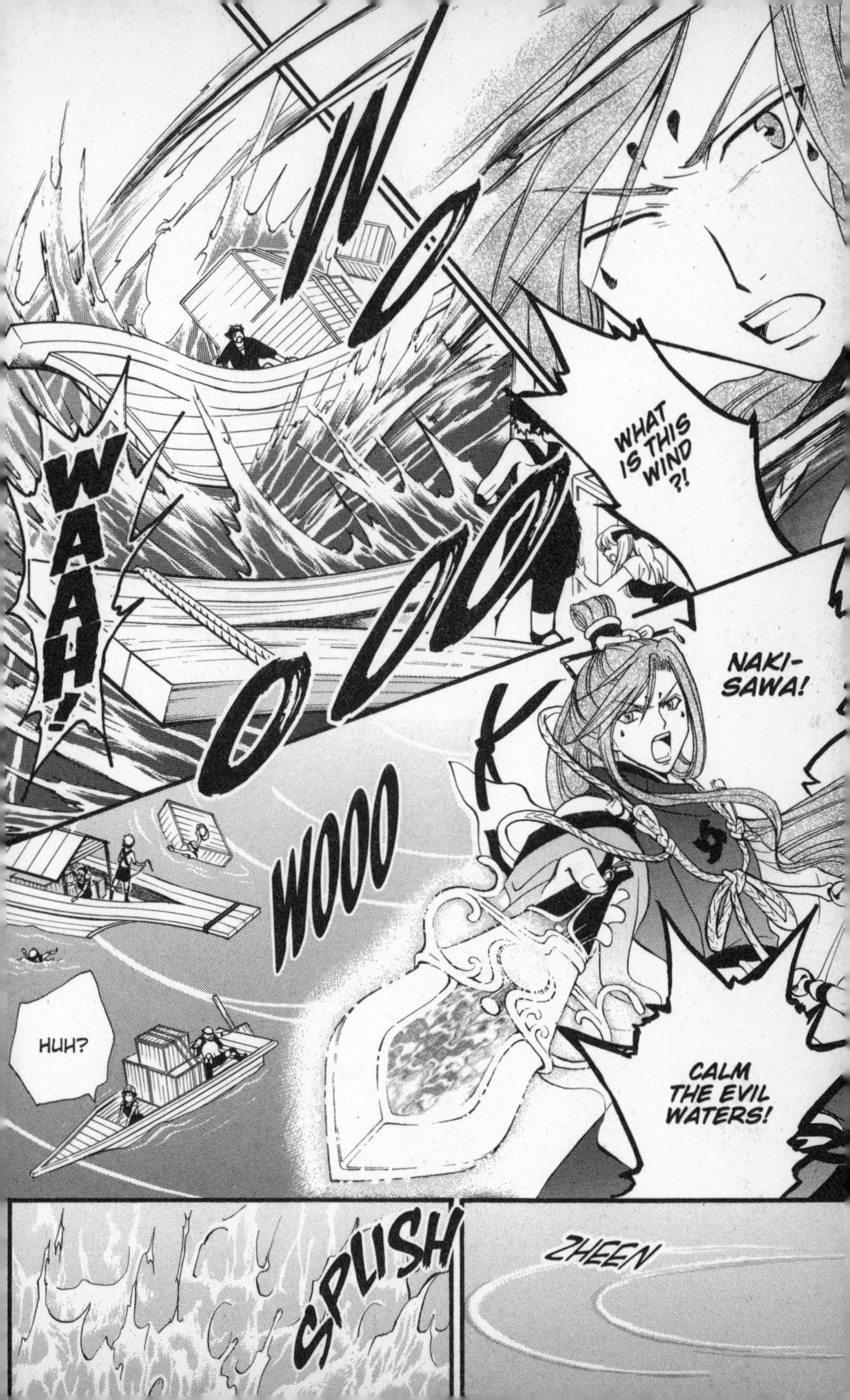
WHAT IS THIS WIND ?!
WAAH!
NAKI-SAWA!
CALM THE EVIL WATERS!
WOOO
HUH?
ZHEEN
SPLISH

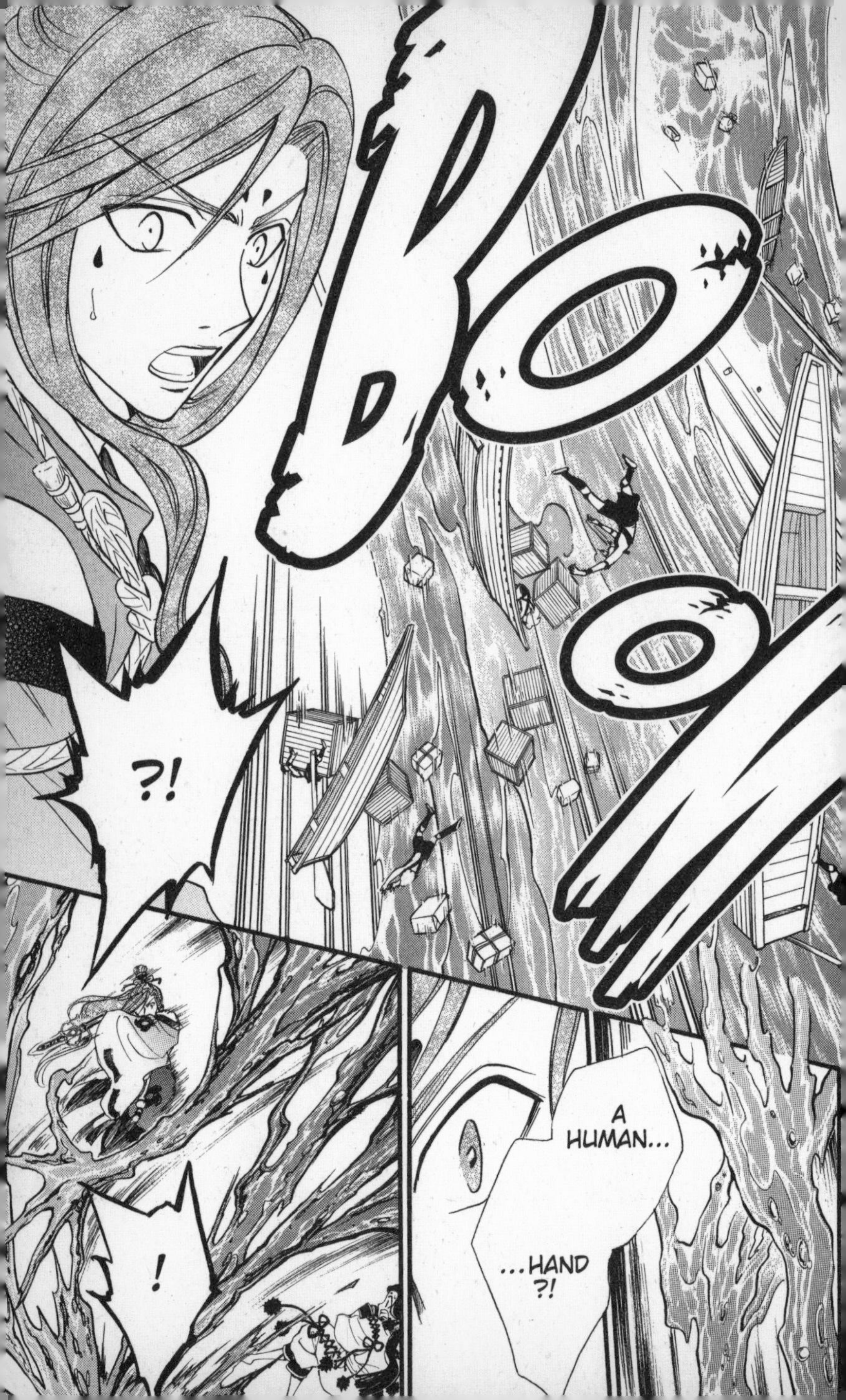
?!
A HUMAN...
...HAND ?!
!

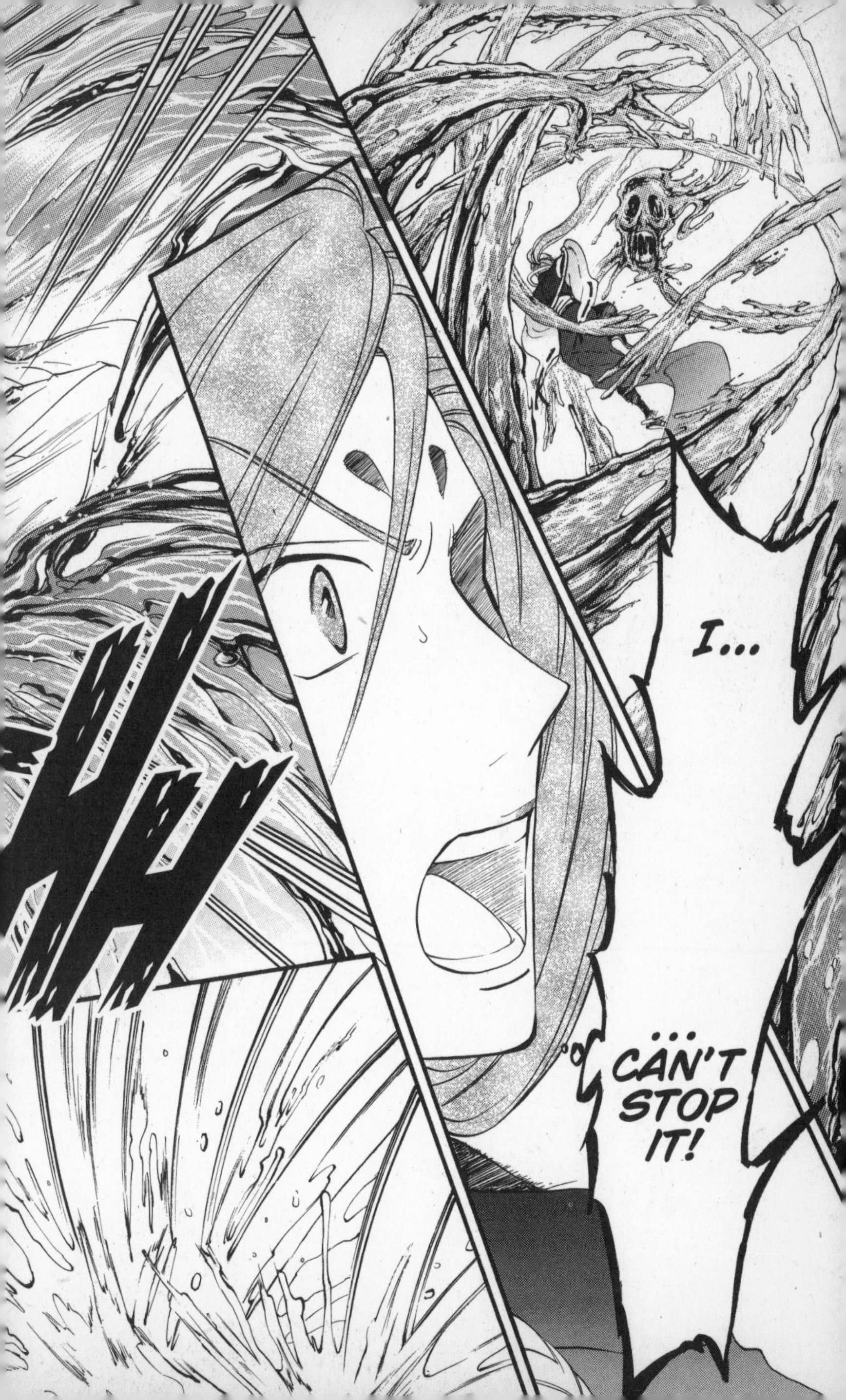
I...
...CAN'T STOP IT!

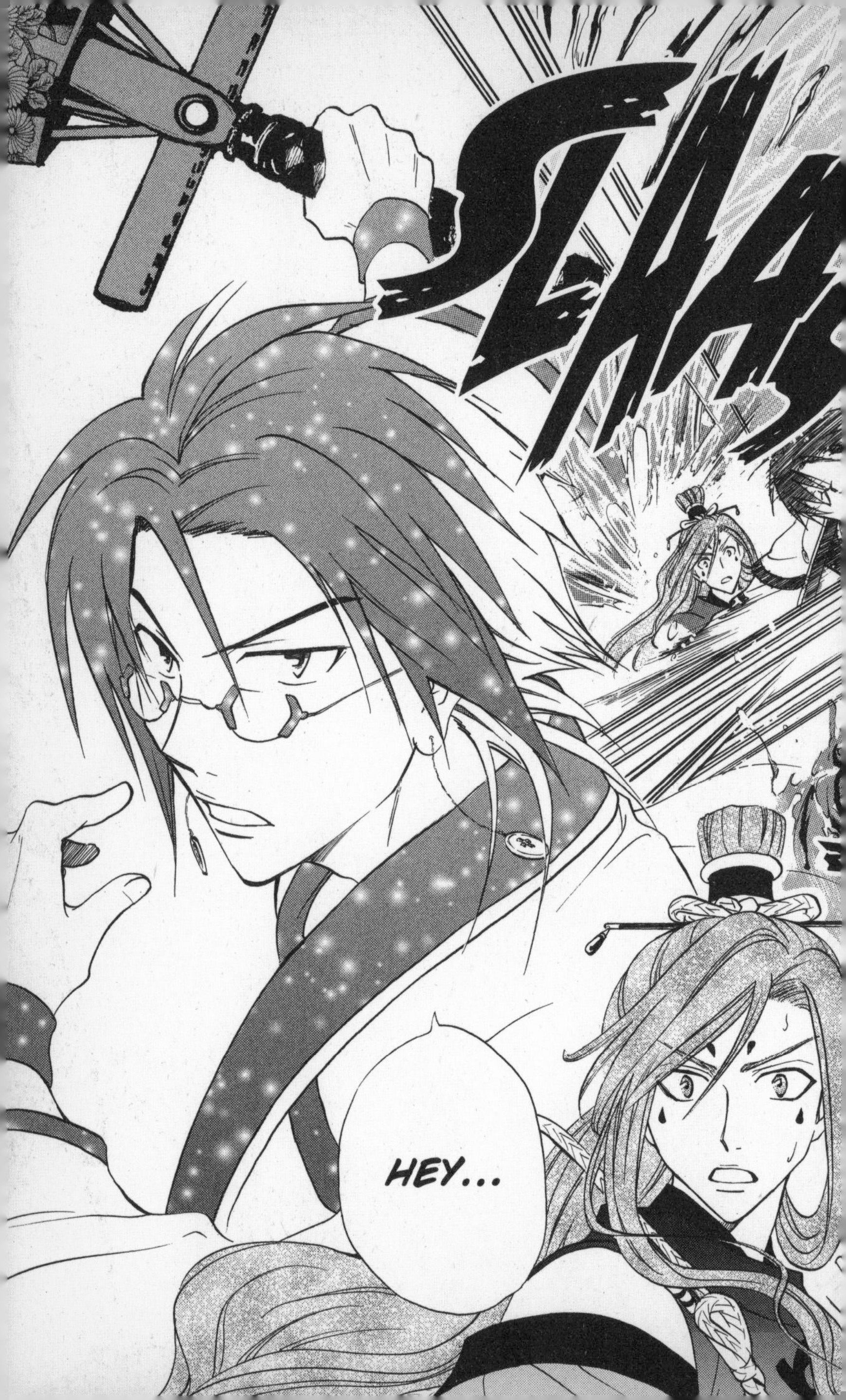
SHA
HEY...

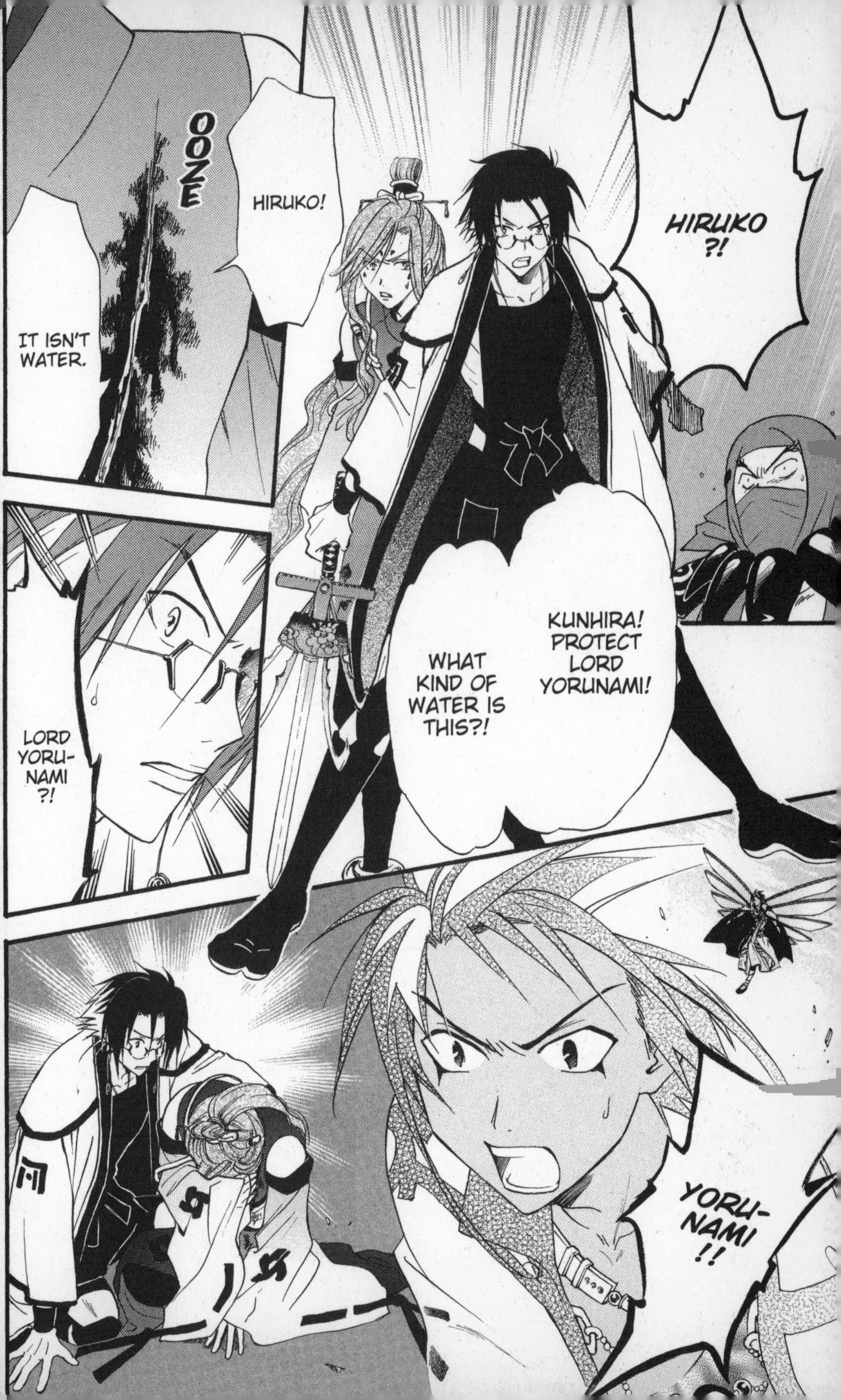
HIRUKO ?!
KUNHIRA! PROTECT LORD YORUNAMI!
WHAT KIND OF WATER IS THIS?!
OOZE
HIRUKO!
IT ISN'T WATER.
LORD YORU-NAMI ?!
YORU-NAMI !!

CHAPTER 131
ONE'S LIFE

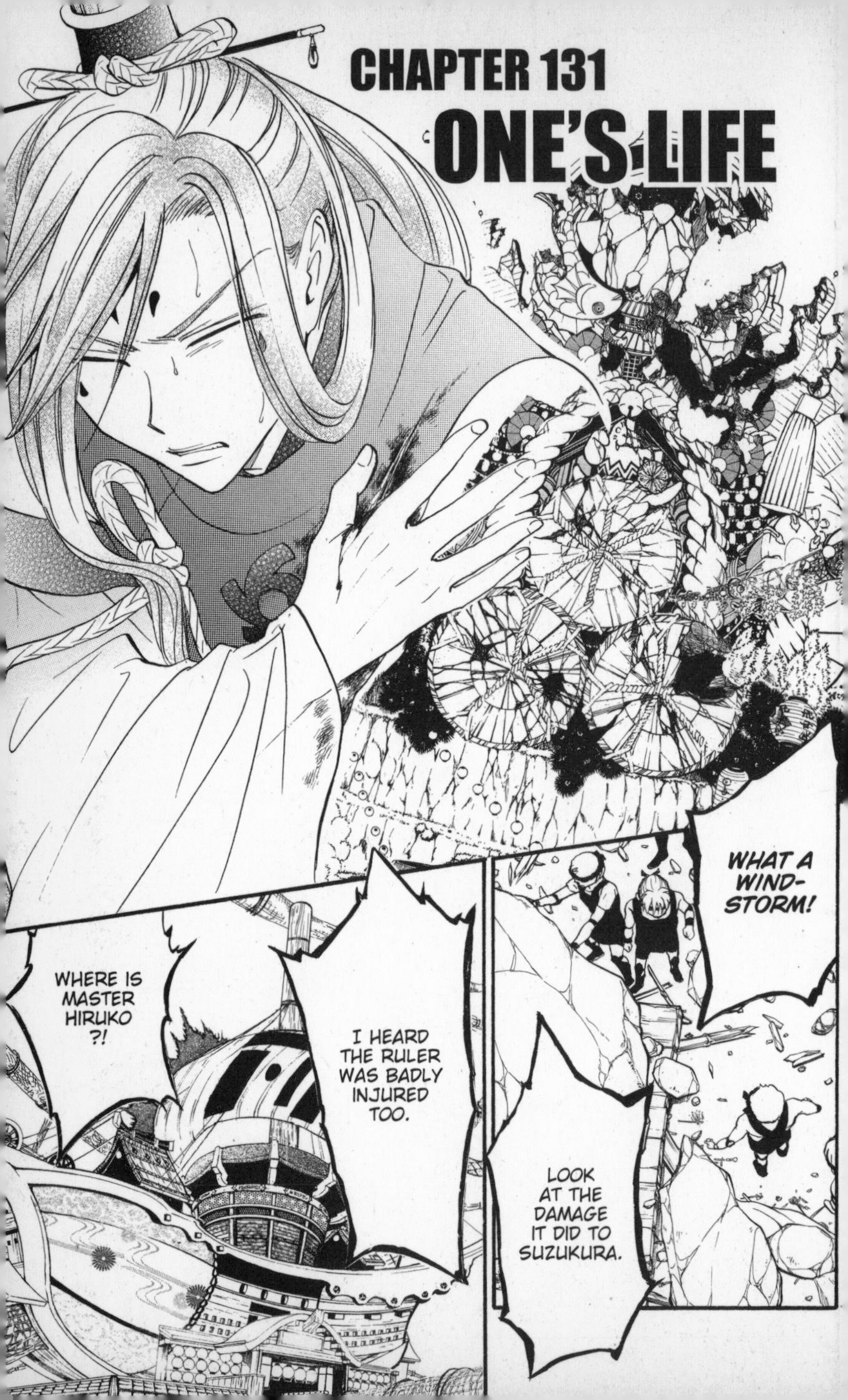
WHAT A WIND-STORM!
LOOK AT THE DAMAGE IT DID TO SUZUKURA.
I HEARD THE RULER WAS BADLY INJURED TOO.
WHERE IS MASTER HIRUKO ?!

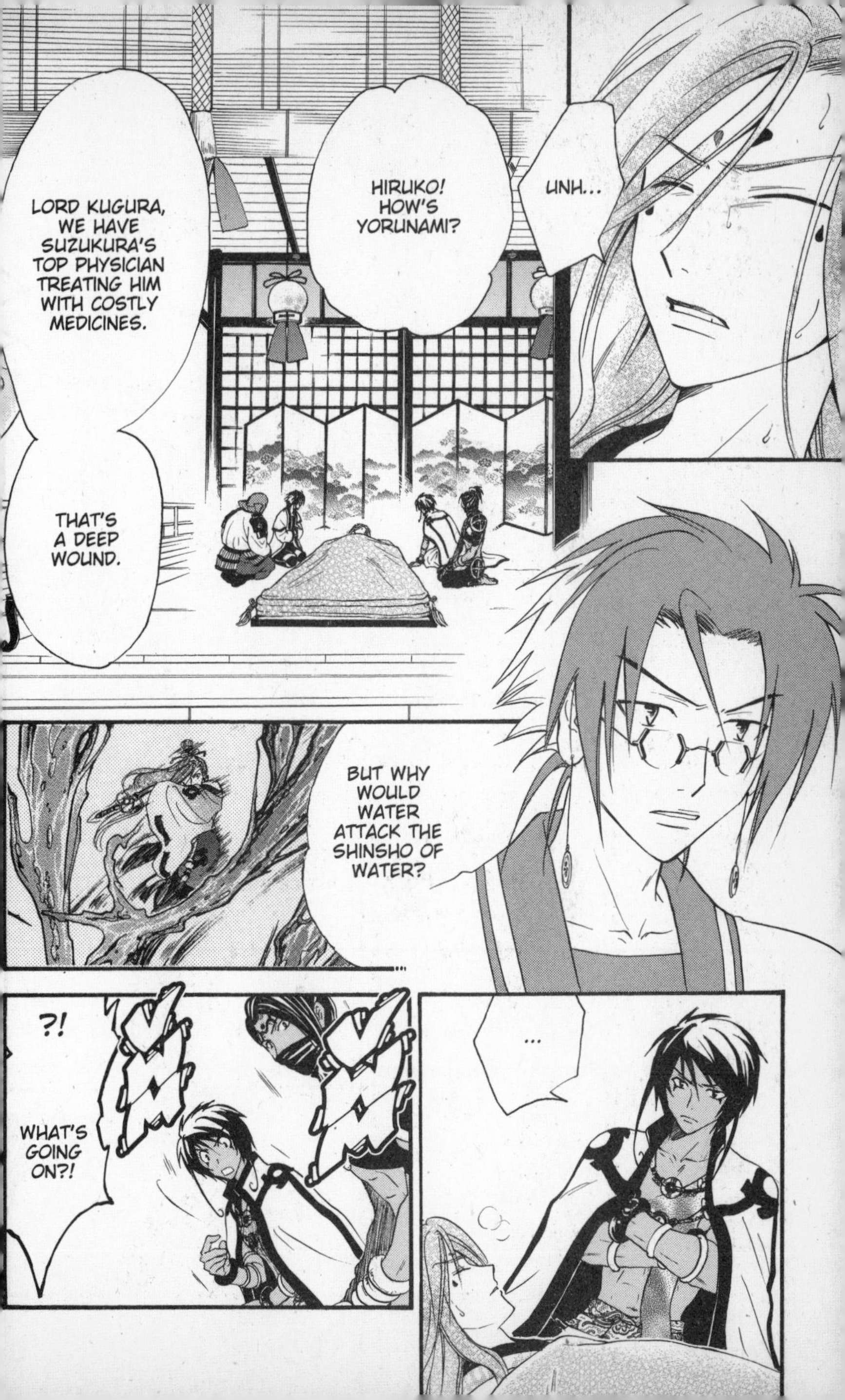
UNH...
HIRUKO! HOW'S YORUNAMI?
LORD KUGURA, WE HAVE SUZUKURA'S TOP PHYSICIAN TREATING HIM WITH COSTLY MEDICINES.
THAT'S A DEEP WOUND.
BUT WHY WOULD WATER ATTACK THE SHINSHO OF WATER?
...
?!
WHAT'S GOING ON?!

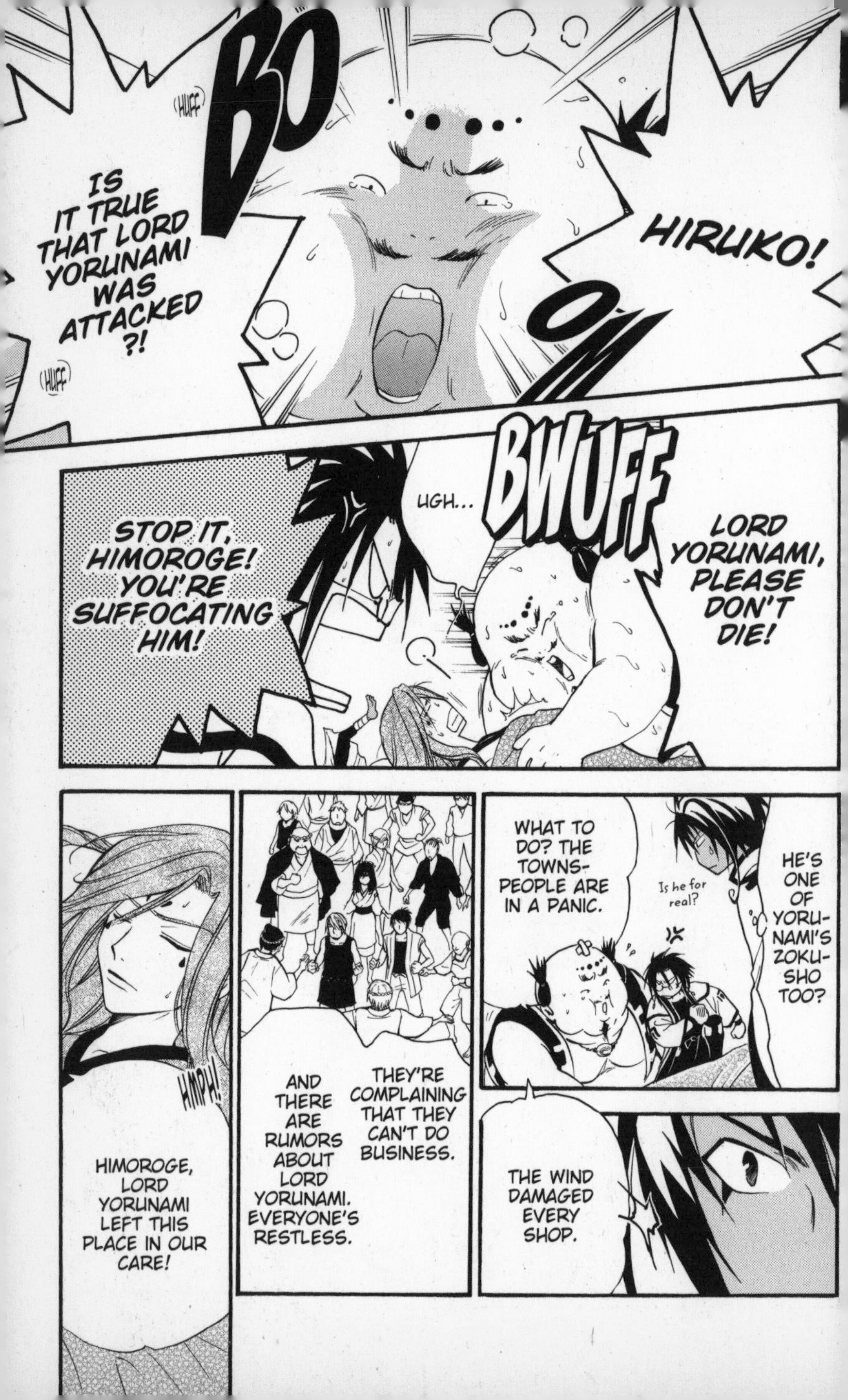
HIRUKO!
(HUFF)
BO
OM
IS IT TRUE THAT LORD YORUNAMI WAS ATTACKED?!
(HUFF)
BWUFF
LORD YORUNAMI, PLEASE DON'T DIE!
UGH...
STOP IT, HIMOROGE! YOU'RE SUFFOCATING HIM!
HE'S ONE OF YORUNAMI'S ZOKUSHO TOO?
Is he for real?
WHAT TO DO? THE TOWNSPEOPLE ARE IN A PANIC.
THE WIND DAMAGED EVERY SHOP.
THEY'RE COMPLAINING THAT THEY CAN'T DO BUSINESS.
AND THERE ARE RUMORS ABOUT LORD YORUNAMI. EVERYONE'S RESTLESS.
HMPH!
HIMOROGE, LORD YORUNAMI LEFT THIS PLACE IN OUR CARE!

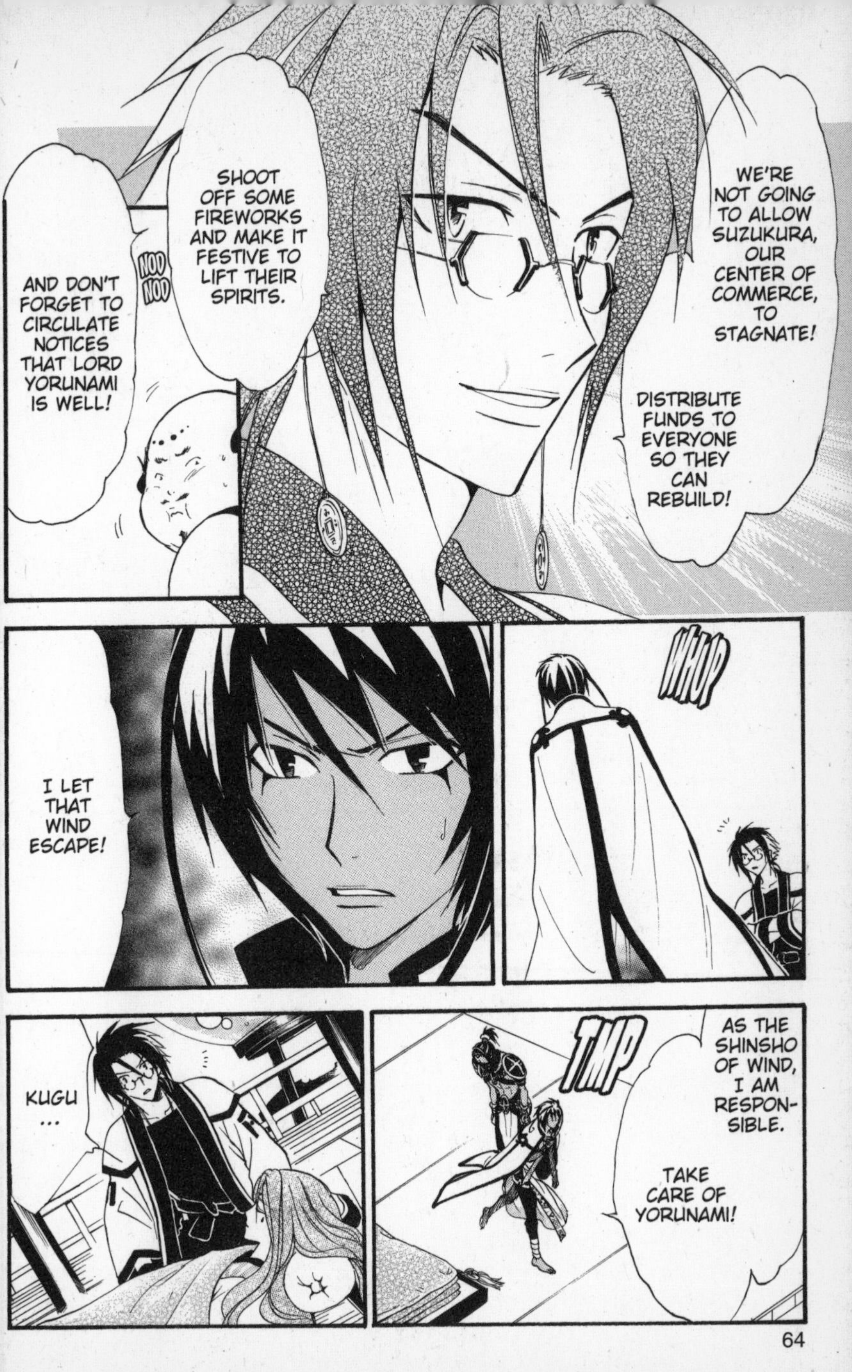
WE'RE NOT GOING TO ALLOW SUZUKURA, OUR CENTER OF COMMERCE, TO STAGNATE!
DISTRIBUTE FUNDS TO EVERYONE SO THEY CAN REBUILD!
SHOOT OFF SOME FIREWORKS AND MAKE IT FESTIVE TO LIFT THEIR SPIRITS.
NOD NOD
AND DON'T FORGET TO CIRCULATE NOTICES THAT LORD YORUNAMI IS WELL!
WHOP
I LET THAT WIND ESCAPE!
TMP
AS THE SHINSHO OF WIND, I AM RESPONSIBLE.
TAKE CARE OF YORUNAMI!
KUGU ...

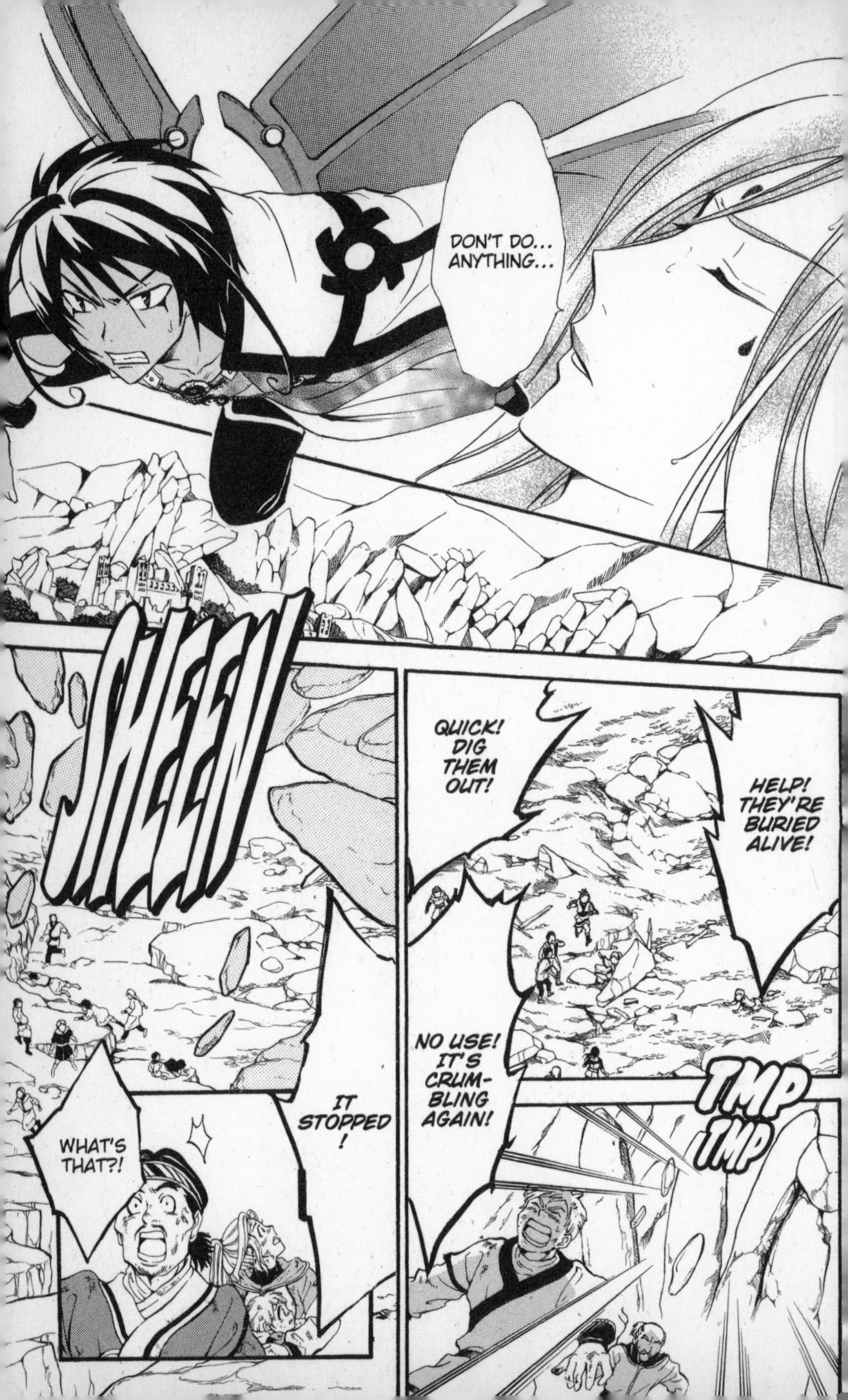
DON'T DO... ANYTHING...
HELP! THEY'RE BURIED ALIVE!
QUICK! DIG THEM OUT!
TMP TMP
NO USE! IT'S CRUMBLING AGAIN!
SHEEN
IT STOPPED!
WHAT'S THAT?!

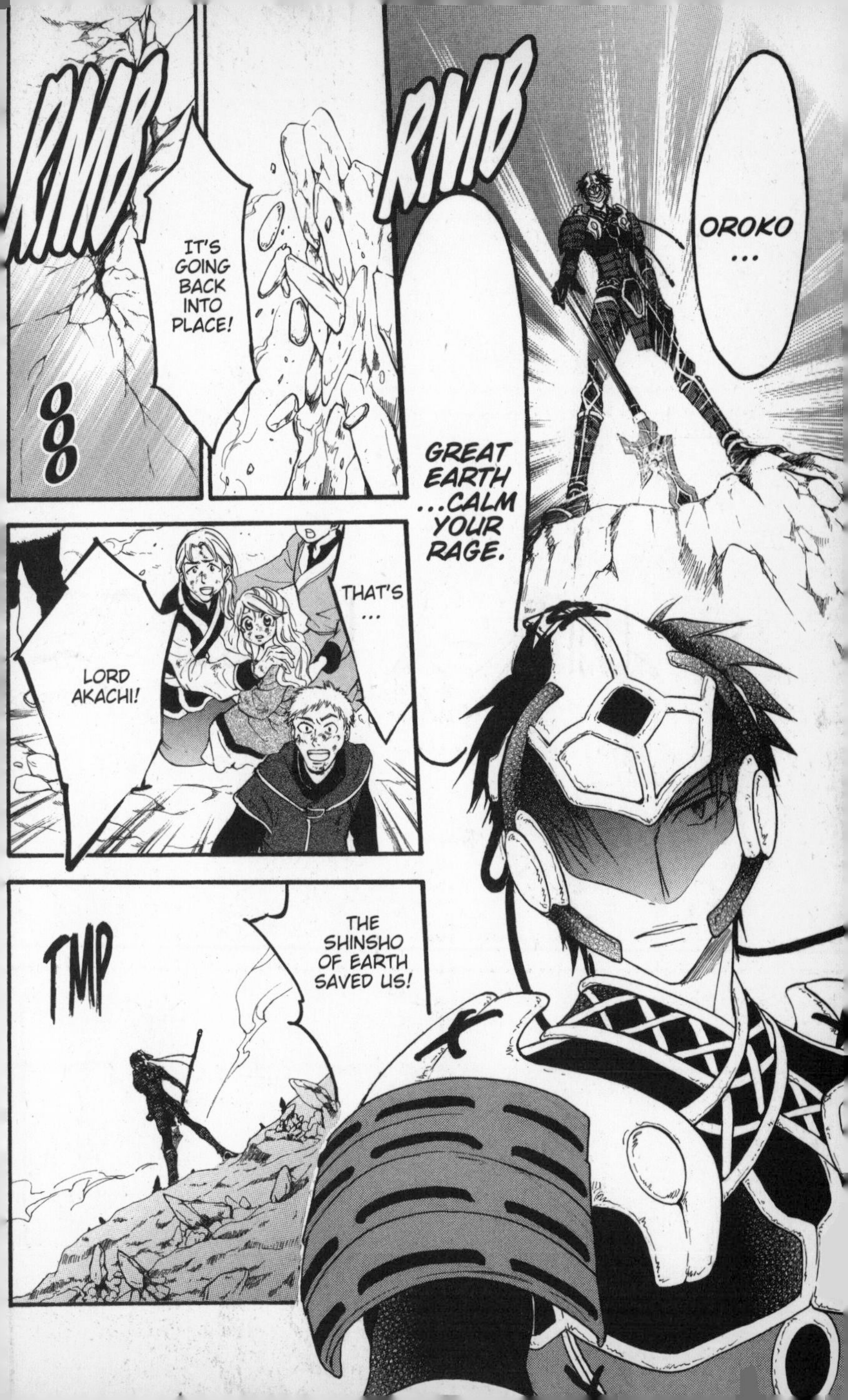
RMB
OROKO ...
GREAT EARTH ...CALM YOUR RAGE.
IT'S GOING BACK INTO PLACE!
RMB
OOO
THAT'S ...
LORD AKACHI!
THE SHINSHO OF EARTH SAVED US!
TMP

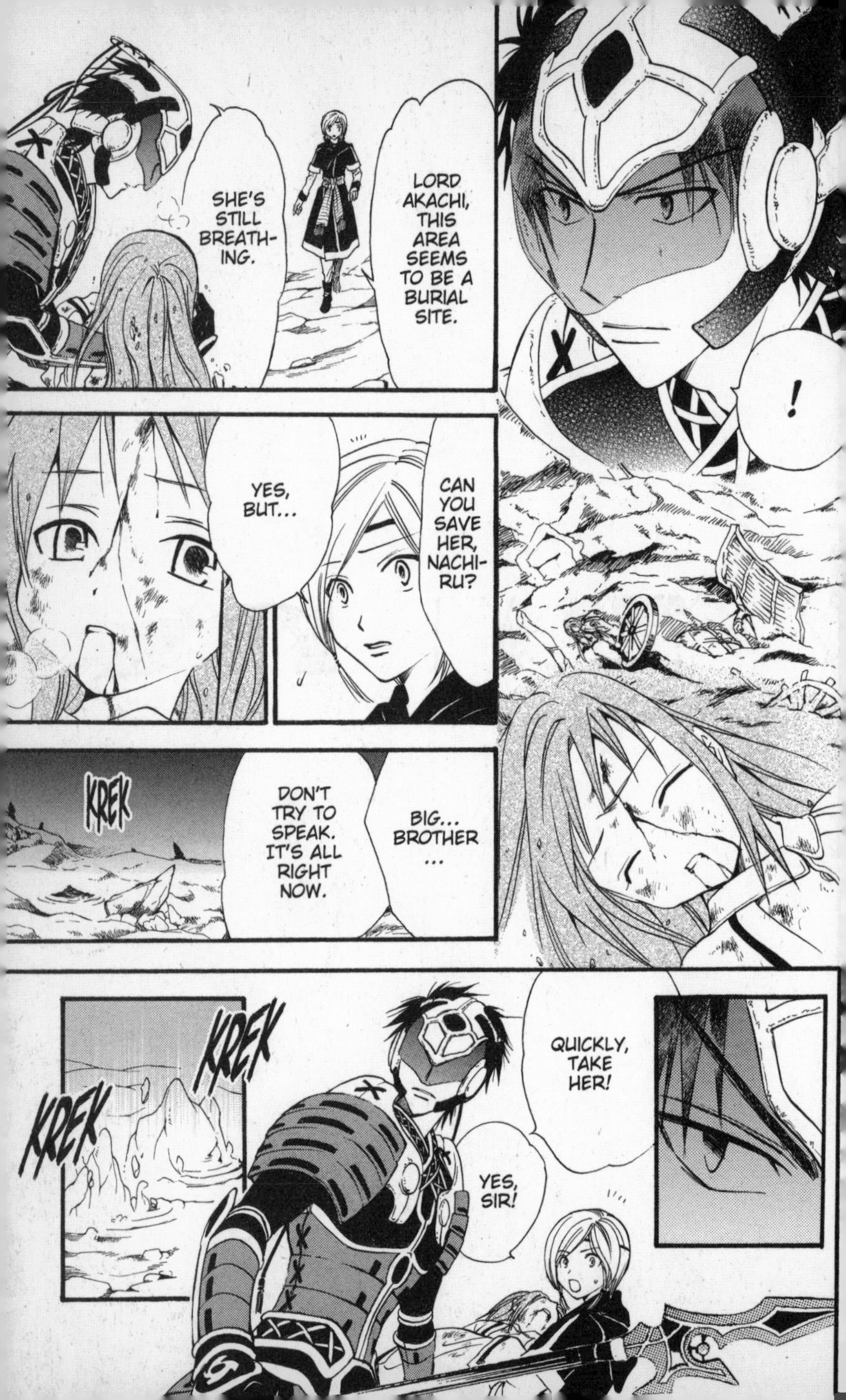
!
LORD AKACHI, THIS AREA SEEMS TO BE A BURIAL SITE.
SHE'S STILL BREATHING.
CAN YOU SAVE HER, NACHIRU?
YES, BUT...
BIG... BROTHER...
DON'T TRY TO SPEAK. IT'S ALL RIGHT NOW.
KREK
QUICKLY, TAKE HER!
YES, SIR!
KREK
KREK

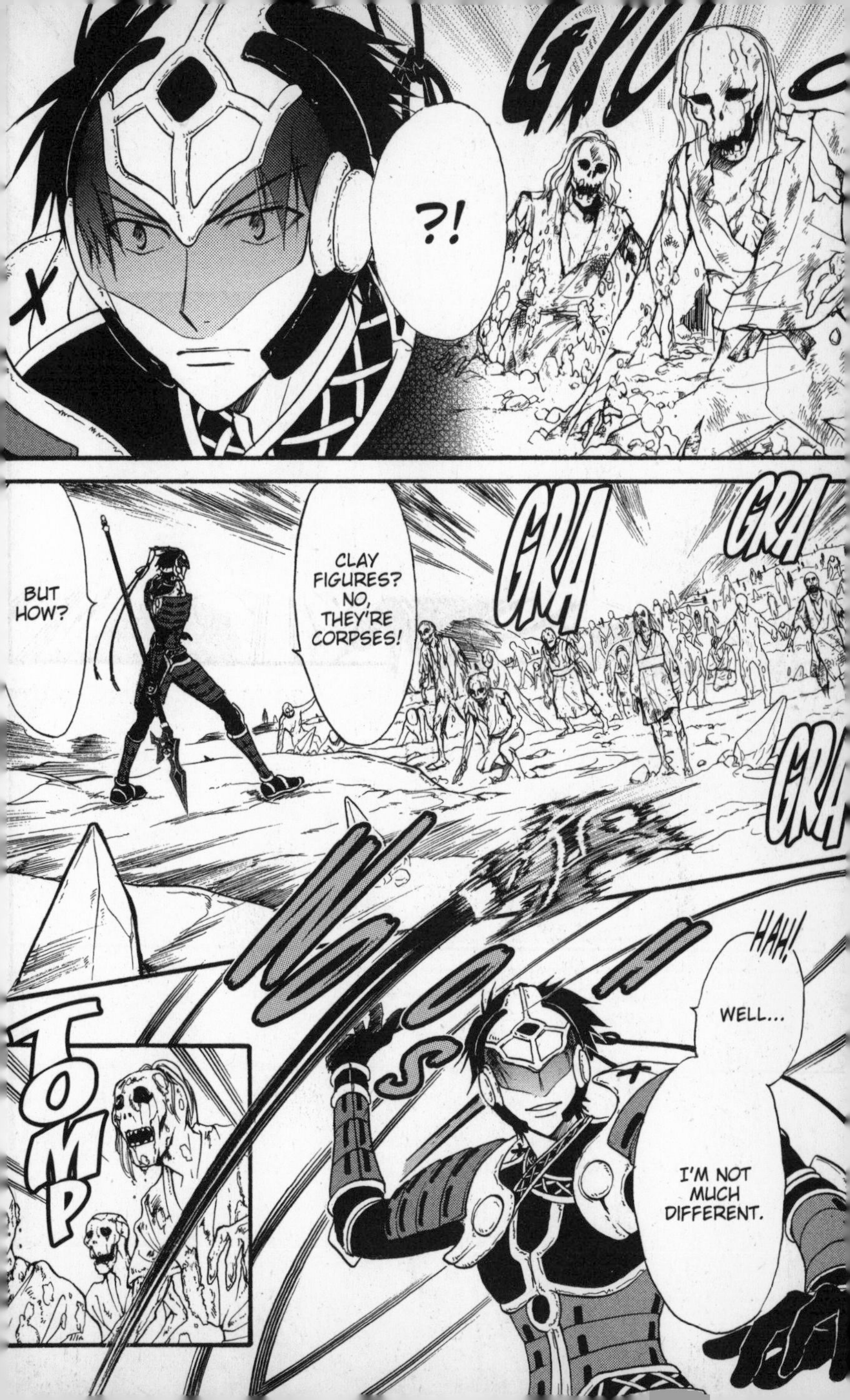
GYU
?!
GRA
GRA
GRA
CLAY FIGURES? NO, THEY'RE CORPSES!
BUT HOW?
HAH!
WELL...
I'M NOT MUCH DIFFERENT.
WHOOSH
TOMP

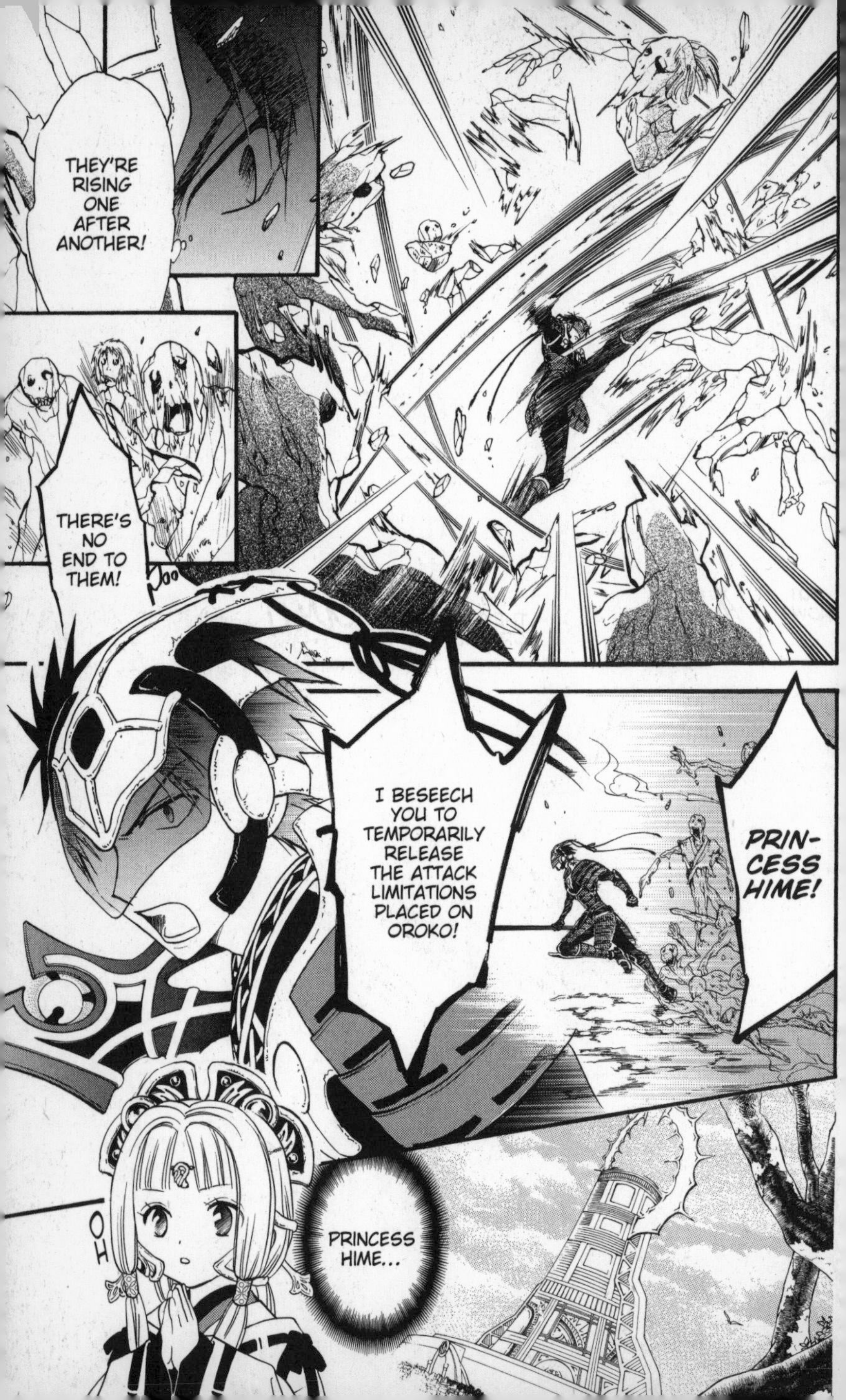
THEY'RE RISING ONE AFTER ANOTHER!
THERE'S NO END TO THEM!
PRIN-CESS HIME!
I BESEECH YOU TO TEMPORARILY RELEASE THE ATTACK LIMITATIONS PLACED ON OROKO!
OH
PRINCESS HIME...

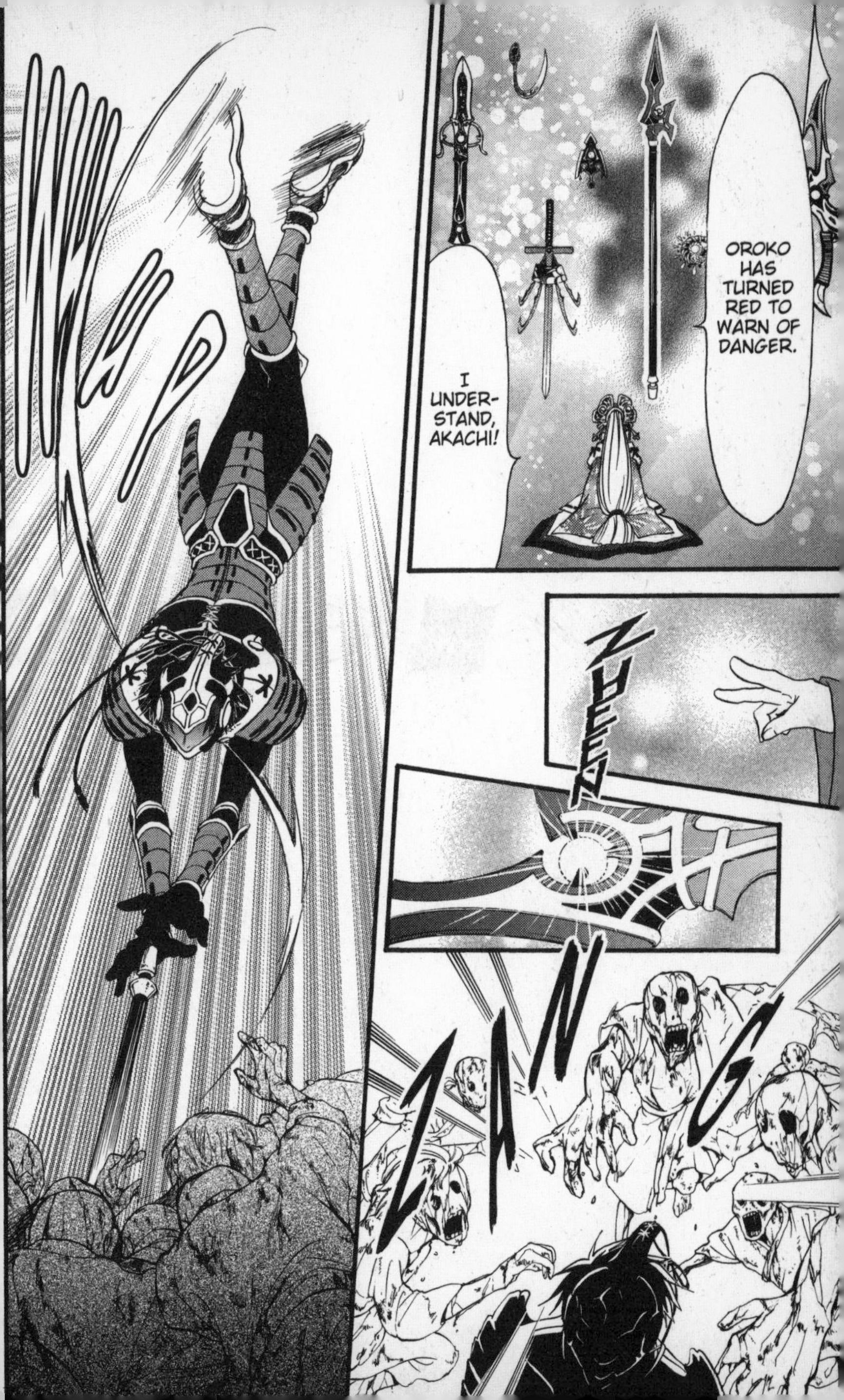
OROKO HAS TURNED RED TO WARN OF DANGER.
I UNDERSTAND, AKACHI!
ZANG
WHAP

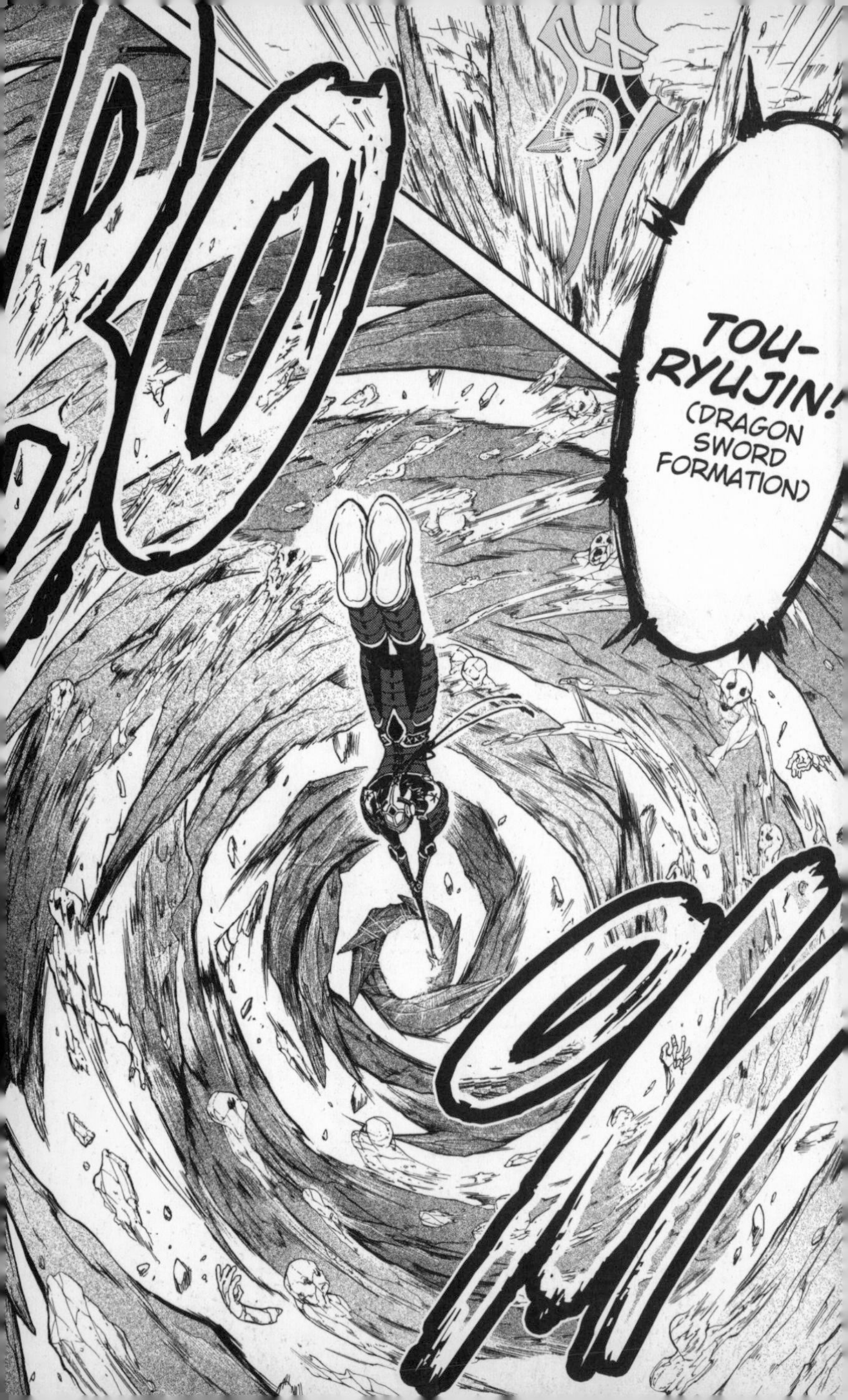
TOU-RYUJIN! (DRAGON SWORD FORMATION)

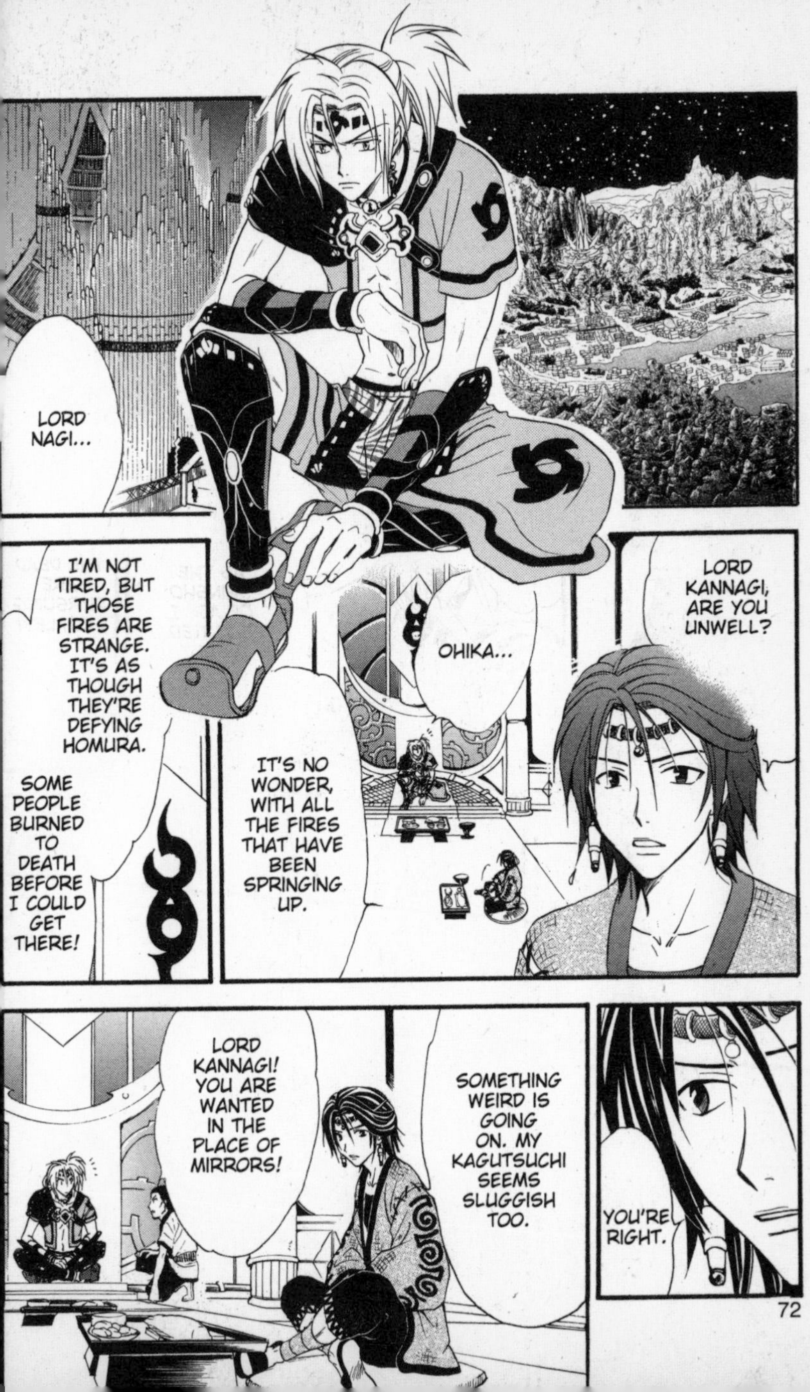
LORD NAGI...
LORD KANNAGI, ARE YOU UNWELL?
OHIKA...
IT'S NO WONDER, WITH ALL THE FIRES THAT HAVE BEEN SPRINGING UP.
I'M NOT TIRED, BUT THOSE FIRES ARE STRANGE. IT'S AS THOUGH THEY'RE DEFYING HOMURA.
SOME PEOPLE BURNED TO DEATH BEFORE I COULD GET THERE!
YOU'RE RIGHT.
SOMETHING WEIRD IS GOING ON. MY KAGUTSUCHI SEEMS SLUGGISH TOO.
LORD KANNAGI! YOU ARE WANTED IN THE PLACE OF MIRRORS!

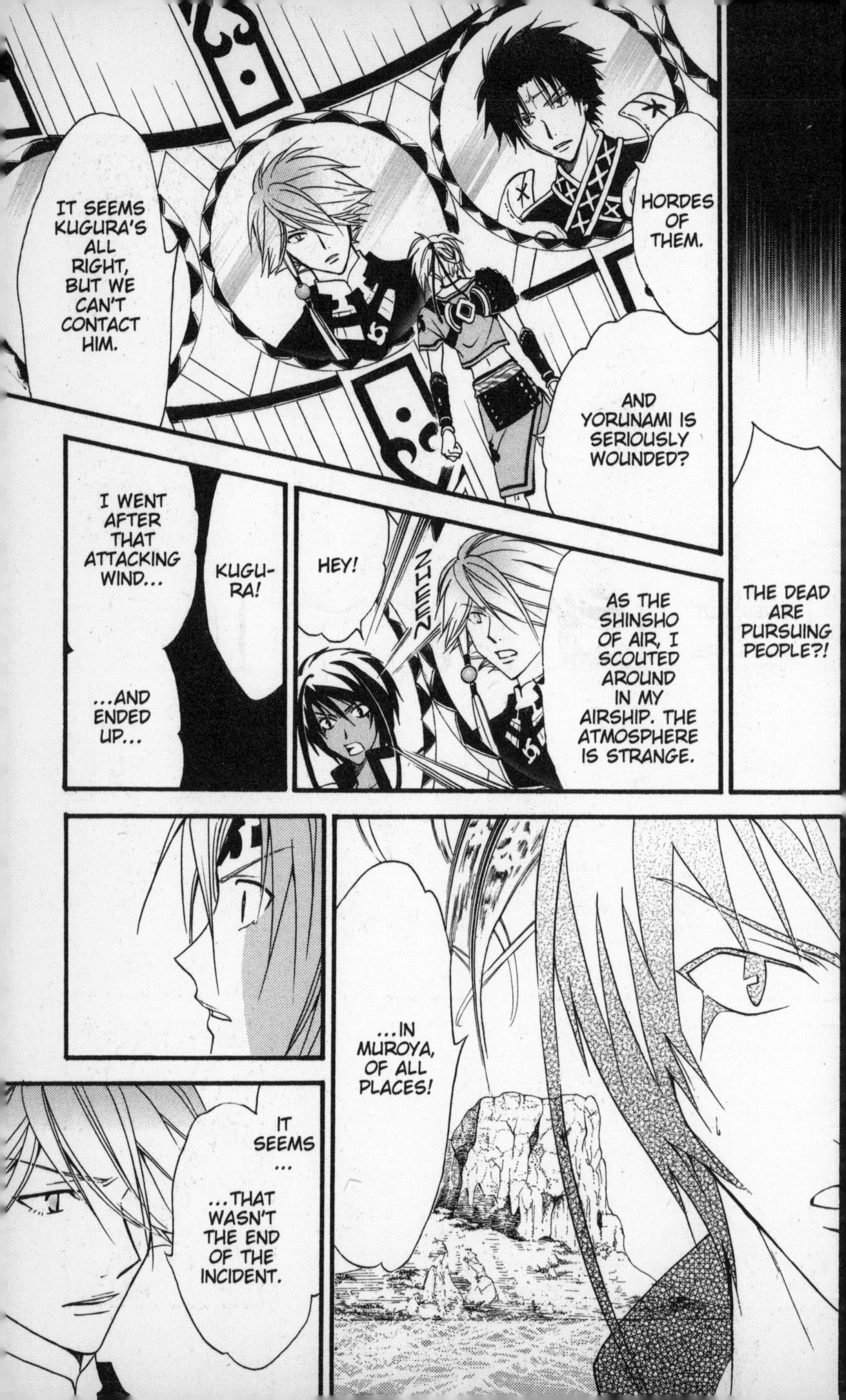
THE DEAD ARE PURSUING PEOPLE?!
HORDES OF THEM.
IT SEEMS KUGURA'S ALL RIGHT, BUT WE CAN'T CONTACT HIM.
AND YORUNAMI IS SERIOUSLY WOUNDED?
AS THE SHINSHO OF AIR, I SCOUTED AROUND IN MY AIRSHIP. THE ATMOSPHERE IS STRANGE.
ZHEEN
HEY!
KUGU-RA!
I WENT AFTER THAT ATTACKING WIND...
...AND ENDED UP...
...IN MUROYA, OF ALL PLACES!
IT SEEMS...
...THAT WASN'T THE END OF THE INCIDENT.

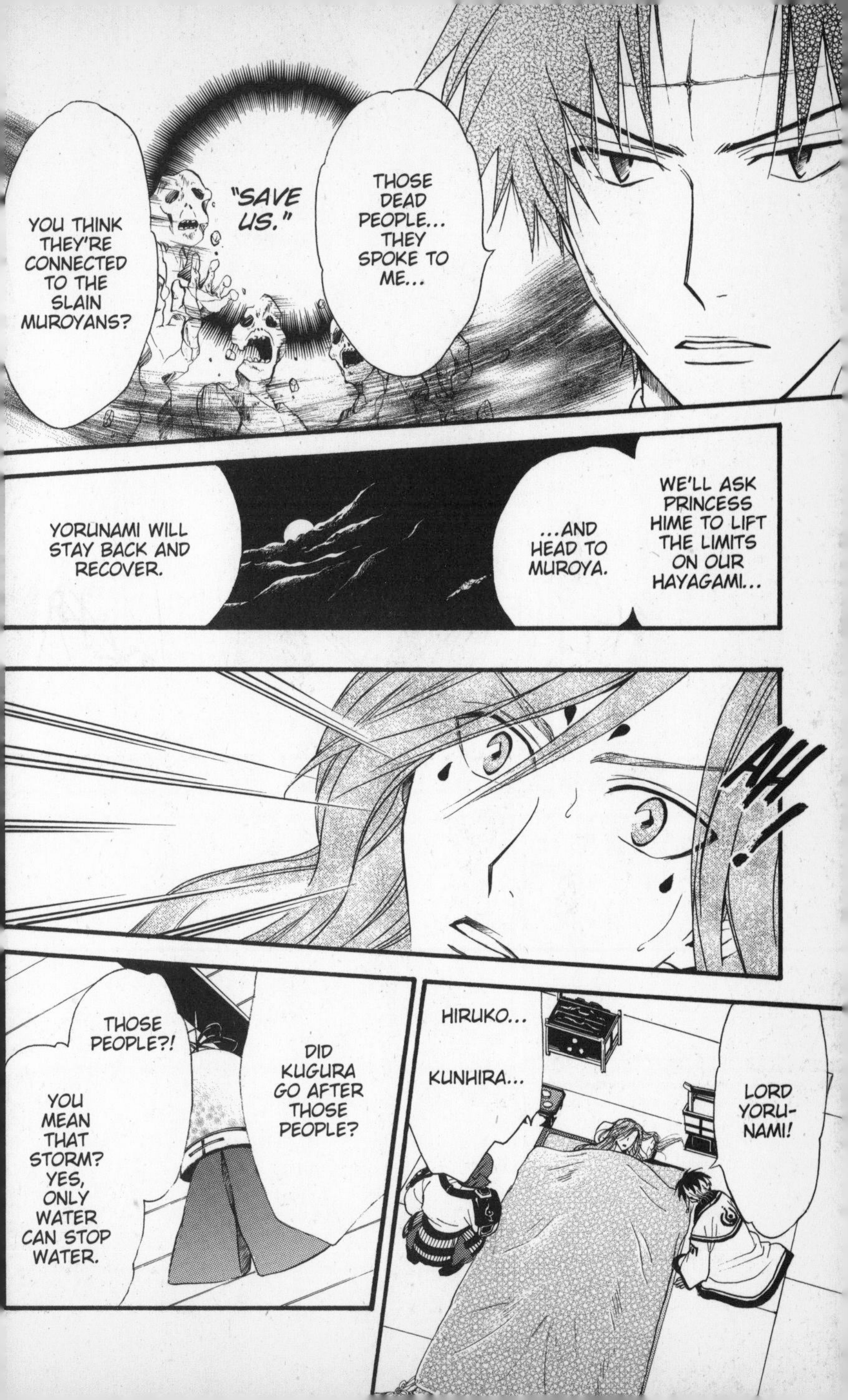
THOSE DEAD PEOPLE... THEY SPOKE TO ME...
"SAVE US."
YOU THINK THEY'RE CONNECTED TO THE SLAIN MUROYANS?
WE'LL ASK PRINCESS HIME TO LIFT THE LIMITS ON OUR HAYAGAMI...
...AND HEAD TO MUROYA.
YORUNAMI WILL STAY BACK AND RECOVER.
AH!!
LORD YORUNAMI!
HIRUKO...
KUNHIRA...
DID KUGURA GO AFTER THOSE PEOPLE?
THOSE PEOPLE?!
YOU MEAN THAT STORM? YES, ONLY WATER CAN STOP WATER.

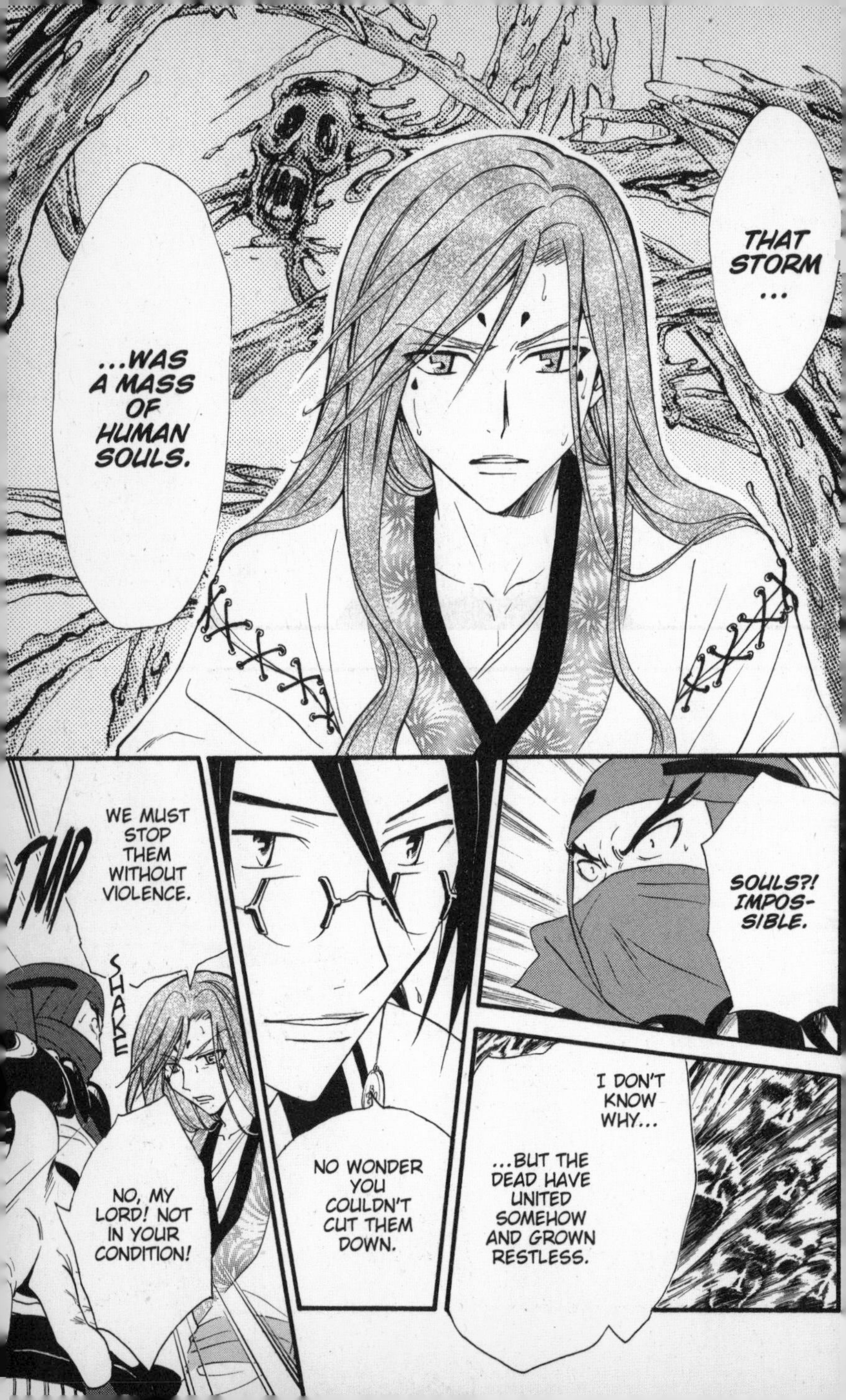
THAT STORM...
...WAS A MASS OF HUMAN SOULS.
SOULS?! IMPOSSIBLE.
I DON'T KNOW WHY...
...BUT THE DEAD HAVE UNITED SOMEHOW AND GROWN RESTLESS.
NO WONDER YOU COULDN'T CUT THEM DOWN.
WE MUST STOP THEM WITHOUT VIOLENCE.
TMP
SHAKE
NO, MY LORD! NOT IN YOUR CONDITION!

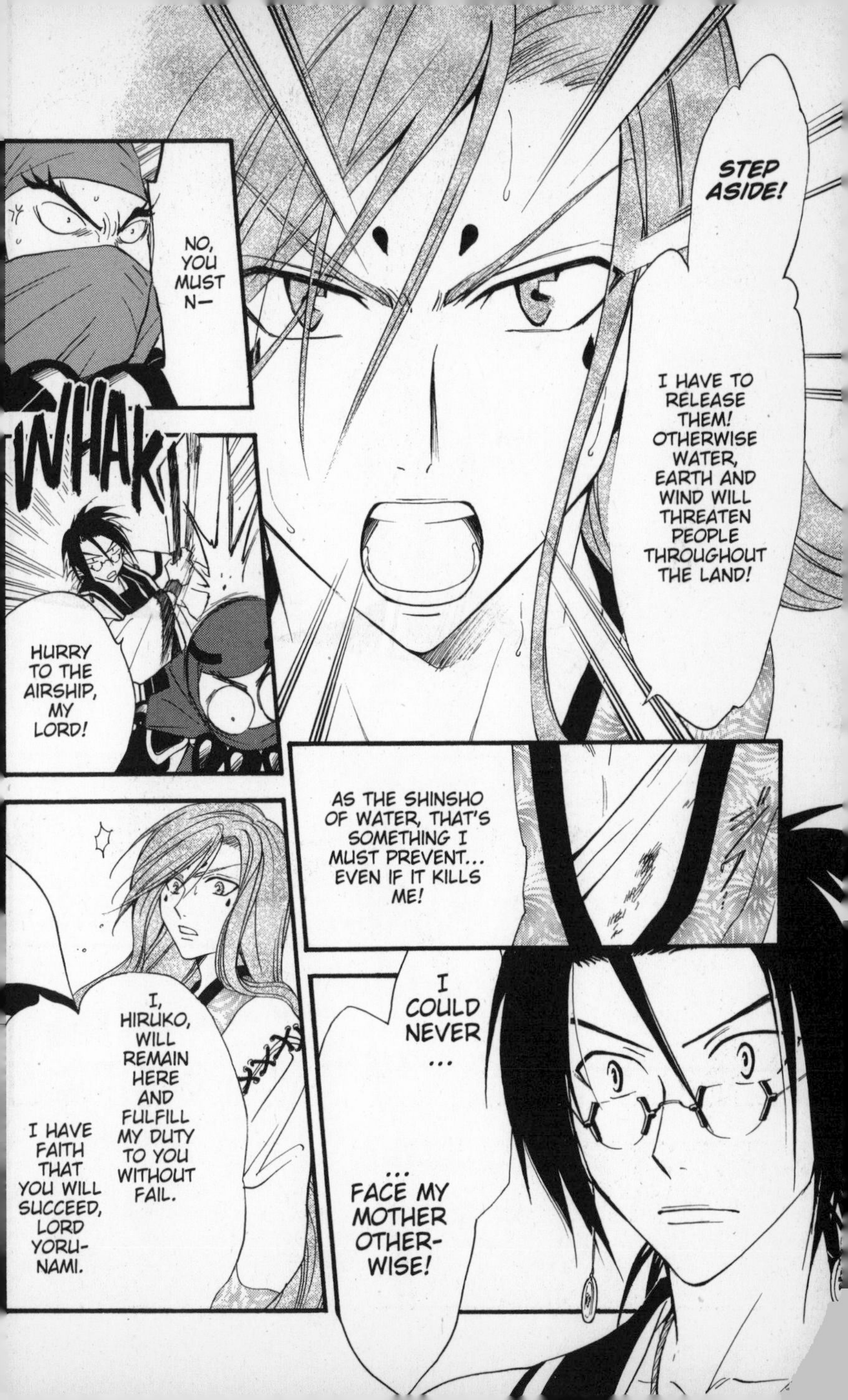
STEP ASIDE!
I HAVE TO RELEASE THEM! OTHERWISE WATER, EARTH AND WIND WILL THREATEN PEOPLE THROUGHOUT THE LAND!
NO, YOU MUST N—
WHAK
HURRY TO THE AIRSHIP, MY LORD!
AS THE SHINSHO OF WATER, THAT'S SOMETHING I MUST PREVENT... EVEN IF IT KILLS ME!
I COULD NEVER...
...FACE MY MOTHER OTHER-WISE!
I, HIRUKO, WILL REMAIN HERE AND FULFILL MY DUTY TO YOU WITHOUT FAIL.
I HAVE FAITH THAT YOU WILL SUCCEED, LORD YORU-NAMI.

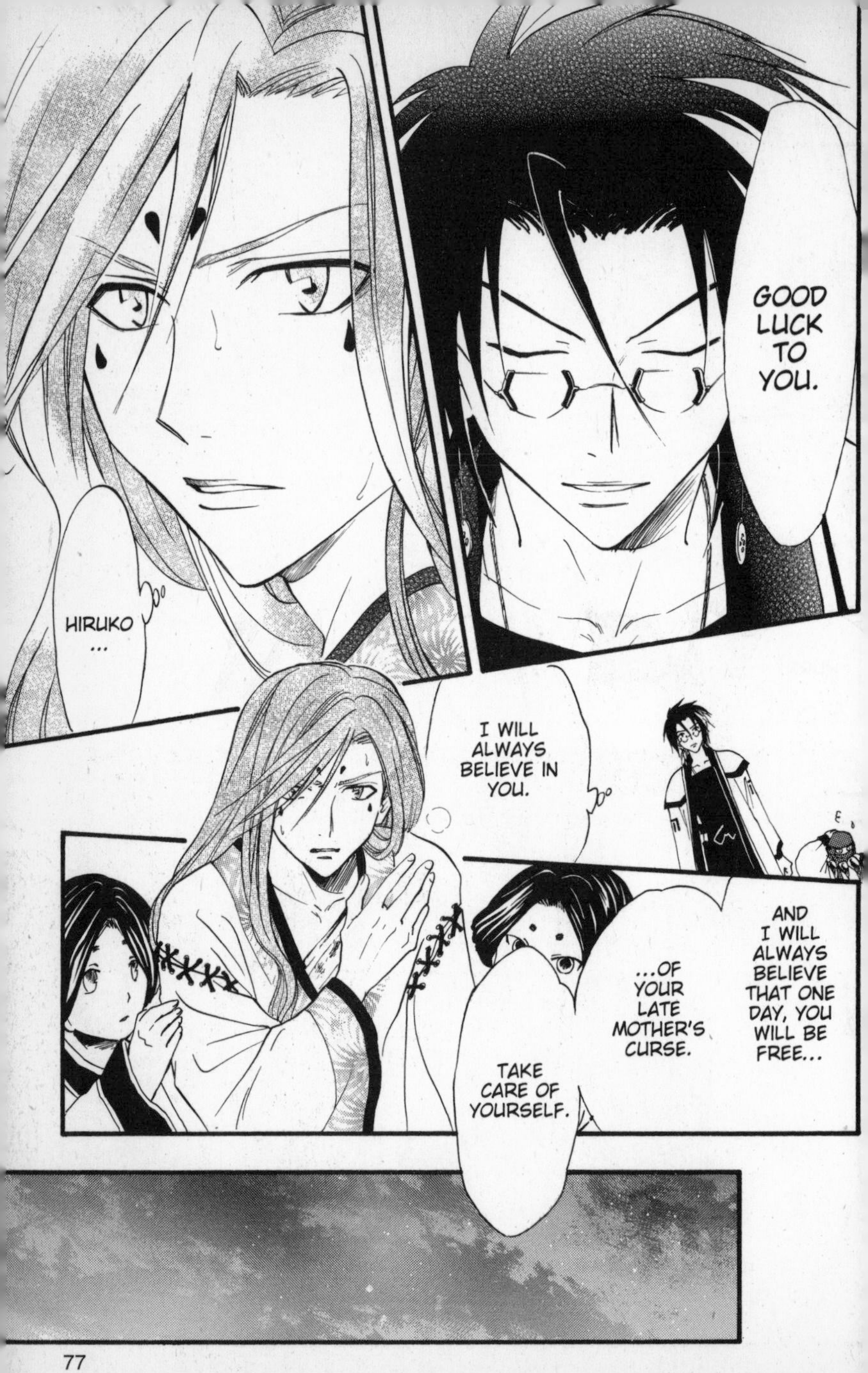
GOOD LUCK TO YOU.
HIRUKO ...
I WILL ALWAYS BELIEVE IN YOU.
AND I WILL ALWAYS BELIEVE THAT ONE DAY, YOU WILL BE FREE...
...OF YOUR LATE MOTHER'S CURSE.
TAKE CARE OF YOURSELF.

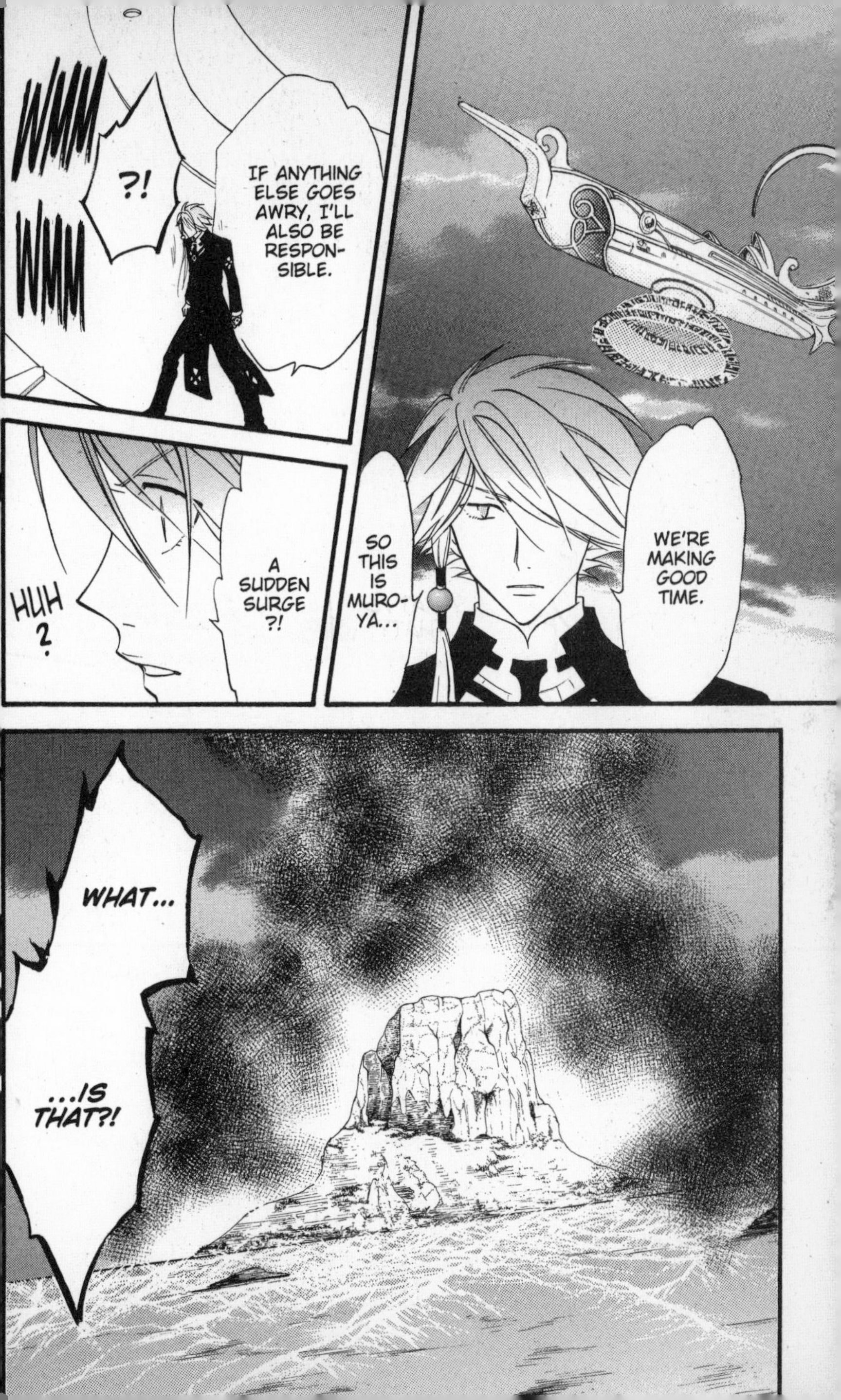
WE'RE MAKING GOOD TIME.
SO THIS IS MURO-YA...
IF ANYTHING ELSE GOES AWRY, I'LL ALSO BE RESPON-SIBLE.
?!
WMM WMM
A SUDDEN SURGE ?!
HUH ?
WHAT...
...IS THAT?!

CHAPTER 132
THE POWER OF THE KAMUI

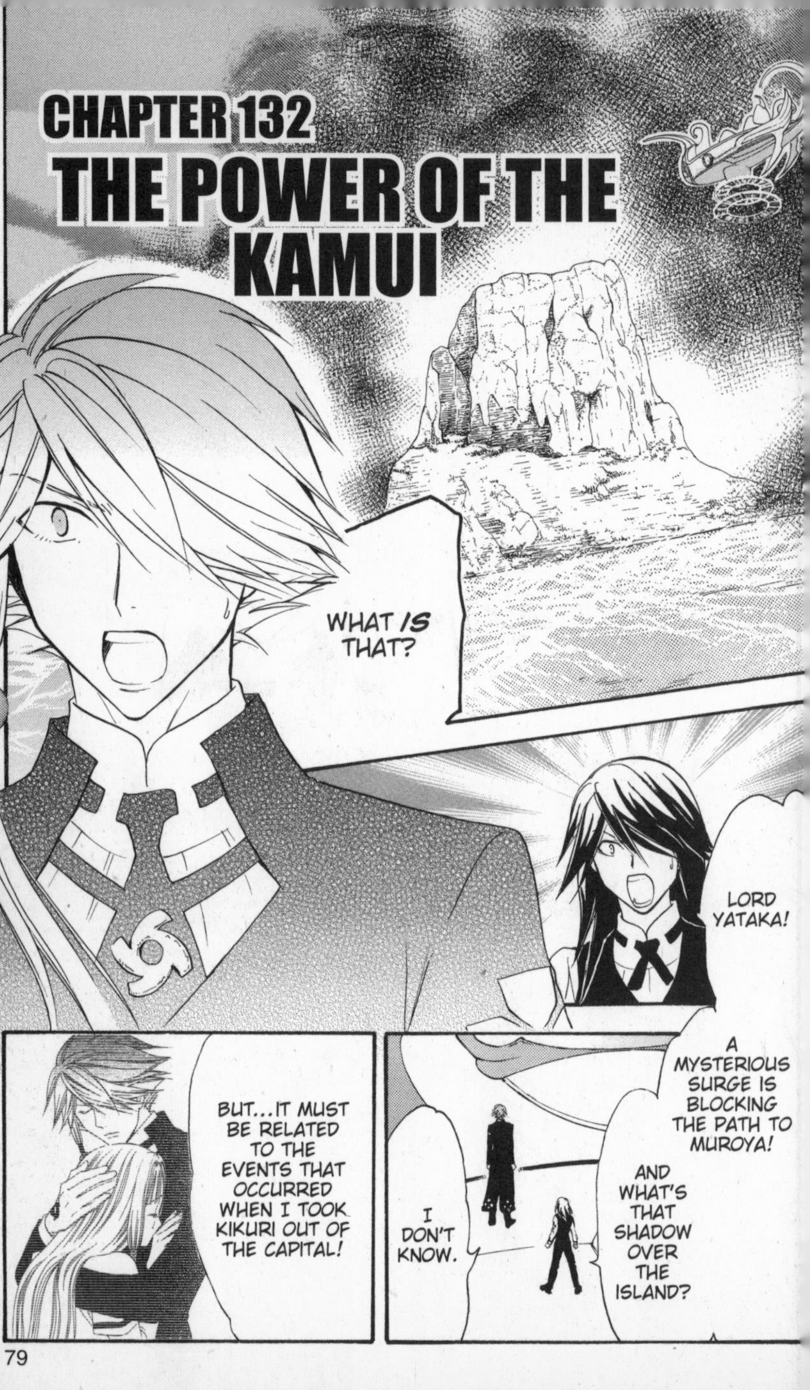

WHAT *IS* THAT?
LORD YATAKA!
A MYSTERIOUS SURGE IS BLOCKING THE PATH TO MUROYA!
AND WHAT'S THAT SHADOW OVER THE ISLAND?
I DON'T KNOW.
BUT...IT MUST BE RELATED TO THE EVENTS THAT OCCURRED WHEN I TOOK KIKURI OUT OF THE CAPITAL!

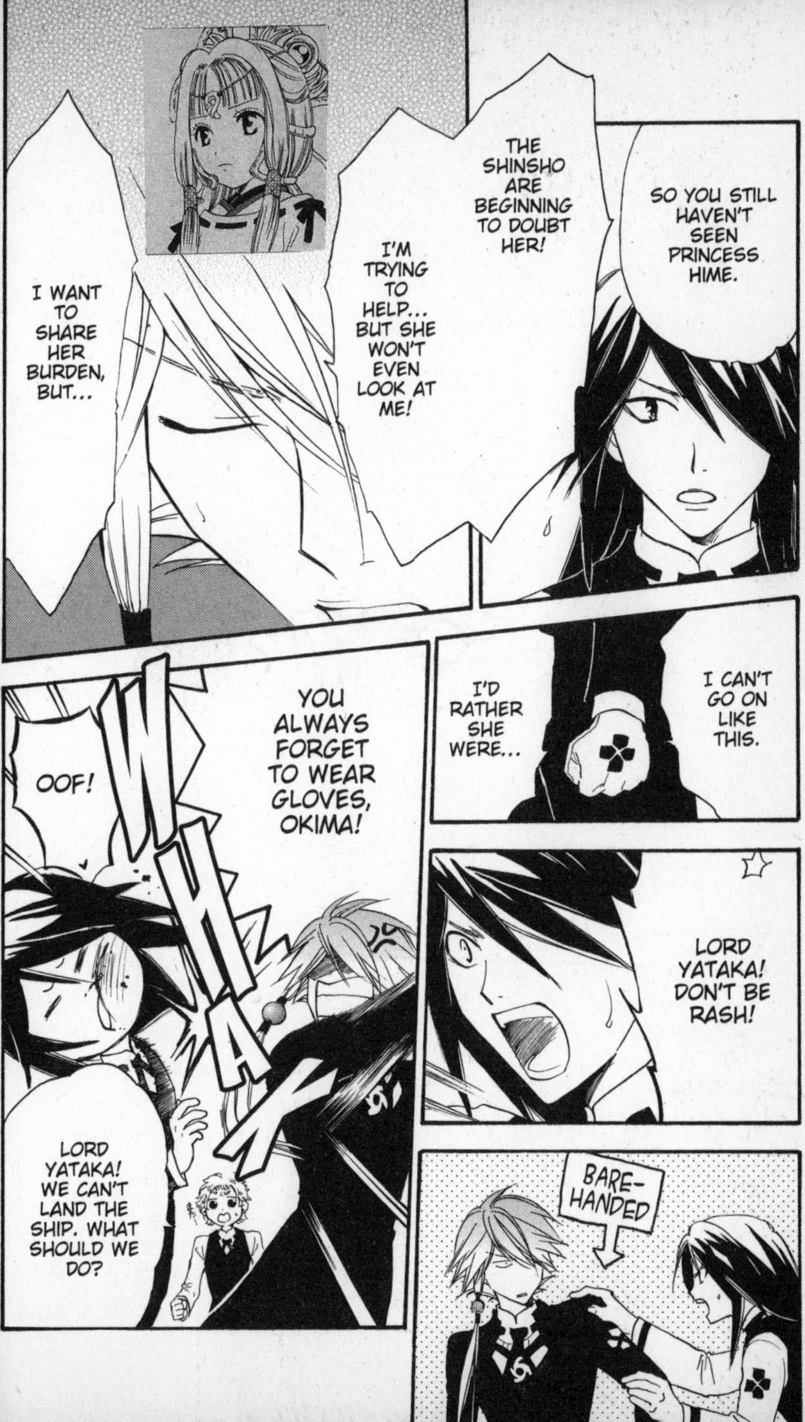
SO YOU STILL HAVEN'T SEEN PRINCESS HIME.
THE SHINSHO ARE BEGINNING TO DOUBT HER!
I'M TRYING TO HELP... BUT SHE WON'T EVEN LOOK AT ME!
I WANT TO SHARE HER BURDEN, BUT...
I CAN'T GO ON LIKE THIS.
I'D RATHER SHE WERE...
LORD YATAKA! DON'T BE RASH!
BARE-HANDED
YOU ALWAYS FORGET TO WEAR GLOVES, OKIMA!
WHAK
OOF!
LORD YATAKA! WE CAN'T LAND THE SHIP. WHAT SHOULD WE DO?

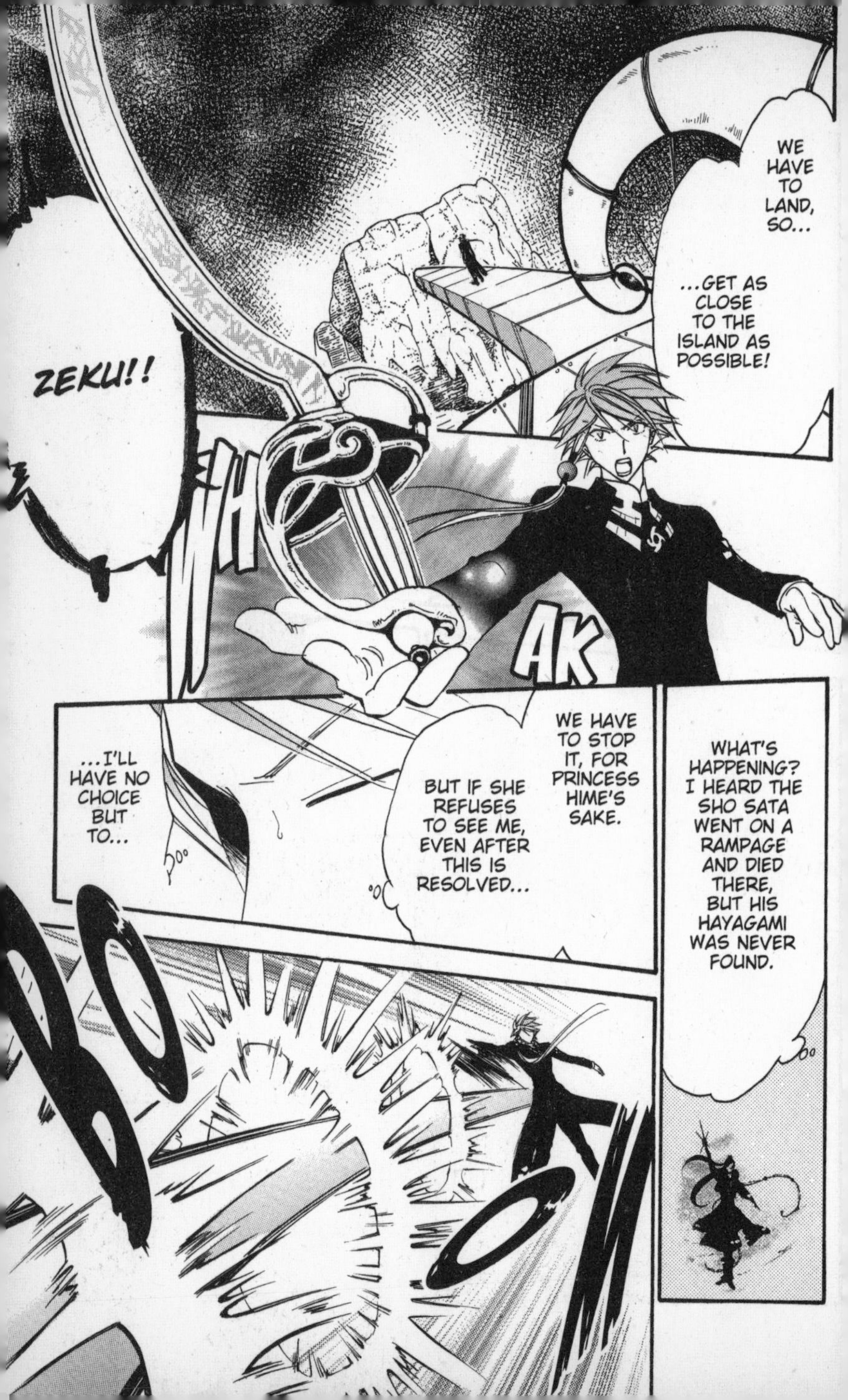
WE HAVE TO LAND, SO...
...GET AS CLOSE TO THE ISLAND AS POSSIBLE!
ZEKU!!
WH
AK
WHAT'S HAPPENING? I HEARD THE SHO SATA WENT ON A RAMPAGE AND DIED THERE, BUT HIS HAYAGAMI WAS NEVER FOUND.
WE HAVE TO STOP IT, FOR PRINCESS HIME'S SAKE.
BUT IF SHE REFUSES TO SEE ME, EVEN AFTER THIS IS RESOLVED...
...I'LL HAVE NO CHOICE BUT TO...

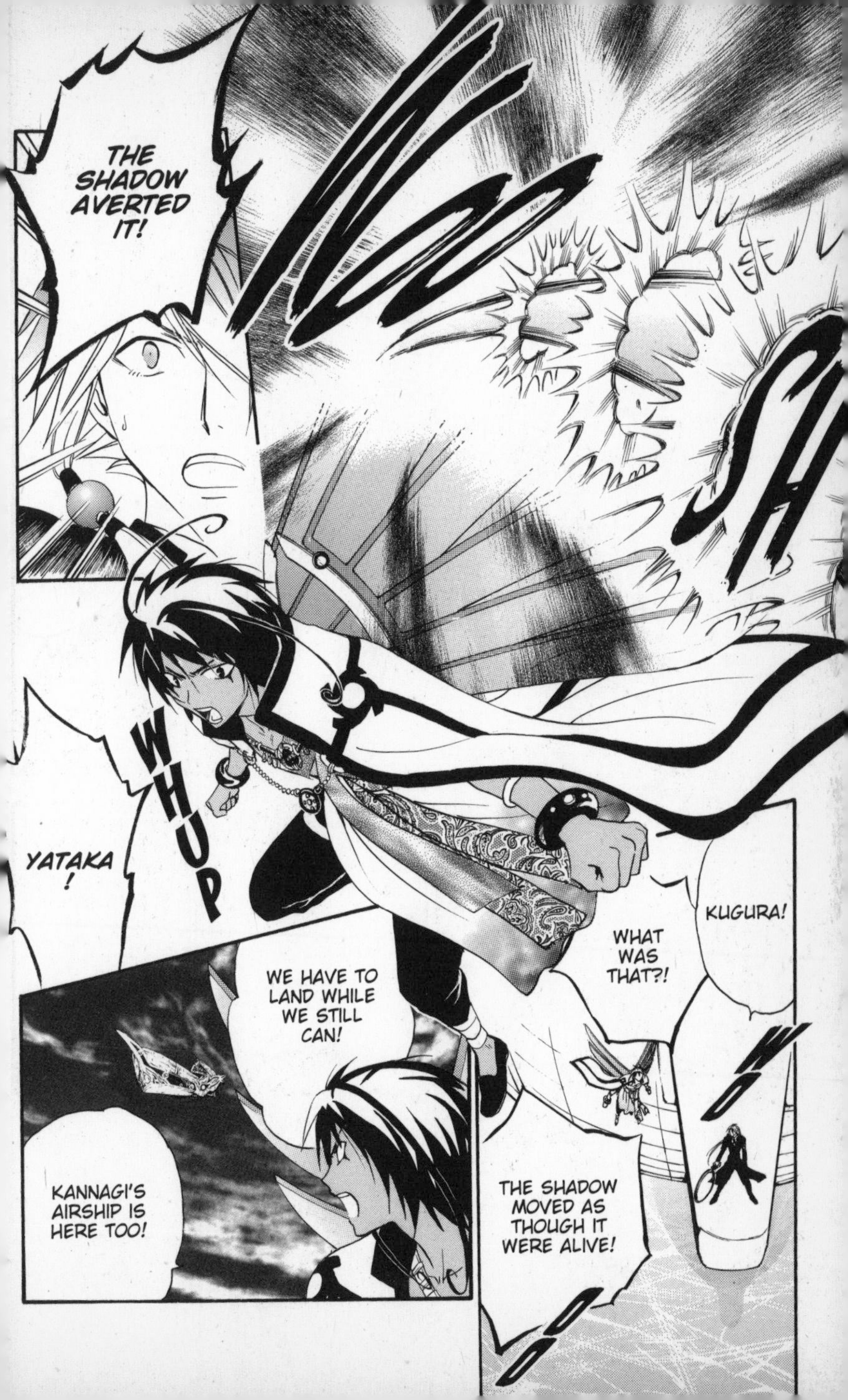
SHA
THE SHADOW AVERTED IT!
KUGURA!
WHAT WAS THAT?!
WHUP
YATAKA!
THE SHADOW MOVED AS THOUGH IT WERE ALIVE!
WE HAVE TO LAND WHILE WE STILL CAN!
KANNAGI'S AIRSHIP IS HERE TOO!

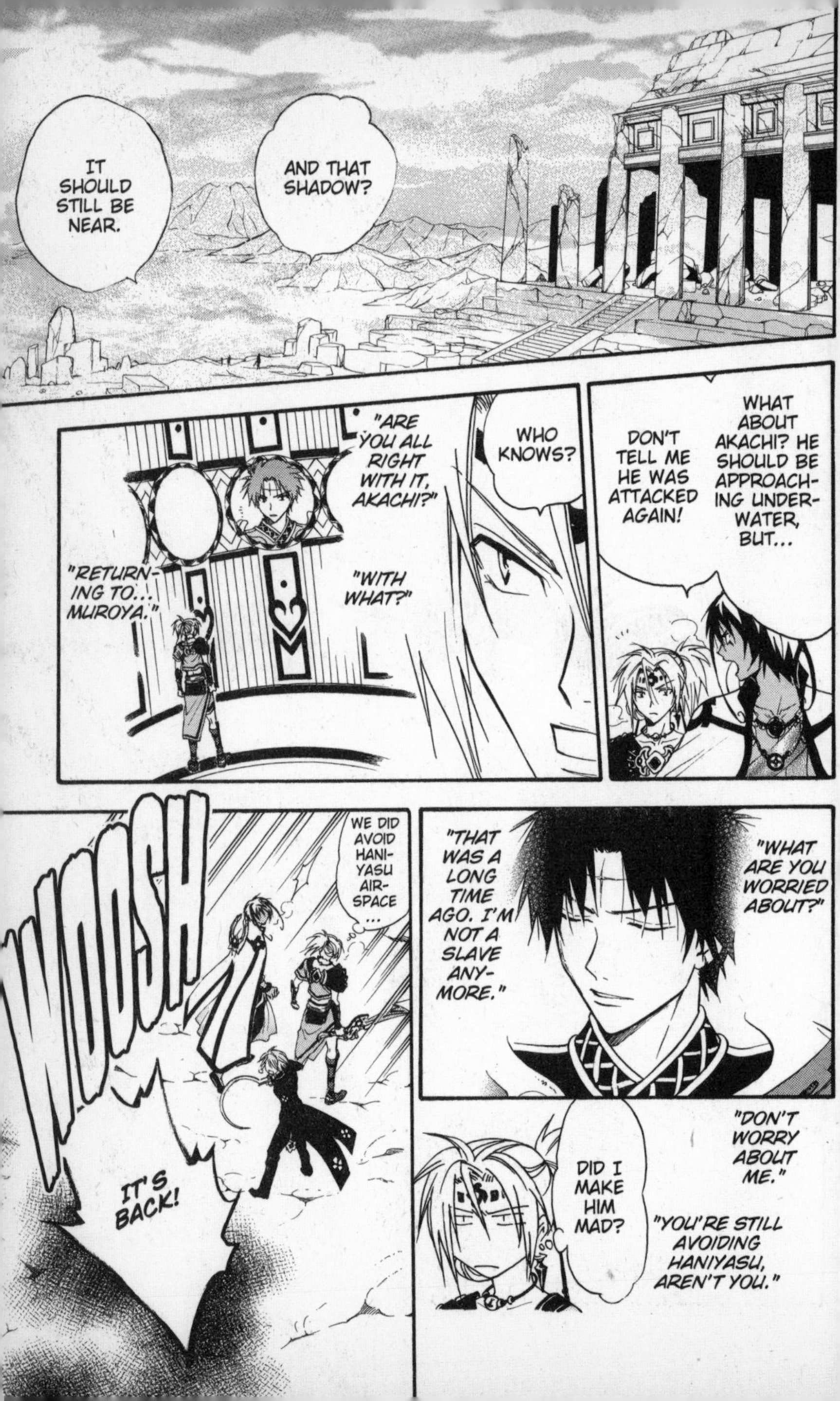
AND THAT SHADOW?
IT SHOULD STILL BE NEAR.
WHAT ABOUT AKACHI? HE SHOULD BE APPROACHING UNDERWATER, BUT...
DON'T TELL ME HE WAS ATTACKED AGAIN!
WHO KNOWS?
"ARE YOU ALL RIGHT WITH IT, AKACHI?"
"WITH WHAT?"
"RETURNING TO... MUROYA."
"WHAT ARE YOU WORRIED ABOUT?"
"THAT WAS A LONG TIME AGO. I'M NOT A SLAVE ANYMORE."
"DON'T WORRY ABOUT ME."
"YOU'RE STILL AVOIDING HANIYASU, AREN'T YOU."
DID I MAKE HIM MAD?
WE DID AVOID HANIYASU AIRSPACE...
WOOSH
IT'S BACK!

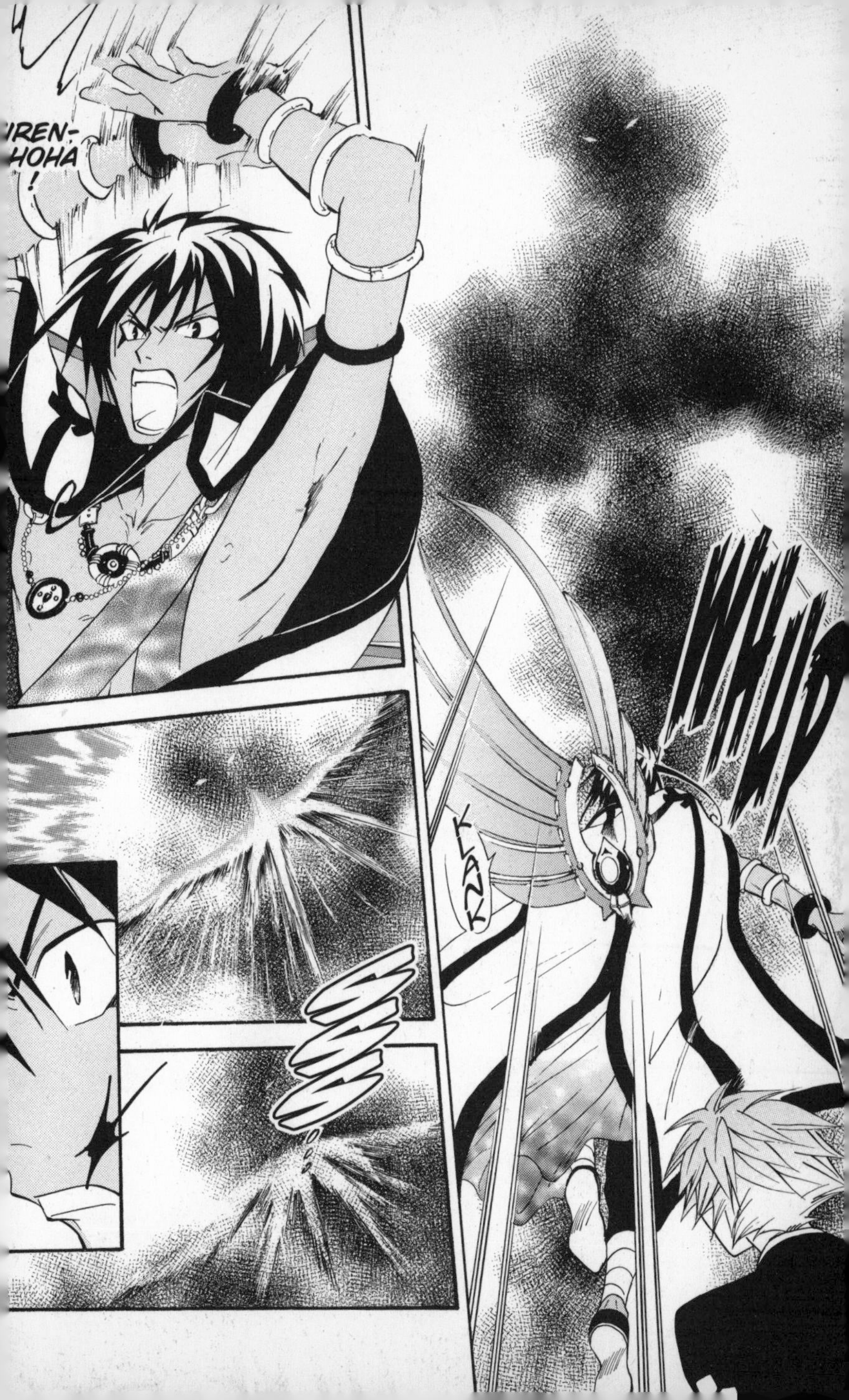
WHIP
KLANK
IREN-HOHA!

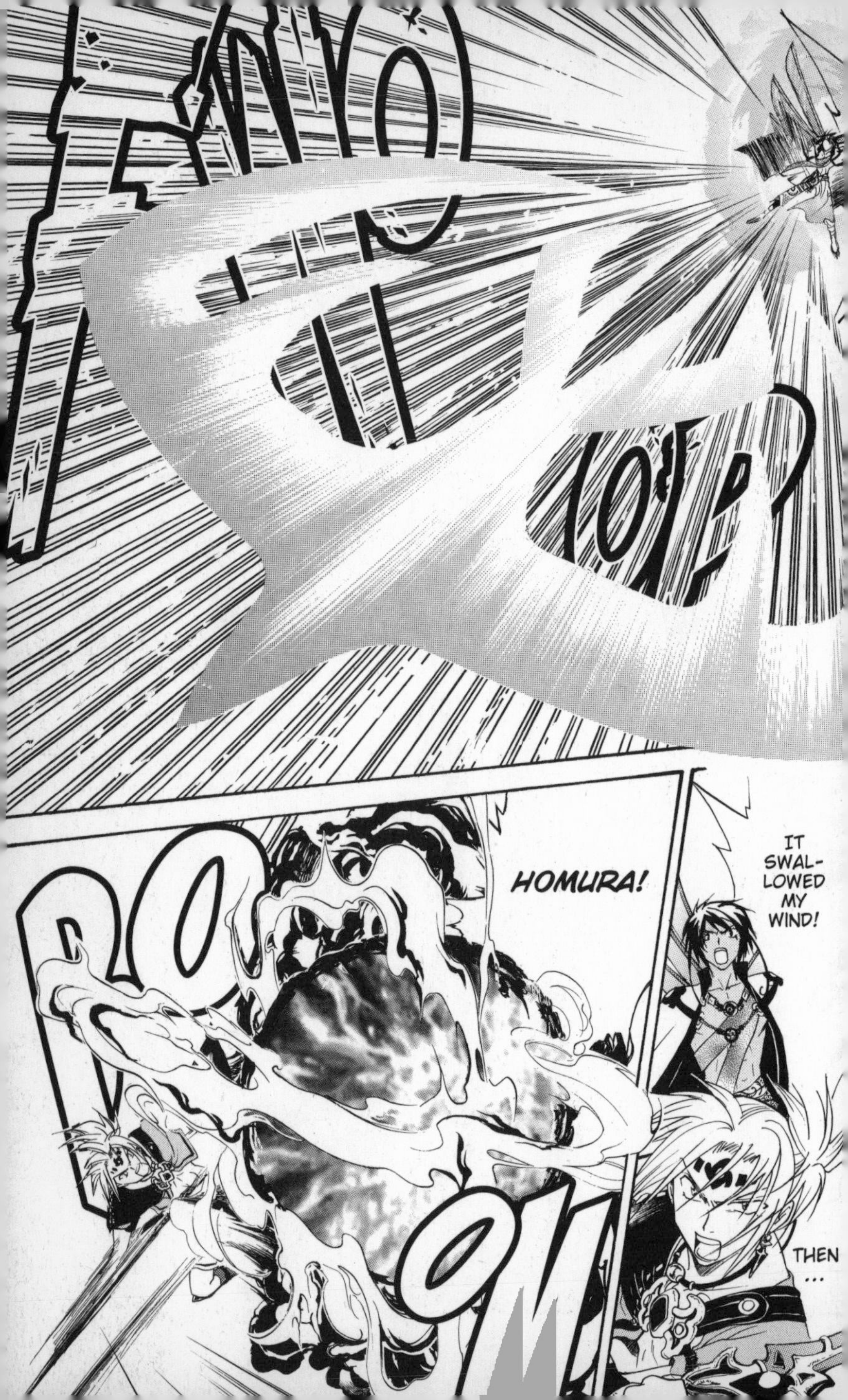
IT SWAL-
LOWED
MY
WIND!
HOMURA!
THEN
...

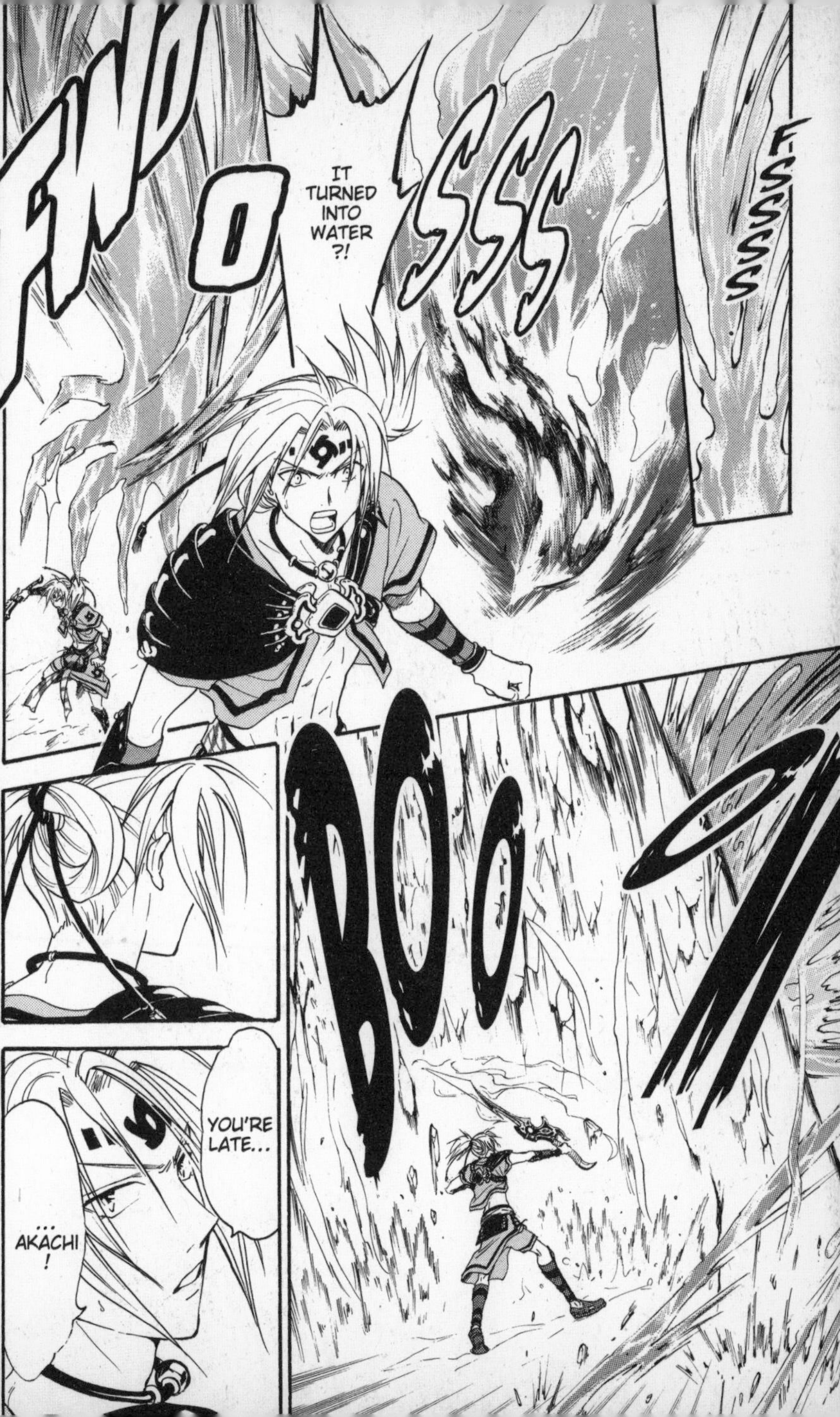
F-SSSSSS
IT TURNED INTO WATER?!
BOOM
YOU'RE LATE...
...AKACHI!

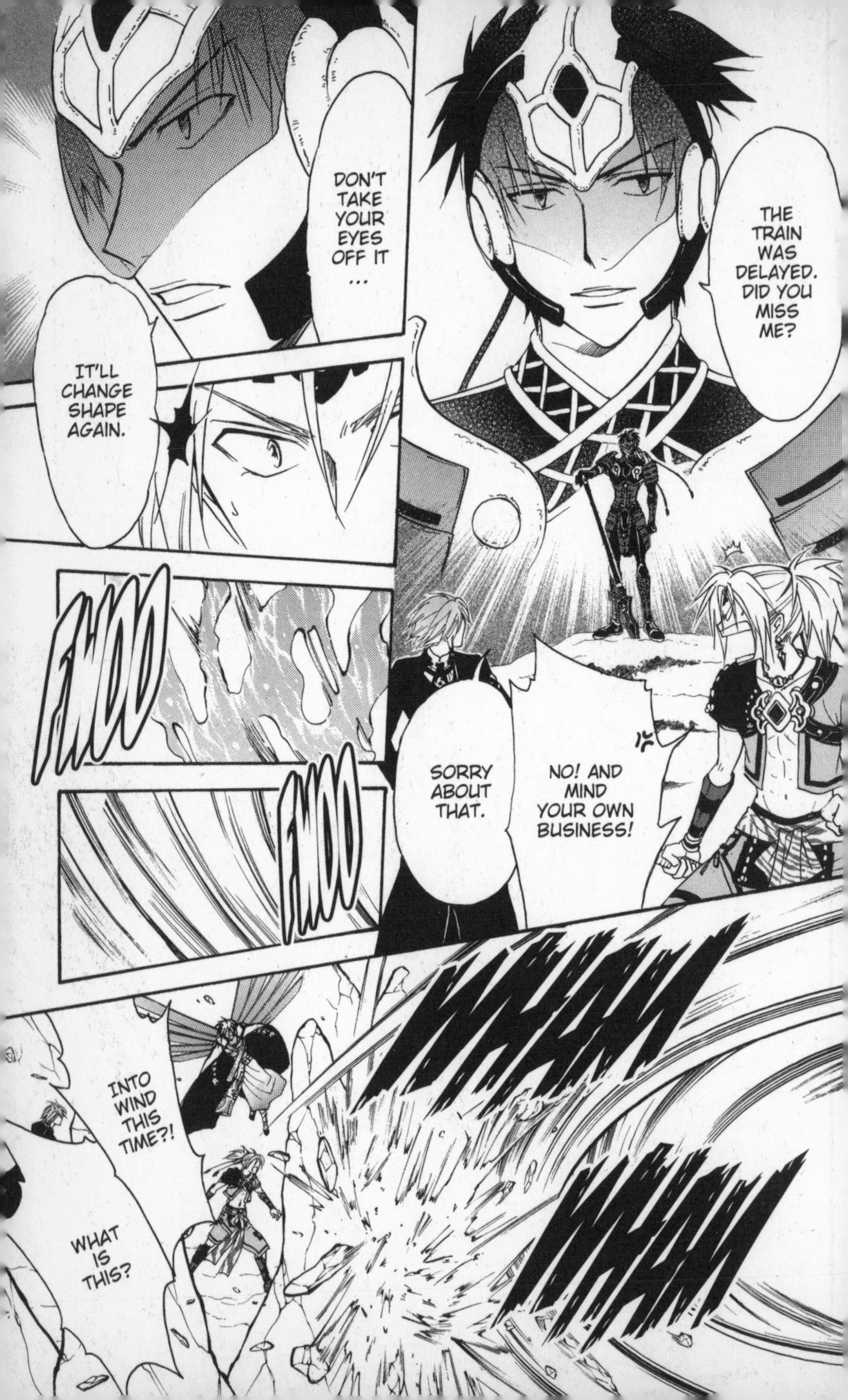
THE TRAIN WAS DELAYED. DID YOU MISS ME?
NO! AND MIND YOUR OWN BUSINESS!
SORRY ABOUT THAT.
DON'T TAKE YOUR EYES OFF IT ...
IT'LL CHANGE SHAPE AGAIN.
FWOO
FWOO
INTO WIND THIS TIME?!
WHAT IS THIS?

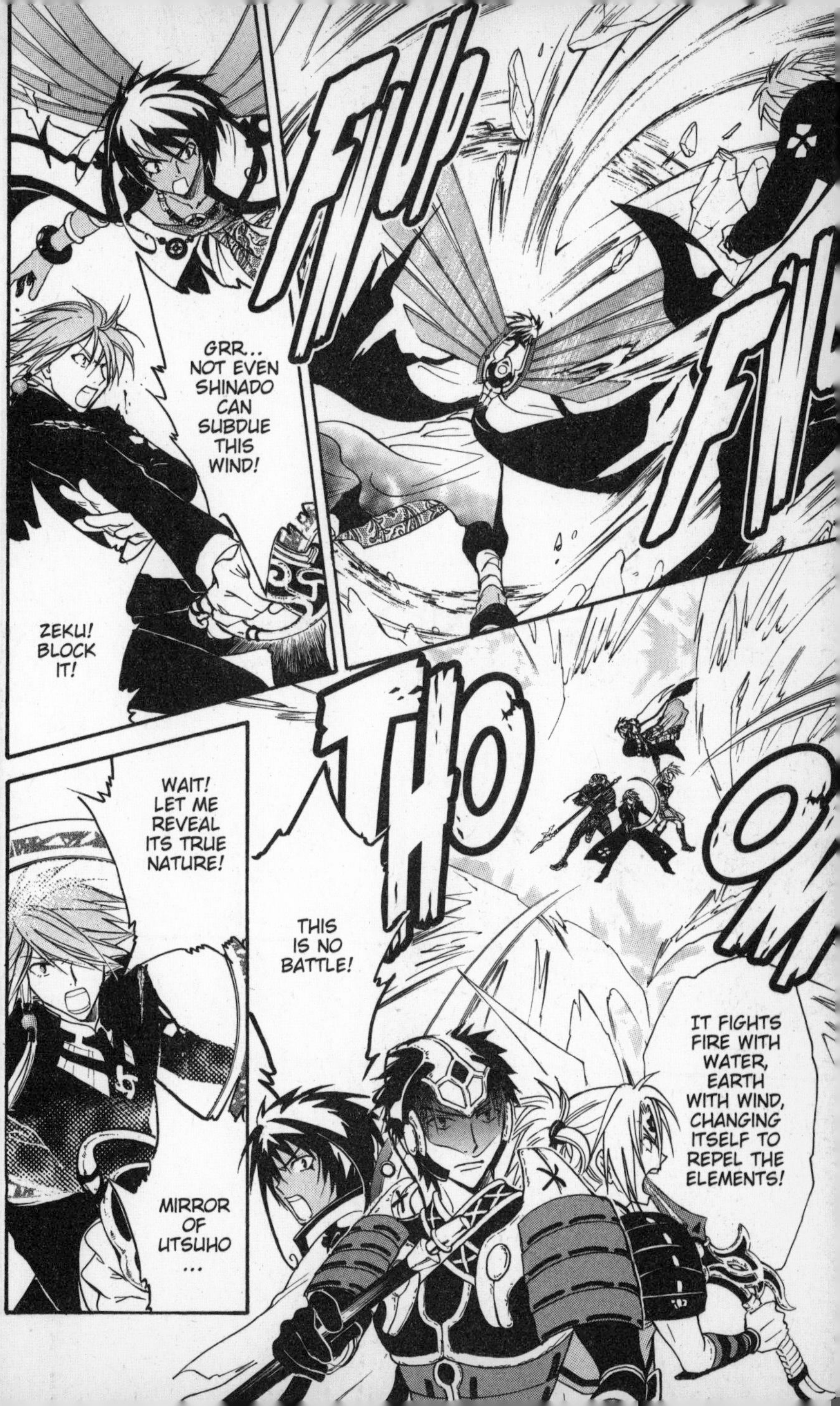
FWIP
FWI
GRR... NOT EVEN SHINADO CAN SUBDUE THIS WIND!
ZEKU! BLOCK IT!
THO
IT FIGHTS FIRE WITH WATER, EARTH WITH WIND, CHANGING ITSELF TO REPEL THE ELEMENTS!
THIS IS NO BATTLE!
WAIT! LET ME REVEAL ITS TRUE NATURE!
MIRROR OF UTSUHO ...

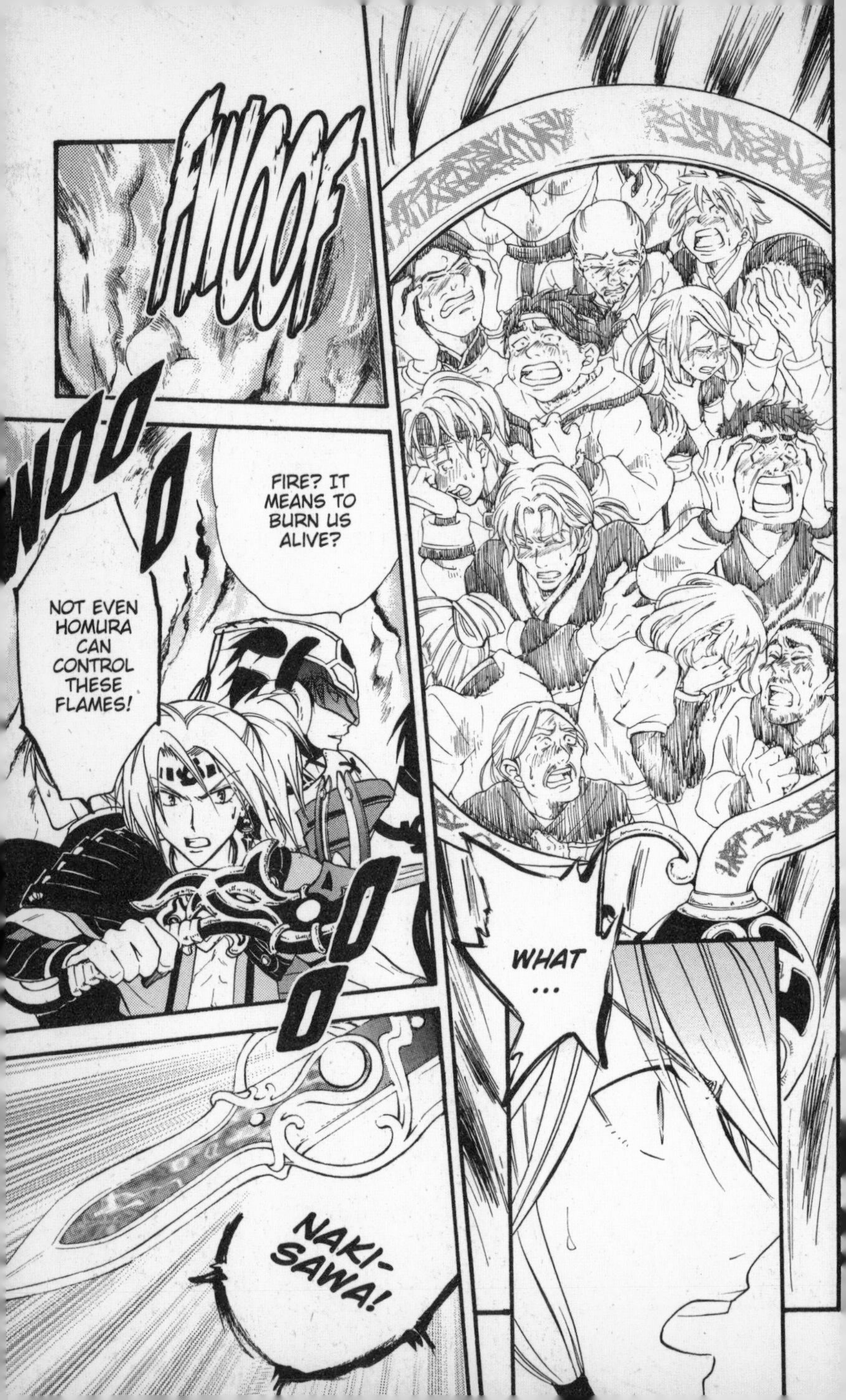
WHAT ...
FWOOF
WOOOOO
FIRE? IT MEANS TO BURN US ALIVE?
NOT EVEN HOMURA CAN CONTROL THESE FLAMES!
NAKI-SAWA!

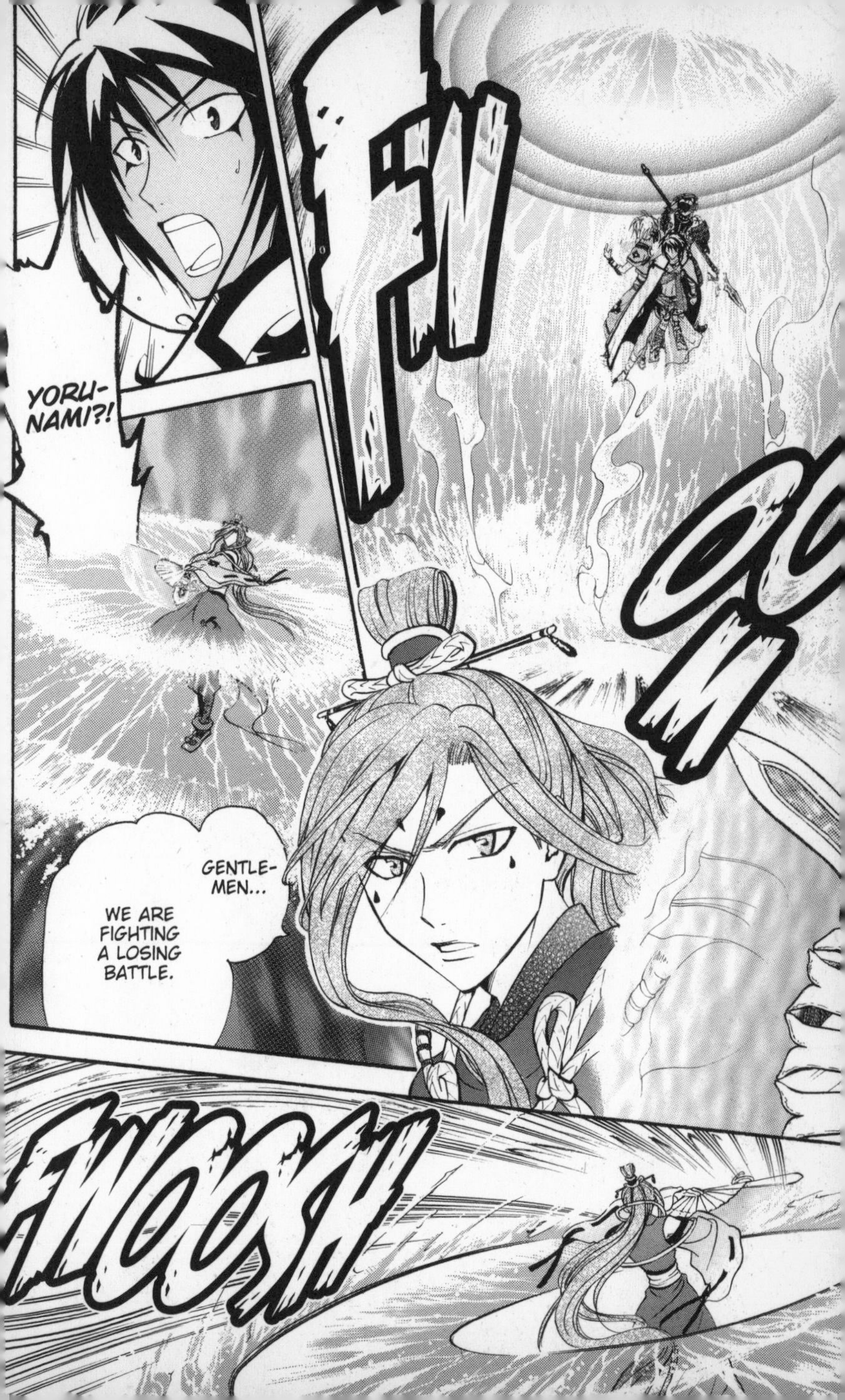

YORU-NAMI?!
GENTLE-MEN...
WE ARE FIGHTING A LOSING BATTLE.
WOOSH

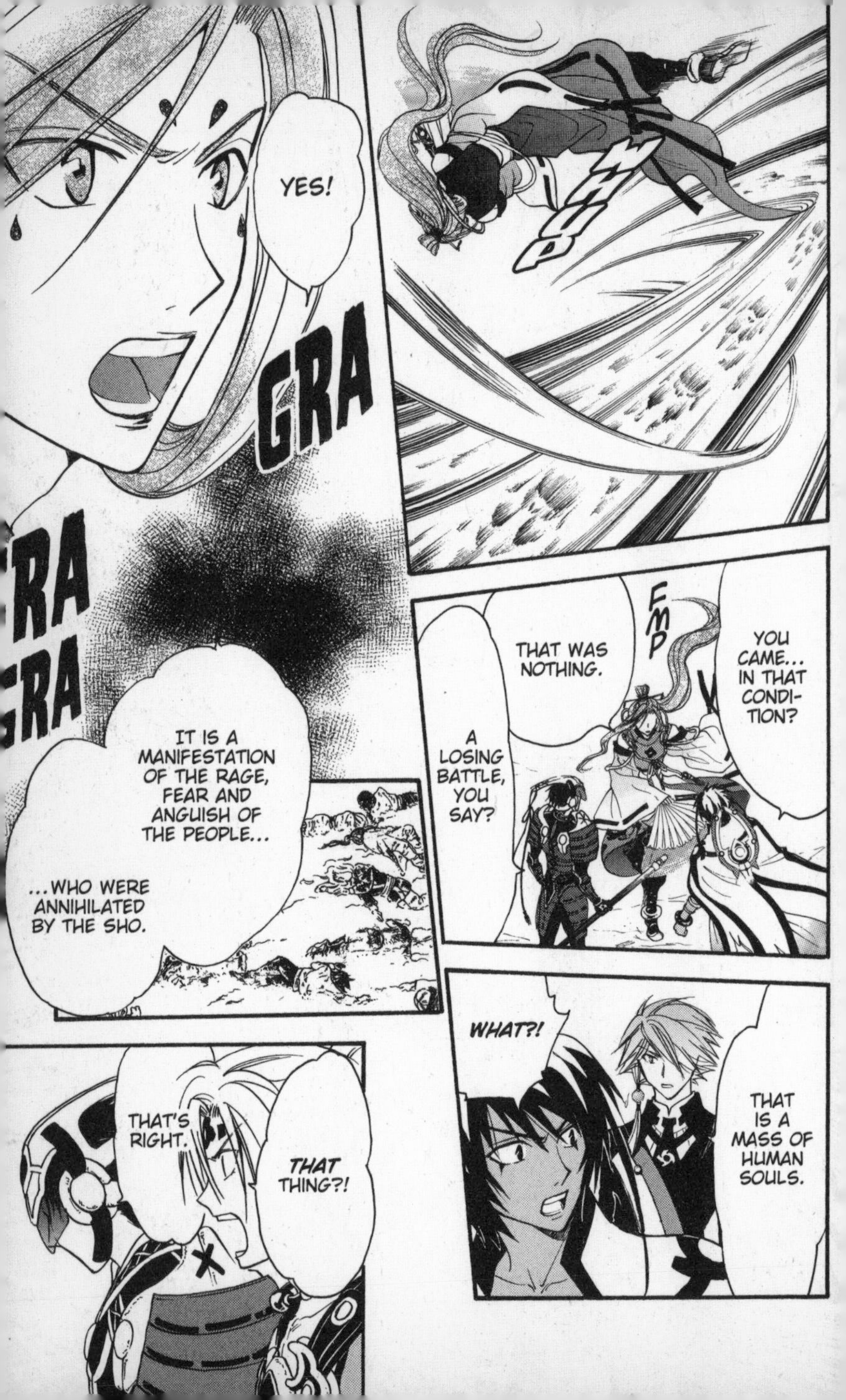
WHUP
FMP
YOU CAME... IN THAT CONDITION?
THAT WAS NOTHING.
A LOSING BATTLE, YOU SAY?
YES!
GRA
GRA
GRA
IT IS A MANIFESTATION OF THE RAGE, FEAR AND ANGUISH OF THE PEOPLE...
...WHO WERE ANNIHILATED BY THE SHO.
THAT IS A MASS OF HUMAN SOULS.
WHAT?!
THAT THING?!
THAT'S RIGHT.

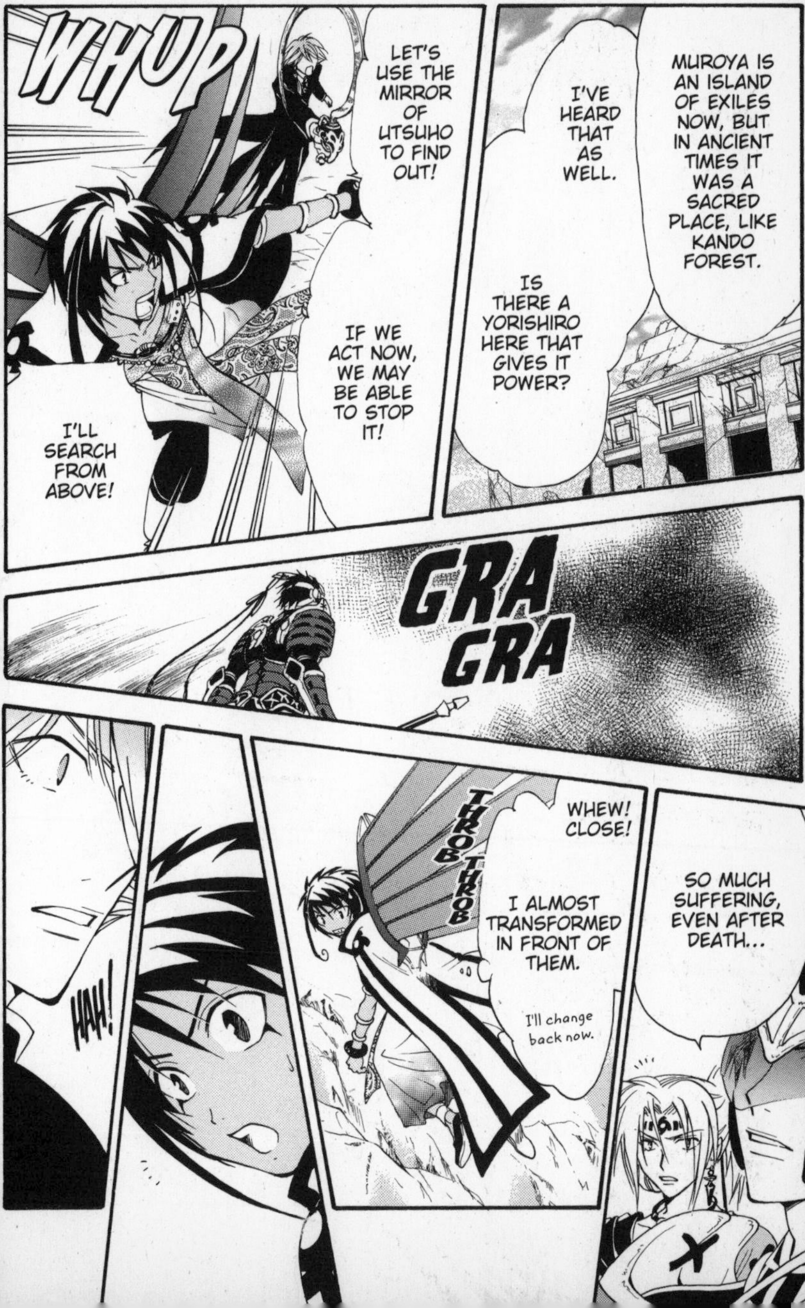
MUROYA IS AN ISLAND OF EXILES NOW, BUT IN ANCIENT TIMES IT WAS A SACRED PLACE, LIKE KANDO FOREST.
I'VE HEARD THAT AS WELL.
IS THERE A YORISHIRO HERE THAT GIVES IT POWER?
LET'S USE THE MIRROR OF UTSUHO TO FIND OUT!
IF WE ACT NOW, WE MAY BE ABLE TO STOP IT!
WHUP
I'LL SEARCH FROM ABOVE!
GRA GRA
SO MUCH SUFFERING, EVEN AFTER DEATH...
WHEW! CLOSE!
I ALMOST TRANSFORMED IN FRONT OF THEM.
I'll change back now.
THROB THROB
HAH!

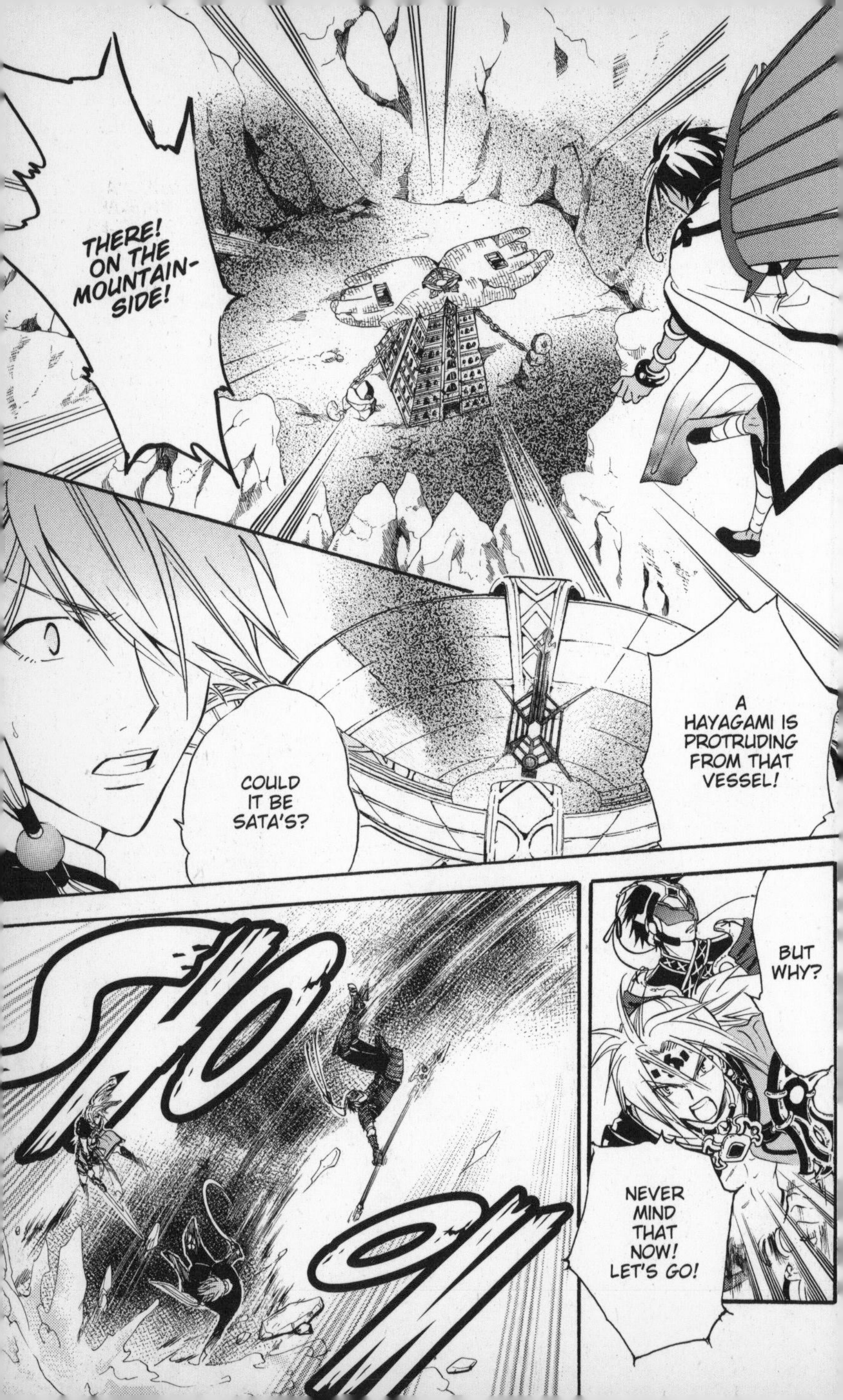
THERE! ON THE MOUNTAIN-SIDE!
A HAYAGAMI IS PROTRUDING FROM THAT VESSEL!
COULD IT BE SATA'S?
BUT WHY?
NEVER MIND THAT NOW! LET'S GO!

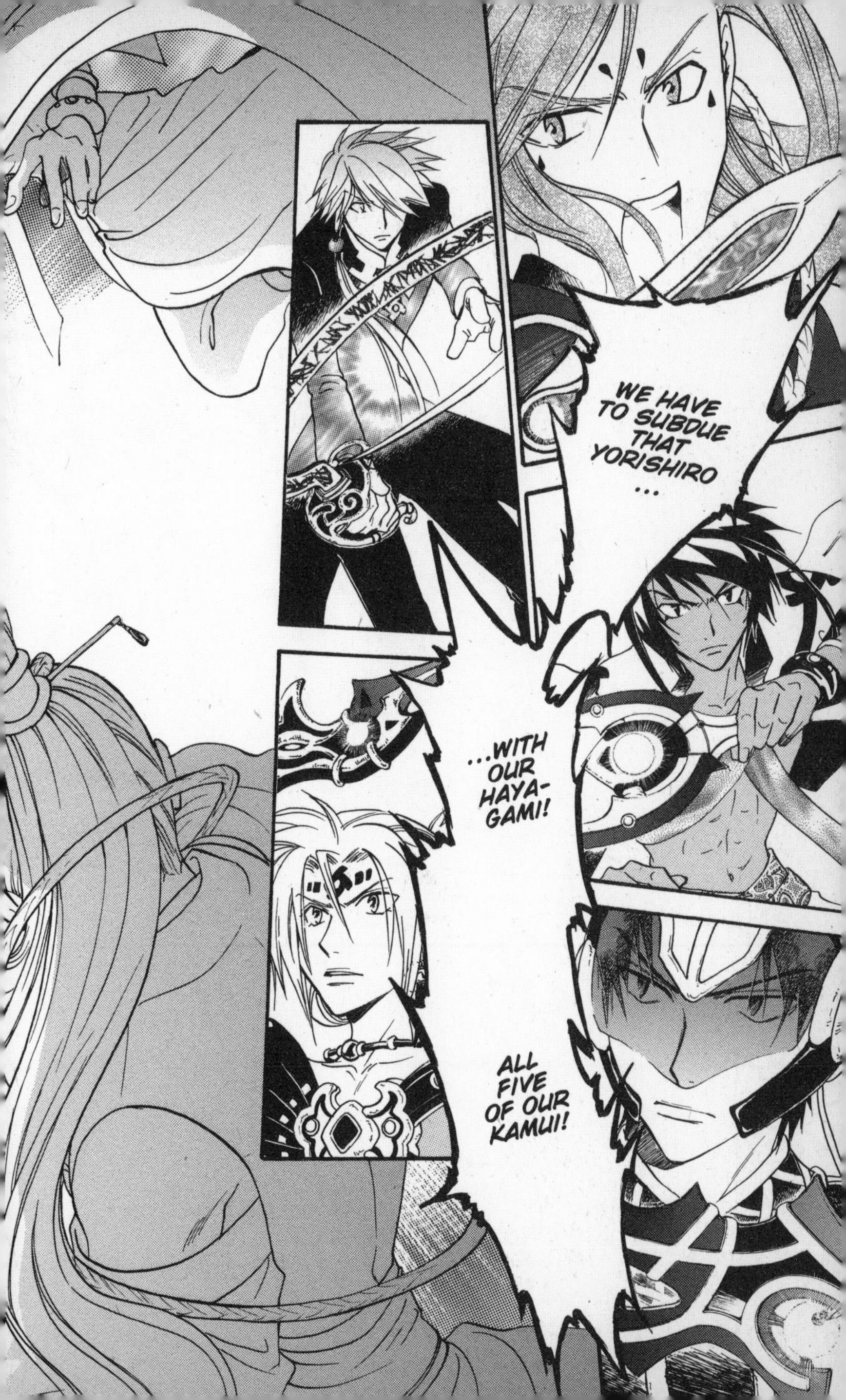
WE HAVE TO SUBDUE THAT YORISHIRO...
...WITH OUR HAYA-GAMI!
ALL FIVE OF OUR KAMUI!

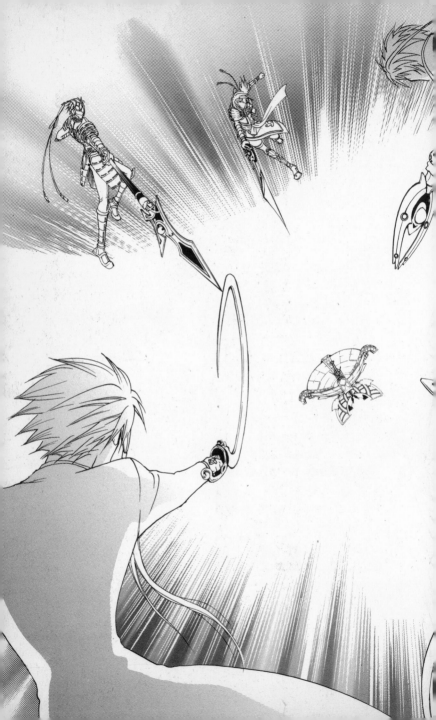

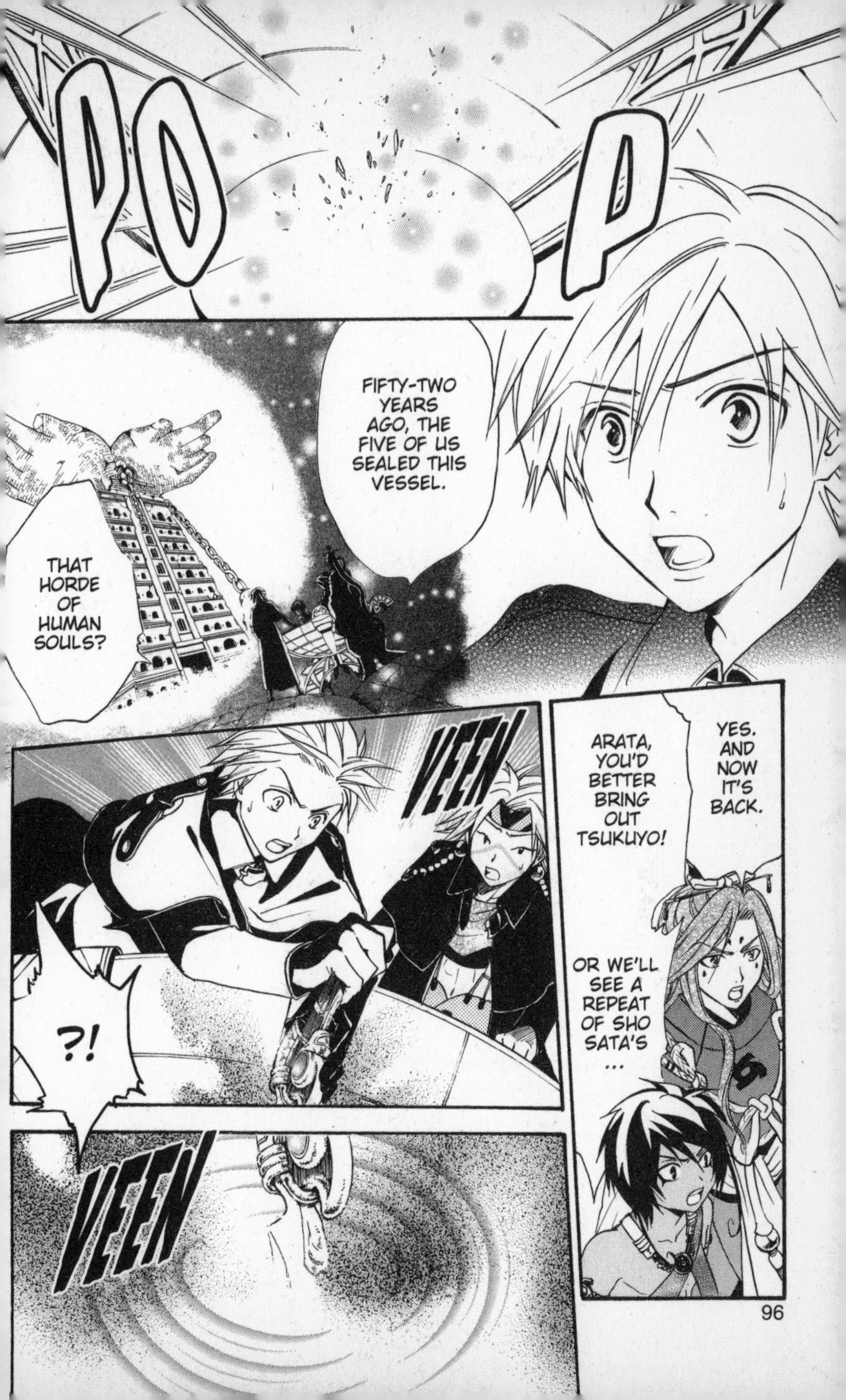
POP
FIFTY-TWO YEARS AGO, THE FIVE OF US SEALED THIS VESSEL.
THAT HORDE OF HUMAN SOULS?
YES. AND NOW IT'S BACK.
ARATA, YOU'D BETTER BRING OUT TSUKUYO!
OR WE'LL SEE A REPEAT OF SHO SATA'S ...
VEEN
?!
VEEN

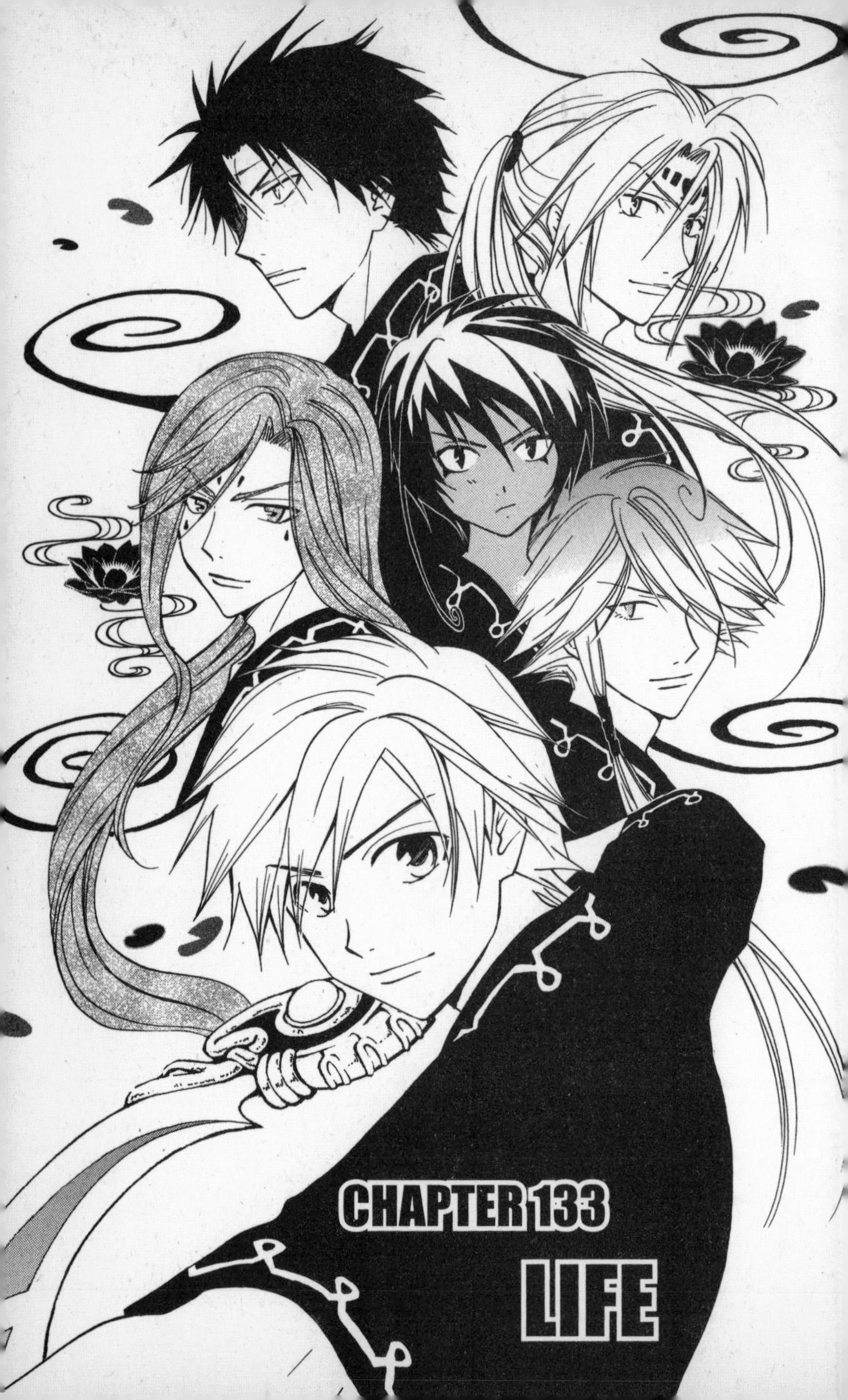
CHAPTER 133
LIFE

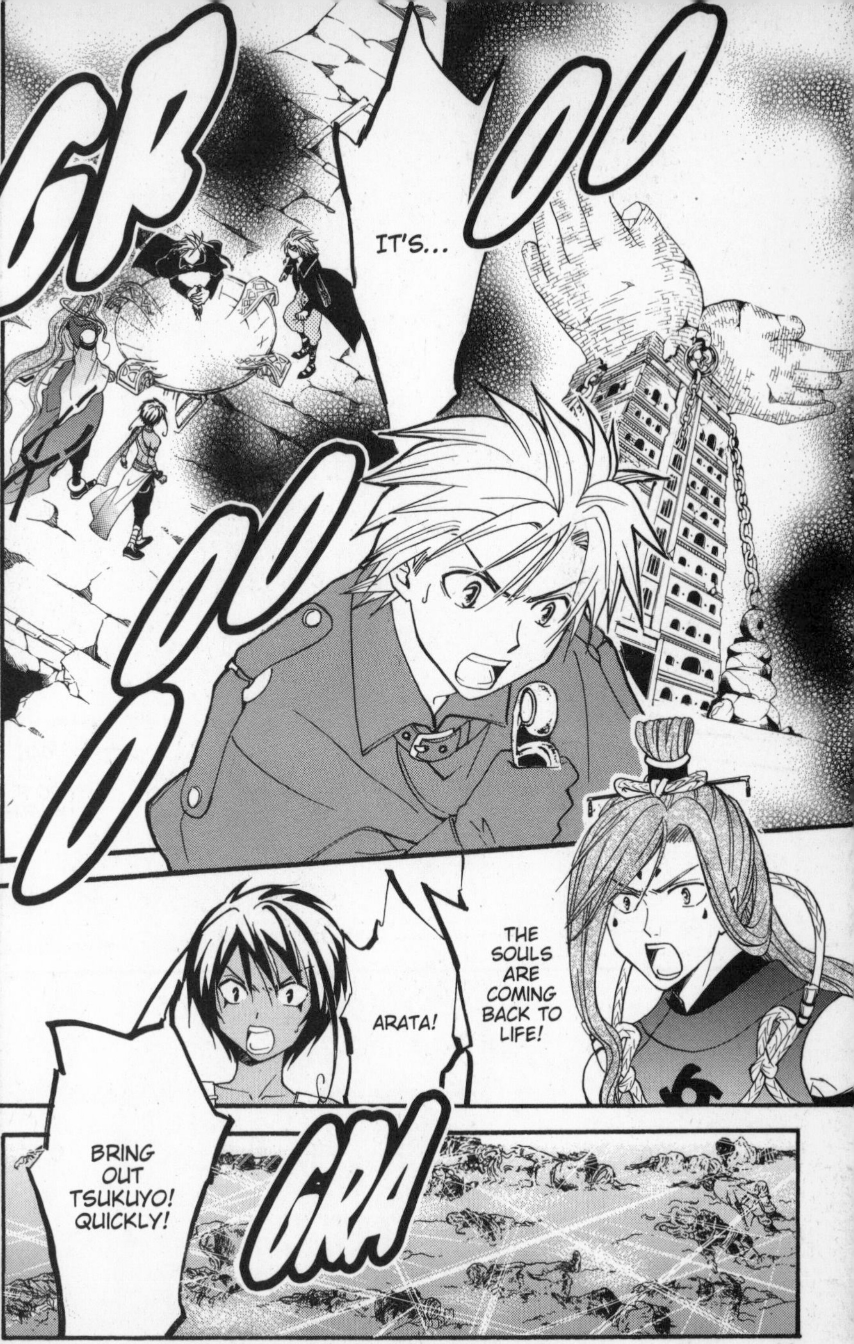
IT'S...
THE SOULS ARE COMING BACK TO LIFE!
ARATA!
BRING OUT TSUKUYO! QUICKLY!
GRA

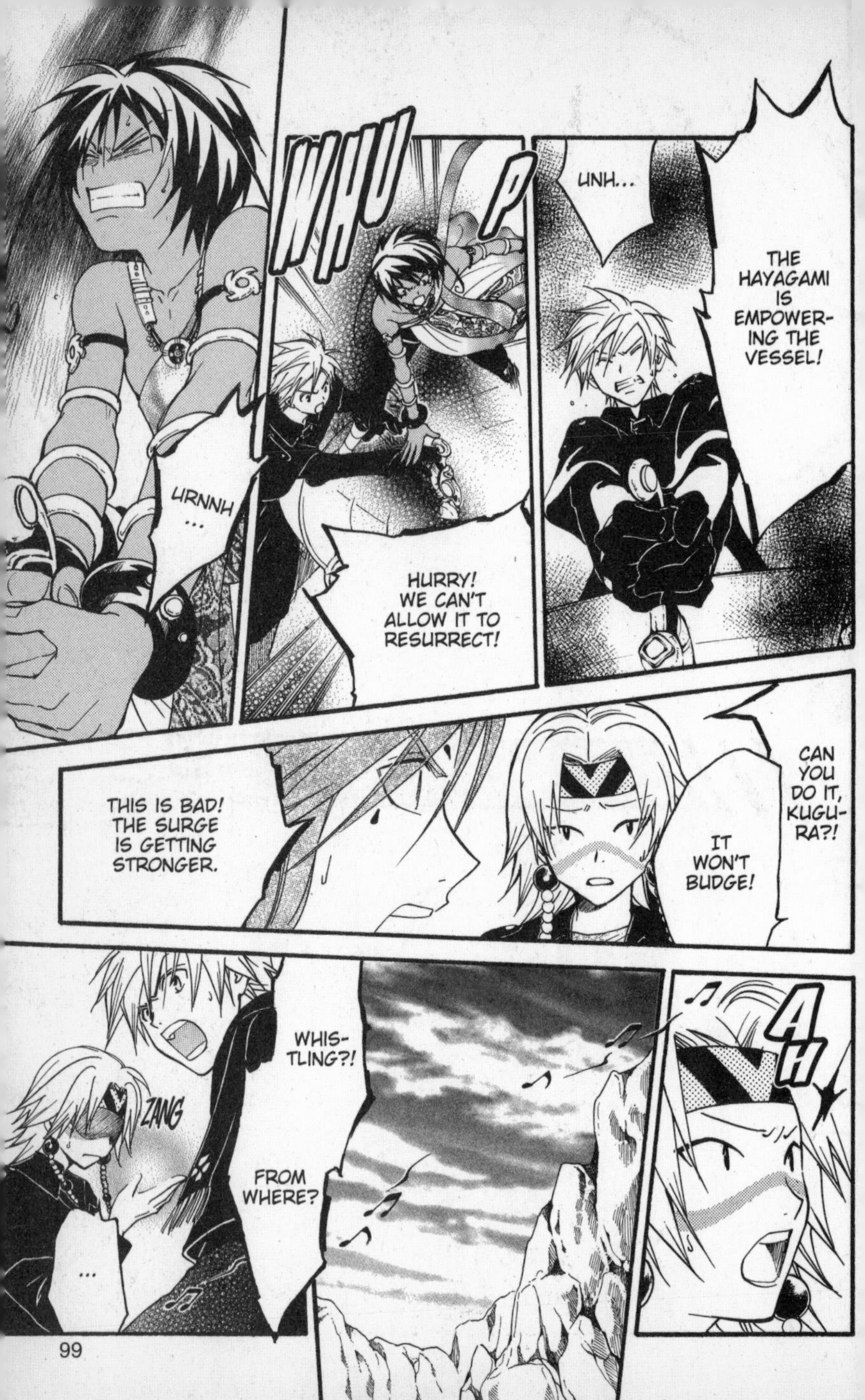
UNH...
THE HAYAGAMI IS EMPOWER-ING THE VESSEL!
WHUP
HURRY! WE CAN'T ALLOW IT TO RESURRECT!
URNNH ...
CAN YOU DO IT, KUGU-RA?!
IT WON'T BUDGE!
THIS IS BAD! THE SURGE IS GETTING STRONGER.
AH
WHIS-TLING?!
FROM WHERE?
ZANG
...

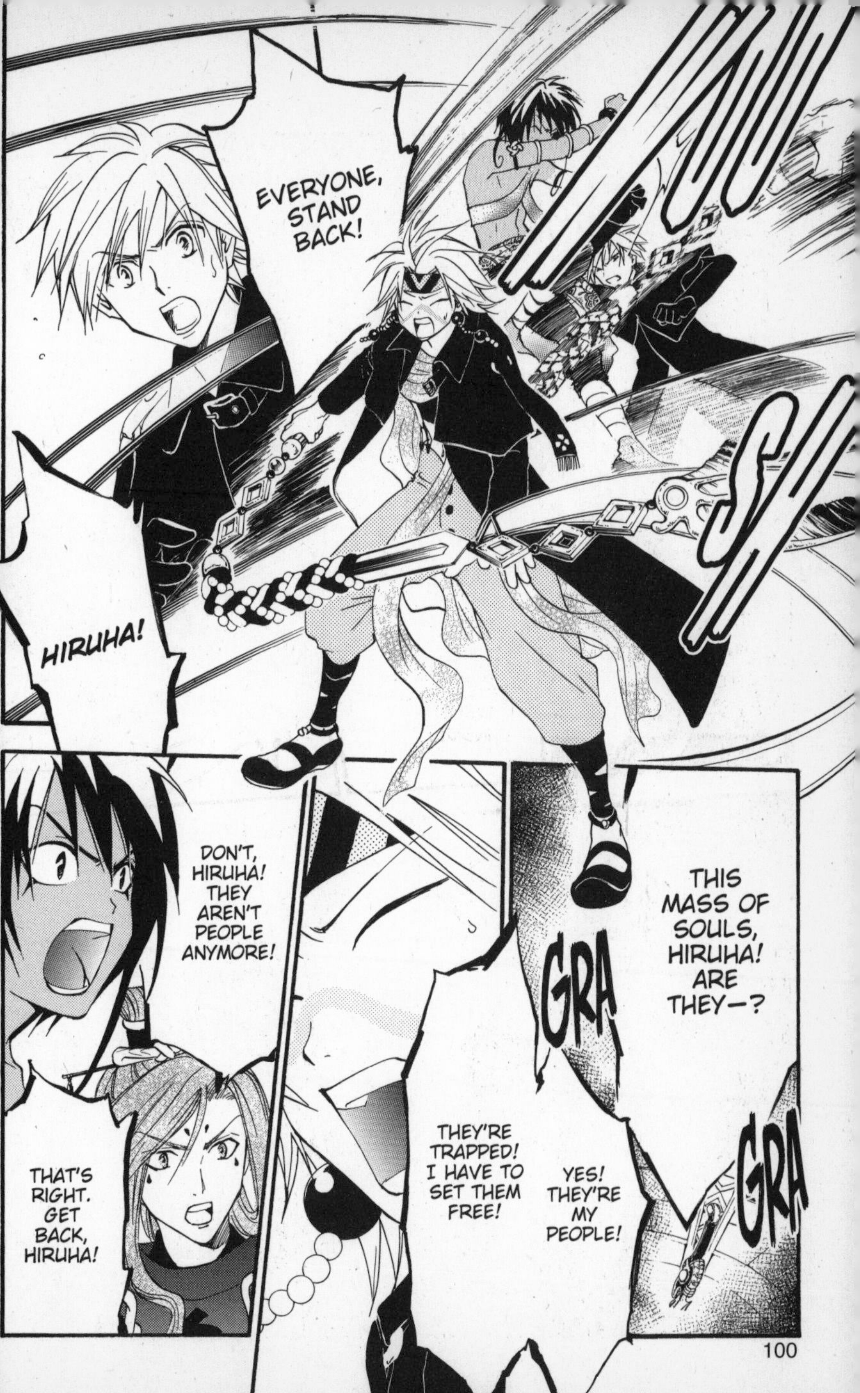
EVERYONE, STAND BACK!
HIRUHA!
THIS MASS OF SOULS, HIRUHA! ARE THEY—?
GRA
GRA
YES! THEY'RE MY PEOPLE!
THEY'RE TRAPPED! I HAVE TO SET THEM FREE!
DON'T, HIRUHA! THEY AREN'T PEOPLE ANYMORE!
THAT'S RIGHT. GET BACK, HIRUHA!

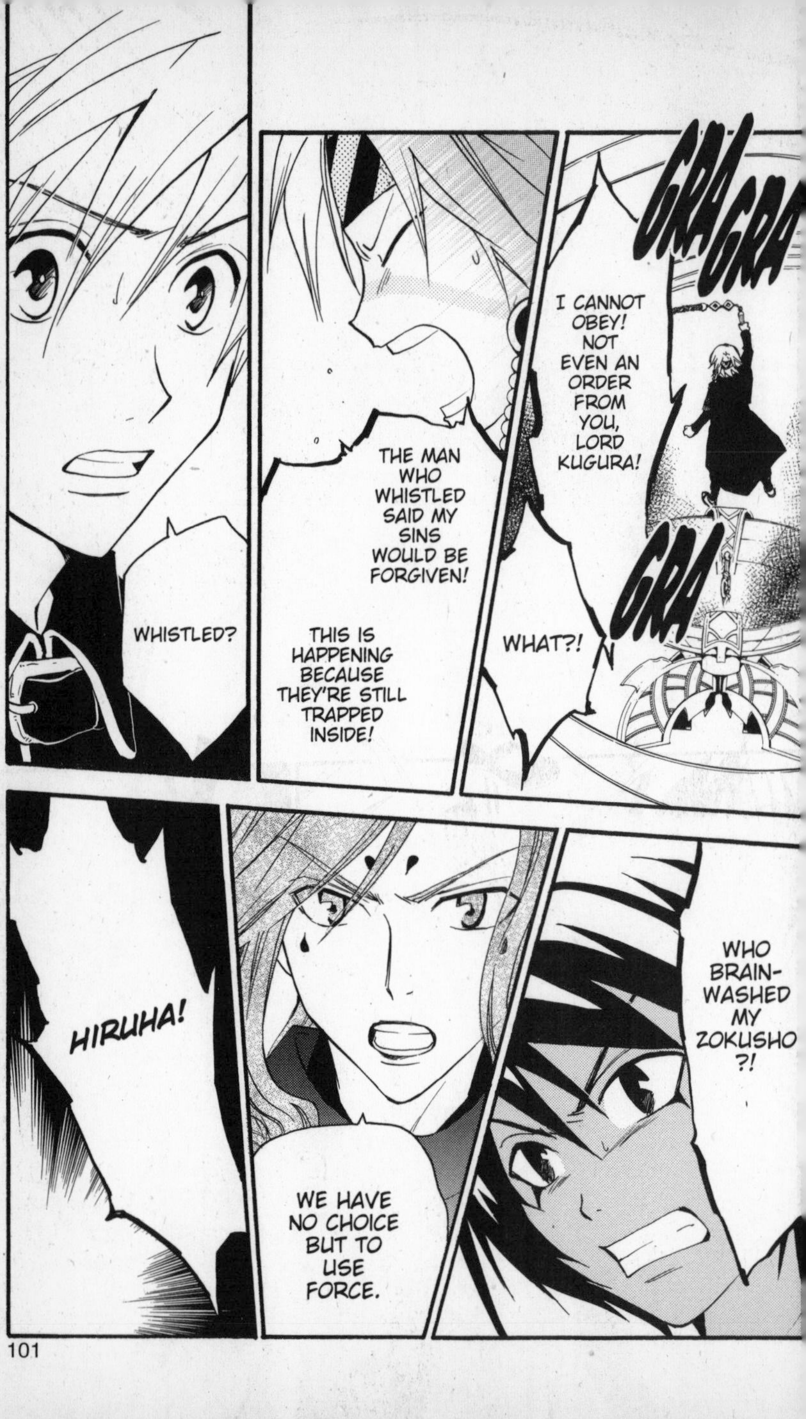
GRA GRA
I CANNOT OBEY! NOT EVEN AN ORDER FROM YOU, LORD KUGURA!
GRA
WHAT?!
THE MAN WHO WHISTLED SAID MY SINS WOULD BE FORGIVEN!
THIS IS HAPPENING BECAUSE THEY'RE STILL TRAPPED INSIDE!
WHISTLED?
WHO BRAIN-WASHED MY ZOKUSHO?!
WE HAVE NO CHOICE BUT TO USE FORCE.
HIRUHA!

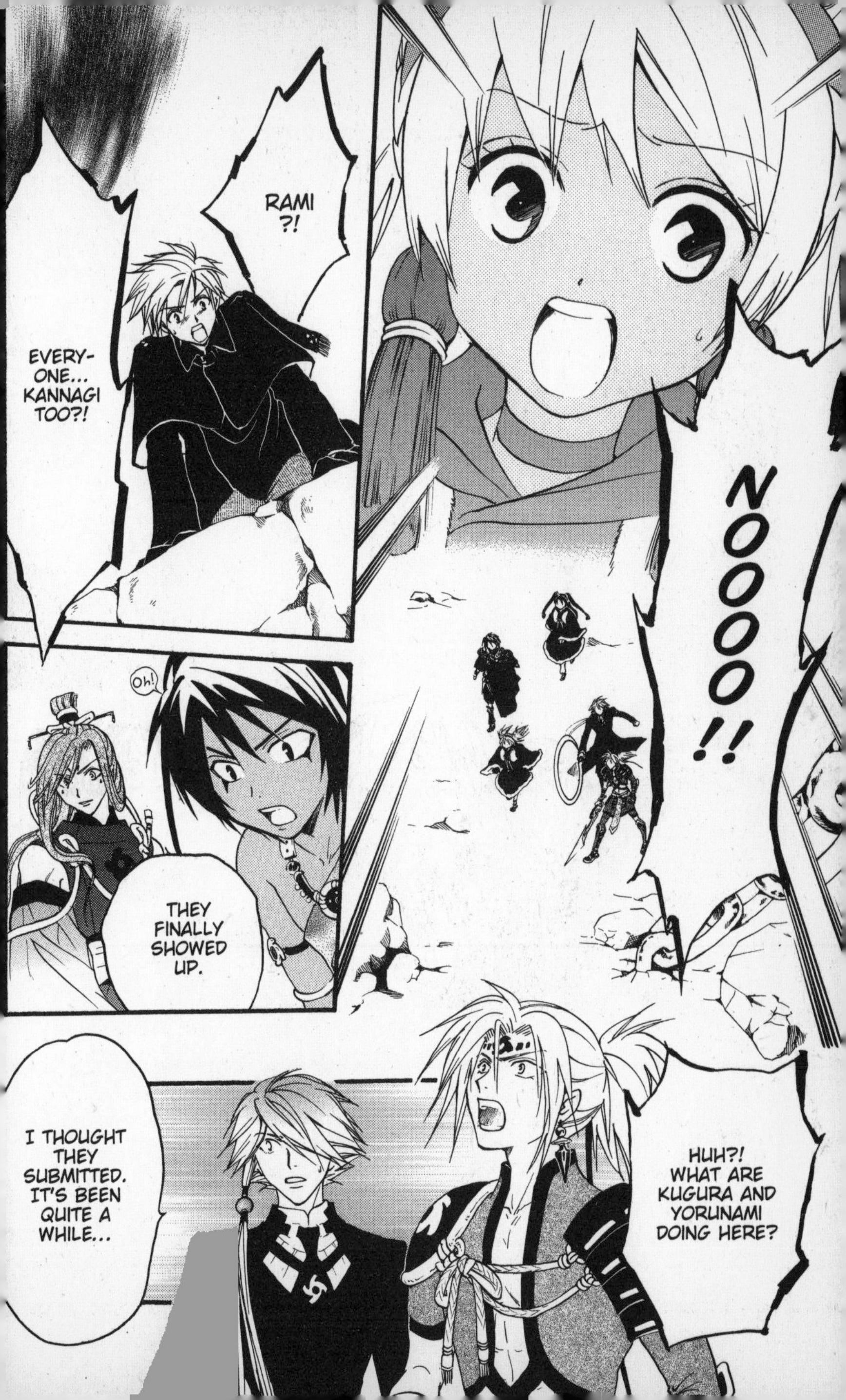
NOOOOO!!
RAMI ?!
EVERY-ONE... KANNAGI TOO?!
Oh!
THEY FINALLY SHOWED UP.
HUH?! WHAT ARE KUGURA AND YORUNAMI DOING HERE?
I THOUGHT THEY SUBMITTED. IT'S BEEN QUITE A WHILE...

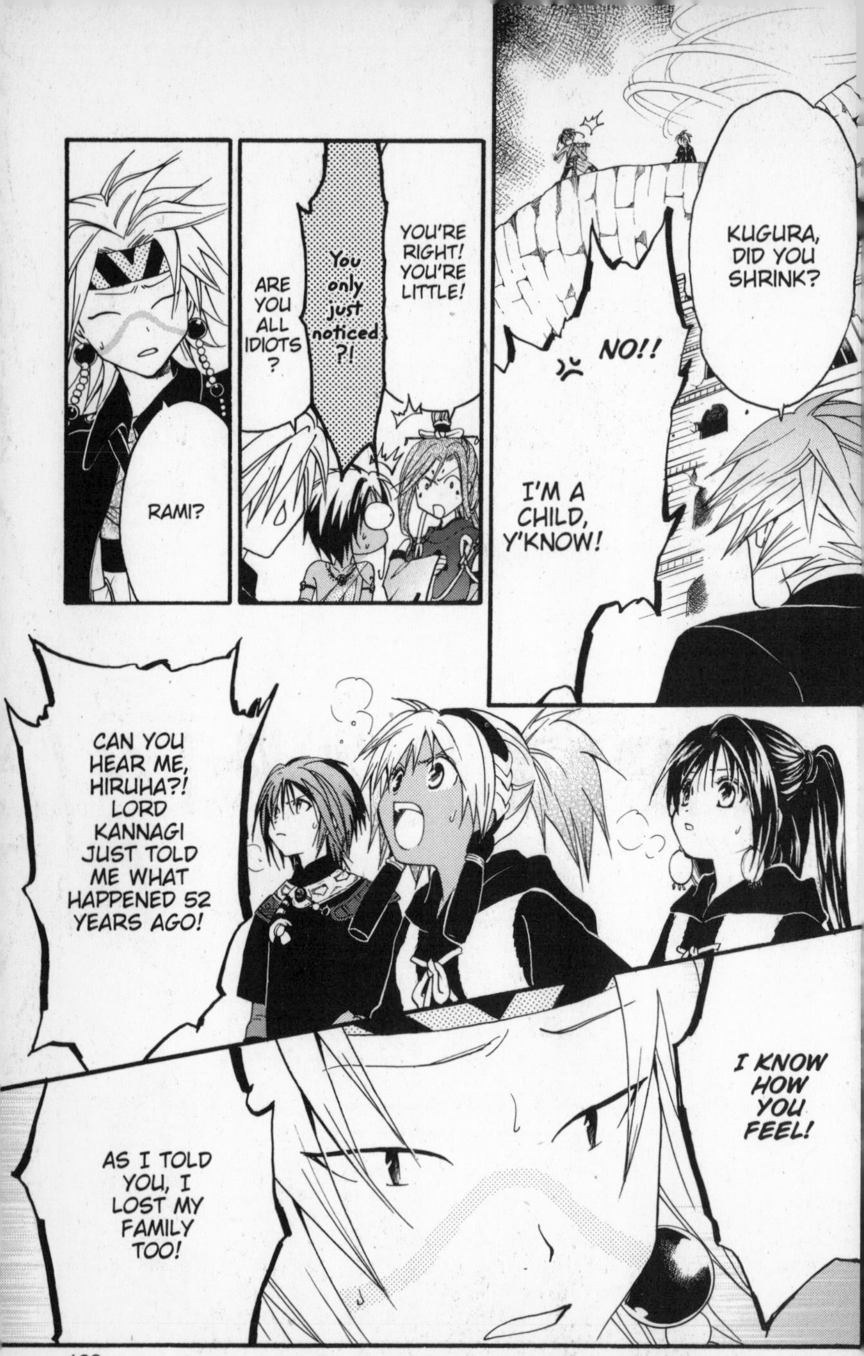
KUGURA, DID YOU SHRINK?
NO!!
I'M A CHILD, Y'KNOW!
YOU'RE RIGHT! YOU'RE LITTLE!
You only just noticed?!
ARE YOU ALL IDIOTS?
RAMI?
CAN YOU HEAR ME, HIRUHA?! LORD KANNAGI JUST TOLD ME WHAT HAPPENED 52 YEARS AGO!
I KNOW HOW YOU FEEL!
AS I TOLD YOU, I LOST MY FAMILY TOO!

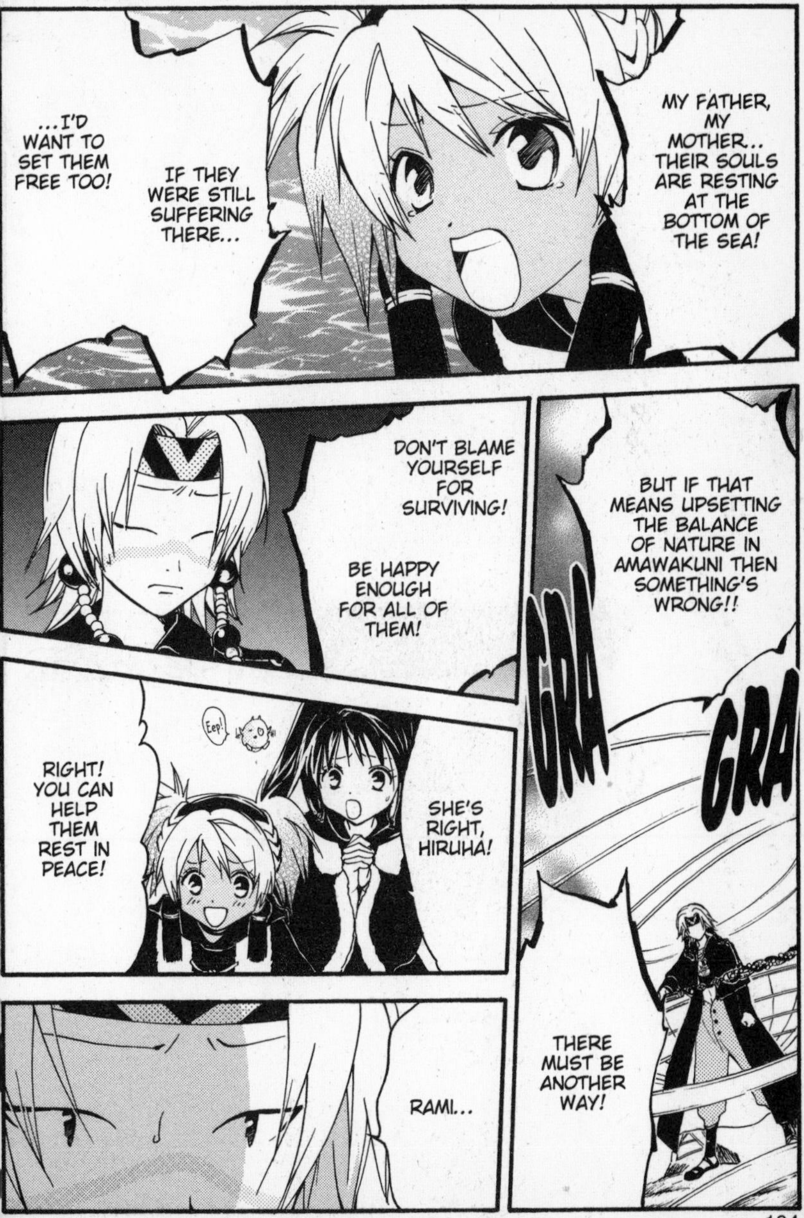
MY FATHER, MY MOTHER.. THEIR SOULS ARE RESTING AT THE BOTTOM OF THE SEA!
IF THEY WERE STILL SUFFERING THERE...
...I'D WANT TO SET THEM FREE TOO!
BUT IF THAT MEANS UPSETTING THE BALANCE OF NATURE IN AMAWAKUNI THEN SOMETHING'S WRONG!!
GRA
GRA
THERE MUST BE ANOTHER WAY!
DON'T BLAME YOURSELF FOR SURVIVING!
BE HAPPY ENOUGH FOR ALL OF THEM!
SHE'S RIGHT, HIRUHA!
Eep!
RIGHT! YOU CAN HELP THEM REST IN PEACE!
RAMI...

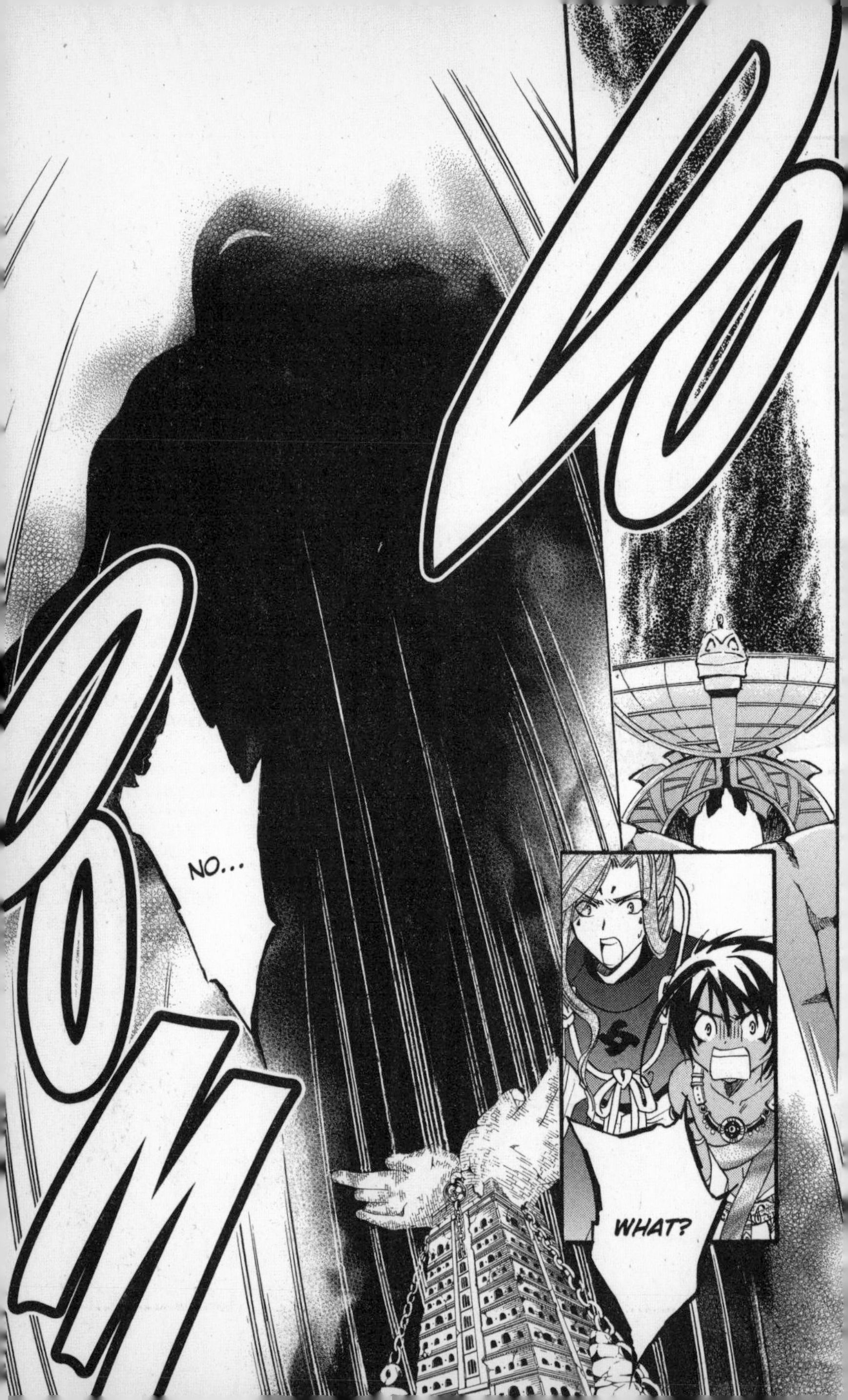
NO...
WHAT?

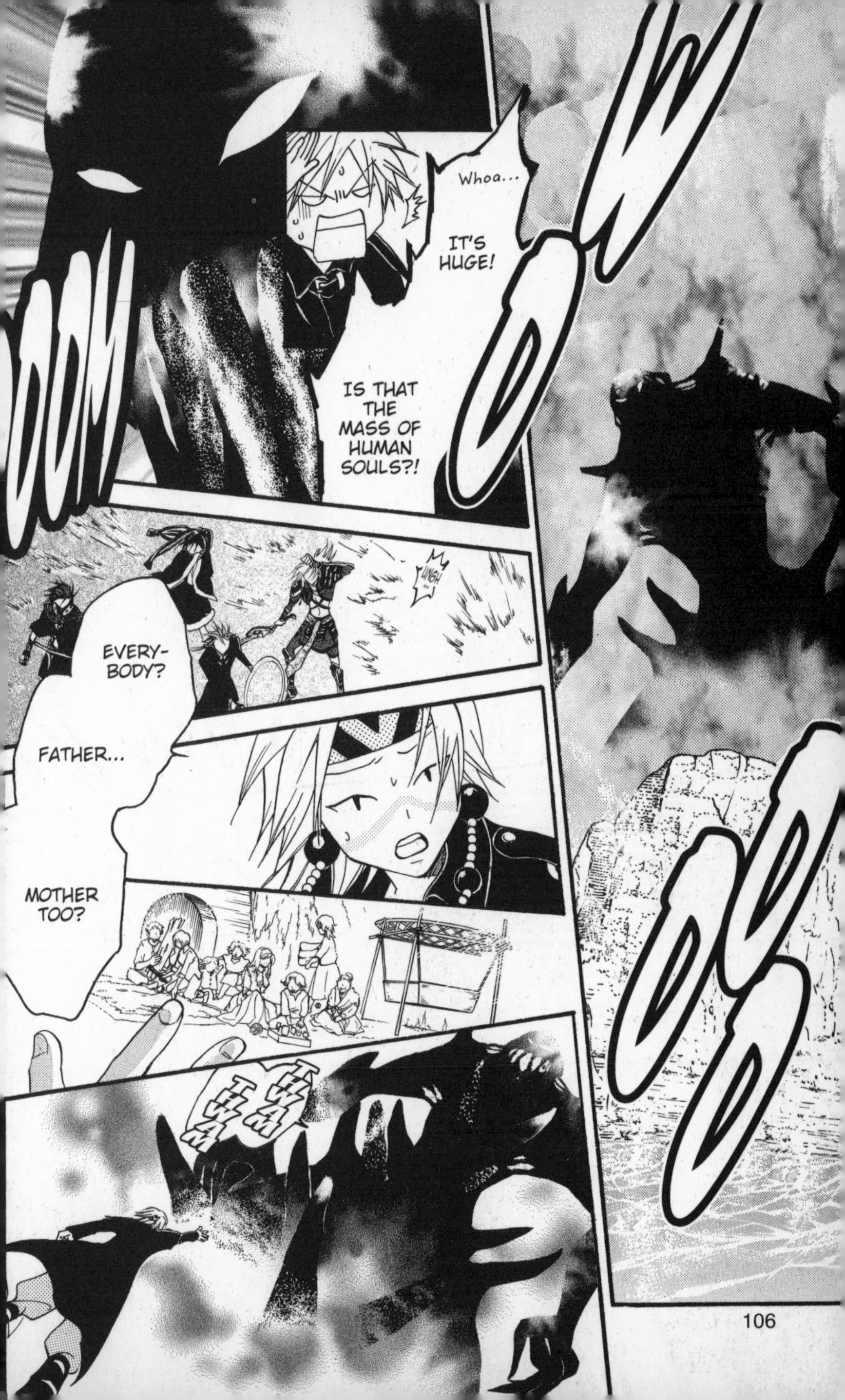

Whoa...
IT'S HUGE!
IS THAT THE MASS OF HUMAN SOULS?!
UNGH
EVERY-BODY?
FATHER...
MOTHER TOO?
THWA THWA

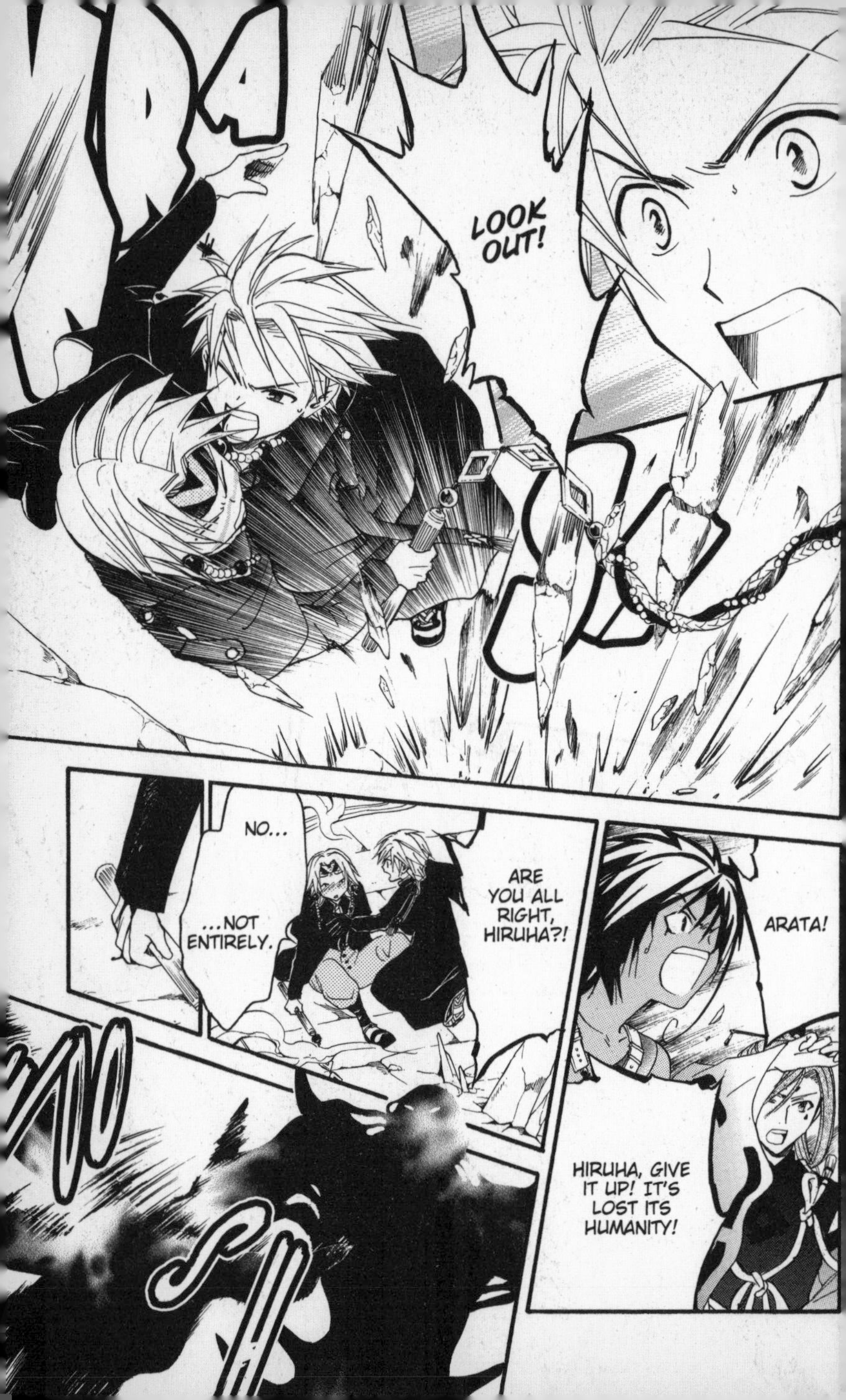
LOOK OUT!
ARATA!
HIRUHA, GIVE IT UP! IT'S LOST ITS HUMANITY!
ARE YOU ALL RIGHT, HIRUHA?!
NO...
...NOT ENTIRELY.

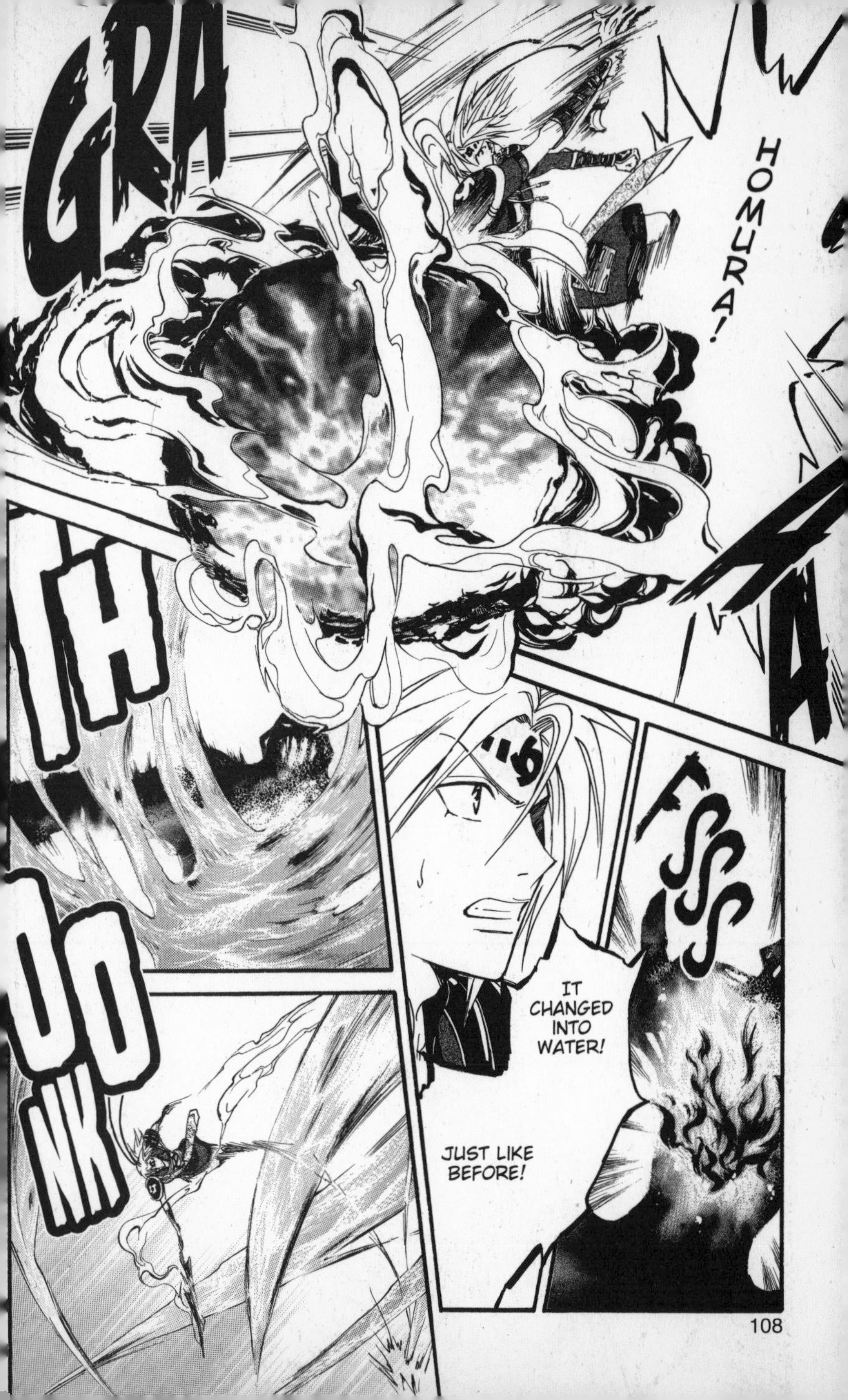
GRA
HOMURA!
FSSS
IT CHANGED INTO WATER!
JUST LIKE BEFORE!

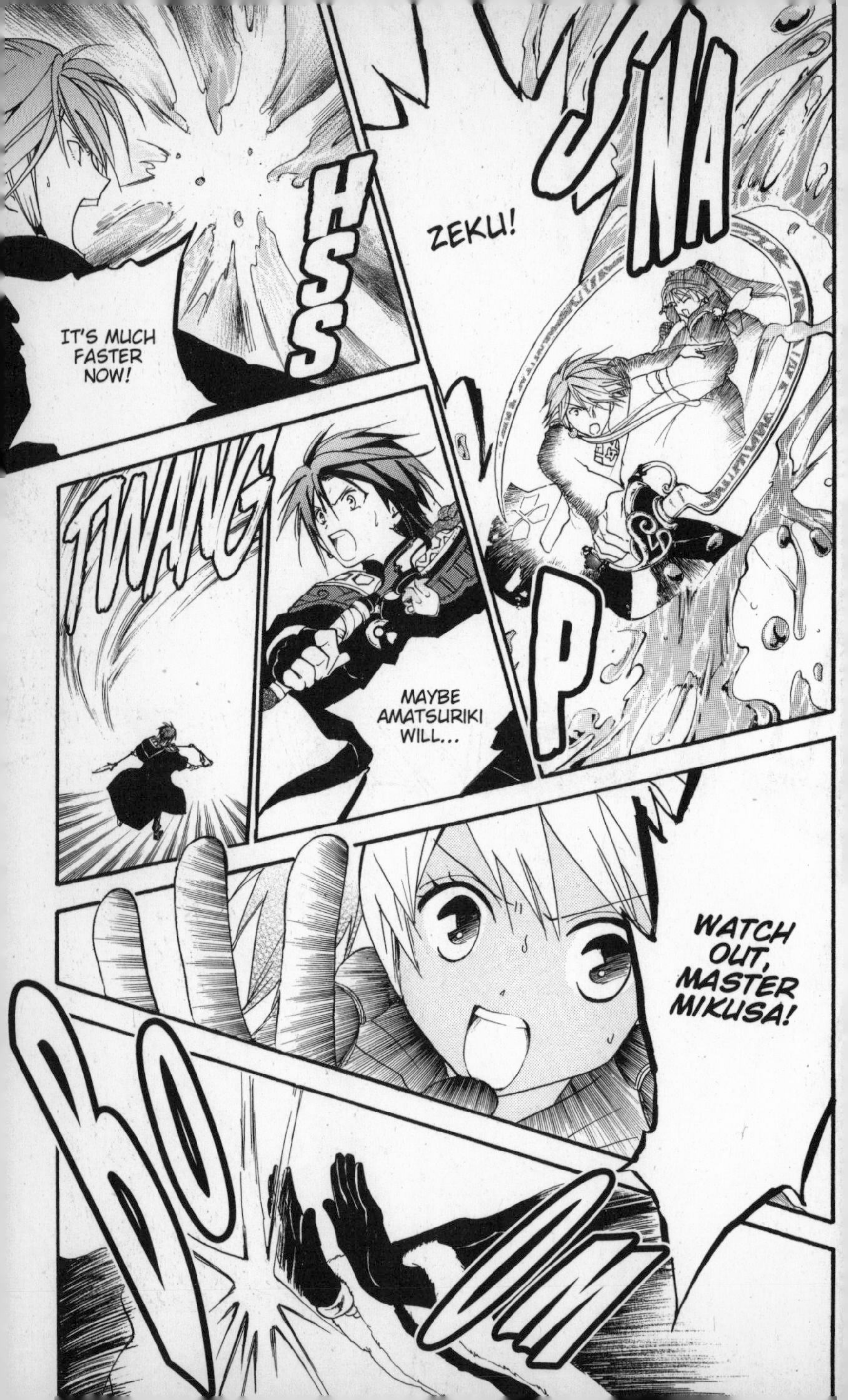

NA
ZEKU!
P
HSS
IT'S MUCH FASTER NOW!
MAYBE AMATSURIKI WILL...
TWANG
WATCH OUT, MASTER MIKUSA!
BOOM

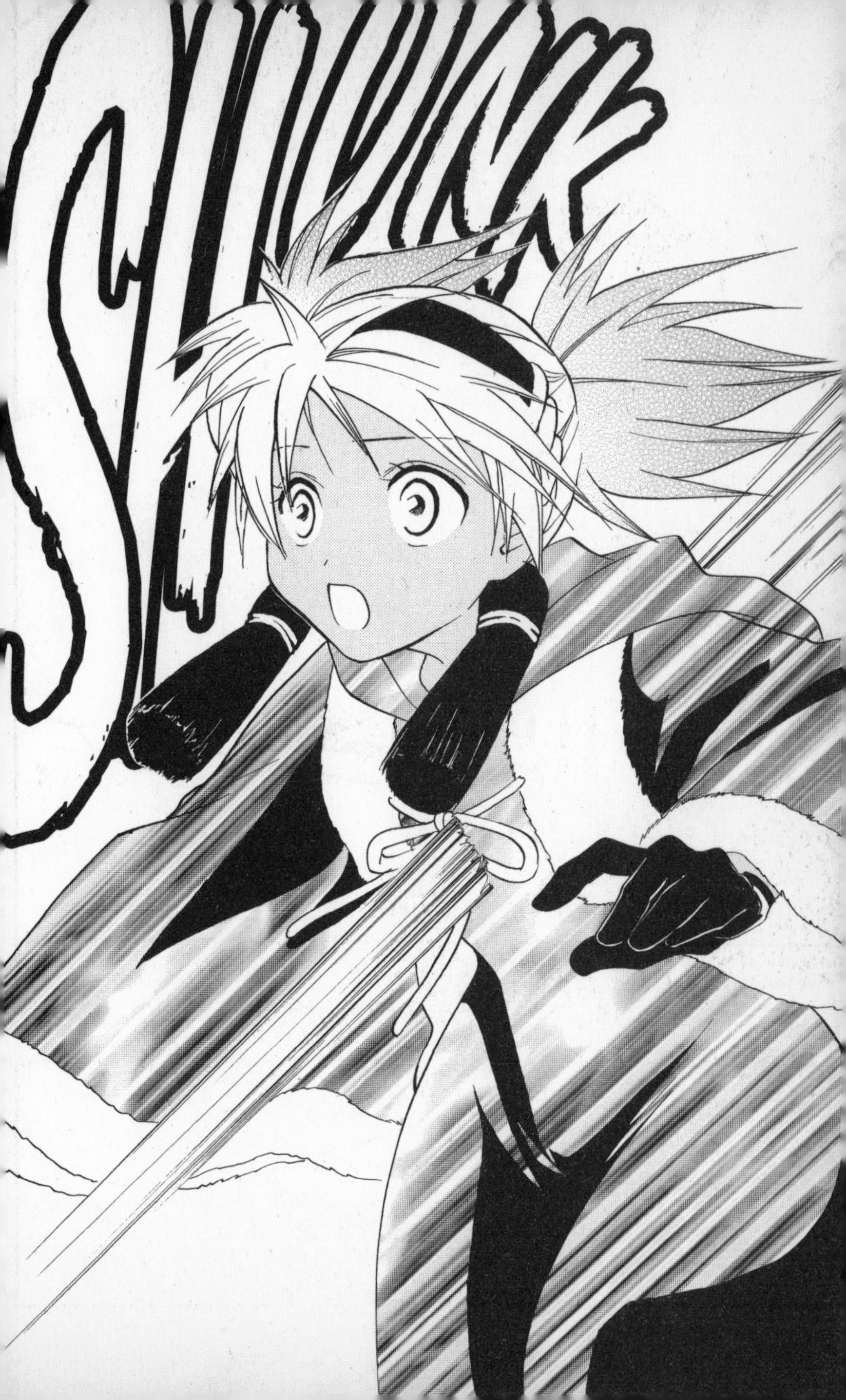

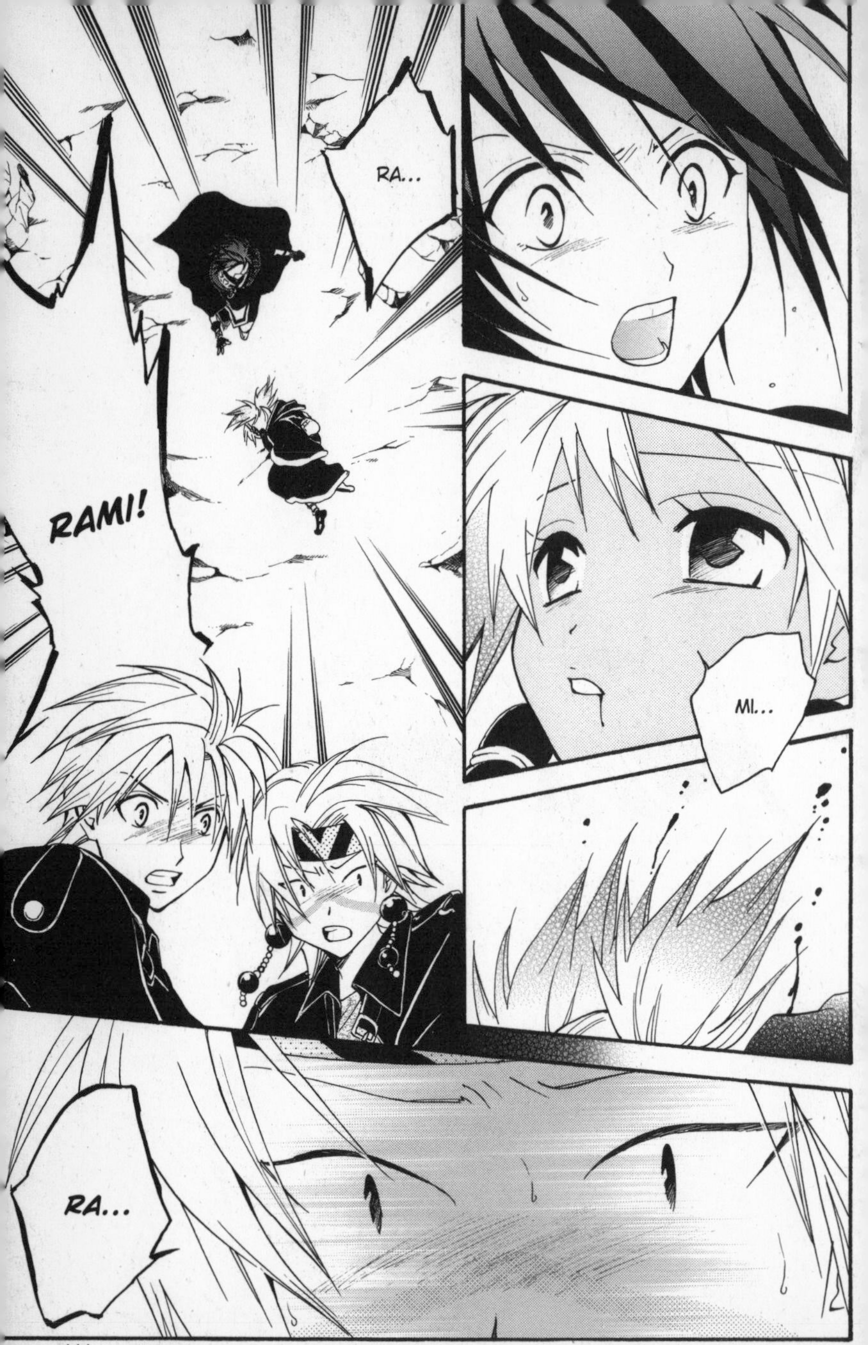
RA...
MI...
RAMI!
RA...

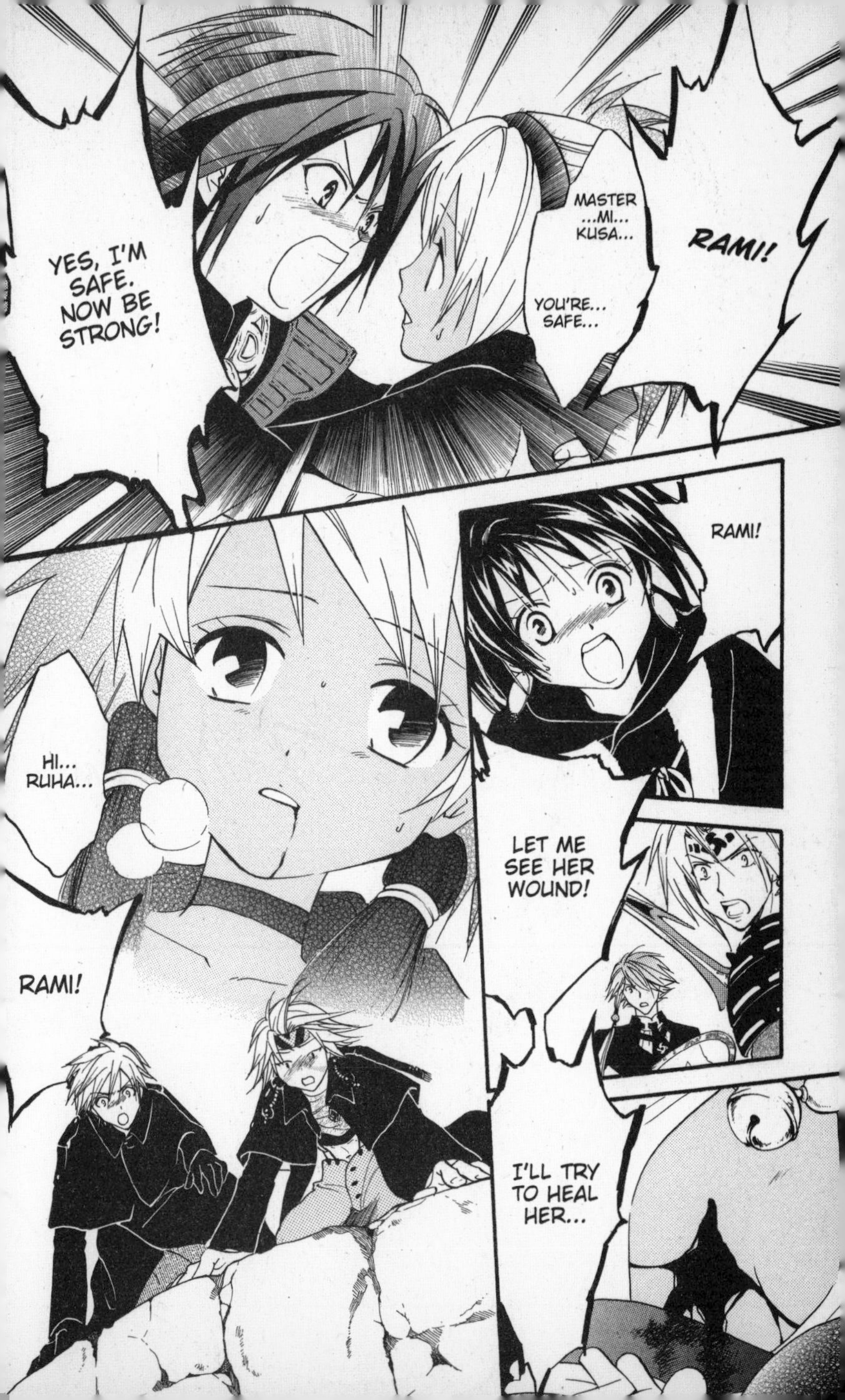
RAMI!
MASTER ...MI... KUSA...
YOU'RE... SAFE...
YES, I'M SAFE. NOW BE STRONG!
RAMI!
LET ME SEE HER WOUND!
I'LL TRY TO HEAL HER...
HI... RUHA...
RAMI!

WHOOSH?

DOMO

HIRUHA?!

IT'S ALL MY FAULT!

I'M SORRY, RAMI!

HUH?!

EVEN IF IT TAKES MY SOUL!

G'RA GRA

I WILL DO IT! I WILL STOP THE KANTAKARA!

IT'S COMING OUT?!

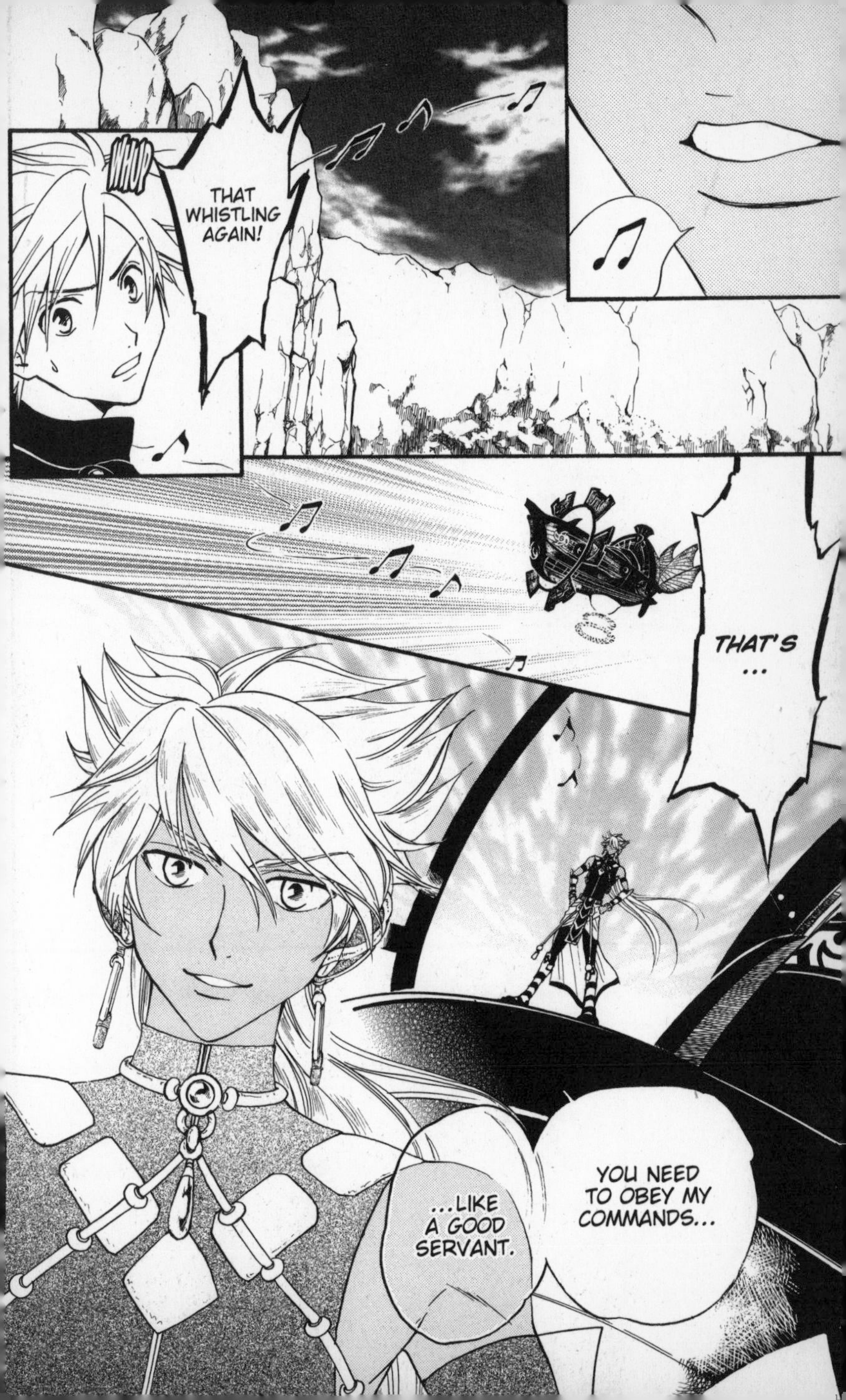
WHOP
THAT WHISTLING AGAIN!
THAT'S ...
YOU NEED TO OBEY MY COMMANDS...
...LIKE A GOOD SERVANT.

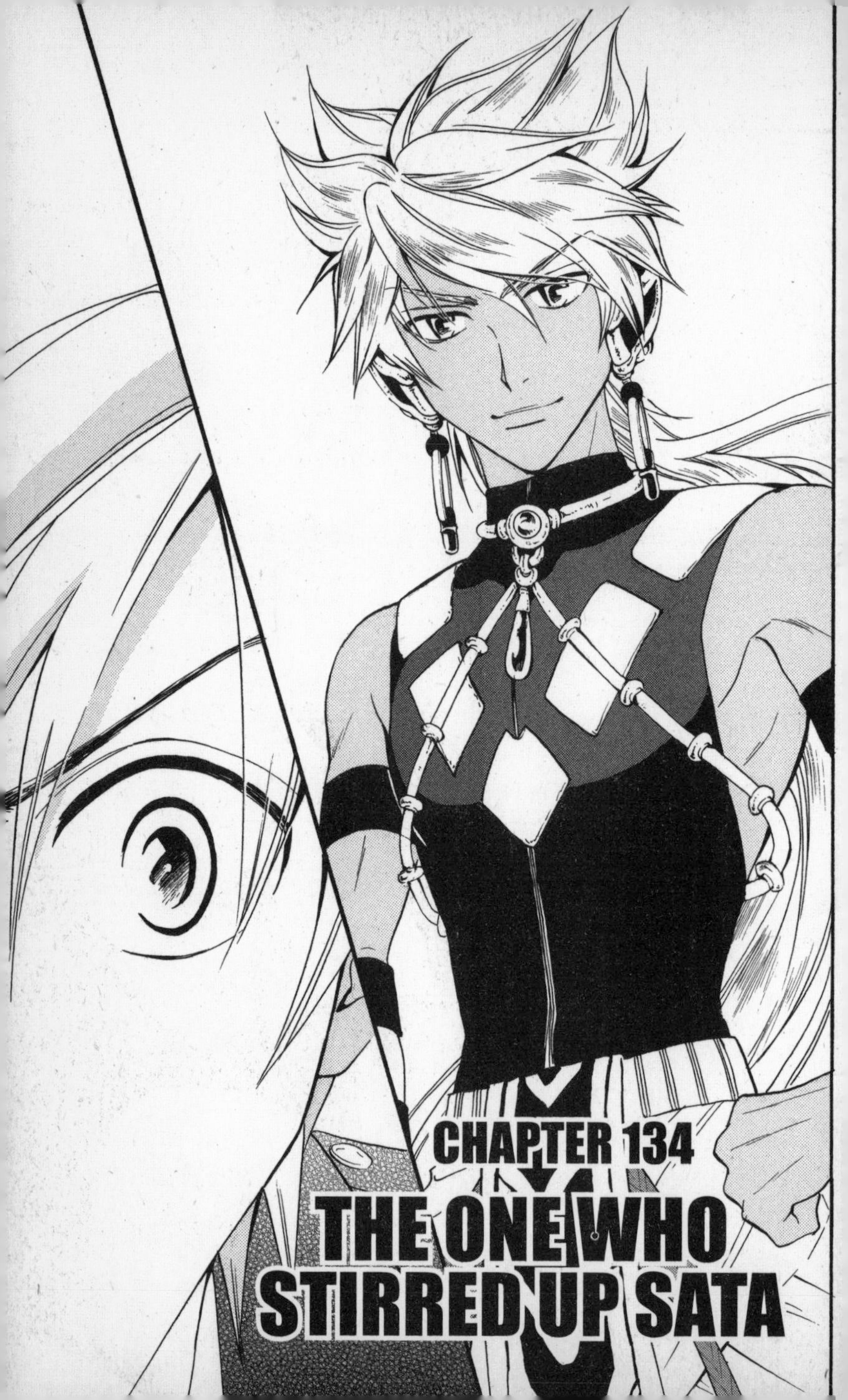
CHAPTER 134
THE ONE WHO STIRRED UP SATA

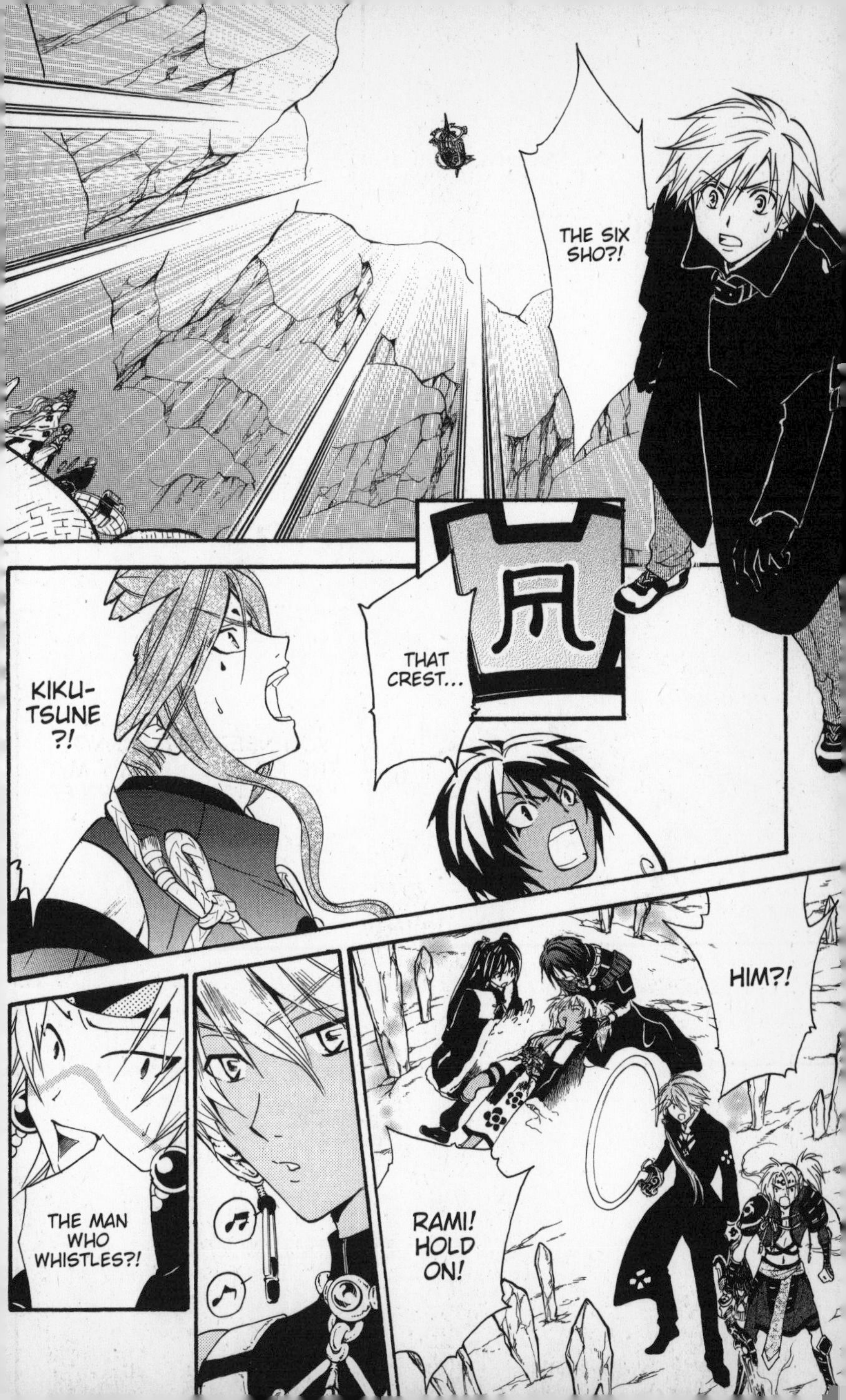
THE SIX SHO?!
THAT CREST...
KIKU-TSUNE ?!
HIM?!
RAMI! HOLD ON!
THE MAN WHO WHISTLES?!

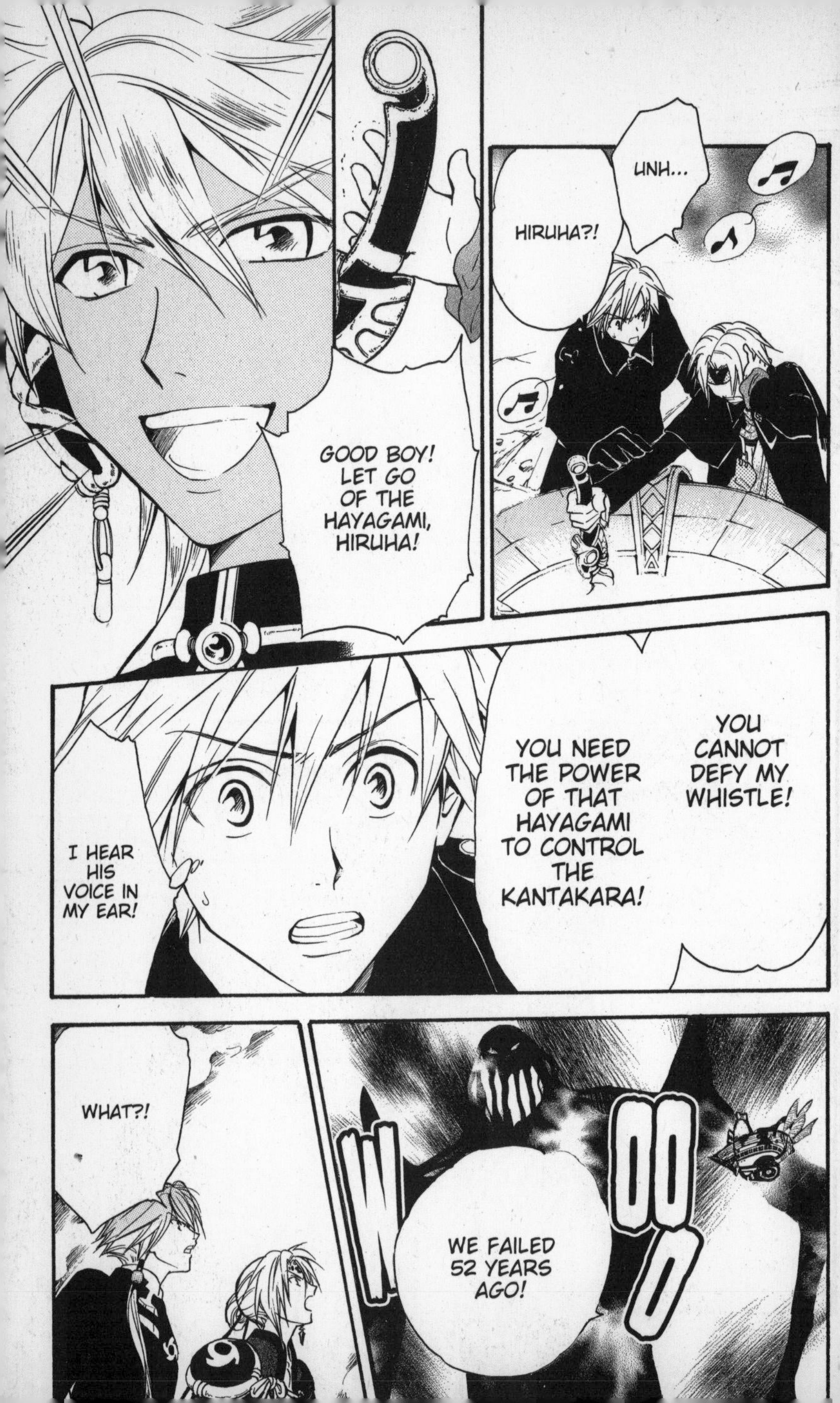
UNH...
HIRUHA?!
GOOD BOY! LET GO OF THE HAYAGAMI, HIRUHA!
YOU CANNOT DEFY MY WHISTLE!
YOU NEED THE POWER OF THAT HAYAGAMI TO CONTROL THE KANTAKARA!
I HEAR HIS VOICE IN MY EAR!
WE FAILED 52 YEARS AGO!
WHAT?!

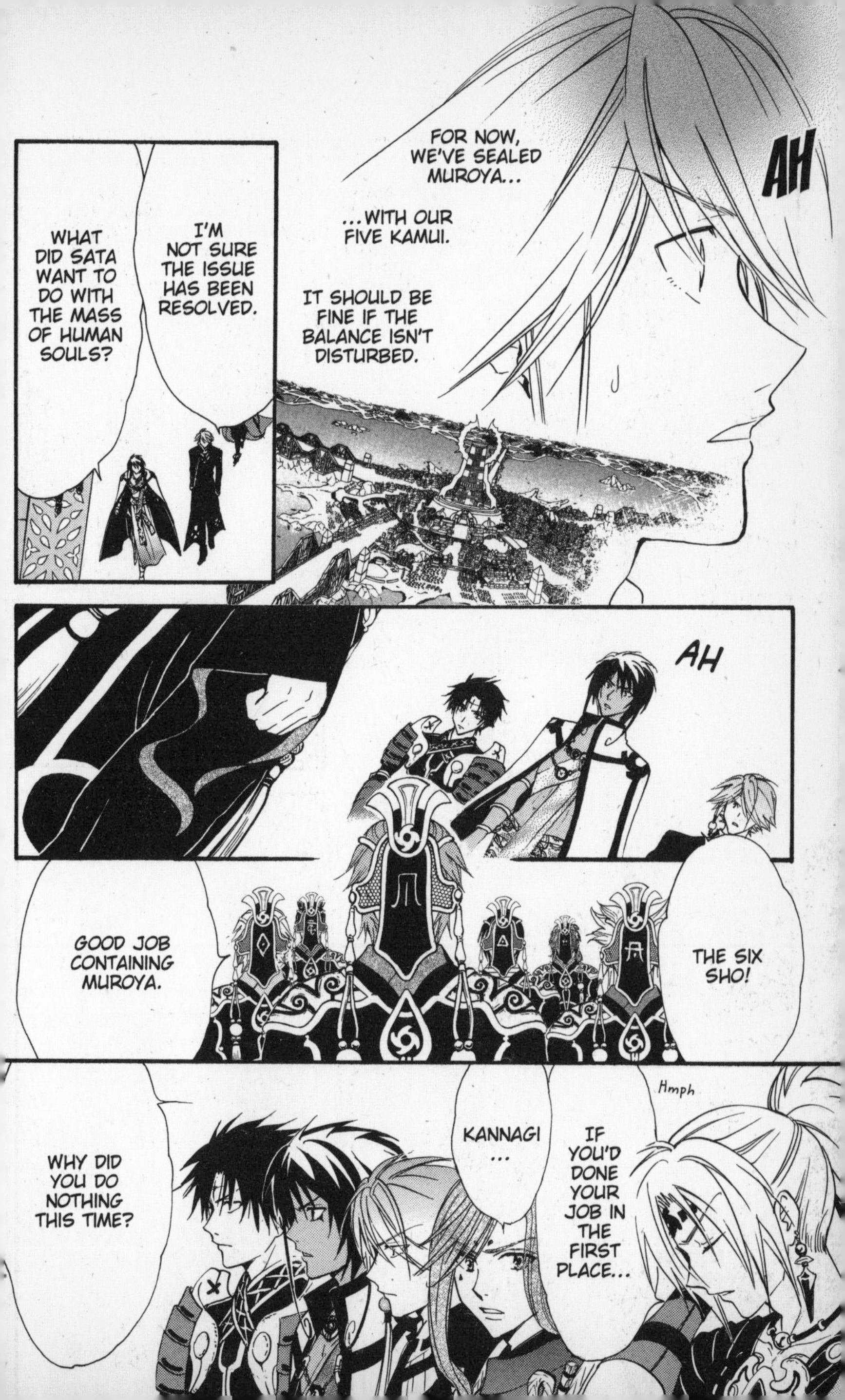
AH
FOR NOW, WE'VE SEALED MUROYA...
...WITH OUR FIVE KAMUI.
IT SHOULD BE FINE IF THE BALANCE ISN'T DISTURBED.
I'M NOT SURE THE ISSUE HAS BEEN RESOLVED.
WHAT DID SATA WANT TO DO WITH THE MASS OF HUMAN SOULS?
AH
THE SIX SHO!
GOOD JOB CONTAINING MUROYA.
Hmph
IF YOU'D DONE YOUR JOB IN THE FIRST PLACE...
KANNAGI...
WHY DID YOU DO NOTHING THIS TIME?

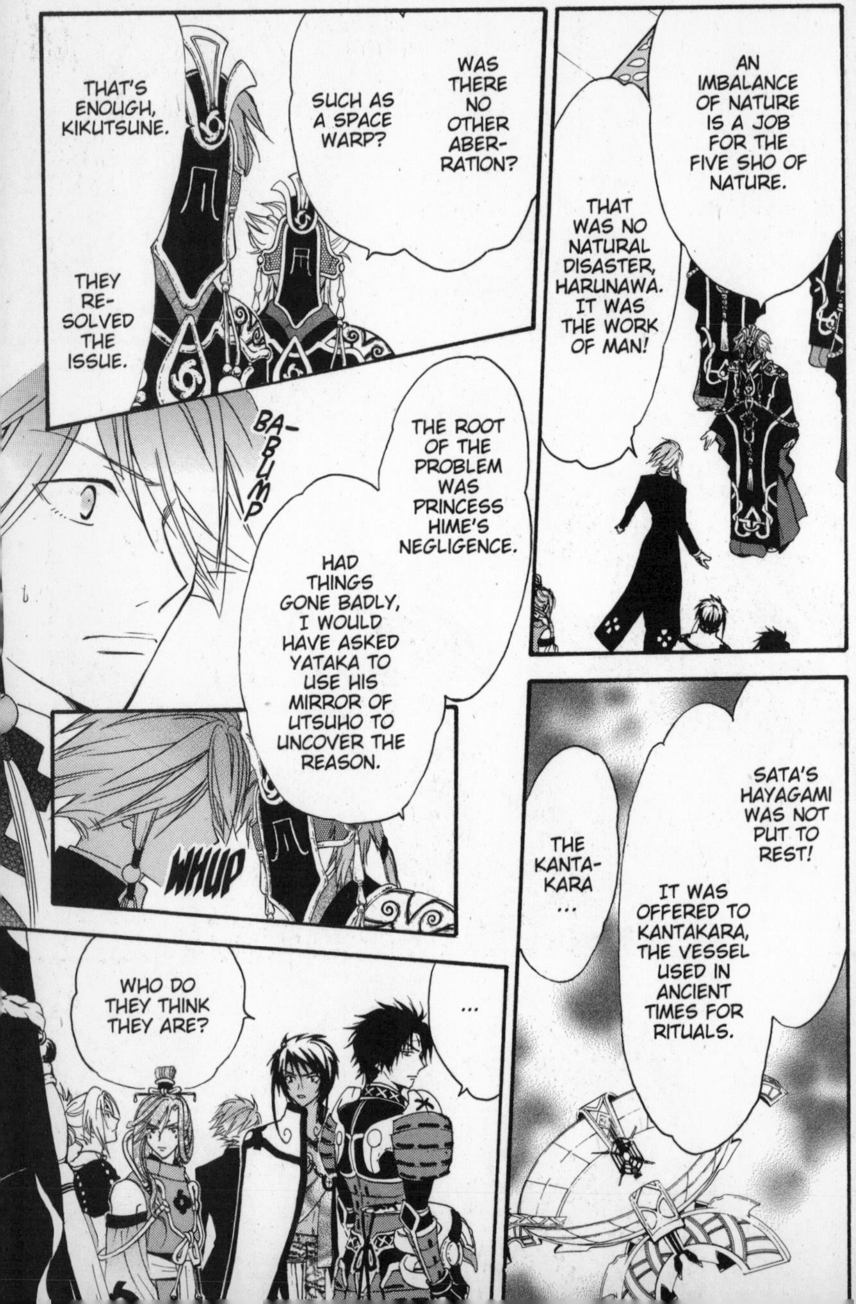
AN IMBALANCE OF NATURE IS A JOB FOR THE FIVE SHO OF NATURE.
THAT WAS NO NATURAL DISASTER, HARUNAWA. IT WAS THE WORK OF MAN!
WAS THERE NO OTHER ABER-RATION?
SUCH AS A SPACE WARP?
THAT'S ENOUGH, KIKUTSUNE.
THEY RE-SOLVED THE ISSUE.
SATA'S HAYAGAMI WAS NOT PUT TO REST!
IT WAS OFFERED TO KANTAKARA, THE VESSEL USED IN ANCIENT TIMES FOR RITUALS.
THE KANTA-KARA ...
BA-BUMP
THE ROOT OF THE PROBLEM WAS PRINCESS HIME'S NEGLIGENCE.
HAD THINGS GONE BADLY, I WOULD HAVE ASKED YATAKA TO USE HIS MIRROR OF UTSUHO TO UNCOVER THE REASON.
WHUP
...
WHO DO THEY THINK THEY ARE?

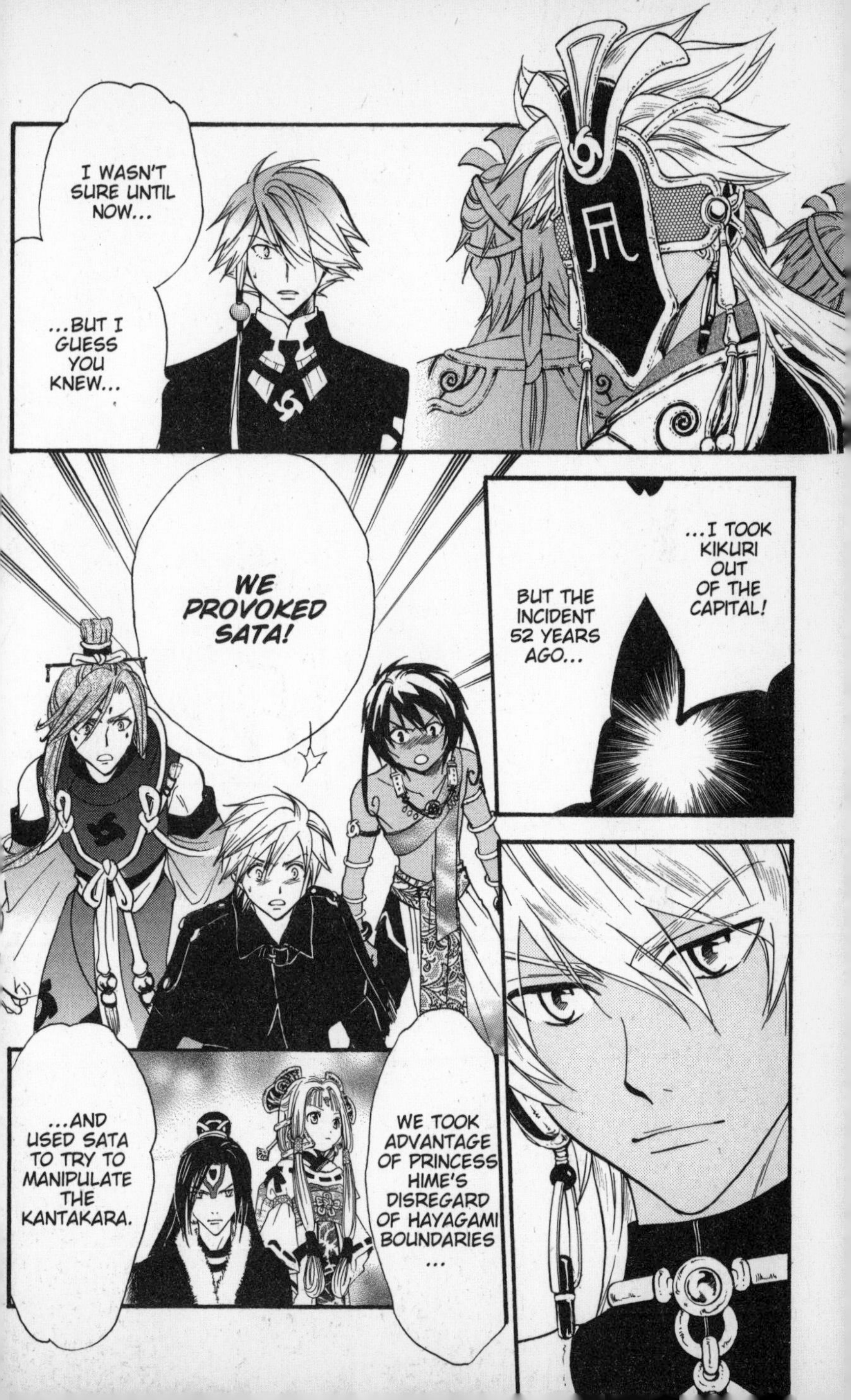
I WASN'T SURE UNTIL NOW...
...BUT I GUESS YOU KNEW...
...I TOOK KIKURI OUT OF THE CAPITAL!
BUT THE INCIDENT 52 YEARS AGO...
WE PROVOKED SATA!
WE TOOK ADVANTAGE OF PRINCESS HIME'S DISREGARD OF HAYAGAMI BOUNDARIES ...
...AND USED SATA TO TRY TO MANIPULATE THE KANTAKARA.

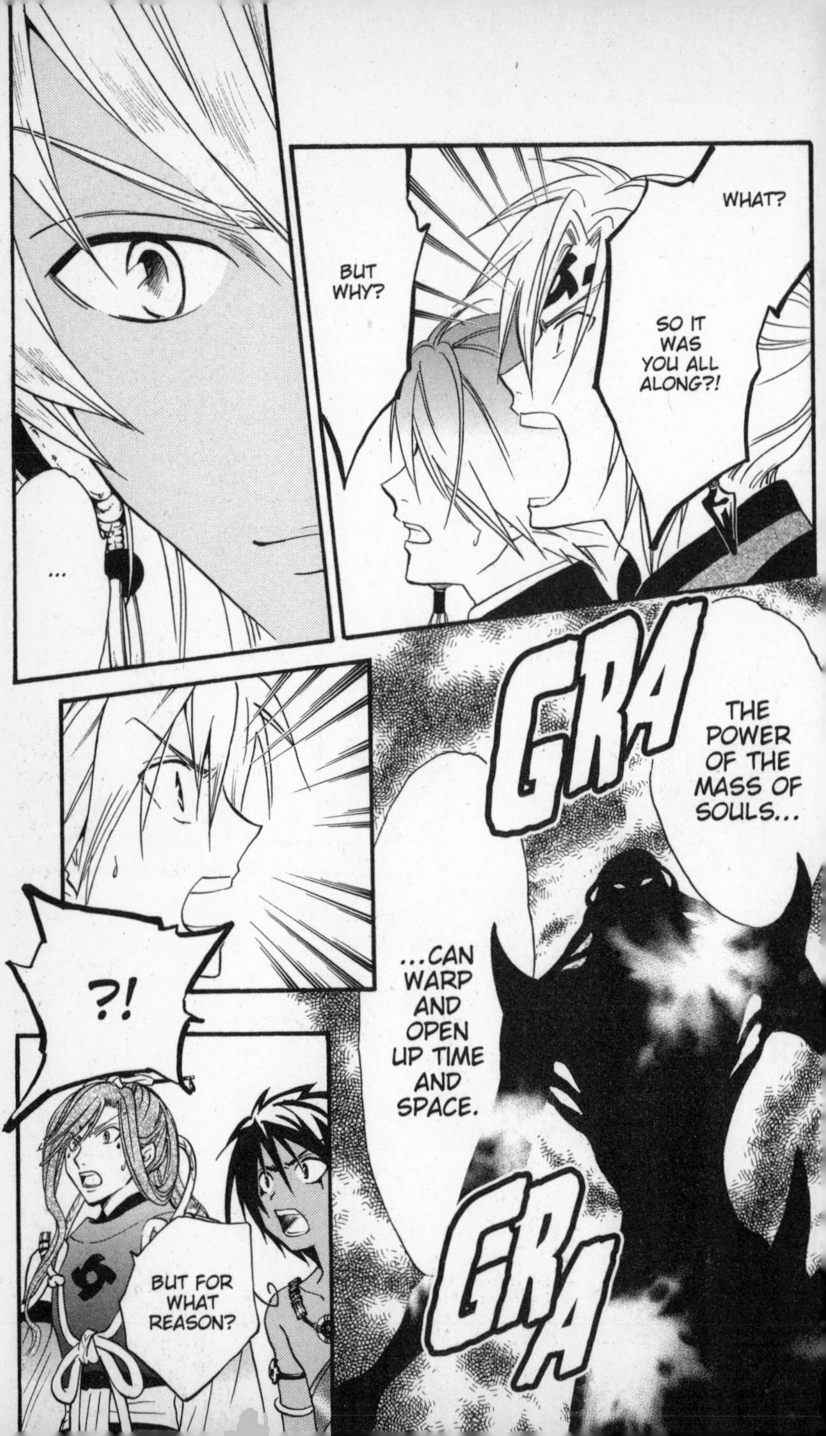
WHAT?
SO IT WAS YOU ALL ALONG?!
BUT WHY?
...
GRA
THE POWER OF THE MASS OF SOULS...
...CAN WARP AND OPEN UP TIME AND SPACE.
GRA
?!
BUT FOR WHAT REASON?

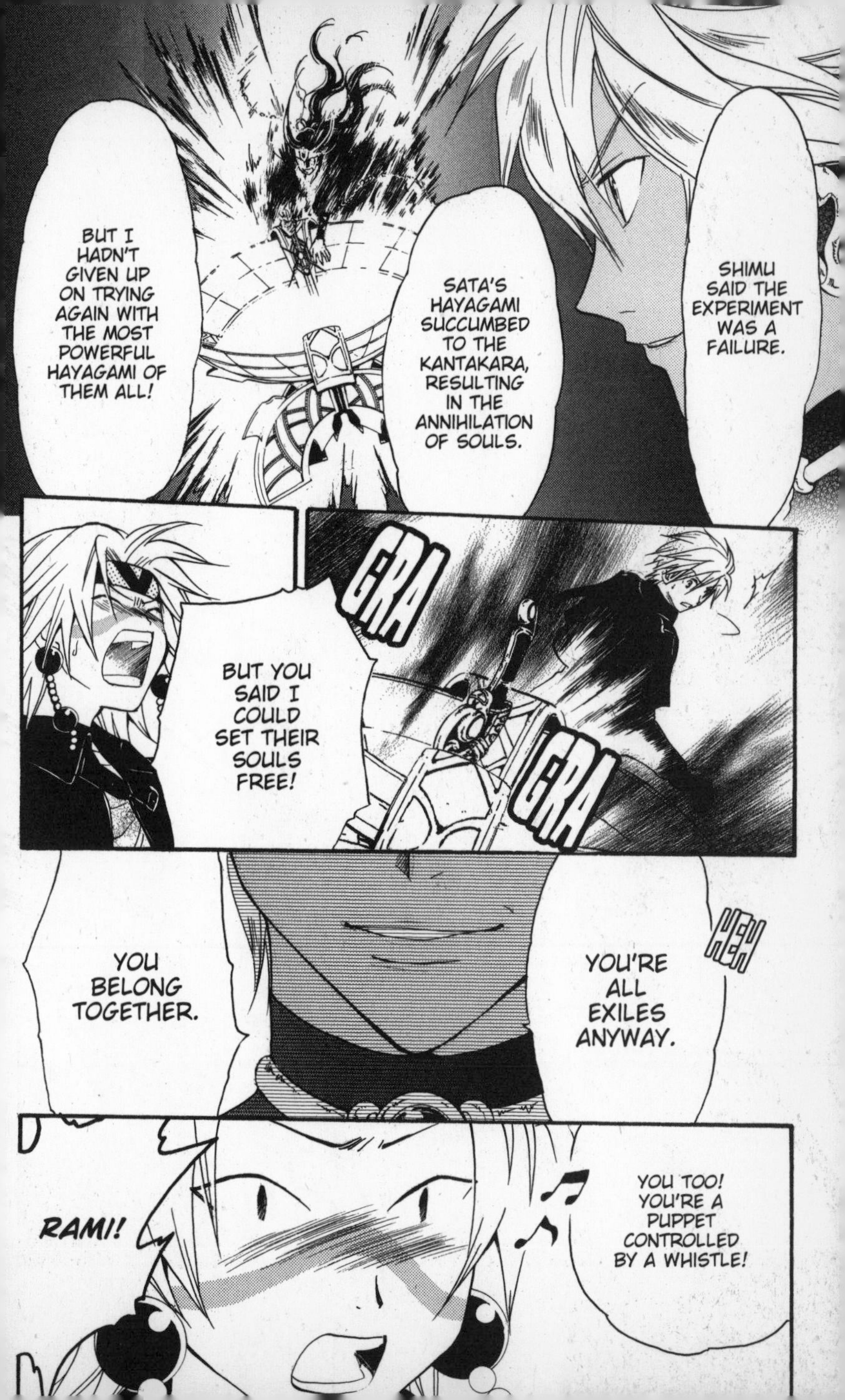
SHIMU SAID THE EXPERIMENT WAS A FAILURE.
SATA'S HAYAGAMI SUCCUMBED TO THE KANTAKARA, RESULTING IN THE ANNIHILATION OF SOULS.
BUT I HADN'T GIVEN UP ON TRYING AGAIN WITH THE MOST POWERFUL HAYAGAMI OF THEM ALL!
GRA
GRA
BUT YOU SAID I COULD SET THEIR SOULS FREE!
HEH
YOU'RE ALL EXILES ANYWAY.
YOU BELONG TOGETHER.
YOU TOO! YOU'RE A PUPPET CONTROLLED BY A WHISTLE!
RAMI!

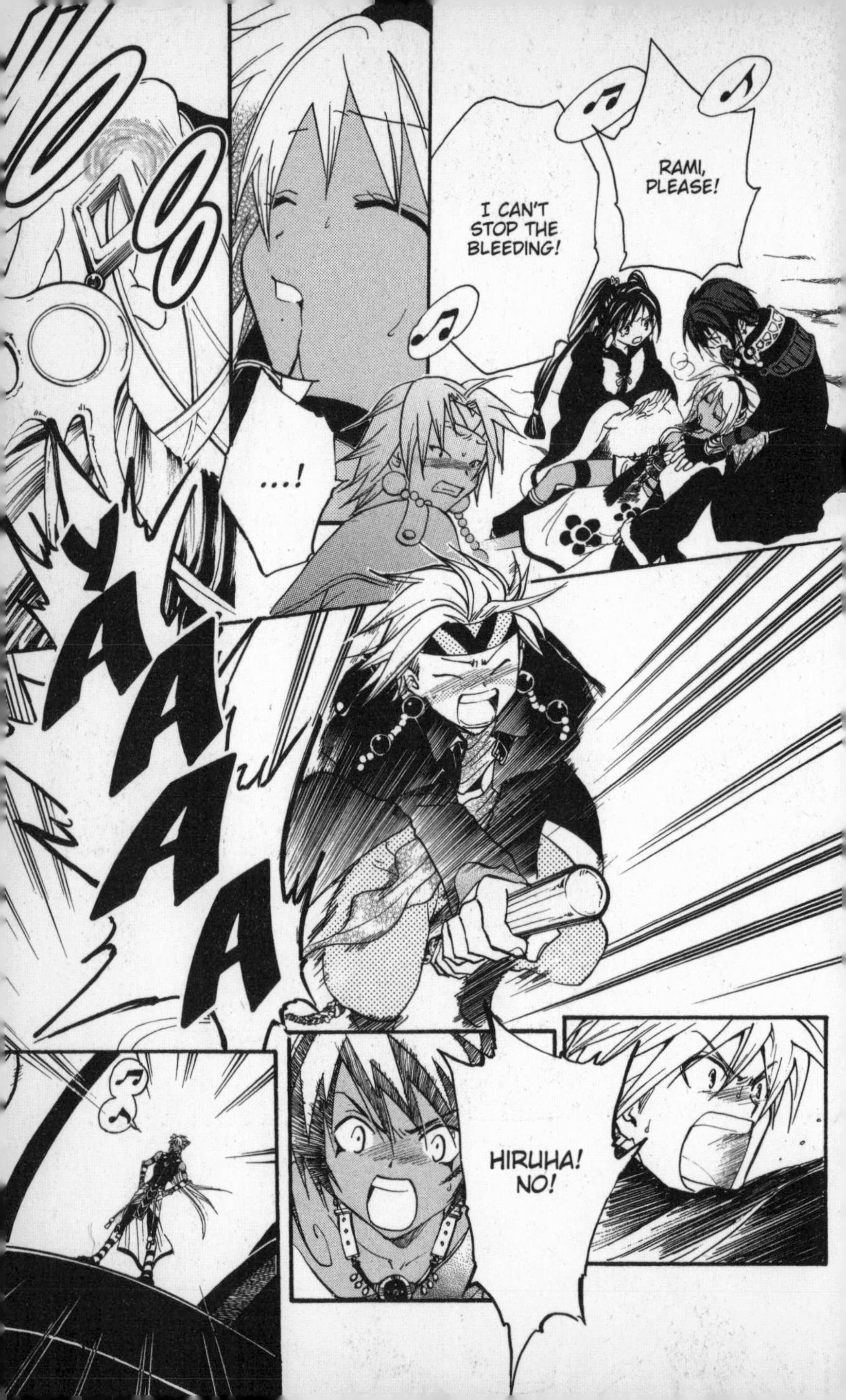
RAMI, PLEASE!
I CAN'T STOP THE BLEEDING!
...!
YAAAA
HIRUHA! NO!

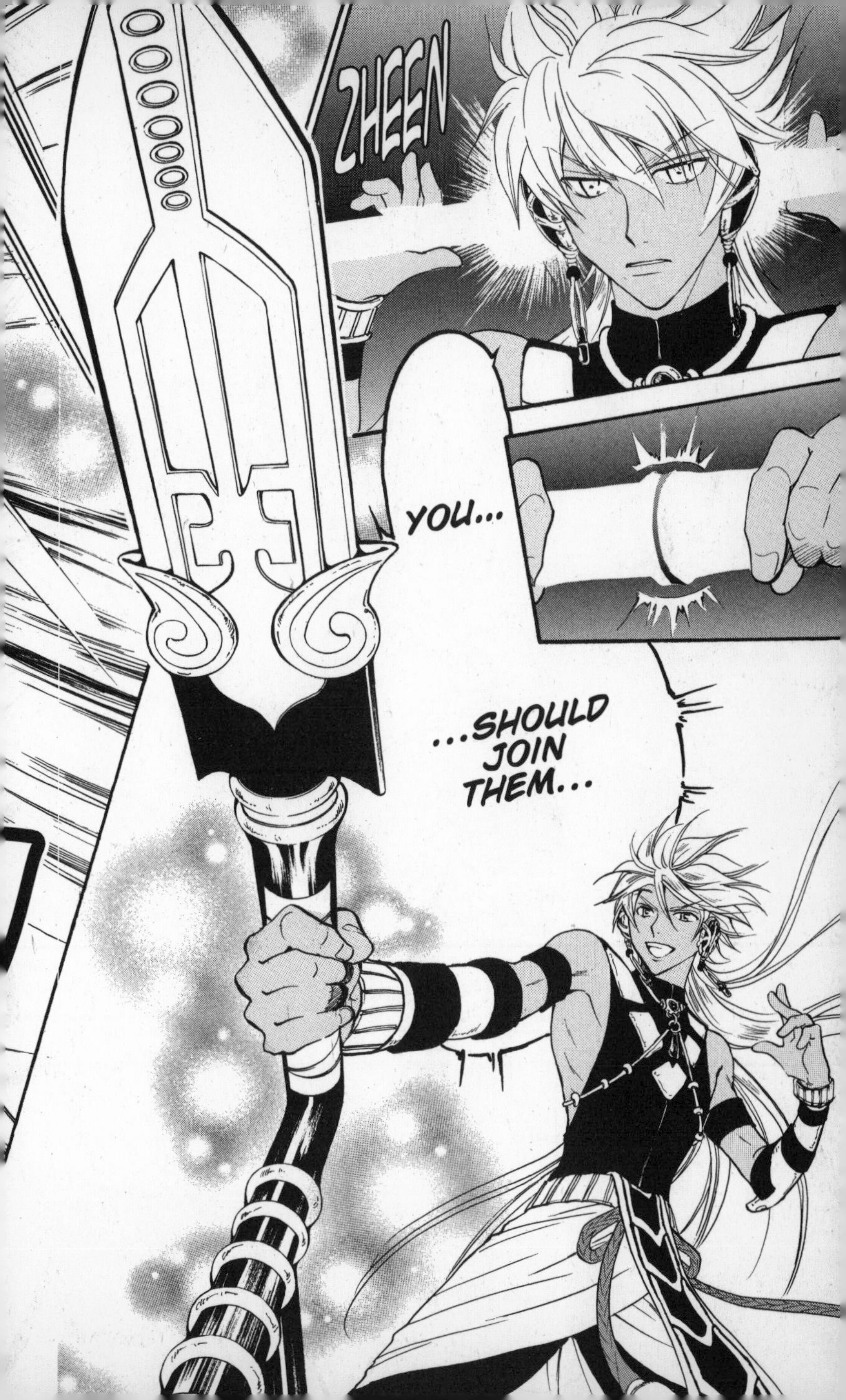
ZHEEN
YOU...
...SHOULD JOIN THEM...

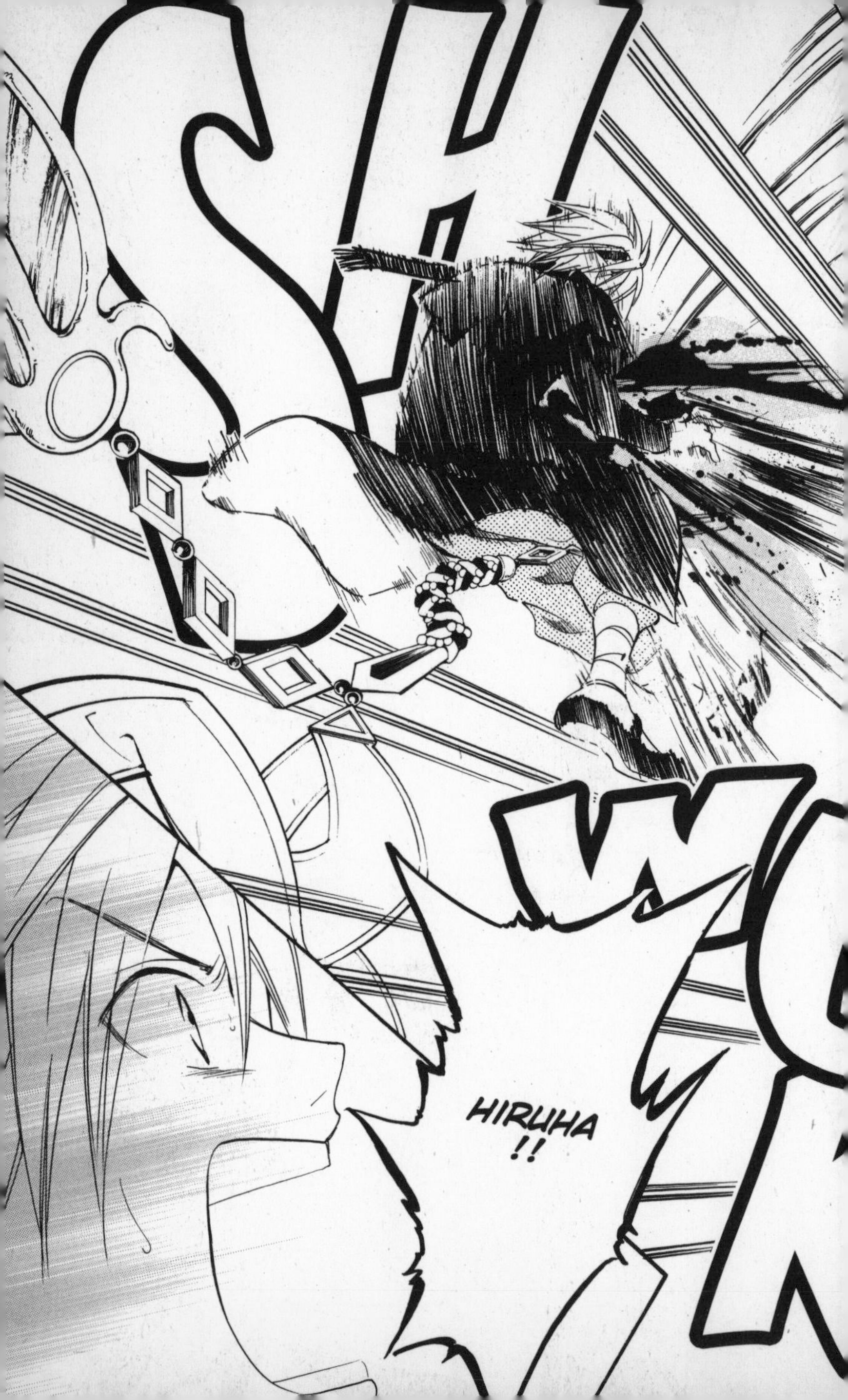
HIRUHA
!!

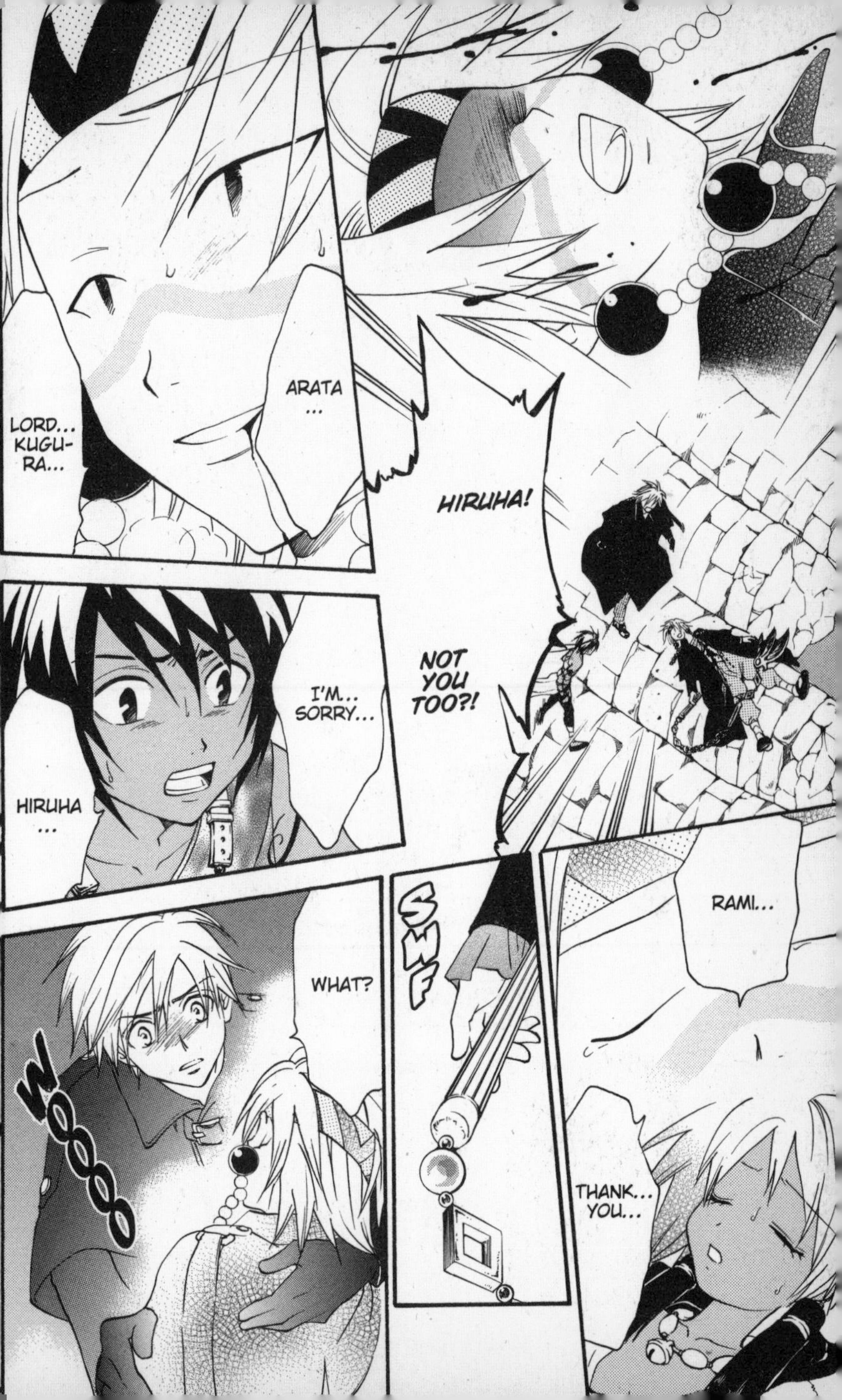
HIRUHA!
NOT YOU TOO?!
ARATA...
LORD... KUGU-RA...
I'M.. SORRY...
HIRUHA...
RAMI...
THANK... YOU...
SWF
WHAT?
WOOOOO

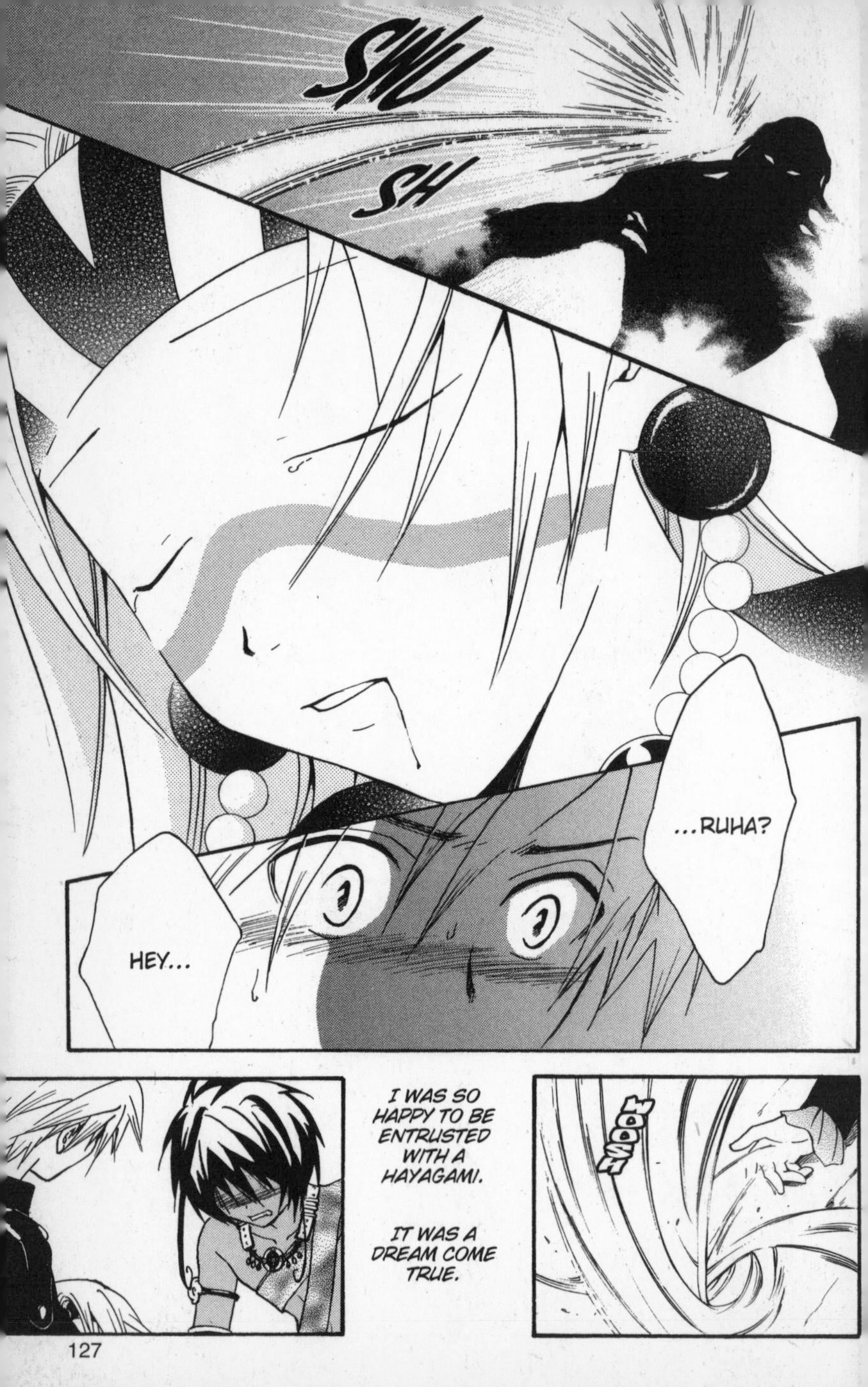
SHU
SH
...RUHA?
HEY...
WOOSH
I WAS SO HAPPY TO BE ENTRUSTED WITH A HAYAGAMI.
IT WAS A DREAM COME TRUE.

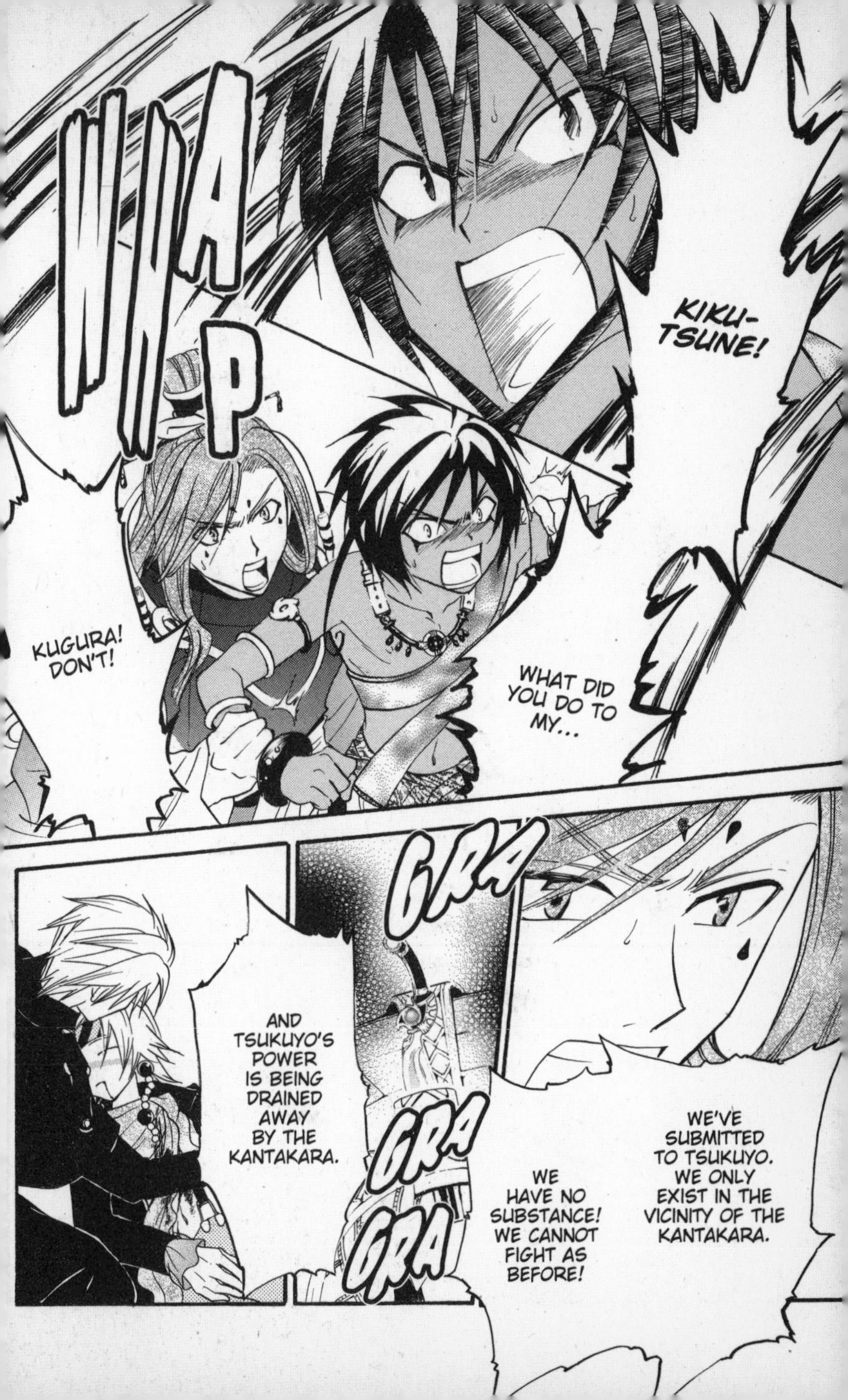
KIKU-TSUNE!
WHAP
WHAT DID YOU DO TO MY...
KUGURA! DON'T!
WE'VE SUBMITTED TO TSUKUYO. WE ONLY EXIST IN THE VICINITY OF THE KANTAKARA.
WE HAVE NO SUBSTANCE! WE CANNOT FIGHT AS BEFORE!
GRA
GRA
GRA
AND TSUKUYO'S POWER IS BEING DRAINED AWAY BY THE KANTAKARA.

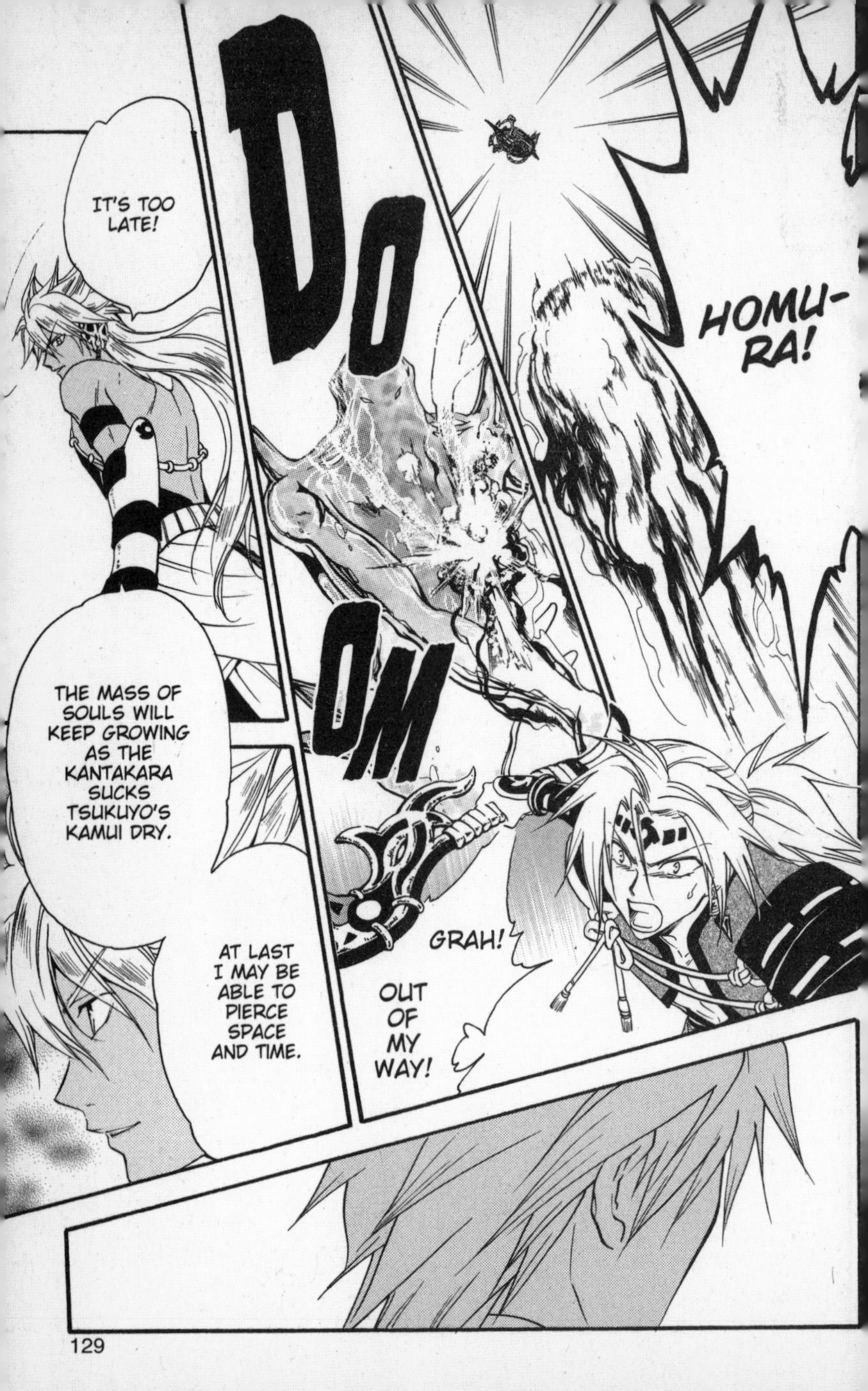
HOMU-RA!
DOOM
GRAH!
OUT OF MY WAY!
IT'S TOO LATE!
THE MASS OF SOULS WILL KEEP GROWING AS THE KANTAKARA SUCKS TSUKUYO'S KAMUI DRY.
AT LAST I MAY BE ABLE TO PIERCE SPACE AND TIME.

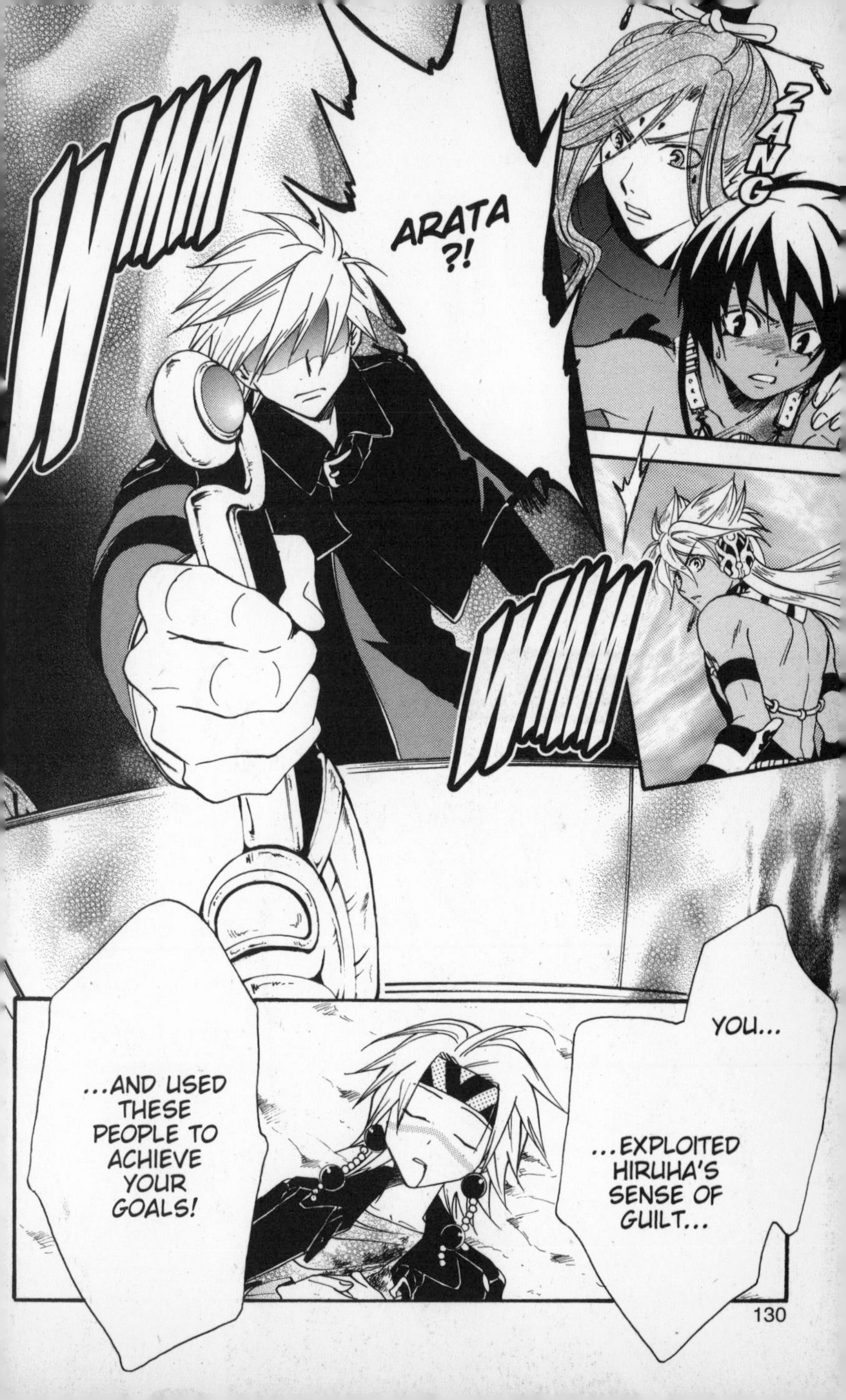
ZANG
ARATA ?!
YOU...
...EXPLOITED HIRUHA'S SENSE OF GUILT...
...AND USED THESE PEOPLE TO ACHIEVE YOUR GOALS!

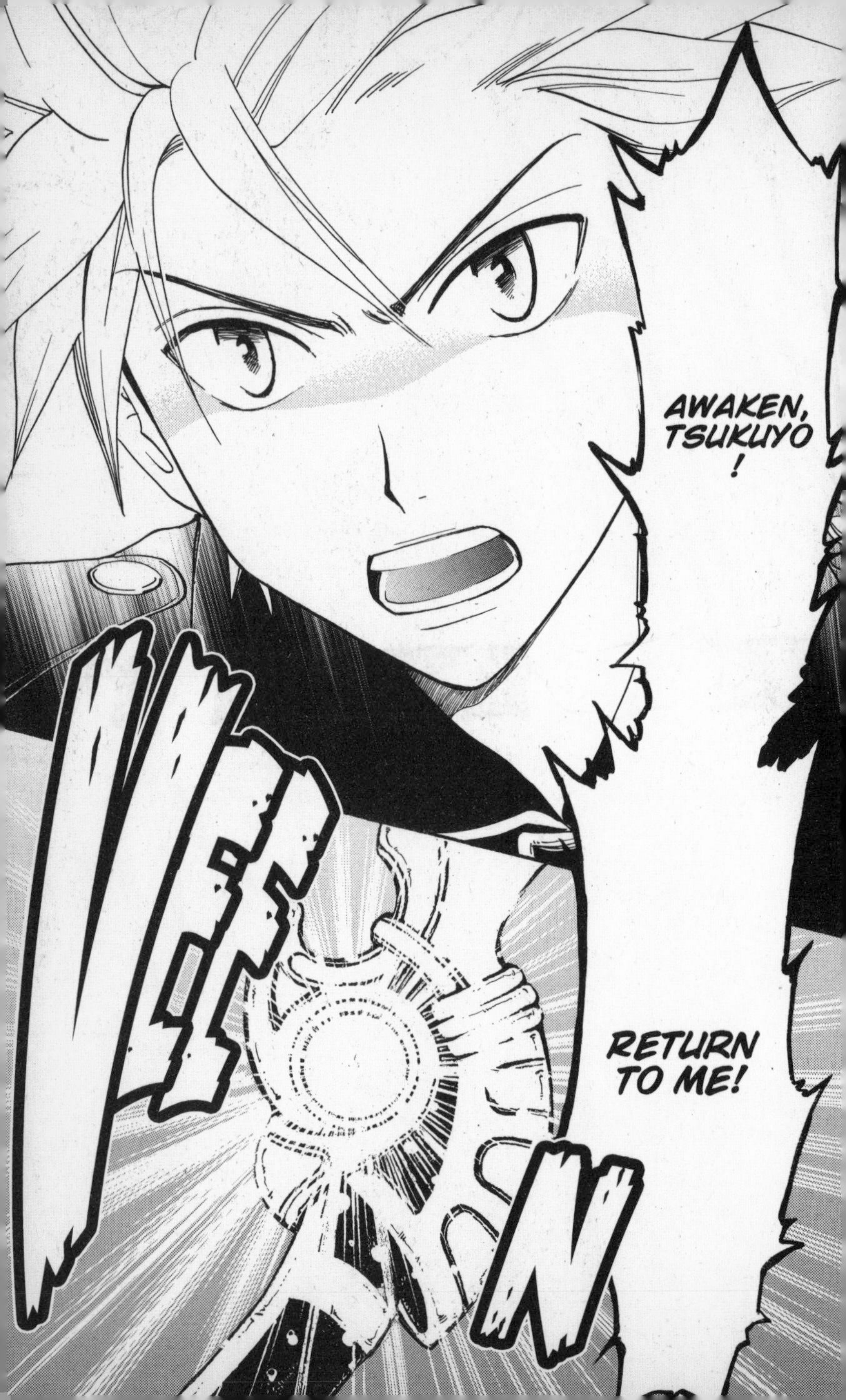
AWAKEN, TSUKUYO!
RETURN TO ME!

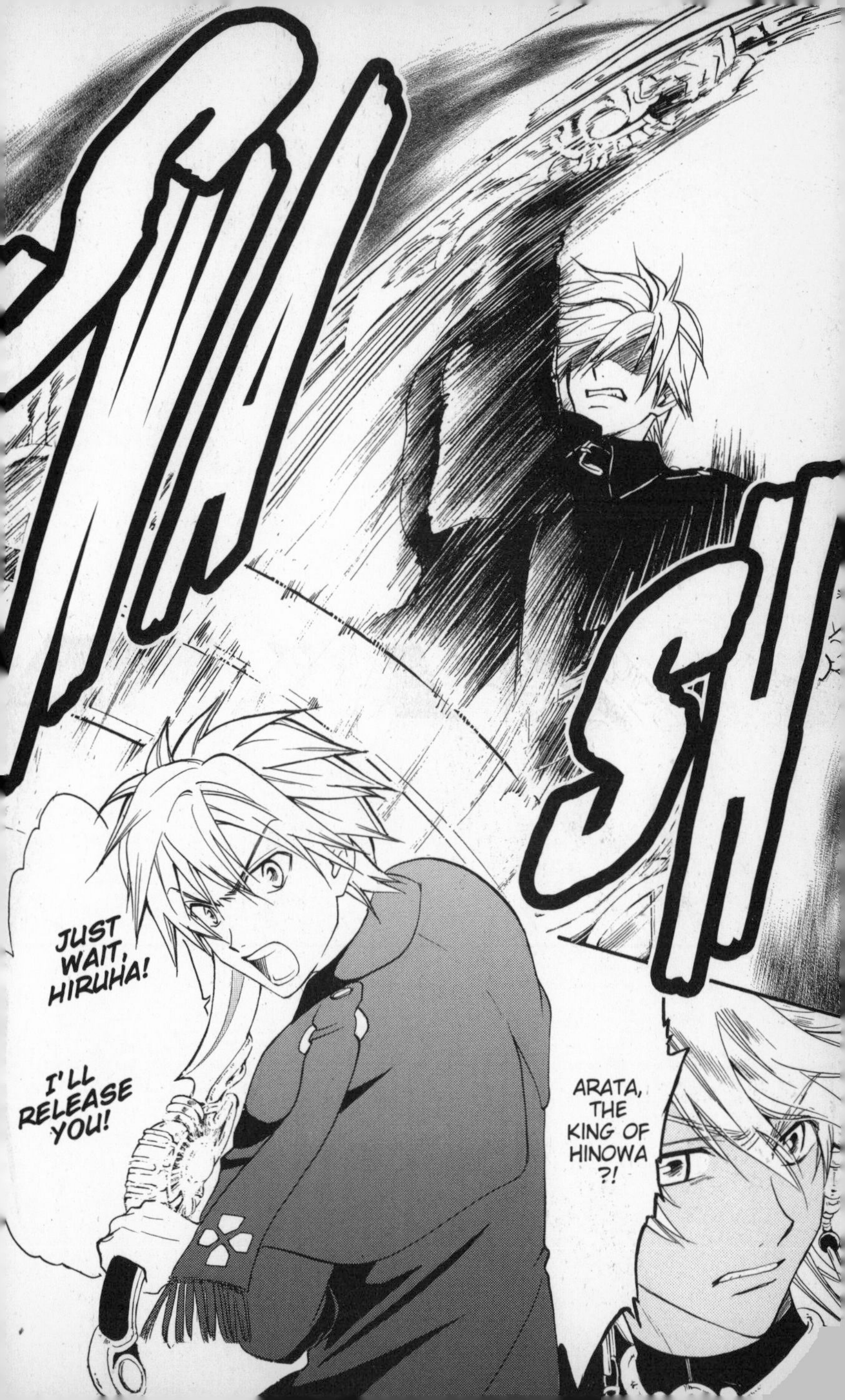
ARATA, THE KING OF HINOWA ?!
JUST WAIT, HIRUHA!
I'LL RELEASE YOU!

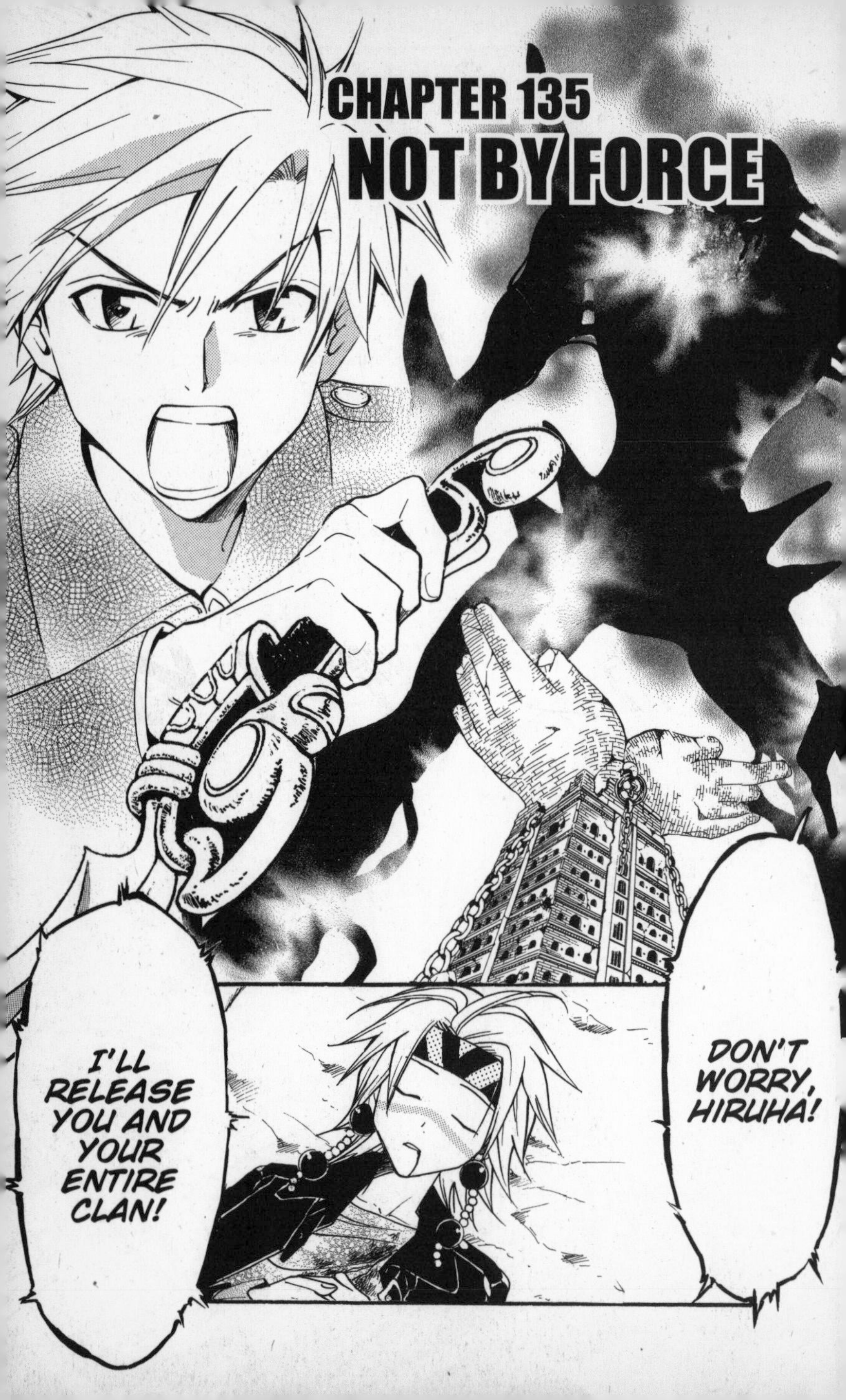
CHAPTER 135
NOT BY FORCE
DON'T WORRY, HIRUHA!
I'LL RELEASE YOU AND YOUR ENTIRE CLAN!

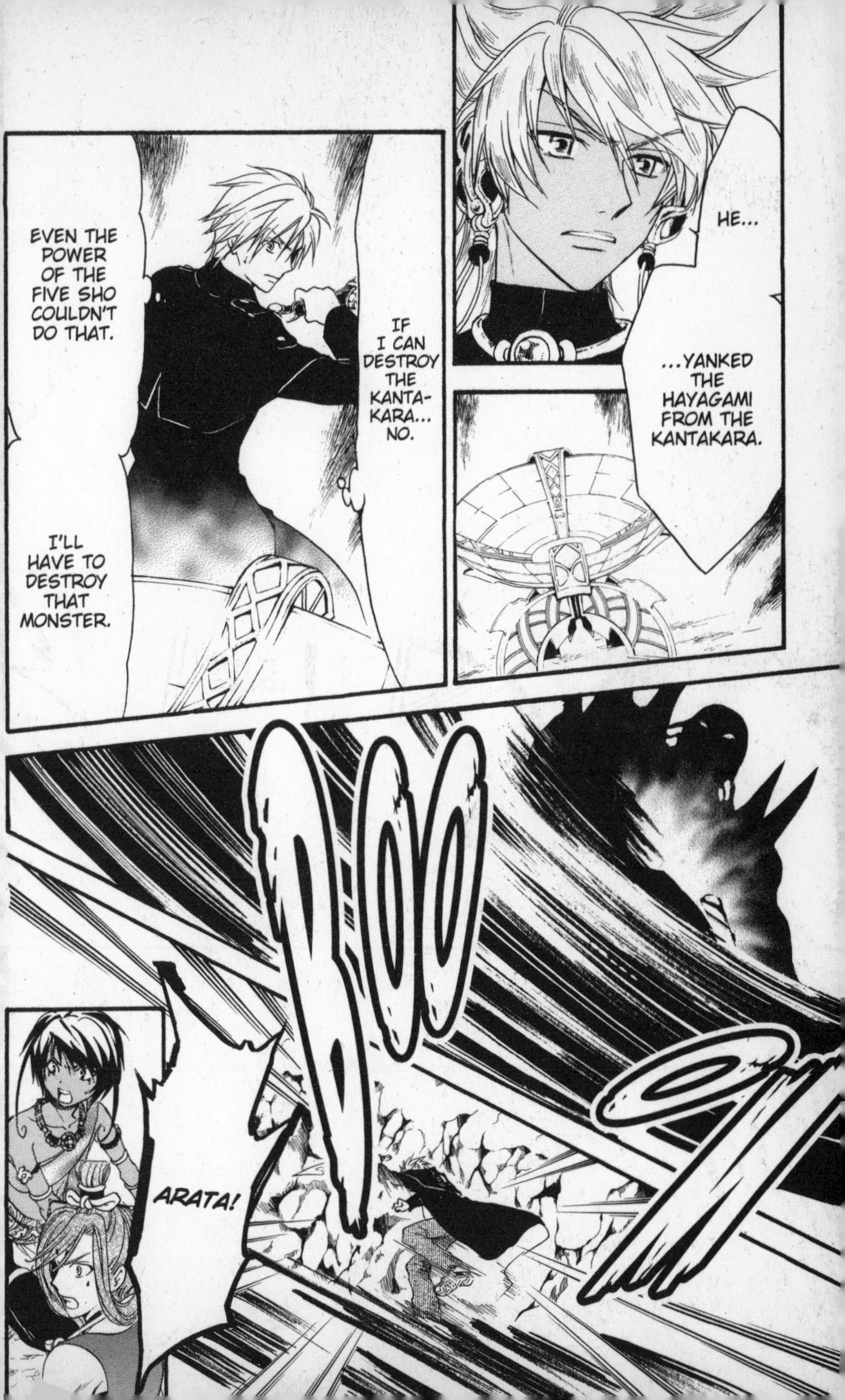
HE...
...YANKED THE HAYAGAMI FROM THE KANTAKARA.
IF I CAN DESTROY THE KANTA-KARA... NO.
EVEN THE POWER OF THE FIVE SHO COULDN'T DO THAT.
I'LL HAVE TO DESTROY THAT MONSTER.
ARATA!

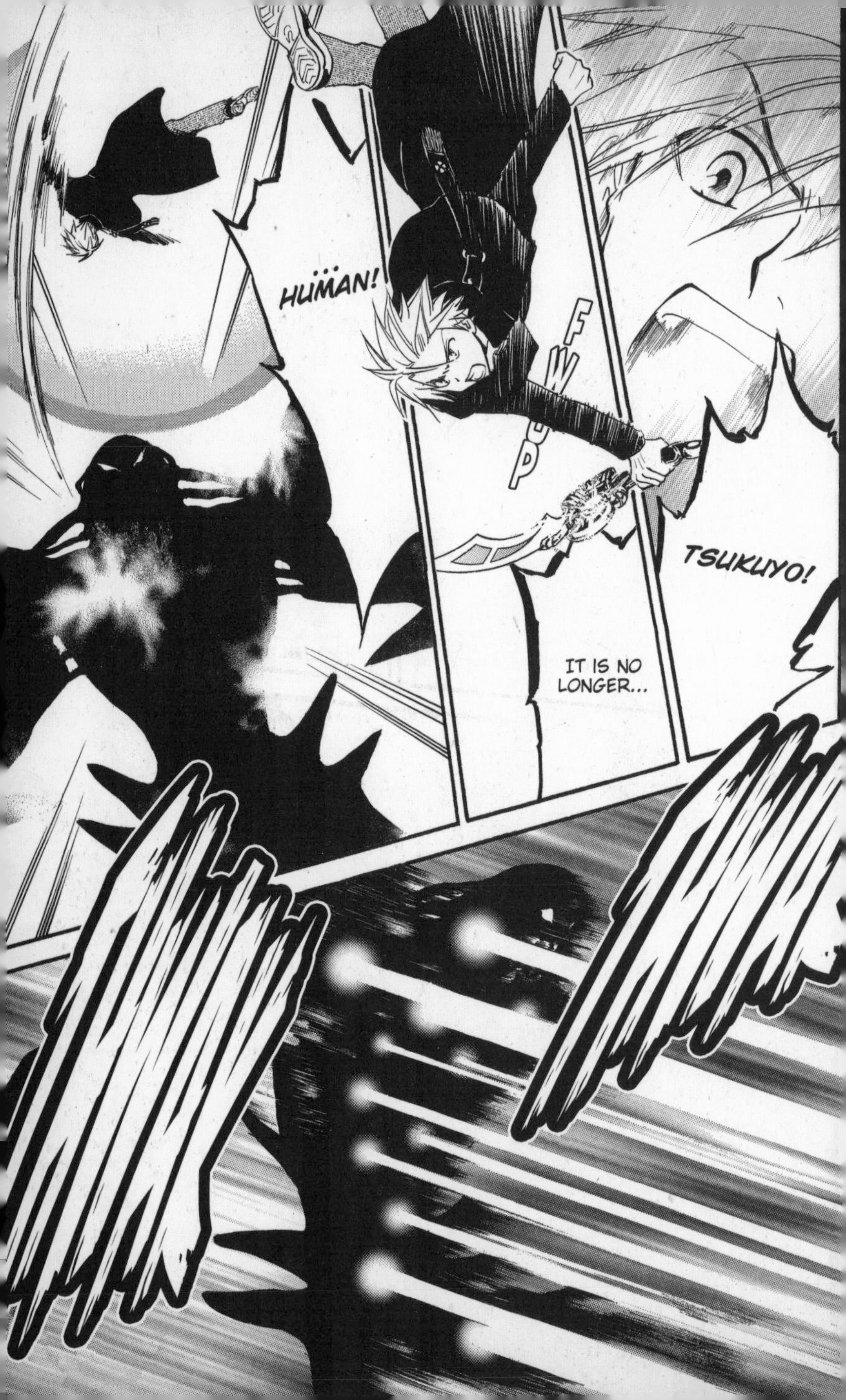
TSUKUYO!
FWUP
IT IS NO LONGER...
HUMAN!

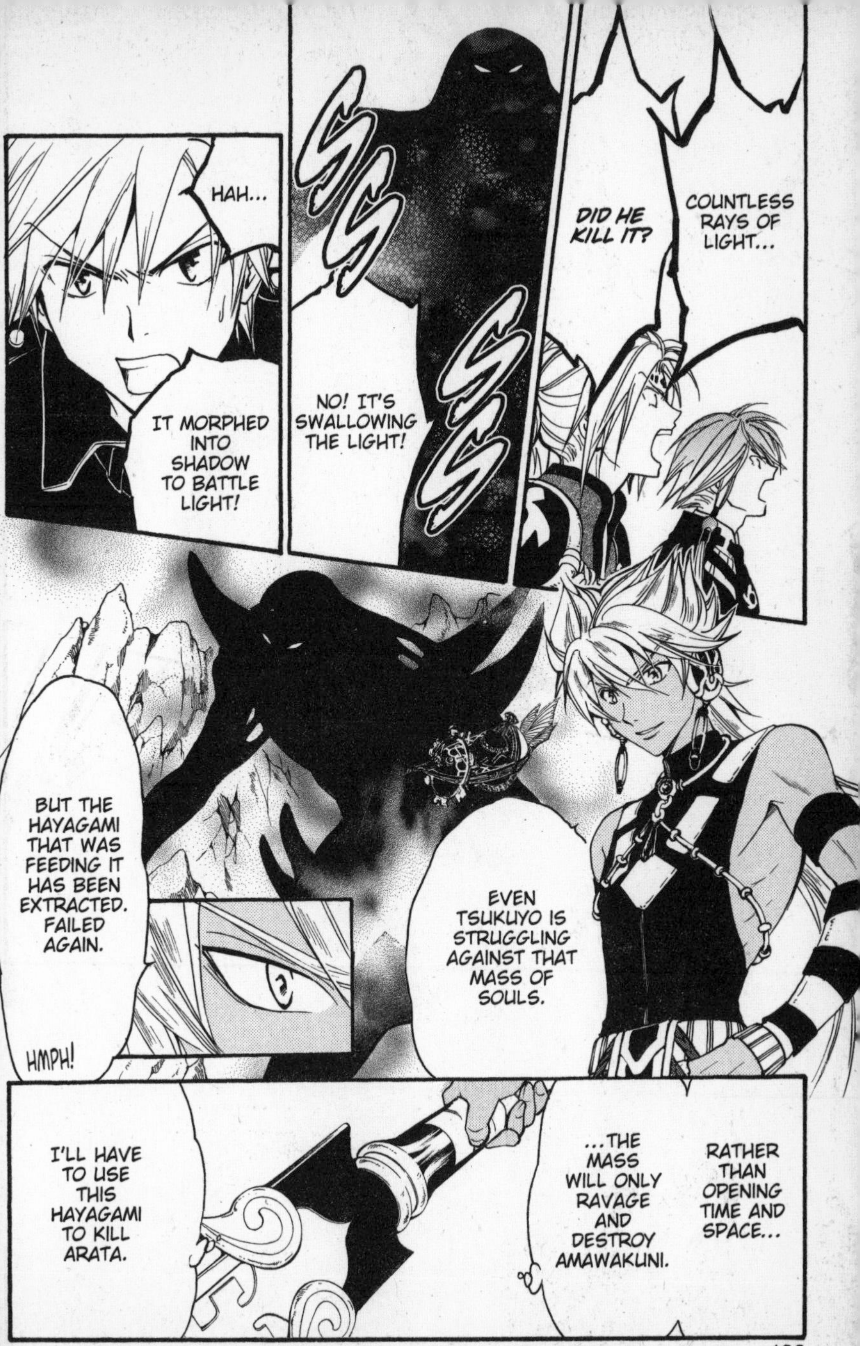
COUNTLESS RAYS OF LIGHT...
DID HE KILL IT?
SSS
SSS
NO! IT'S SWALLOWING THE LIGHT!
HAH...
IT MORPHED INTO SHADOW TO BATTLE LIGHT!
EVEN TSUKUYO IS STRUGGLING AGAINST THAT MASS OF SOULS.
BUT THE HAYAGAMI THAT WAS FEEDING IT HAS BEEN EXTRACTED. FAILED AGAIN.
HMPH!
RATHER THAN OPENING TIME AND SPACE...
...THE MASS WILL ONLY RAVAGE AND DESTROY AMAWAKUNI.
I'LL HAVE TO USE THIS HAYAGAMI TO KILL ARATA.

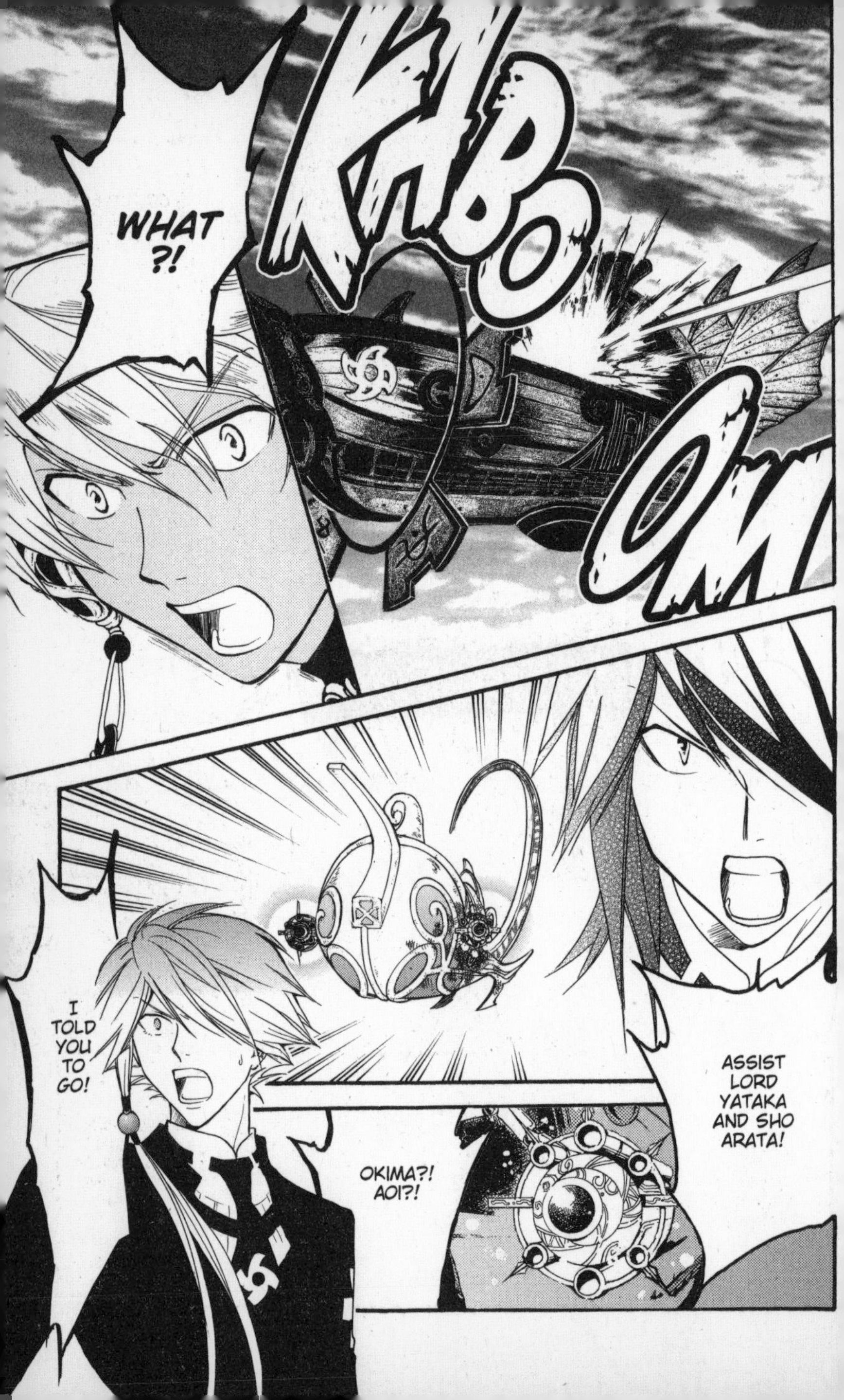
KABOOM
WHAT ?!
ASSIST LORD YATAKA AND SHO ARATA!
I TOLD YOU TO GO!
OKIMA?! AOI?!

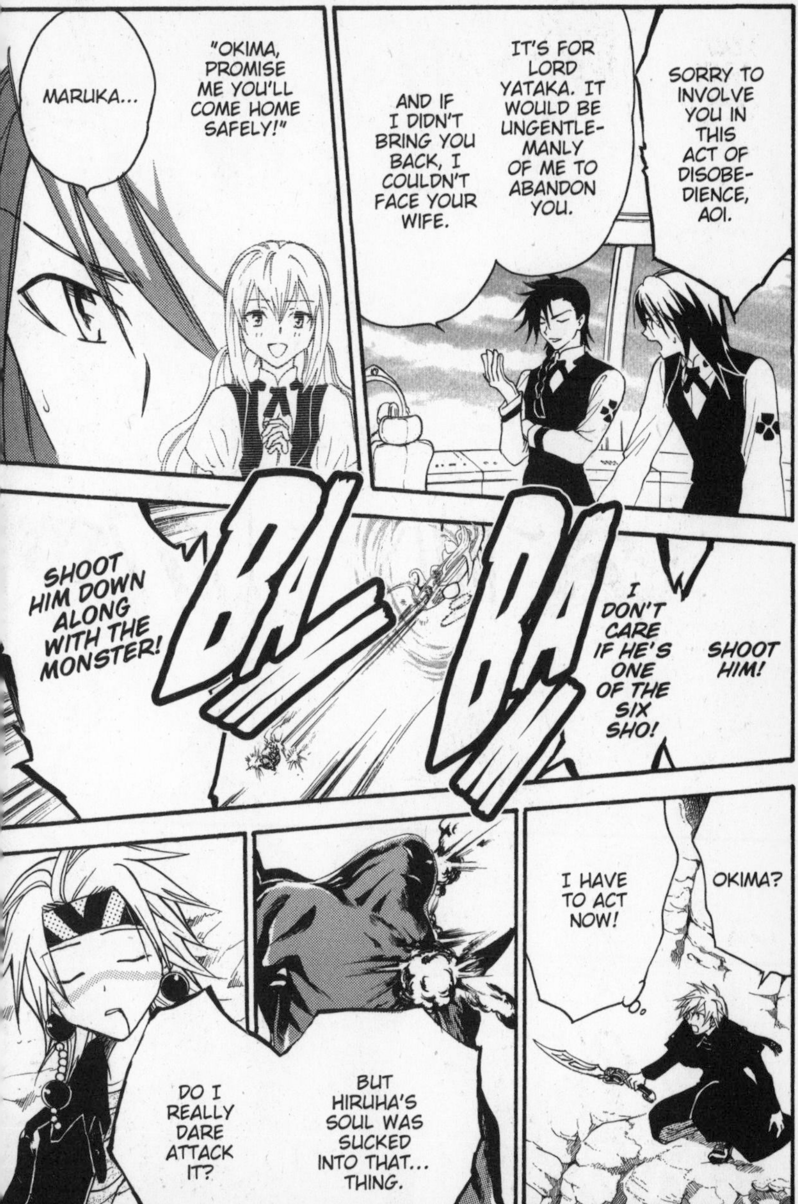
SORRY TO INVOLVE YOU IN THIS ACT OF DISOBEDIENCE, AOI.
IT'S FOR LORD YATAKA. IT WOULD BE UNGENTLEMANLY OF ME TO ABANDON YOU.
AND IF I DIDN'T BRING YOU BACK, I COULDN'T FACE YOUR WIFE.
"OKIMA, PROMISE ME YOU'LL COME HOME SAFELY!"
MARUKA...
SHOOT HIM!
I DON'T CARE IF HE'S ONE OF THE SIX SHO!
BA- BA
SHOOT HIM DOWN ALONG WITH THE MONSTER!
OKIMA?
I HAVE TO ACT NOW!
BUT HIRUHA'S SOUL WAS SUCKED INTO THAT... THING.
DO I REALLY DARE ATTACK IT?

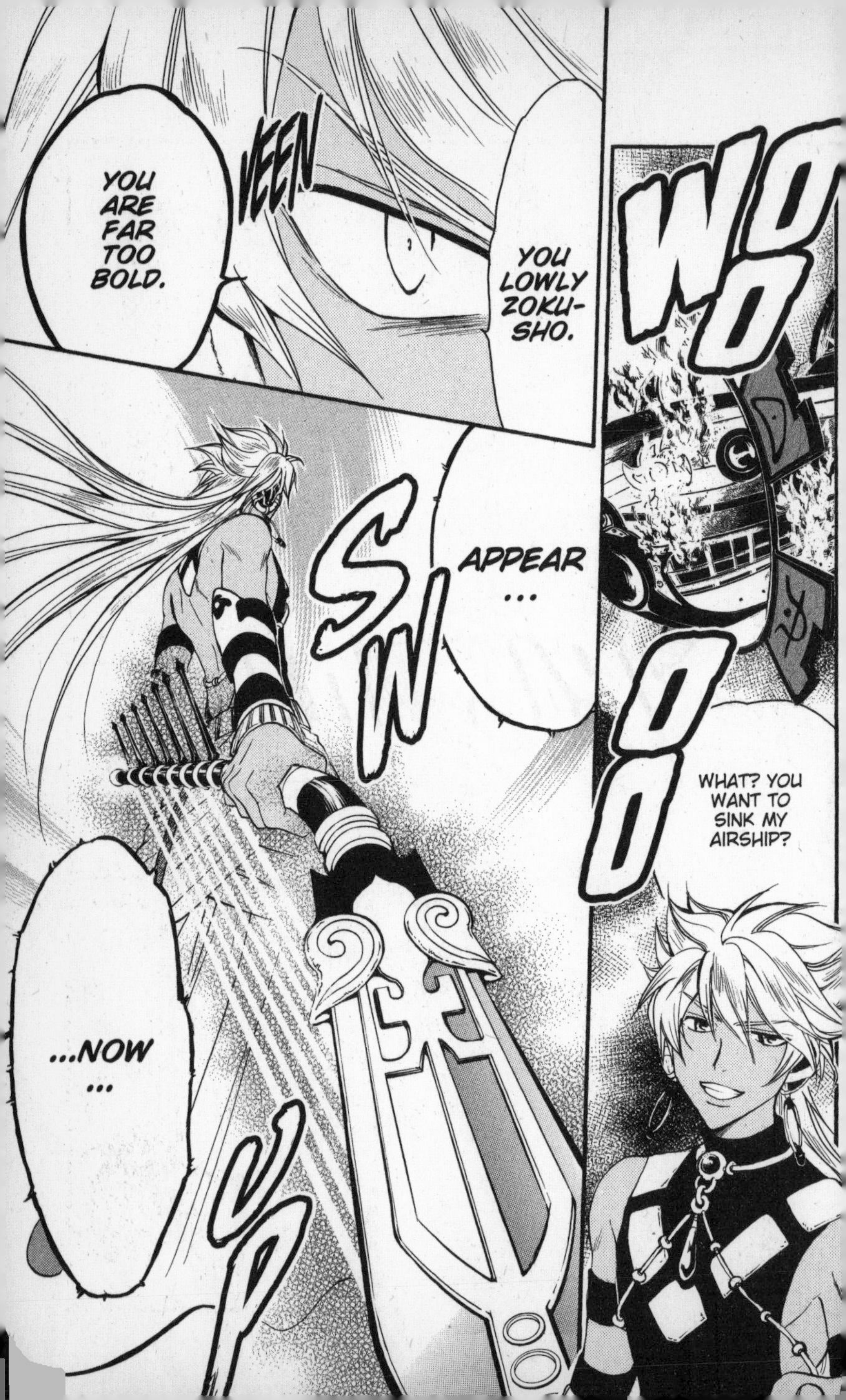
WOOOOO
WHAT? YOU WANT TO SINK MY AIRSHIP?
YOU ARE FAR TOO BOLD.
VEEN
YOU LOWLY ZOKU-SHO.
APPEAR ...
SW
...NOW ...
S

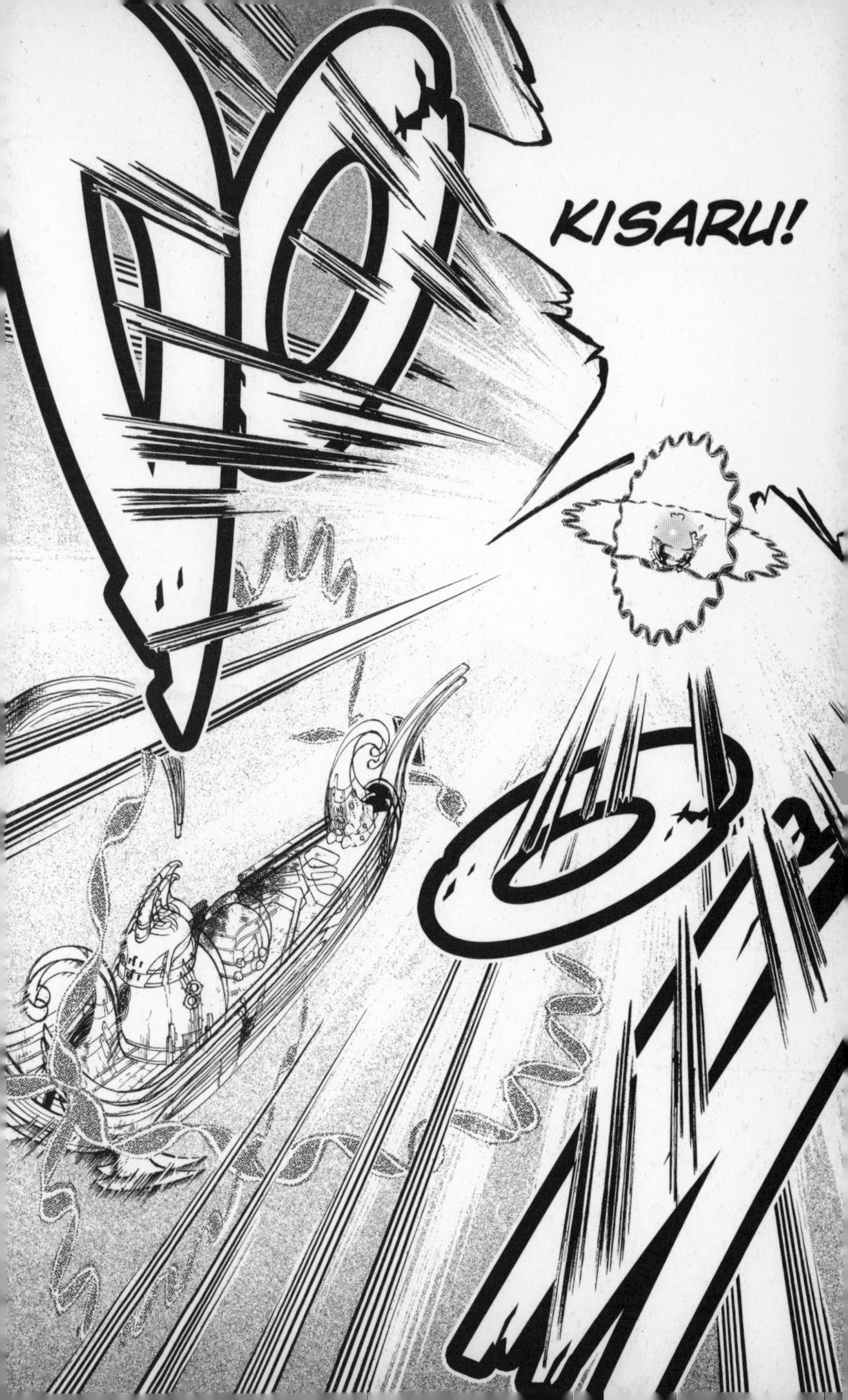
KISARU!

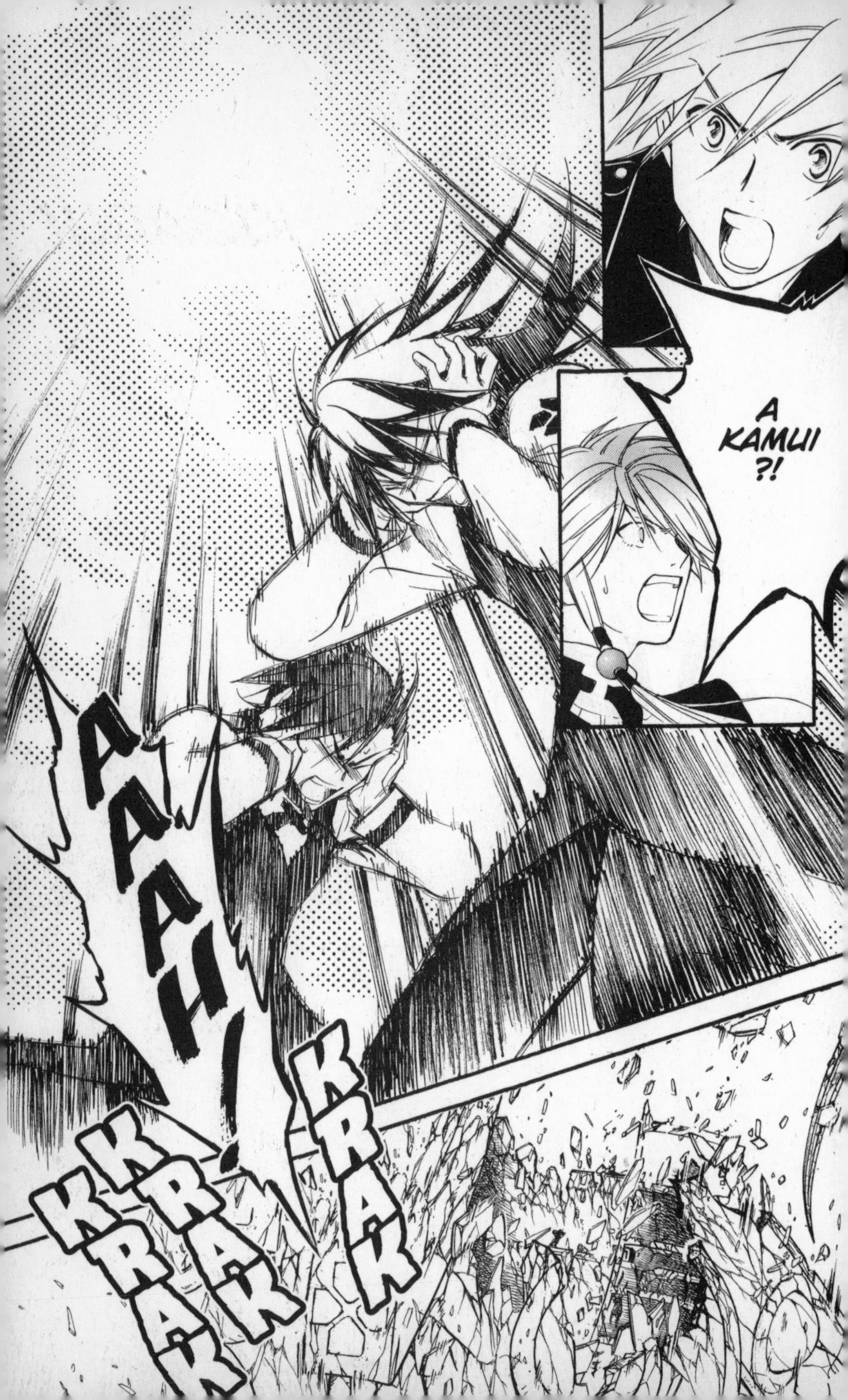
A KAMUI ?!
AAAH!
KRAK
KRAK
KRAK

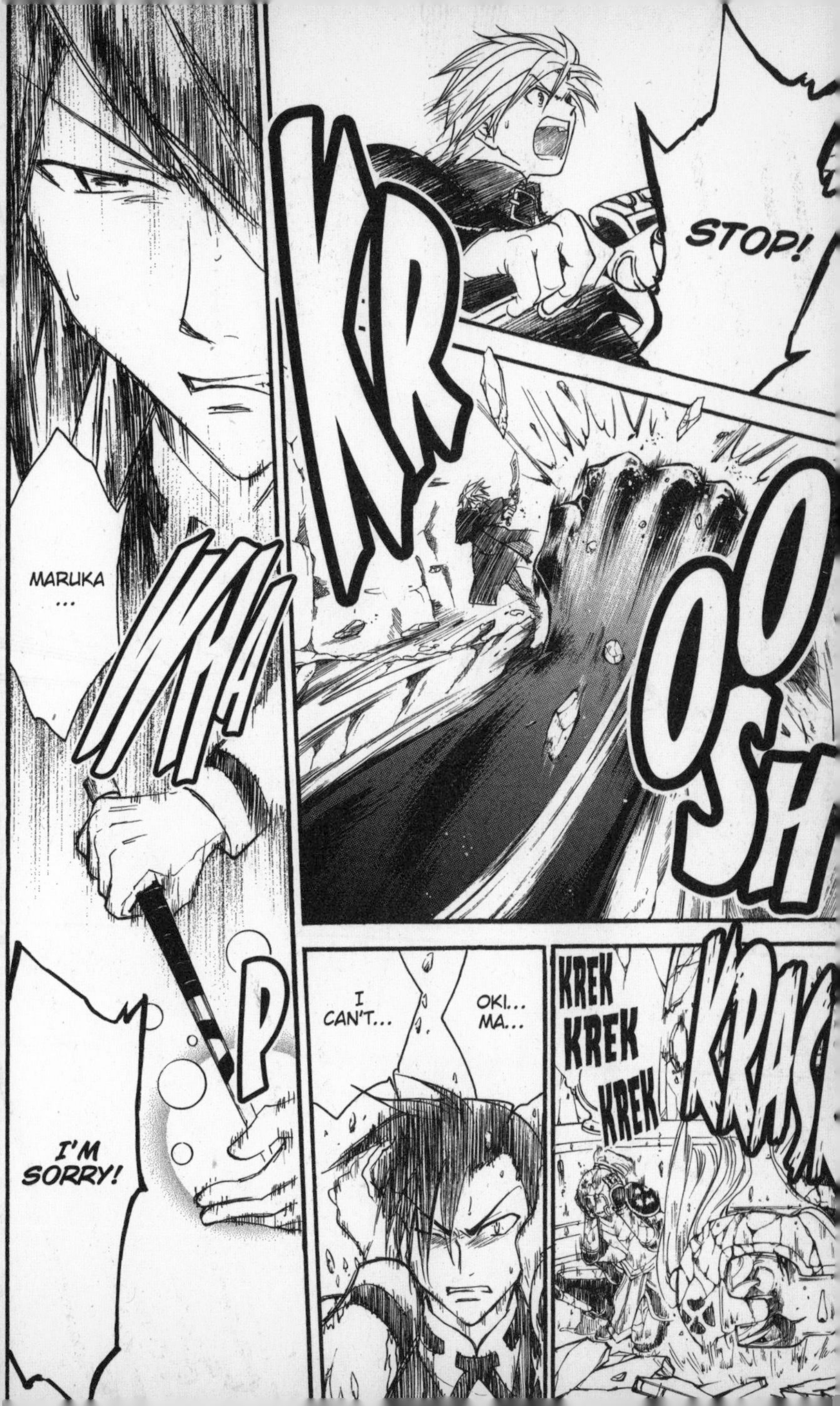
STOP!
KR
OOOSH
KREK KREK KREK
KRAS
OKI... MA...
I CAN'T...
MARUKA...
WHA
P
I'M SORRY!

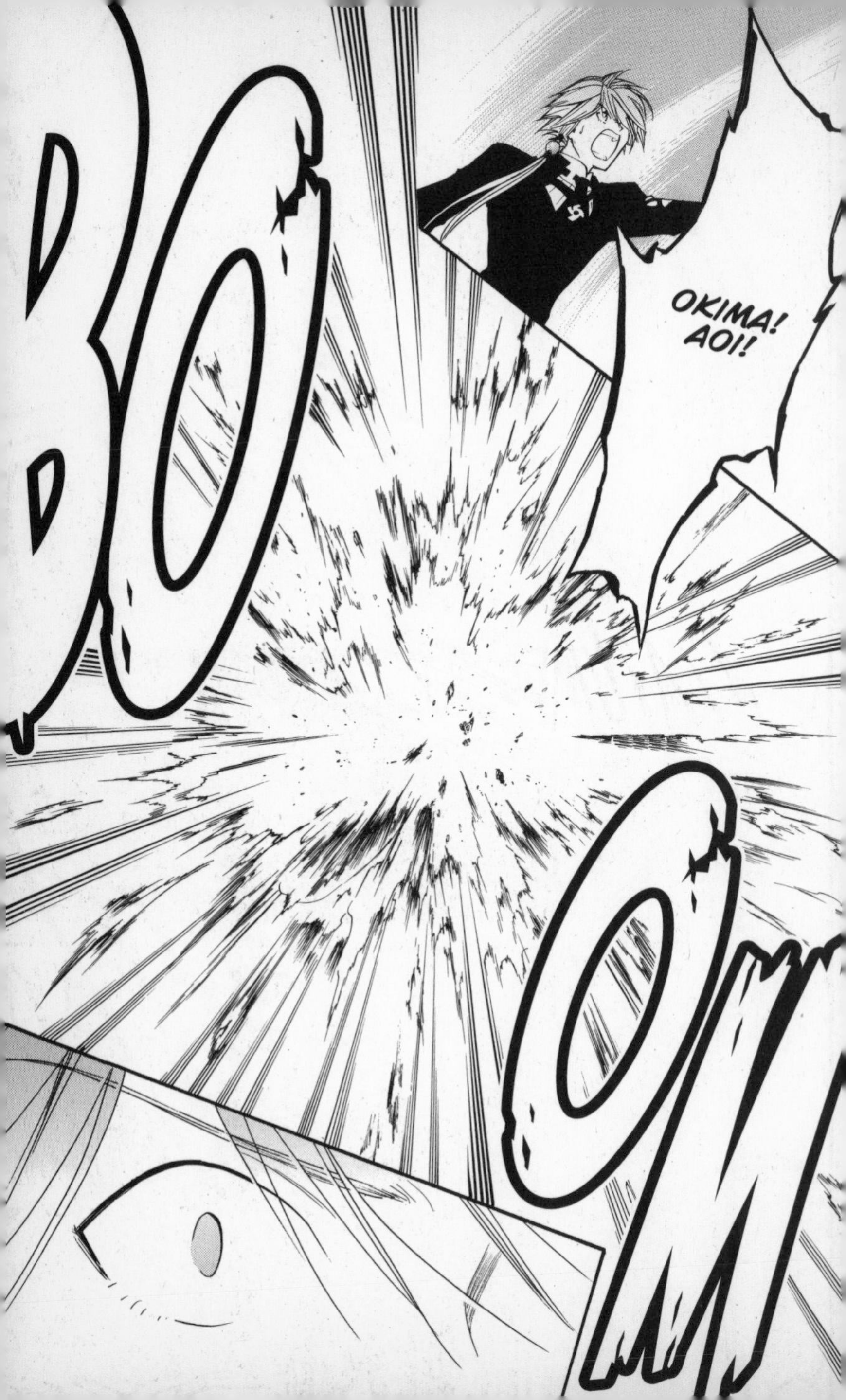
OKIMA! AOI!
BOOM

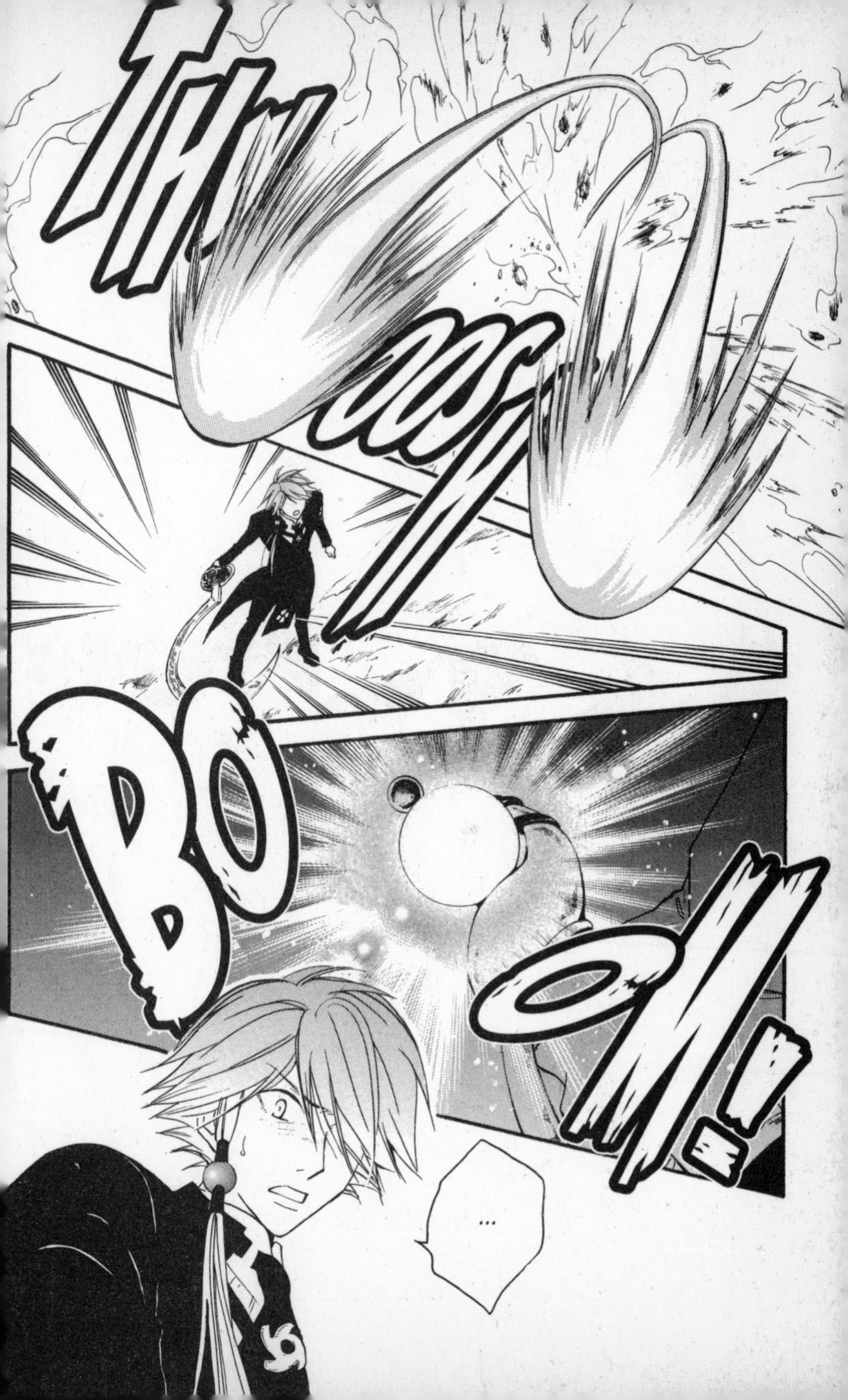
THWOOSH
BOOOM!!
...

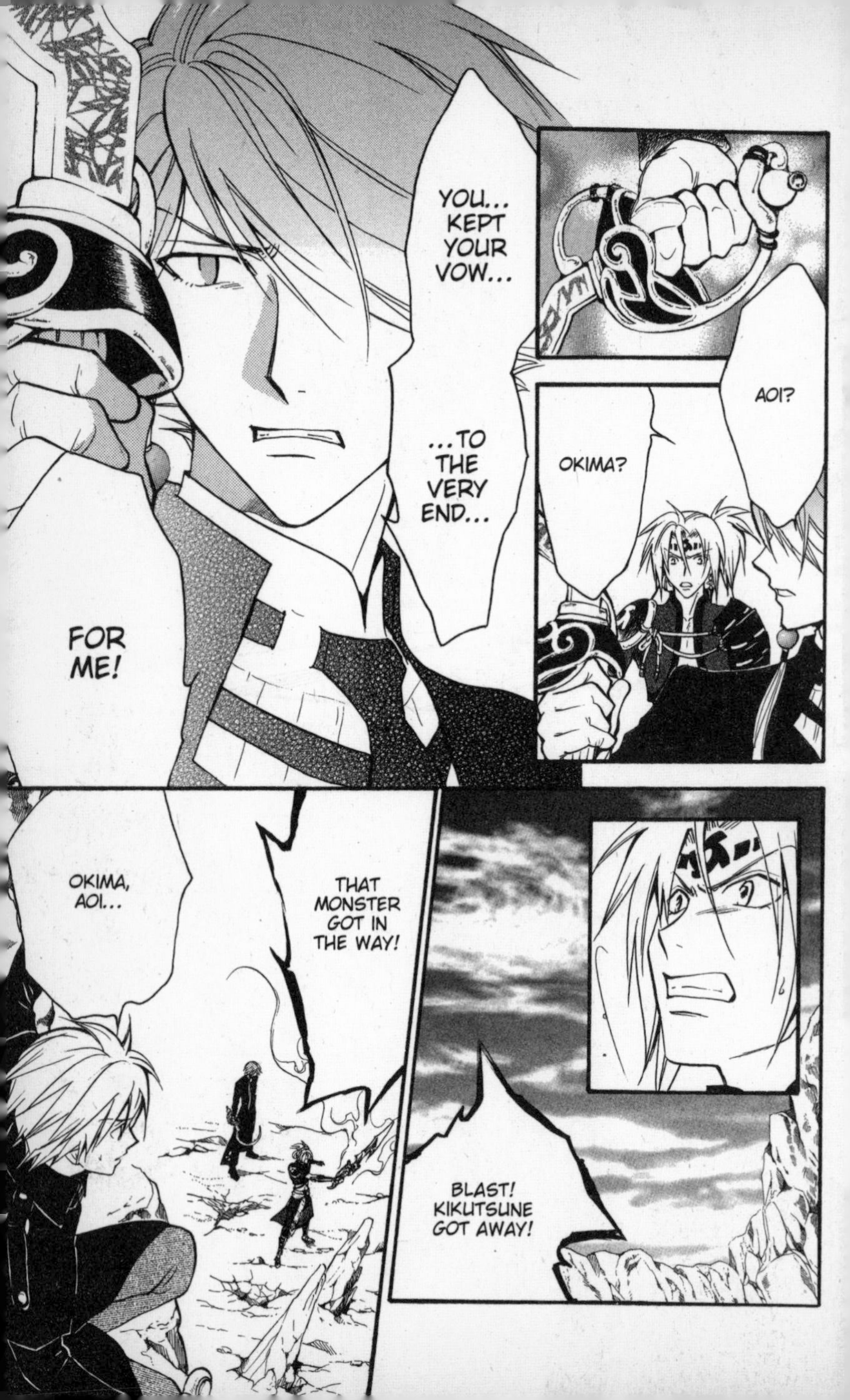
AOI?
OKIMA?
YOU... KEPT YOUR VOW...
...TO THE VERY END...
FOR ME!
BLAST! KIKUTSUNE GOT AWAY!
THAT MONSTER GOT IN THE WAY!
OKIMA, AOI...

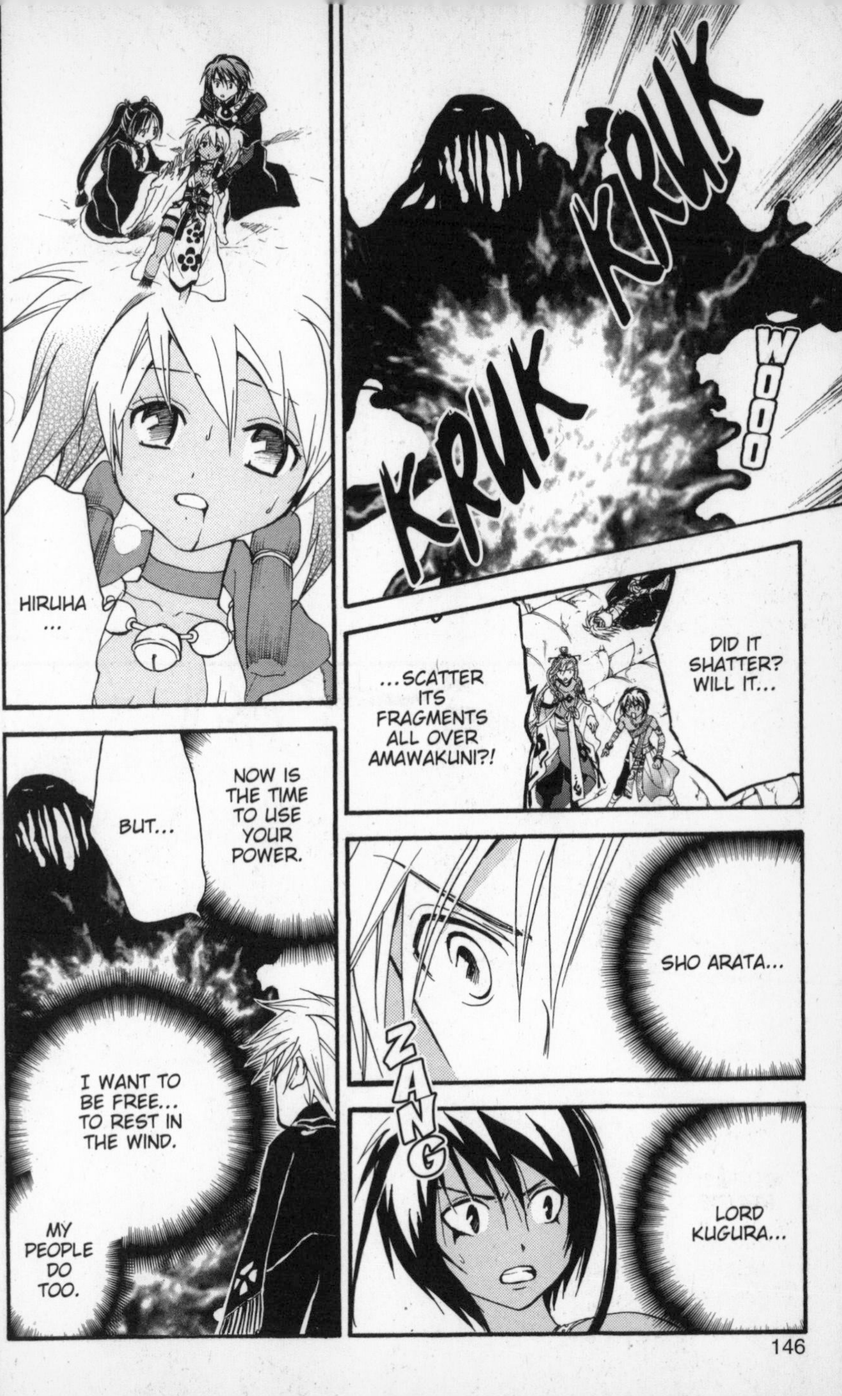
KRUK KRUK
WOOO
KRUK
DID IT SHATTER? WILL IT...
...SCATTER ITS FRAGMENTS ALL OVER AMAWAKUNI?!
HIRUHA ...
SHO ARATA...
ZANG
LORD KUGURA...
NOW IS THE TIME TO USE YOUR POWER.
BUT...
I WANT TO BE FREE... TO REST IN THE WIND.
MY PEOPLE DO TOO.

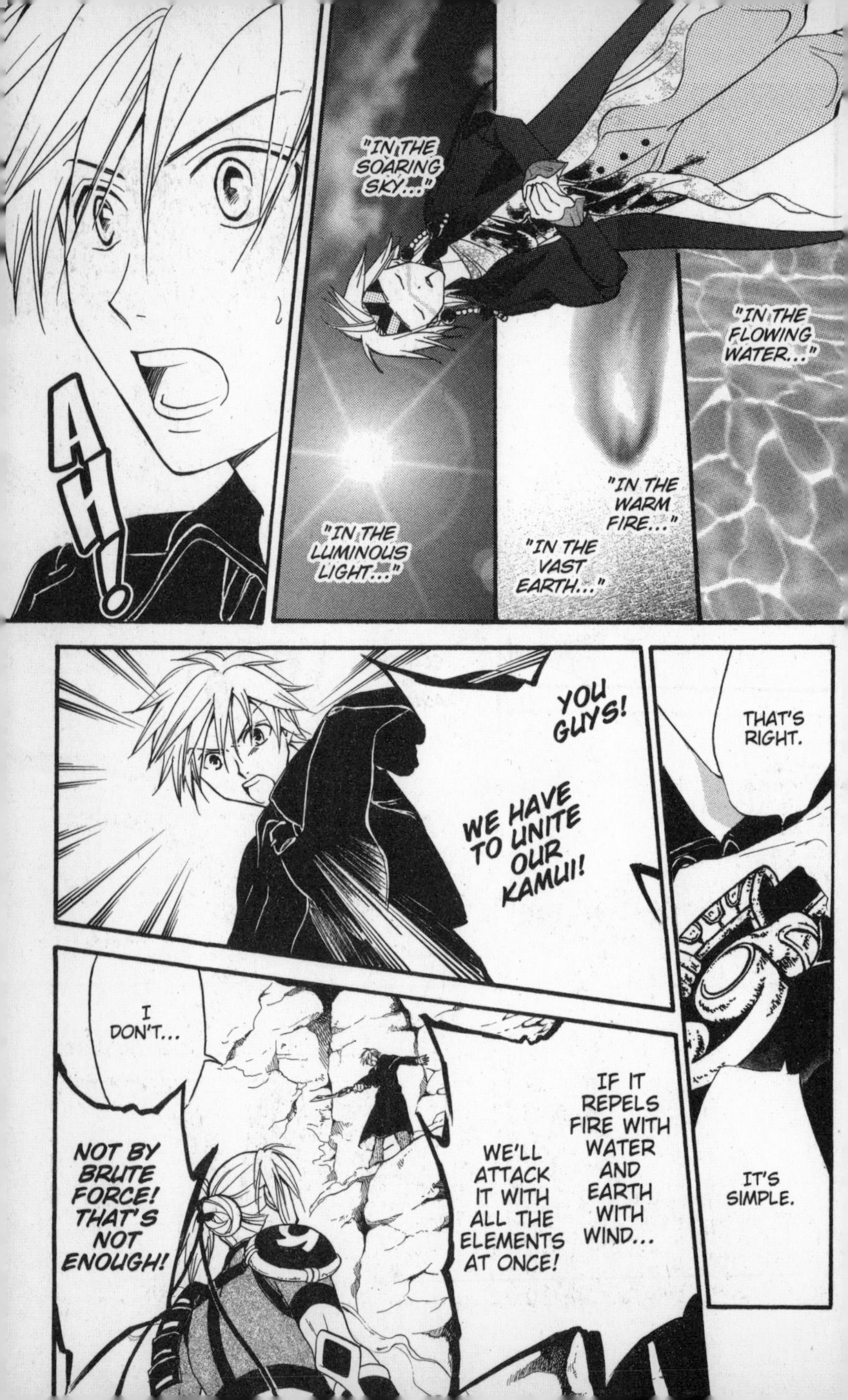
"IN THE FLOWING WATER..."
"IN THE WARM FIRE..."
"IN THE VAST EARTH..."
"IN THE SOARING SKY..."
"IN THE LUMINOUS LIGHT..."
AH!
THAT'S RIGHT.
IT'S SIMPLE.
YOU GUYS!
WE HAVE TO UNITE OUR KAMUI!
IF IT REPELS FIRE WITH WATER AND EARTH WITH WIND...
WE'LL ATTACK IT WITH ALL THE ELEMENTS AT ONCE!
I DON'T...
NOT BY BRUTE FORCE! THAT'S NOT ENOUGH!

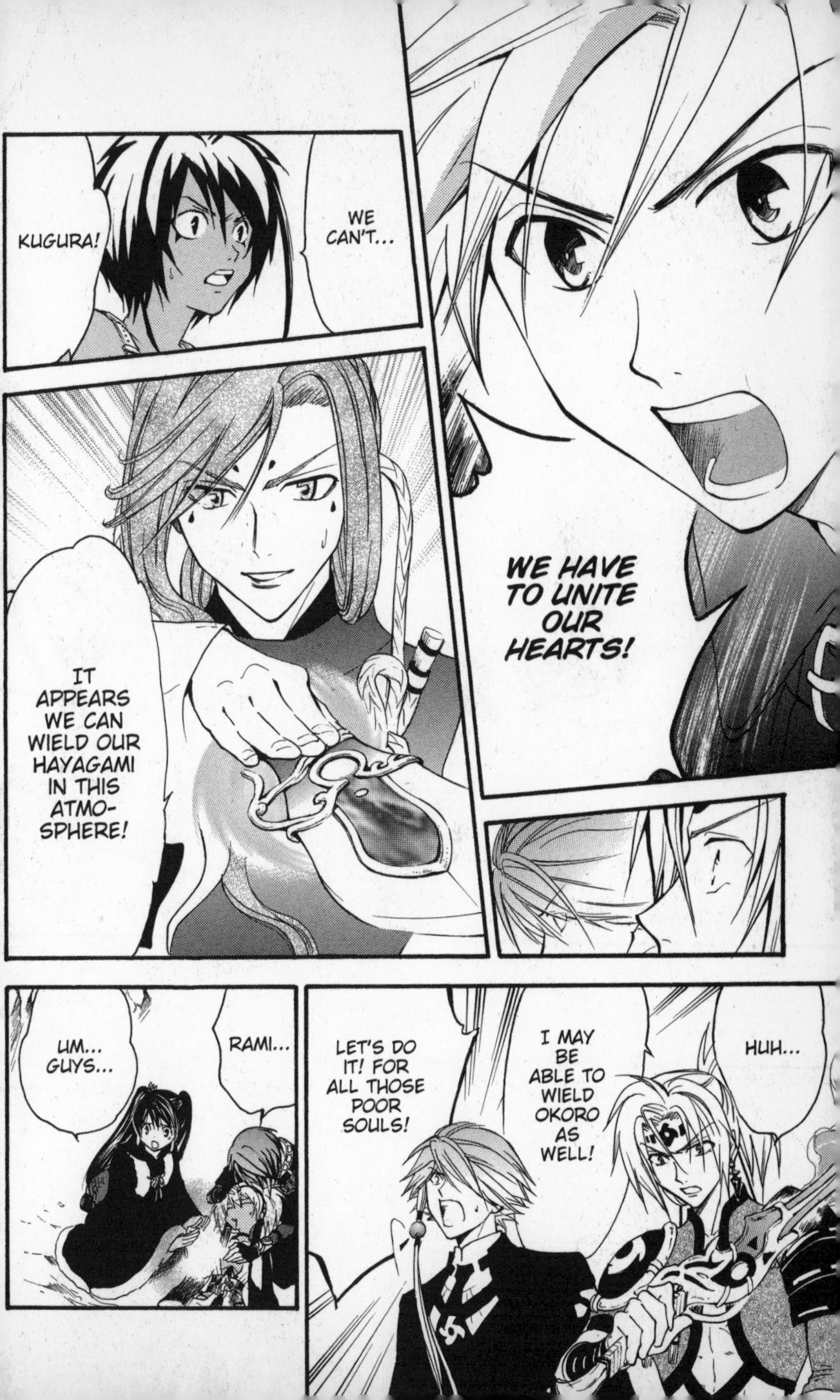
WE HAVE TO UNITE OUR HEARTS!
WE CAN'T...
KUGURA!
IT APPEARS WE CAN WIELD OUR HAYAGAMI IN THIS ATMO-SPHERE!
HUH...
I MAY BE ABLE TO WIELD OKORO AS WELL!
LET'S DO IT! FOR ALL THOSE POOR SOULS!
RAMI...
UM... GUYS...

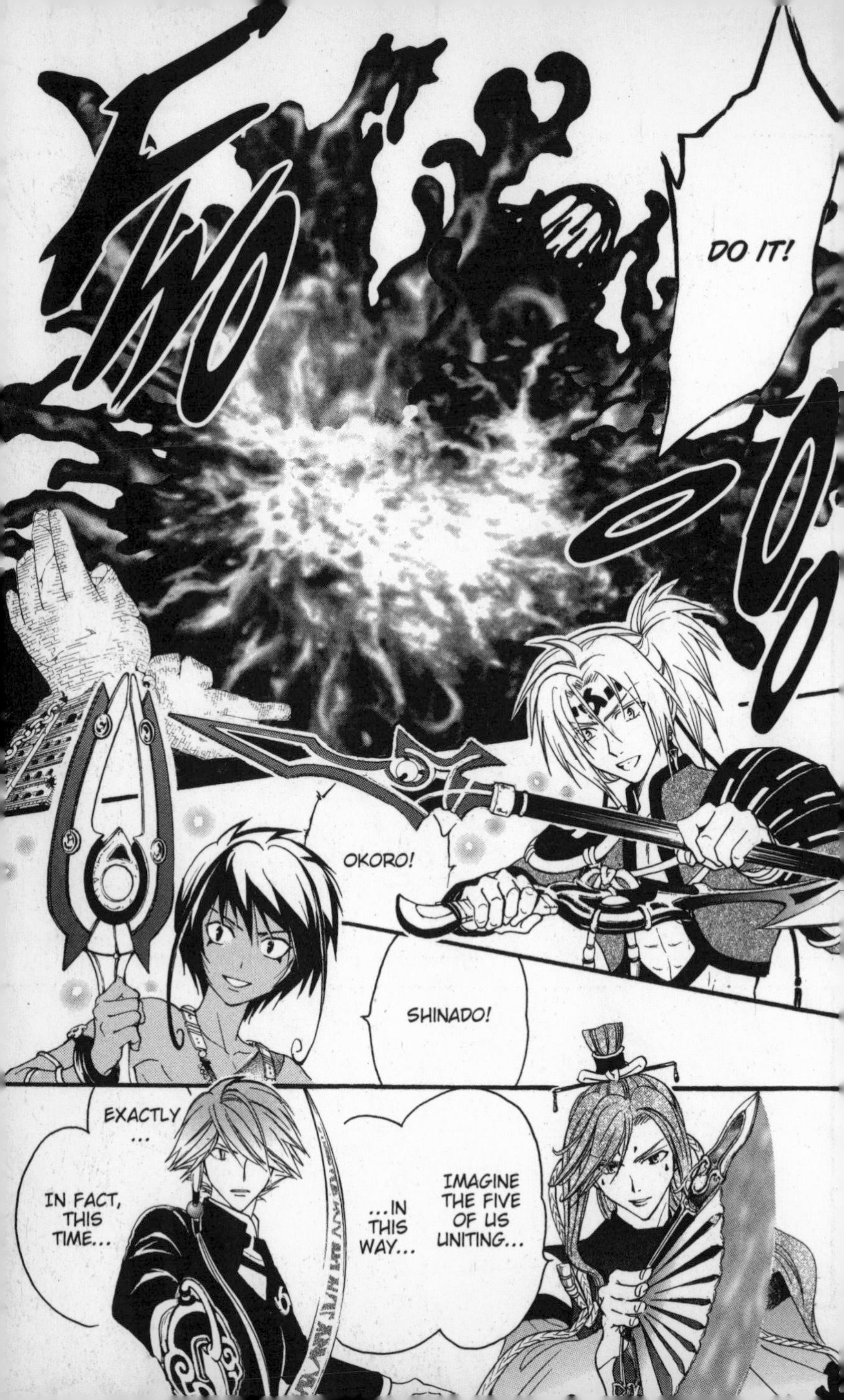
DO IT!
OKORO!
SHINADO!
IMAGINE THE FIVE OF US UNITING...
...IN THIS WAY...
EXACTLY ...
IN FACT, THIS TIME...

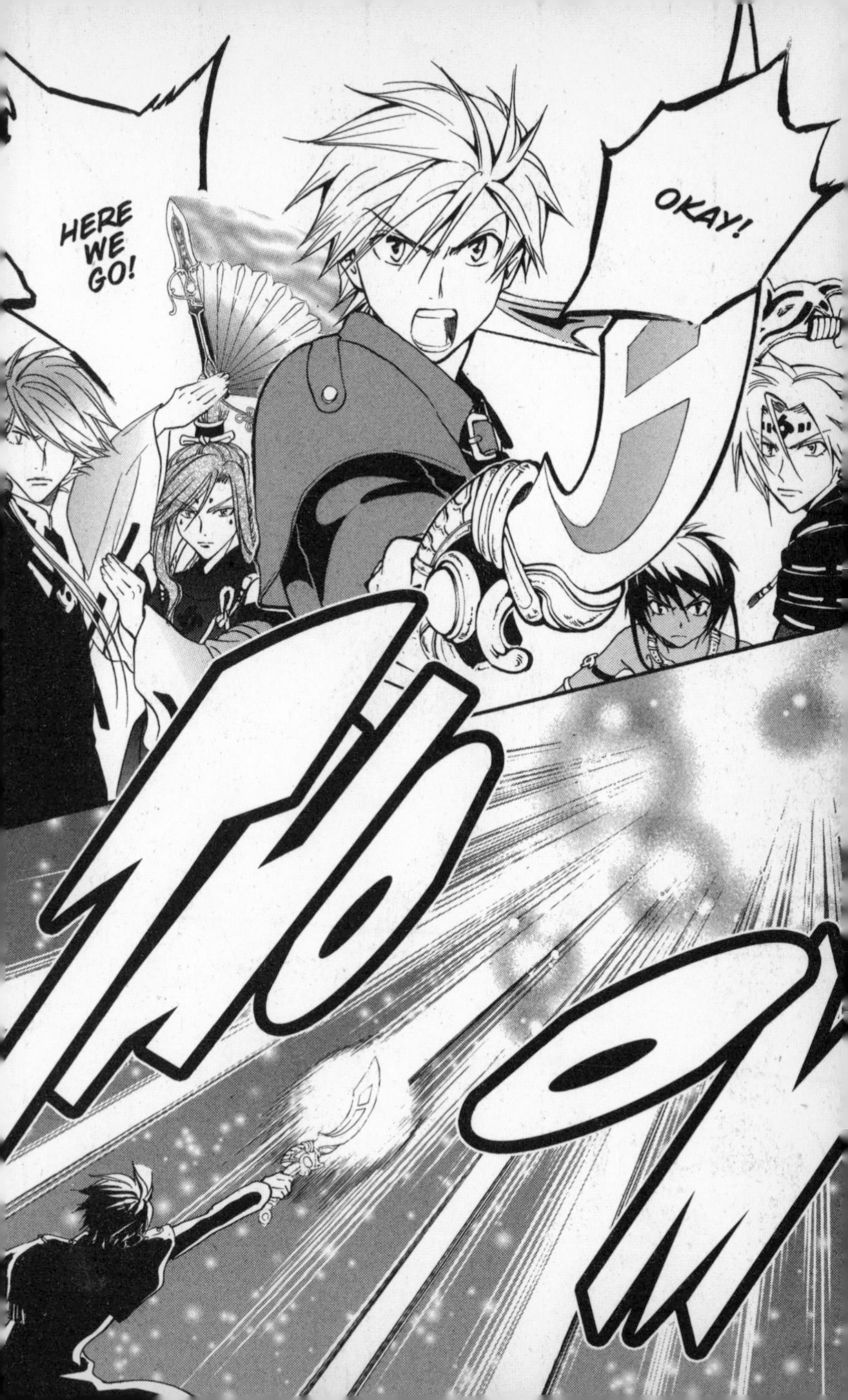
OKAY!
HERE WE GO!

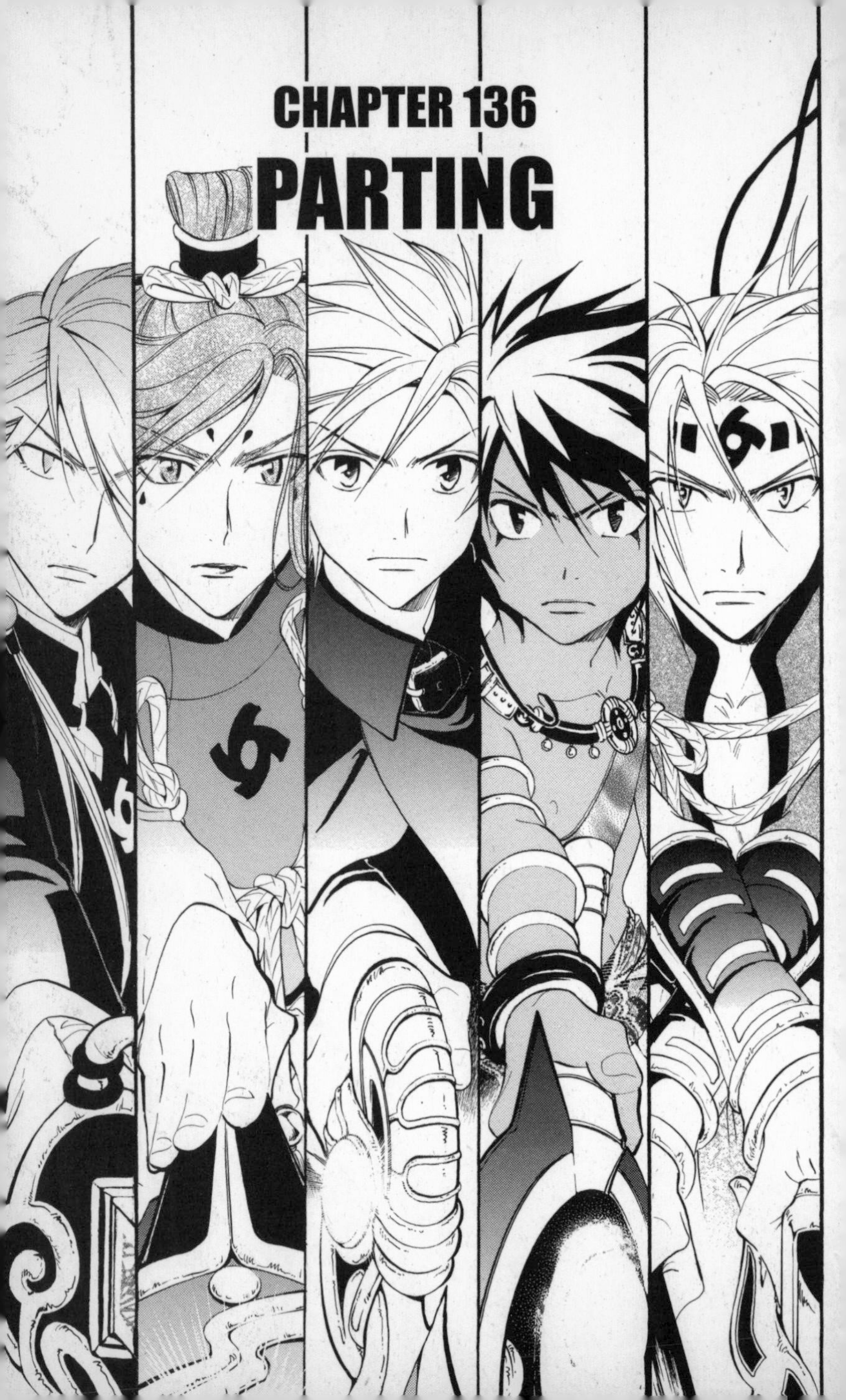

CHAPTER 136
PARTING

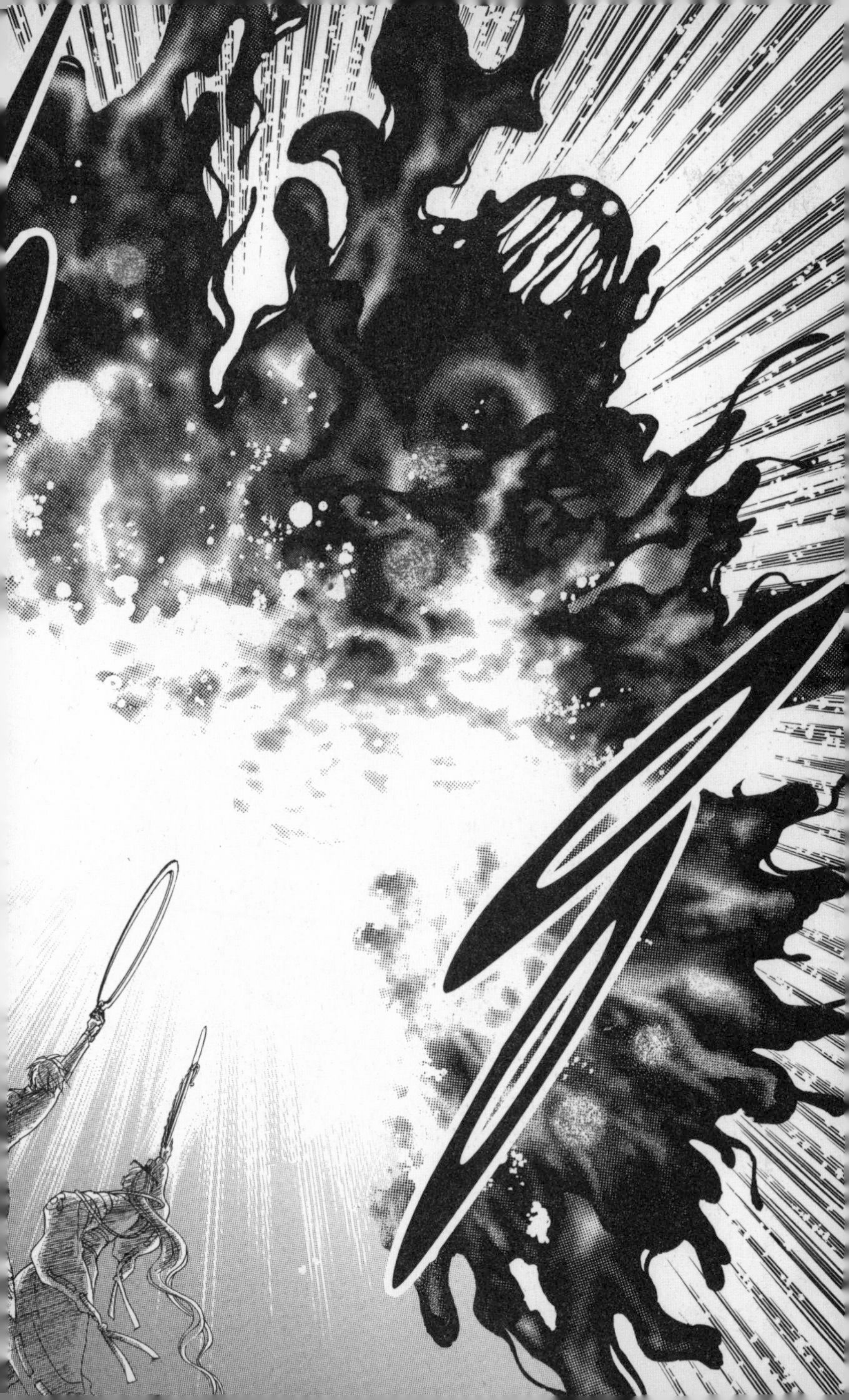

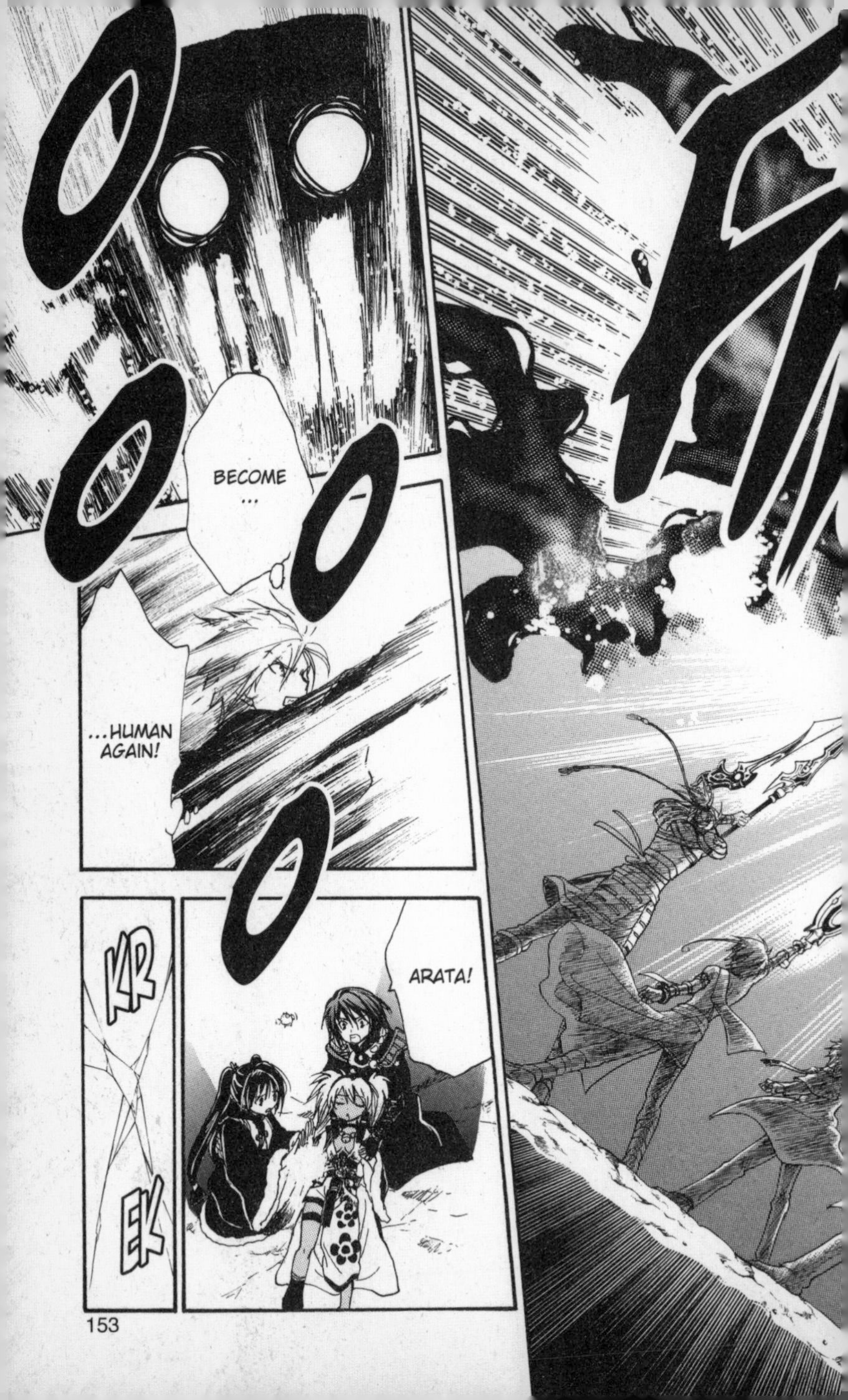
BECOME ...
...HUMAN AGAIN!
ARATA!
KR EK

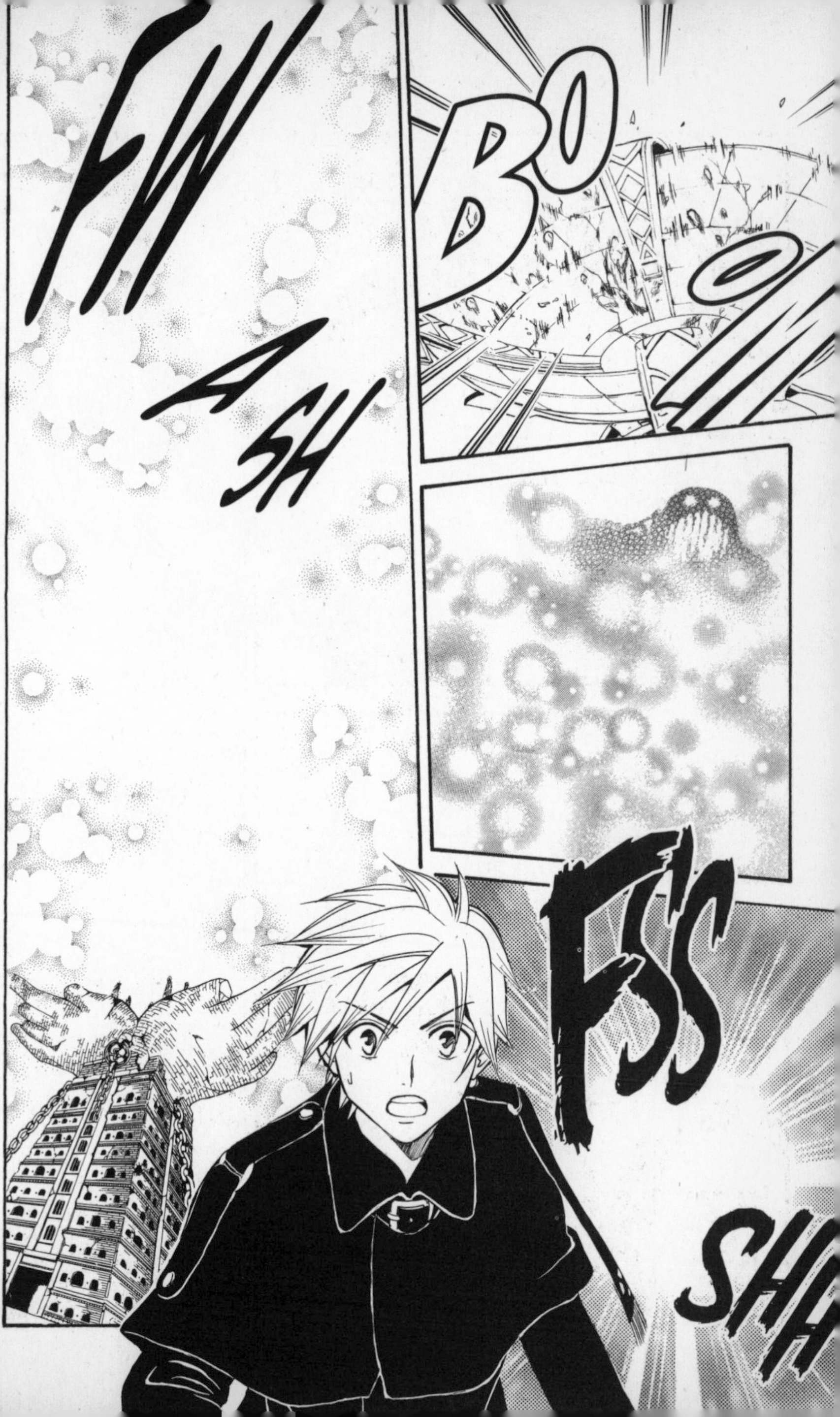
BOOM
FSSSH
FWASH

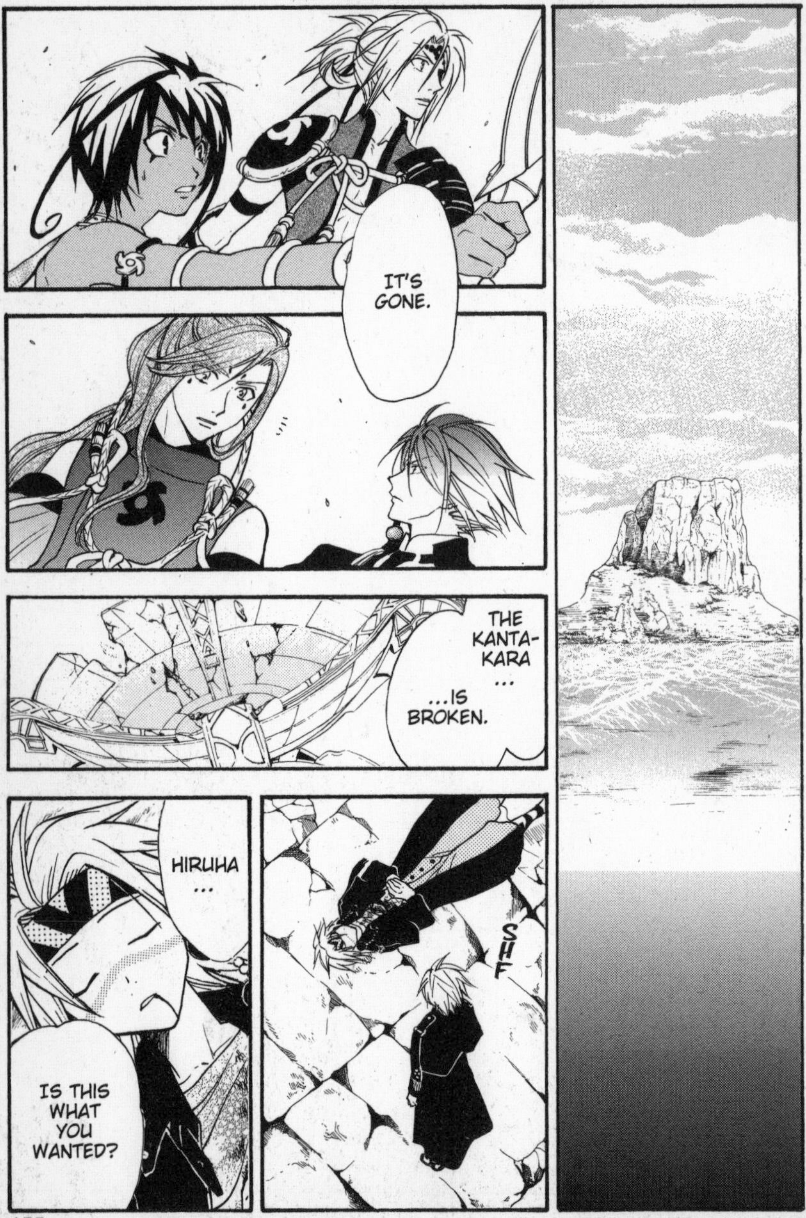
IT'S GONE.
THE KANTA-KARA ...
...IS BROKEN.
SHF
HIRUHA ...
IS THIS WHAT YOU WANTED?

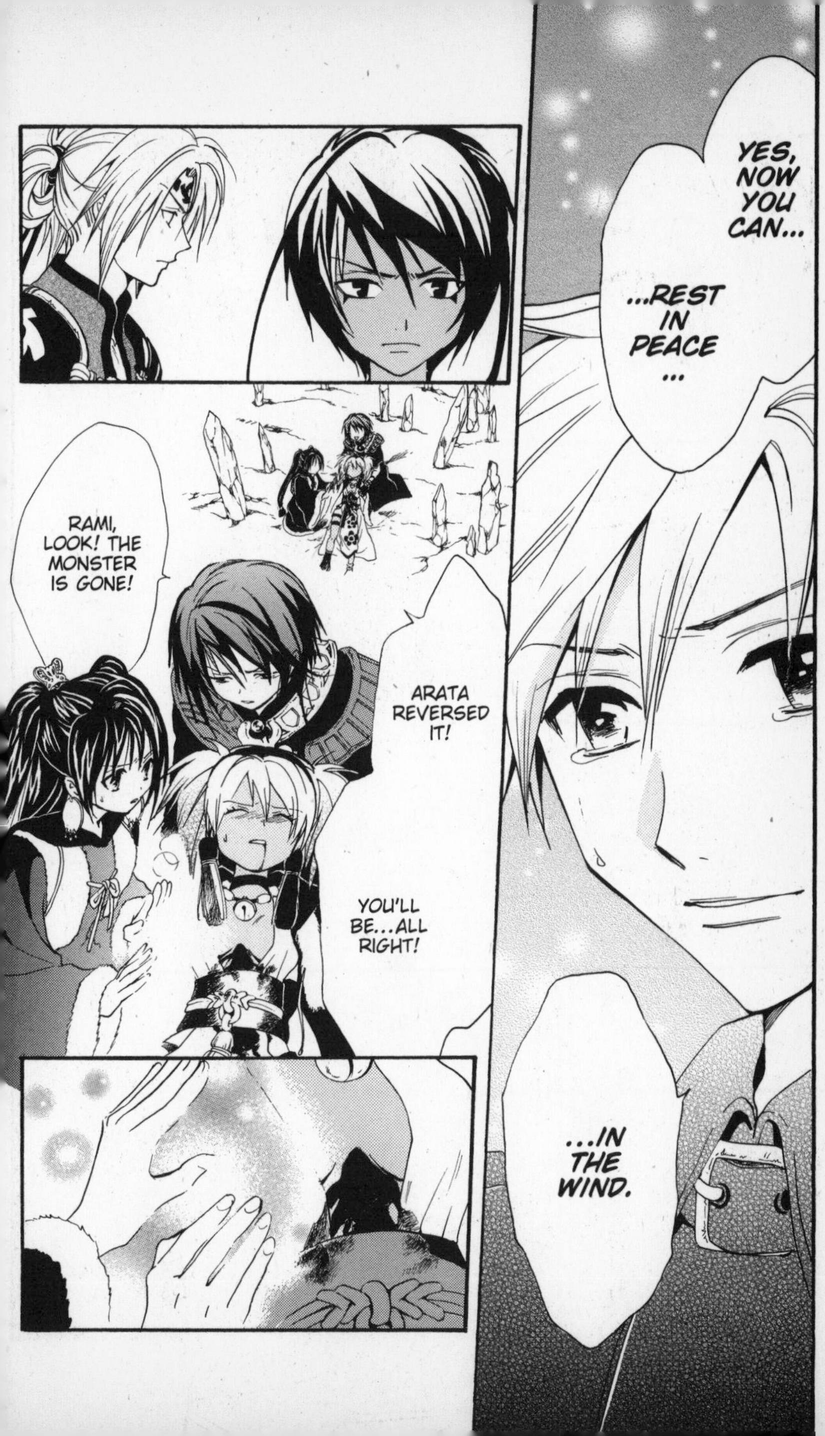
YES, NOW YOU CAN...
...REST IN PEACE...
...IN THE WIND.
RAMI, LOOK! THE MONSTER IS GONE!
ARATA REVERSED IT!
YOU'LL BE...ALL RIGHT!

RAMI!

SHE'S TOO...

RAMI, I'M SORRY!

SHE'S TOO FAR GONE! MY POWERS CAN'T SAVE HER!

KOTOHA...

IT'S...ALL RIGHT.

I...

RAMI!

...MUST LEAVE YOU.

MASTER...

...MIKUSA...

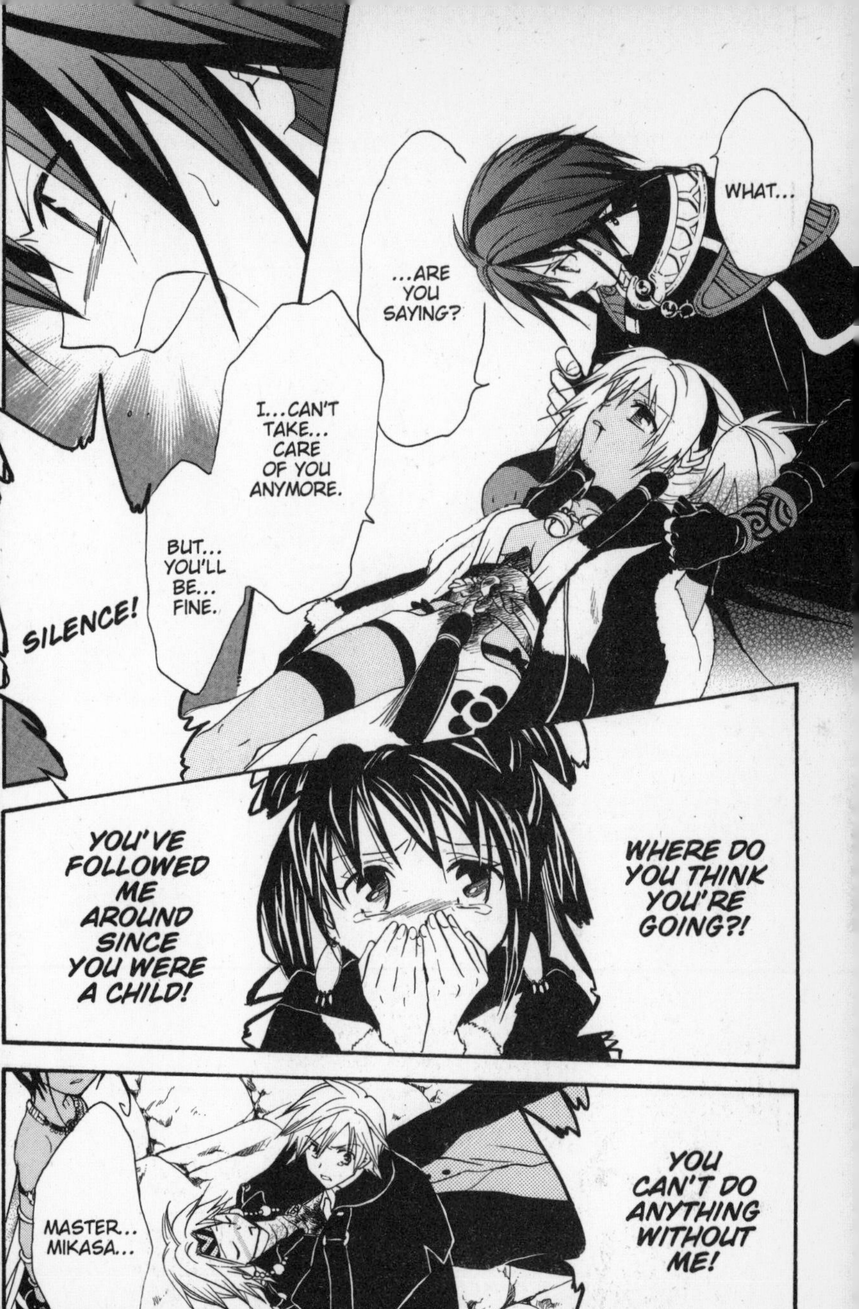
WHAT...
...ARE YOU SAYING?
I...CAN'T TAKE... CARE OF YOU ANYMORE.
BUT... YOU'LL BE... FINE.
SILENCE!
WHERE DO YOU THINK YOU'RE GOING?!
YOU'VE FOLLOWED ME AROUND SINCE YOU WERE A CHILD!
YOU CAN'T DO ANYTHING WITHOUT ME!
MASTER... MIKASA...

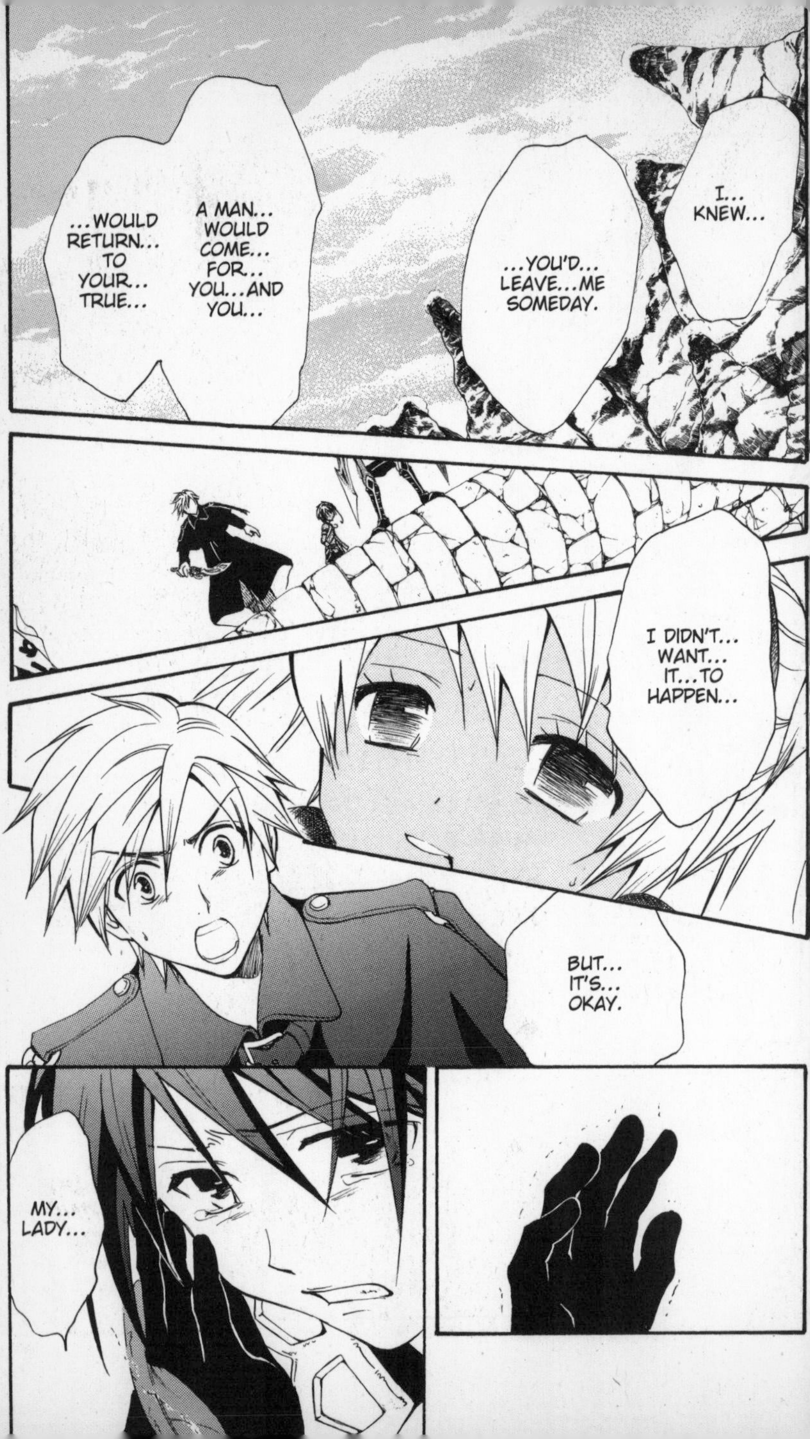
I... KNEW...
...YOU'D... LEAVE...ME SOMEDAY.
A MAN... WOULD COME... FOR... YOU...AND YOU...
...WOULD RETURN... TO YOUR... TRUE...
I DIDN'T... WANT... IT...TO HAPPEN...
BUT... IT'S... OKAY.
MY... LADY...

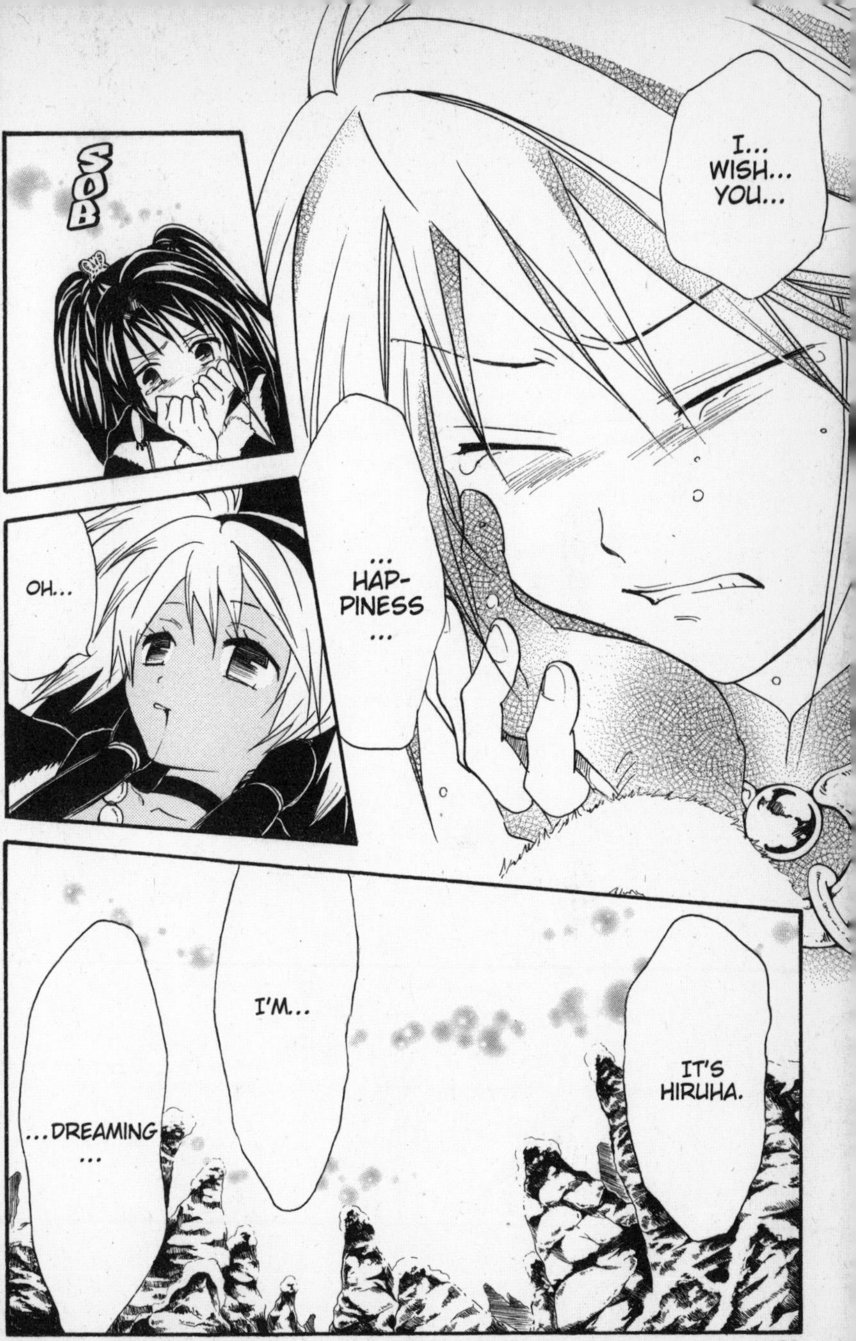
I... WISH... YOU...
... HAP-PINESS ...
SOB
OH...
IT'S HIRUHA.
I'M...
...DREAMING ...

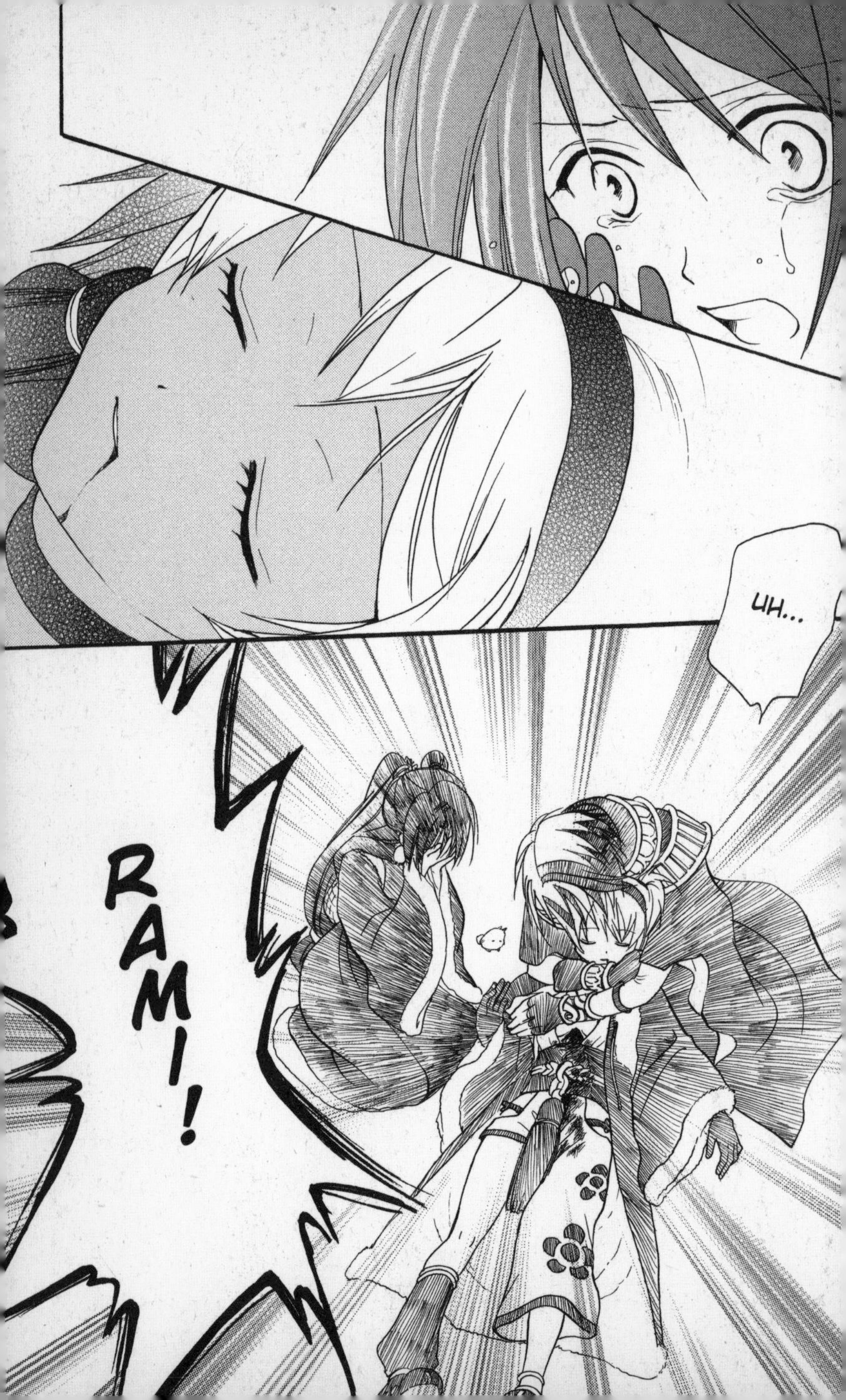
UH...
RAMI!

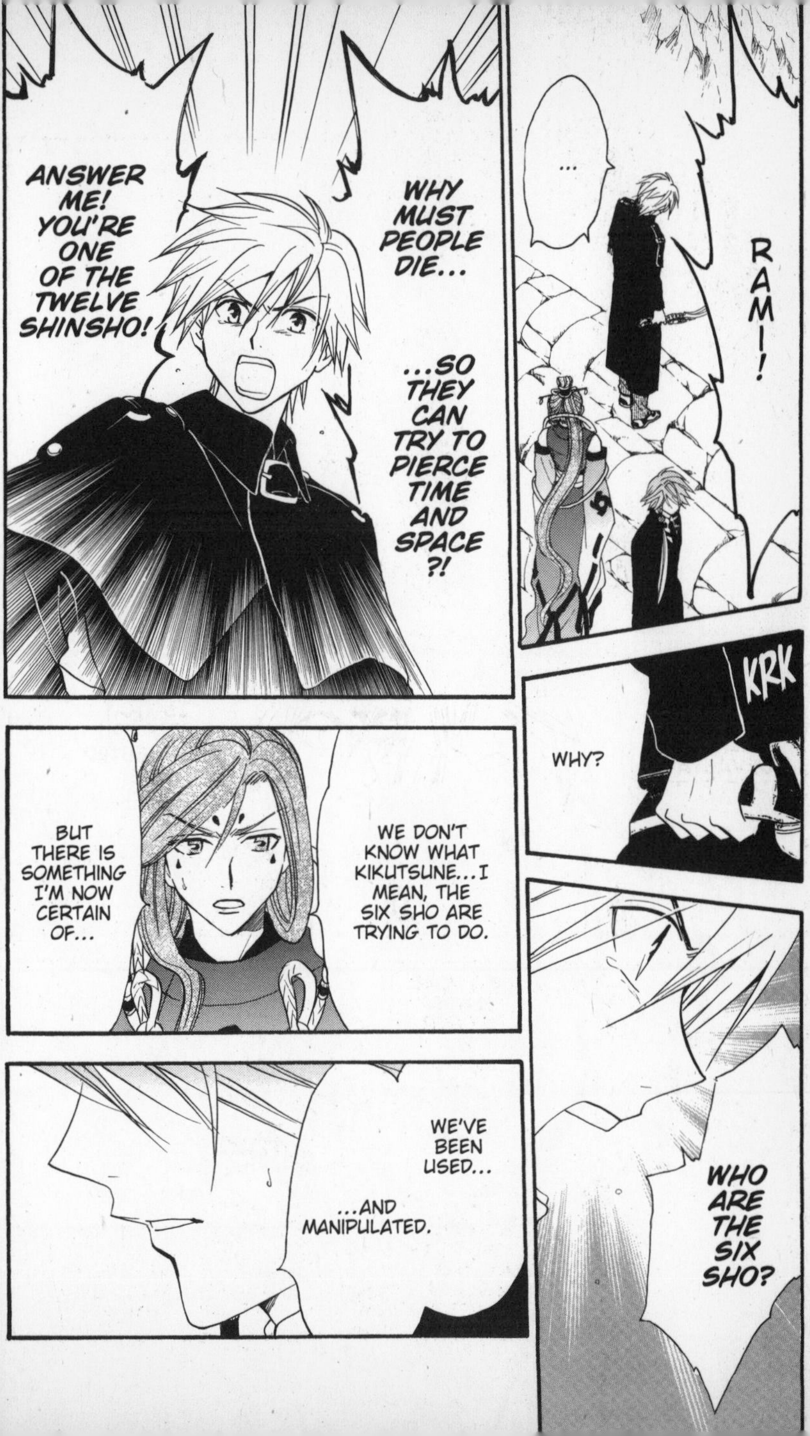
...
RAMI!
WHY MUST PEOPLE DIE...
...SO THEY CAN TRY TO PIERCE TIME AND SPACE?!
ANSWER ME! YOU'RE ONE OF THE TWELVE SHINSHO!
KRK
WHY?
WHO ARE THE SIX SHO?
WE DON'T KNOW WHAT KIKUTSUNE...I MEAN, THE SIX SHO ARE TRYING TO DO.
BUT THERE IS SOMETHING I'M NOW CERTAIN OF...
WE'VE BEEN USED...
...AND MANIPULATED.

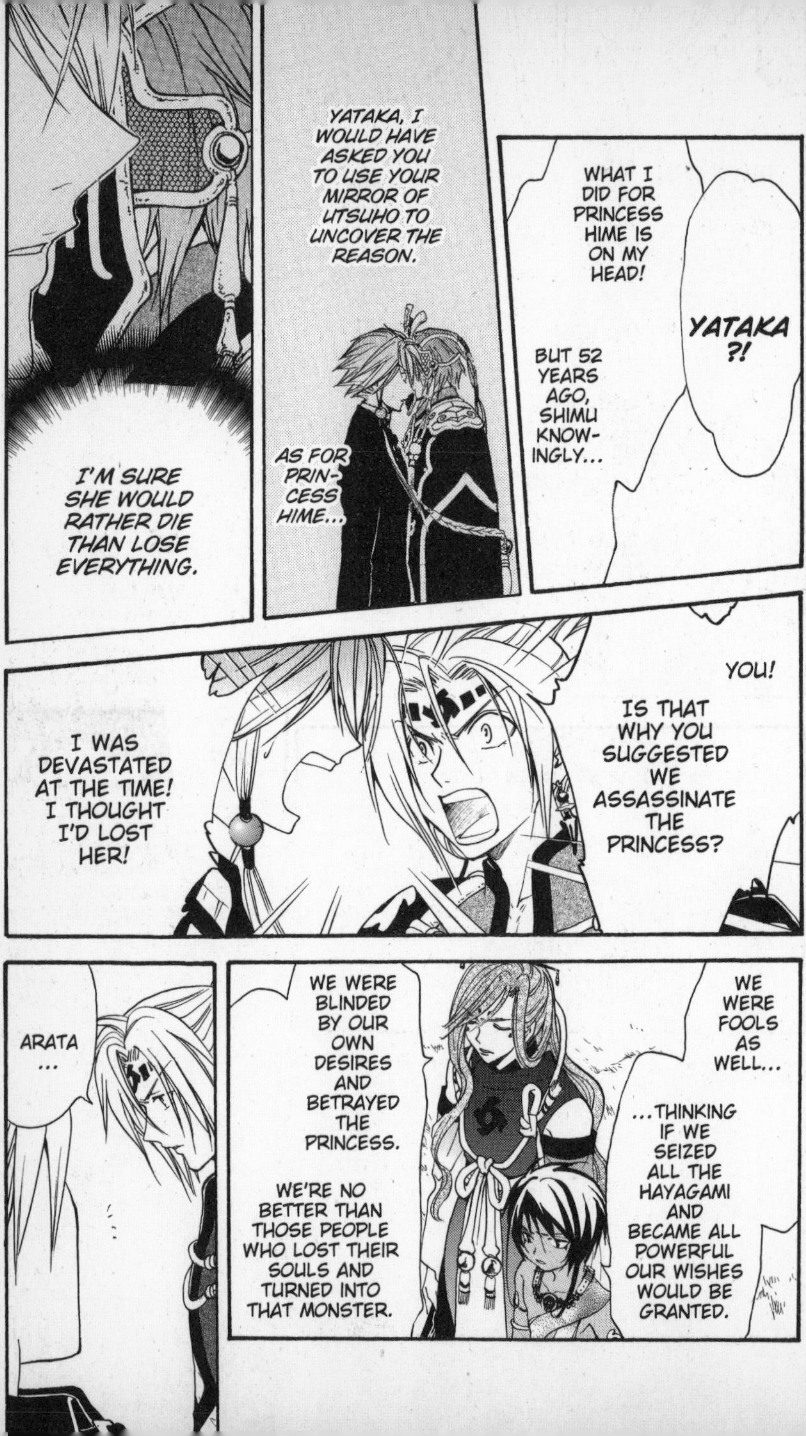
YATAKA ?!
WHAT I DID FOR PRINCESS HIME IS ON MY HEAD!
BUT 52 YEARS AGO, SHIMU KNOWINGLY...
YATAKA, I WOULD HAVE ASKED YOU TO USE YOUR MIRROR OF UTSUHO TO UNCOVER THE REASON.
AS FOR PRINCESS HIME...
I'M SURE SHE WOULD RATHER DIE THAN LOSE EVERYTHING.
YOU!
IS THAT WHY YOU SUGGESTED WE ASSASSINATE THE PRINCESS?
I WAS DEVASTATED AT THE TIME! I THOUGHT I'D LOST HER!
WE WERE FOOLS AS WELL...
...THINKING IF WE SEIZED ALL THE HAYAGAMI AND BECAME ALL POWERFUL OUR WISHES WOULD BE GRANTED.
WE WERE BLINDED BY OUR OWN DESIRES AND BETRAYED THE PRINCESS.
WE'RE NO BETTER THAN THOSE PEOPLE WHO LOST THEIR SOULS AND TURNED INTO THAT MONSTER.
ARATA ...

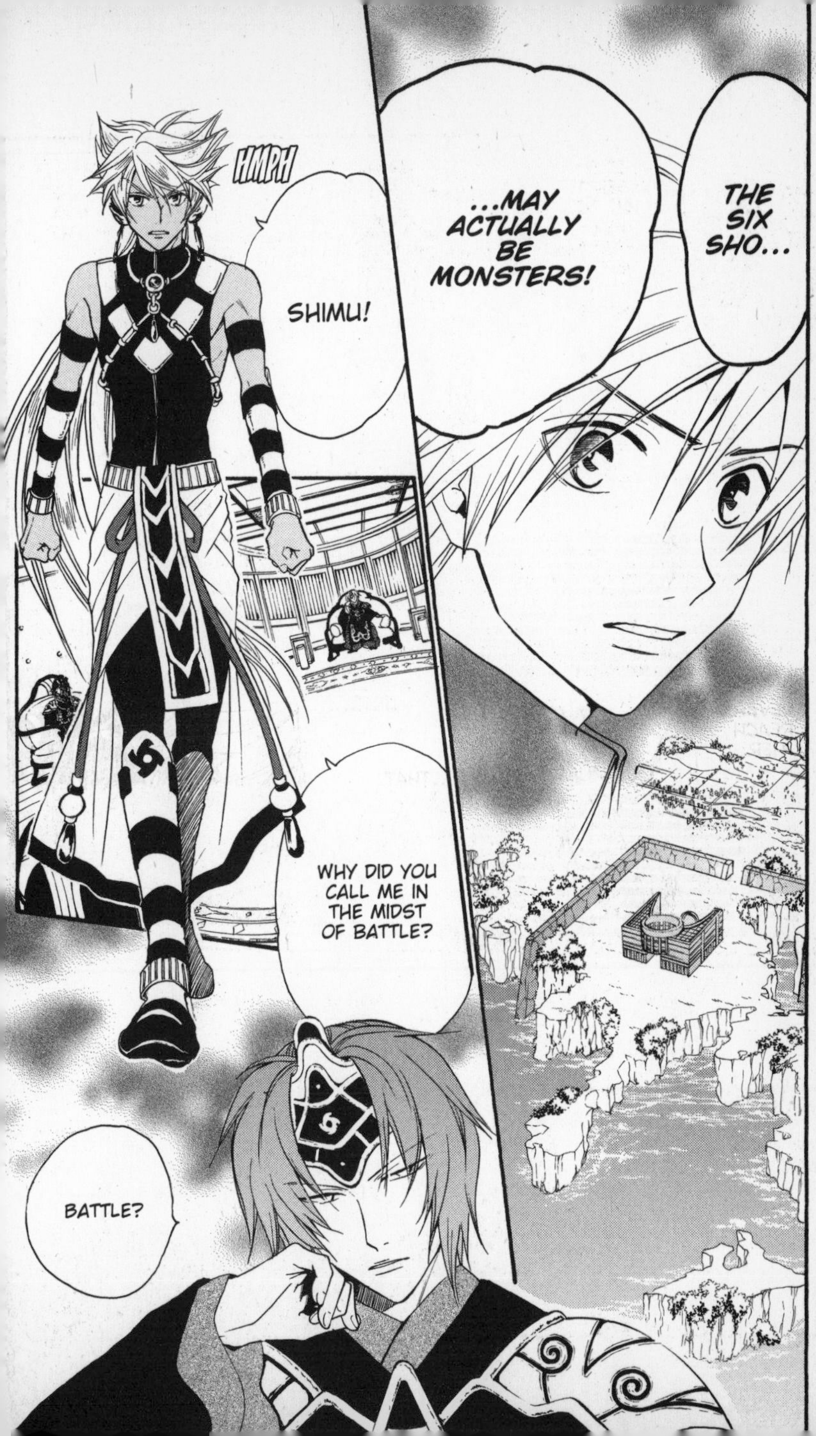
THE SIX SHO...
...MAY ACTUALLY BE MONSTERS!
HMPH
SHIMU!
WHY DID YOU CALL ME IN THE MIDST OF BATTLE?
BATTLE?

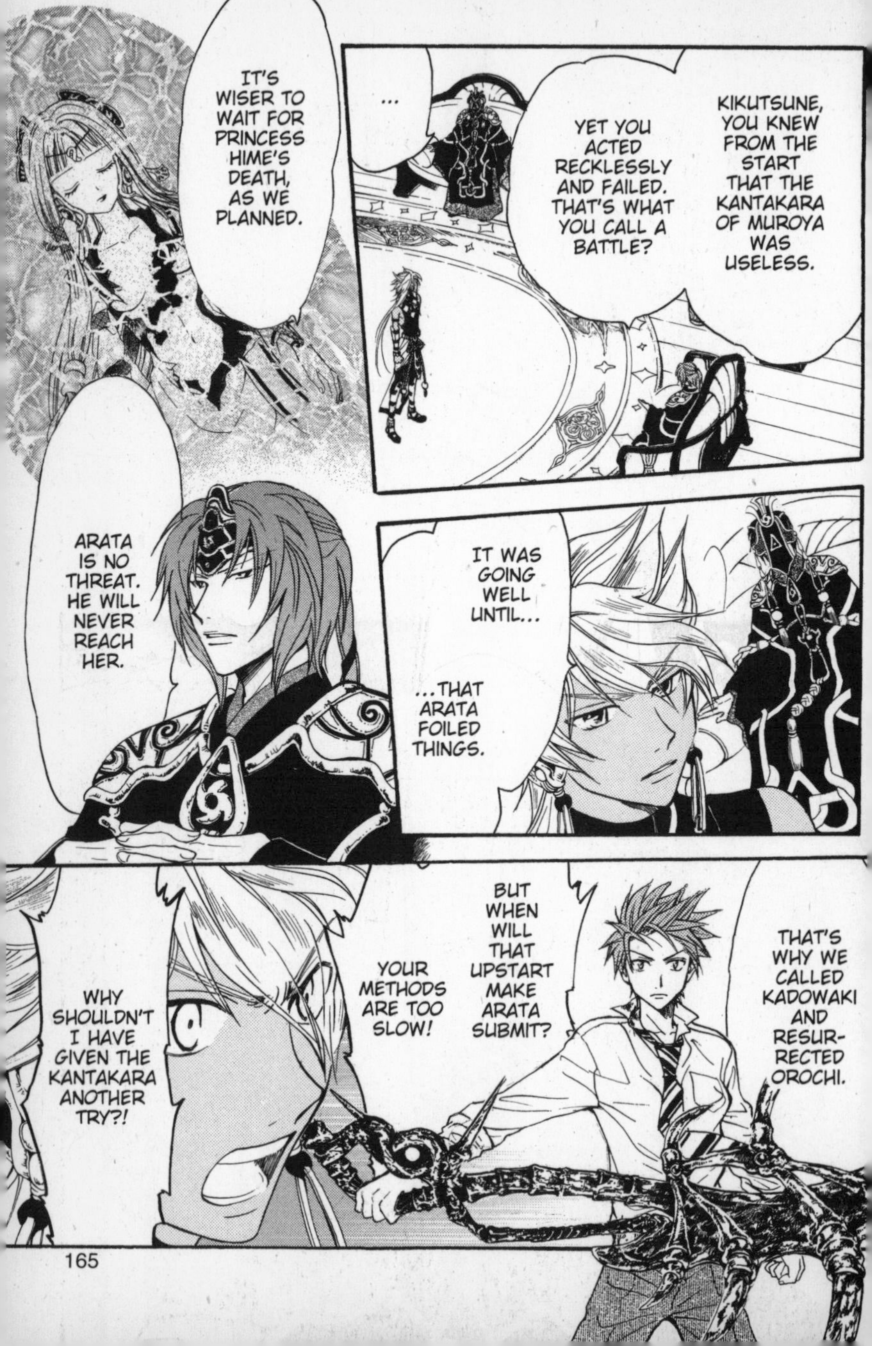

KIKUTSUNE, YOU KNEW FROM THE START THAT THE KANTAKARA OF MUROYA WAS USELESS.
YET YOU ACTED RECKLESSLY AND FAILED. THAT'S WHAT YOU CALL A BATTLE?
...
IT WAS GOING WELL UNTIL...
...THAT ARATA FOILED THINGS.
IT'S WISER TO WAIT FOR PRINCESS HIME'S DEATH, AS WE PLANNED.
ARATA IS NO THREAT. HE WILL NEVER REACH HER.
THAT'S WHY WE CALLED KADOWAKI AND RESURRECTED OROCHI.
BUT WHEN WILL THAT UPSTART MAKE ARATA SUBMIT?
YOUR METHODS ARE TOO SLOW!
WHY SHOULDN'T I HAVE GIVEN THE KANTAKARA ANOTHER TRY?!

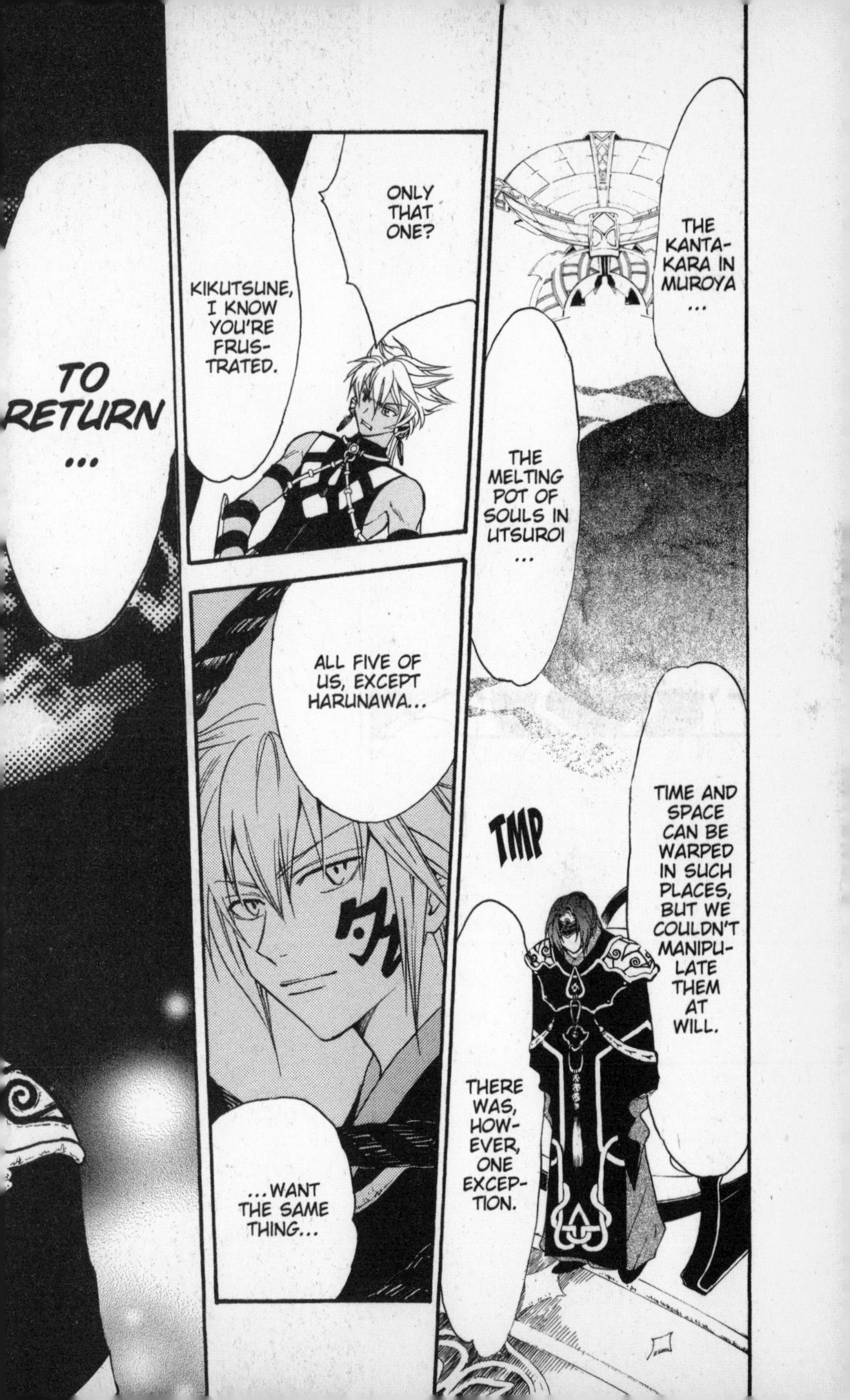

THE KANTA-KARA IN MUROYA...
THE MELTING POT OF SOULS IN UTSUROI...
TIME AND SPACE CAN BE WARPED IN SUCH PLACES, BUT WE COULDN'T MANIPU-LATE THEM AT WILL.
TMP
THERE WAS, HOW-EVER, ONE EXCEP-TION.
ONLY THAT ONE?
KIKUTSUNE, I KNOW YOU'RE FRUS-TRATED.
ALL FIVE OF US, EXCEPT HARUNAWA...
...WANT THE SAME THING...
TO RETURN...

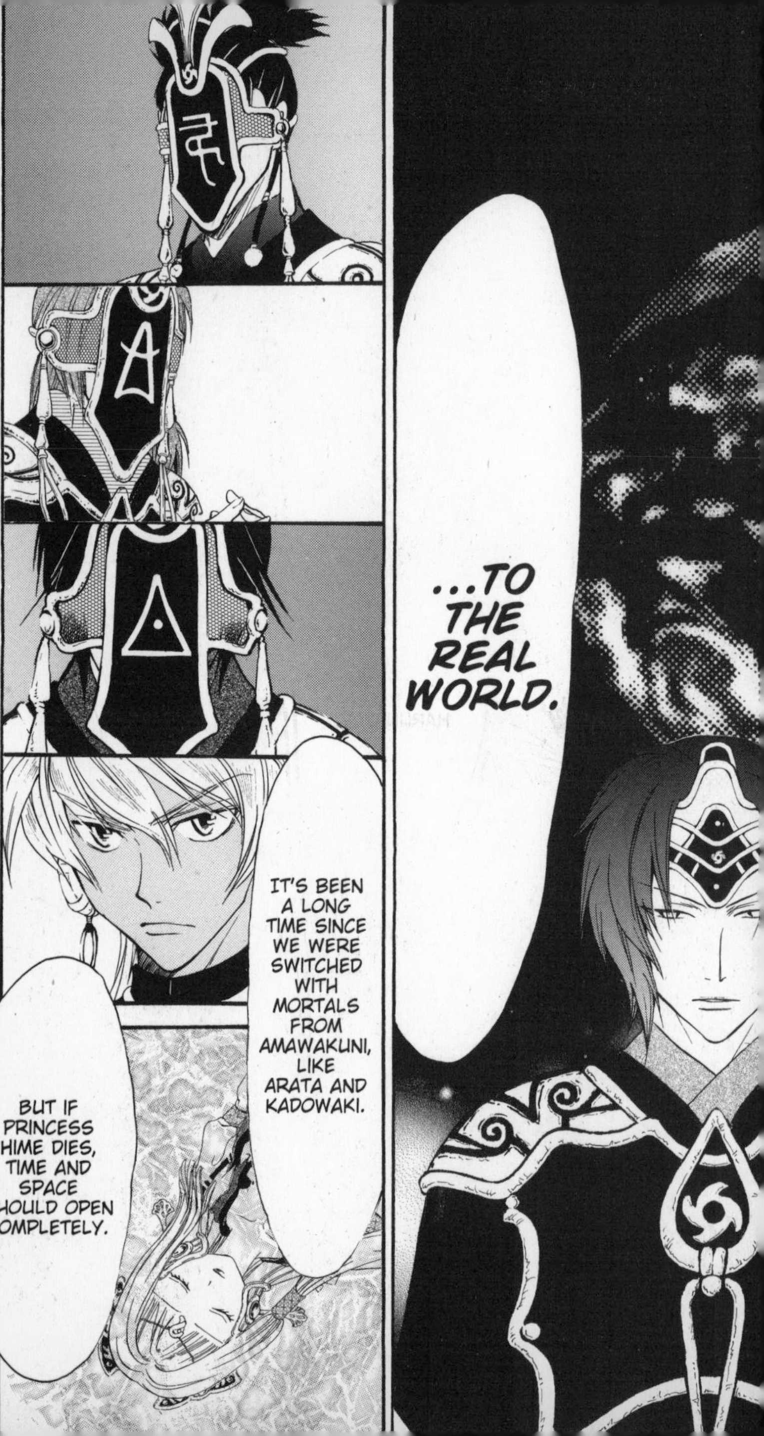
...TO THE REAL WORLD.
IT'S BEEN A LONG TIME SINCE WE WERE SWITCHED WITH MORTALS FROM AMAWAKUNI, LIKE ARATA AND KADOWAKI.
BUT IF PRINCESS HIME DIES, TIME AND SPACE SHOULD OPEN COMPLETELY.

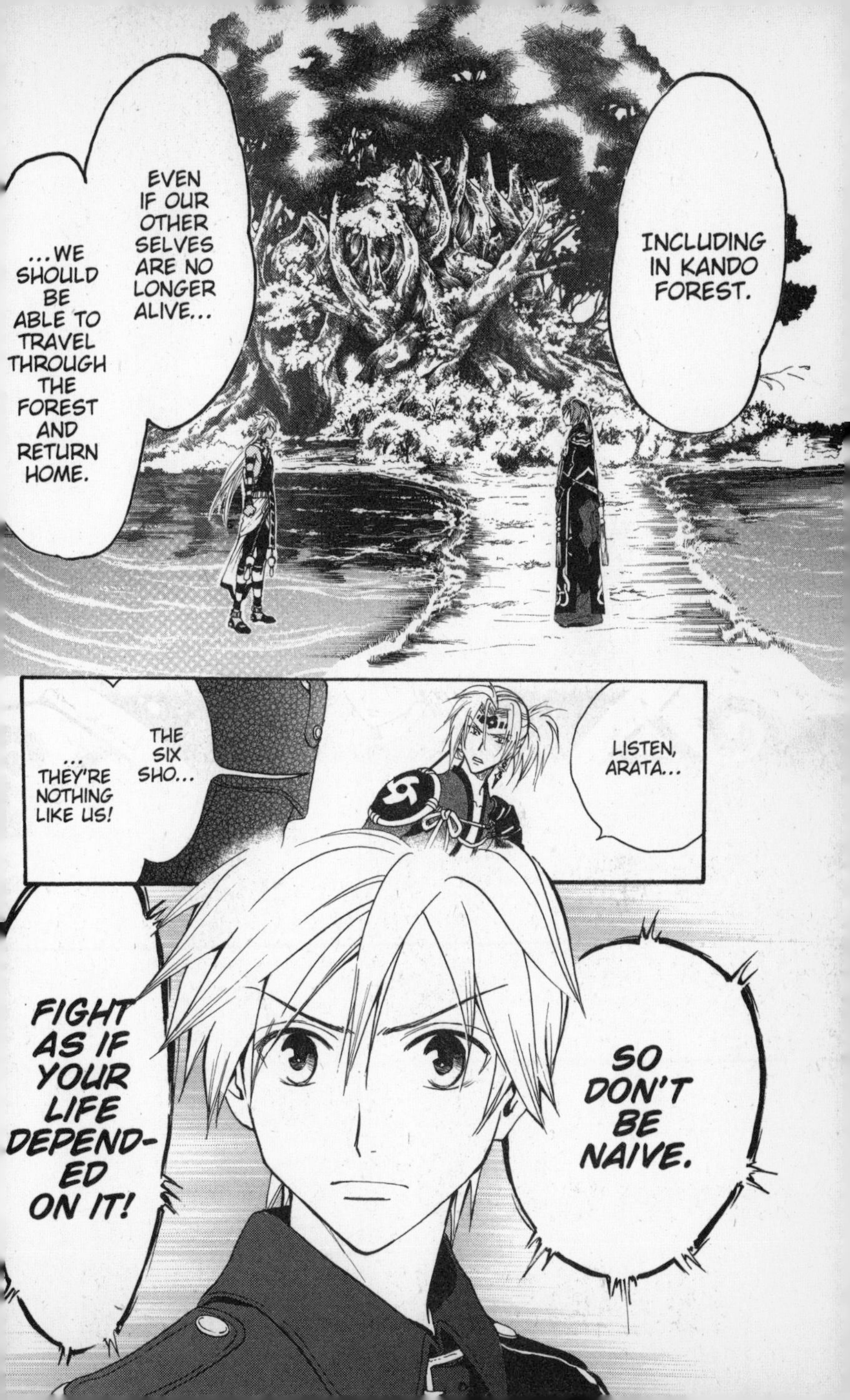
INCLUDING IN KANDO FOREST.
EVEN IF OUR OTHER SELVES ARE NO LONGER ALIVE...
...WE SHOULD BE ABLE TO TRAVEL THROUGH THE FOREST AND RETURN HOME.
LISTEN, ARATA...
THE SIX SHO...
...THEY'RE NOTHING LIKE US!
SO DON'T BE NAIVE.
FIGHT AS IF YOUR LIFE DEPEND-ED ON IT!

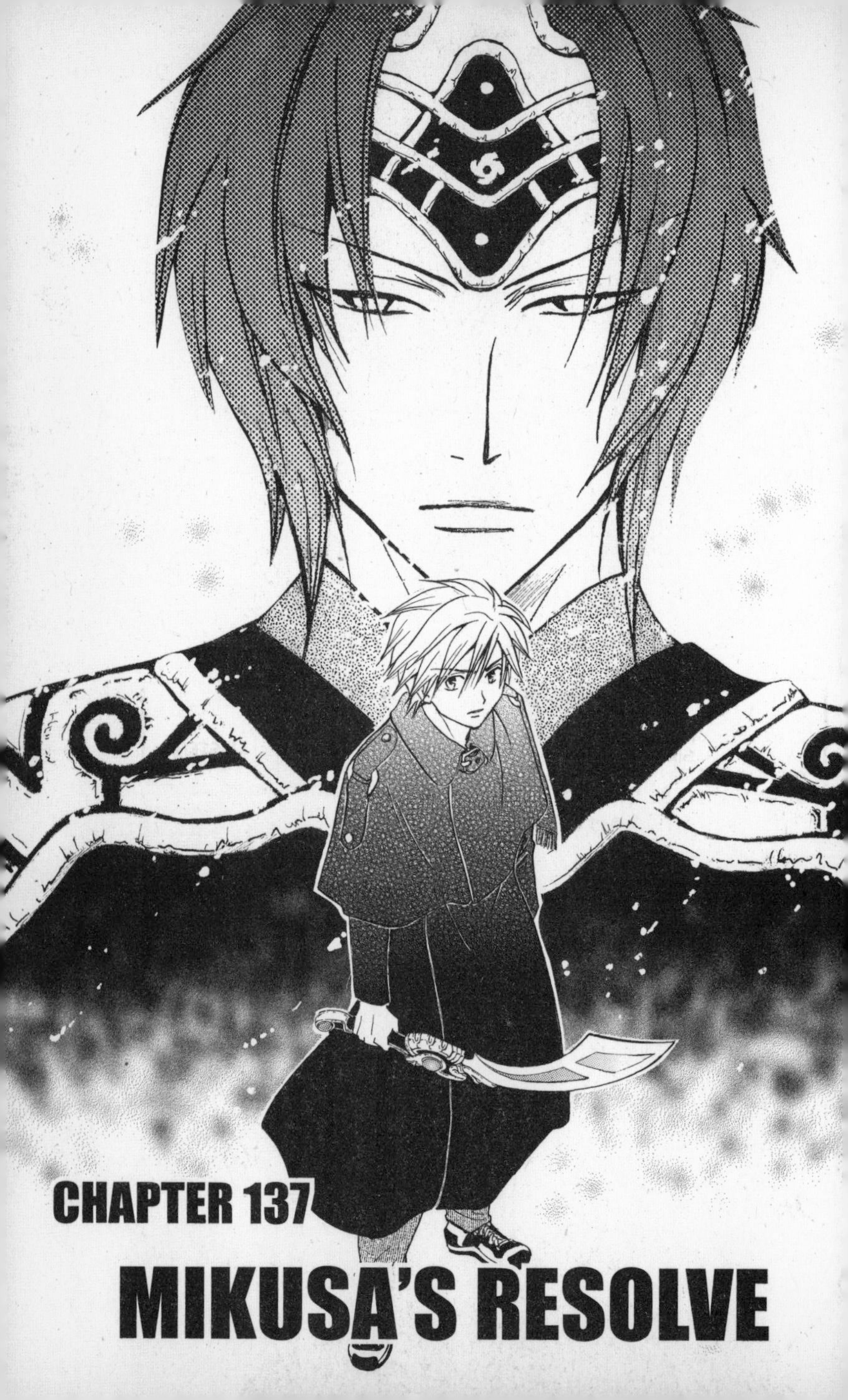
CHAPTER 137
MIKUSA'S RESOLVE

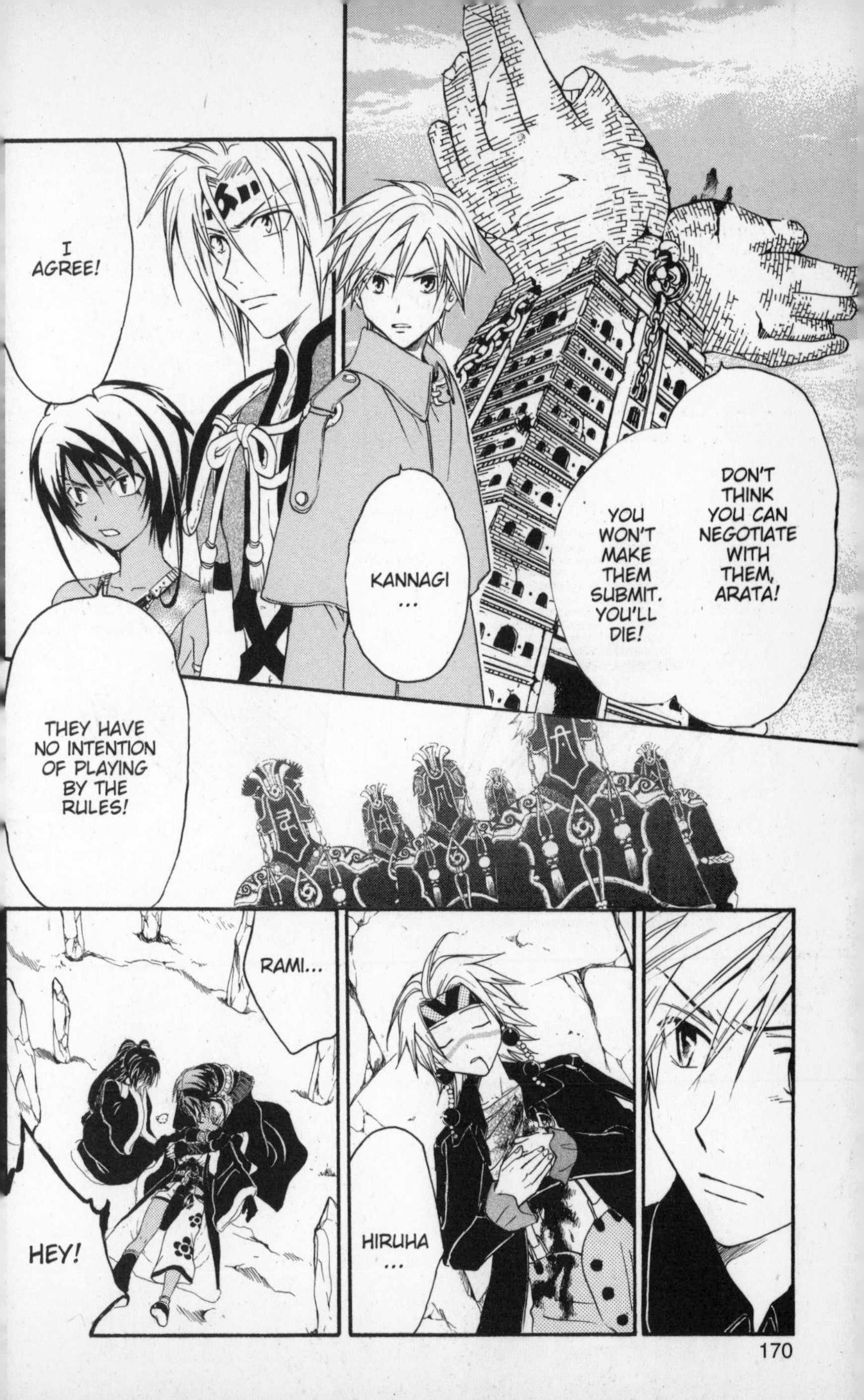
DON'T THINK YOU CAN NEGOTIATE WITH THEM, ARATA!
YOU WON'T MAKE THEM SUBMIT. YOU'LL DIE!
KANNAGI ...
I AGREE!
THEY HAVE NO INTENTION OF PLAYING BY THE RULES!
HIRUHA ...
RAMI...
HEY!

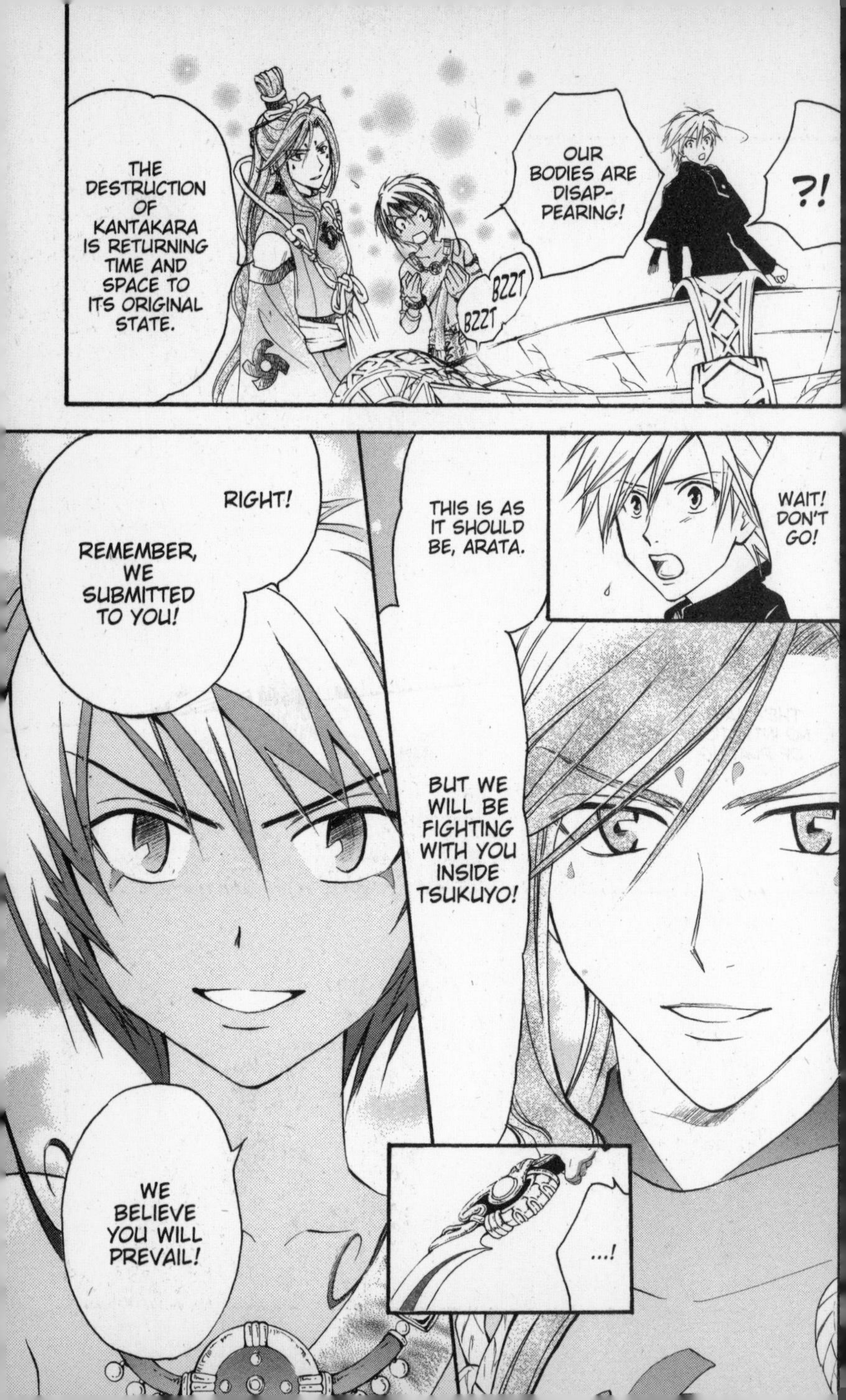
?!
OUR BODIES ARE DISAP-PEARING!
BZZT
BZZT
THE DESTRUCTION OF KANTAKARA IS RETURNING TIME AND SPACE TO ITS ORIGINAL STATE.
WAIT! DON'T GO!
THIS IS AS IT SHOULD BE, ARATA.
BUT WE WILL BE FIGHTING WITH YOU INSIDE TSUKUYO!
RIGHT!
REMEMBER, WE SUBMITTED TO YOU!
WE BELIEVE YOU WILL PREVAIL!
...!

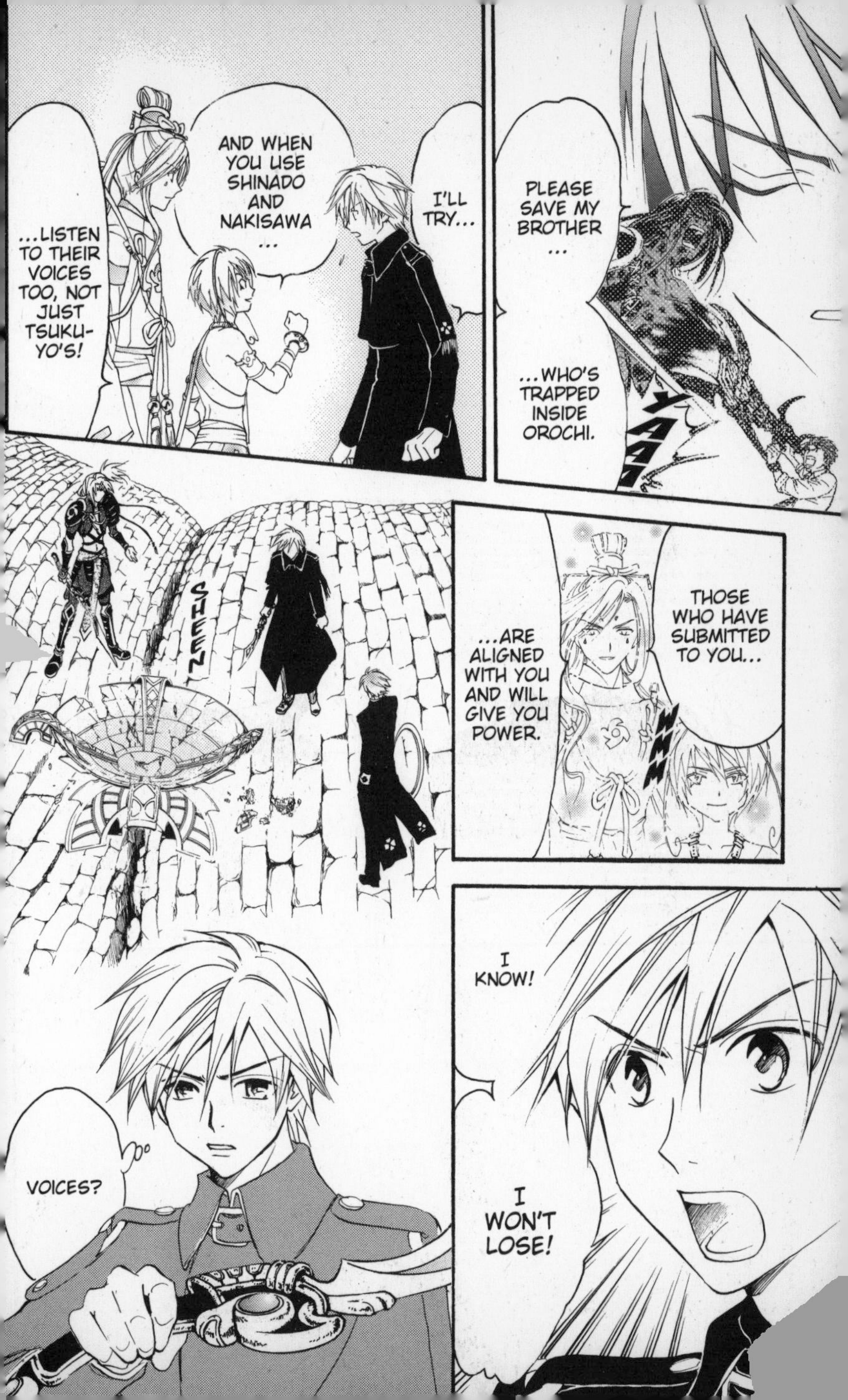

PLEASE SAVE MY BROTHER ...
...WHO'S TRAPPED INSIDE OROCHI.
YAAA
I'LL TRY...
AND WHEN YOU USE SHINADO AND NAKISAWA ...
...LISTEN TO THEIR VOICES TOO, NOT JUST TSUKUYO'S!
THOSE WHO HAVE SUBMITTED TO YOU...
...ARE ALIGNED WITH YOU AND WILL GIVE YOU POWER.
SHEEN
I KNOW!
I WON'T LOSE!
VOICES?

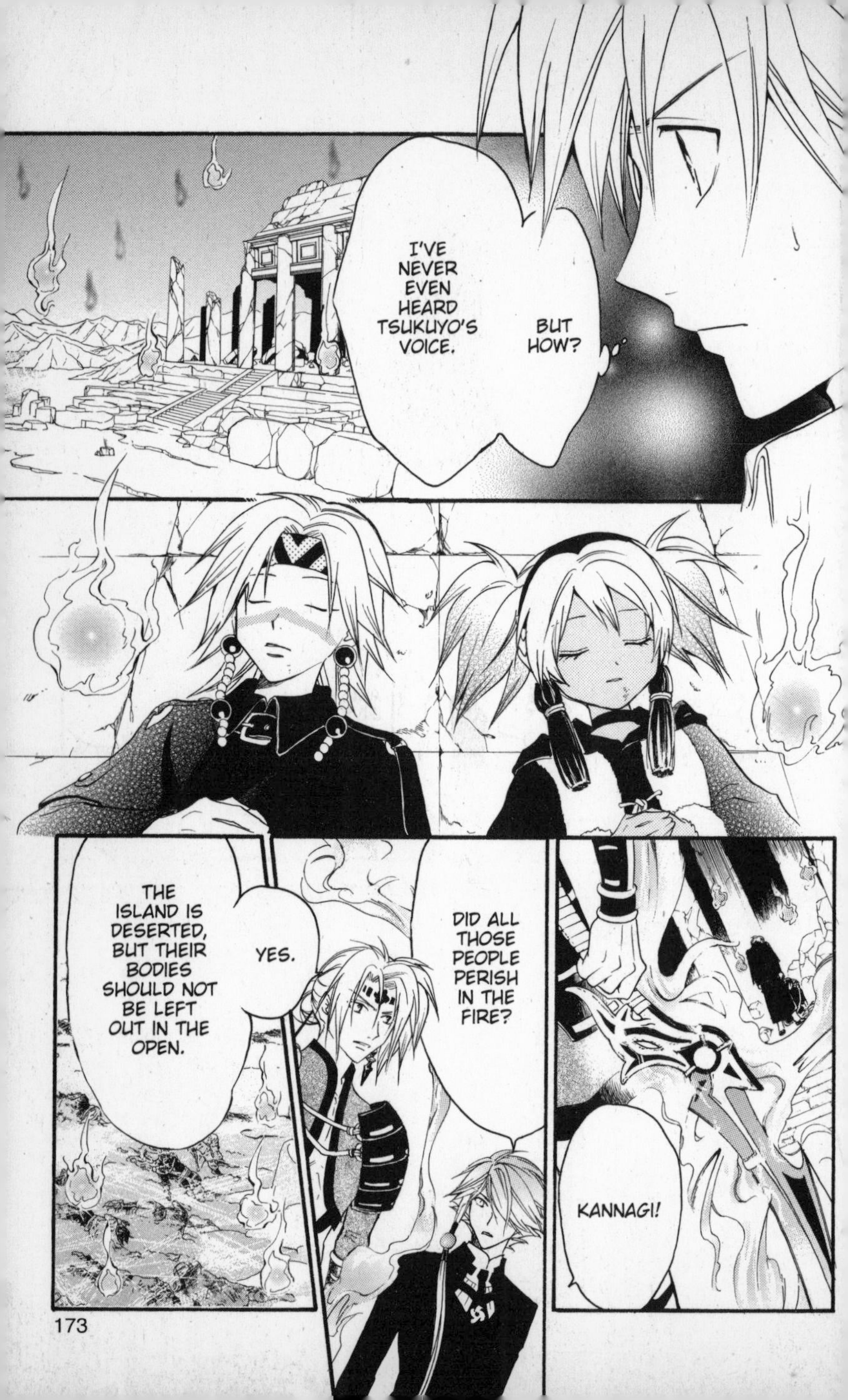
BUT HOW?
I'VE NEVER EVEN HEARD TSUKUYO'S VOICE.
KANNAGI!
DID ALL THOSE PEOPLE PERISH IN THE FIRE?
YES.
THE ISLAND IS DESERTED, BUT THEIR BODIES SHOULD NOT BE LEFT OUT IN THE OPEN.

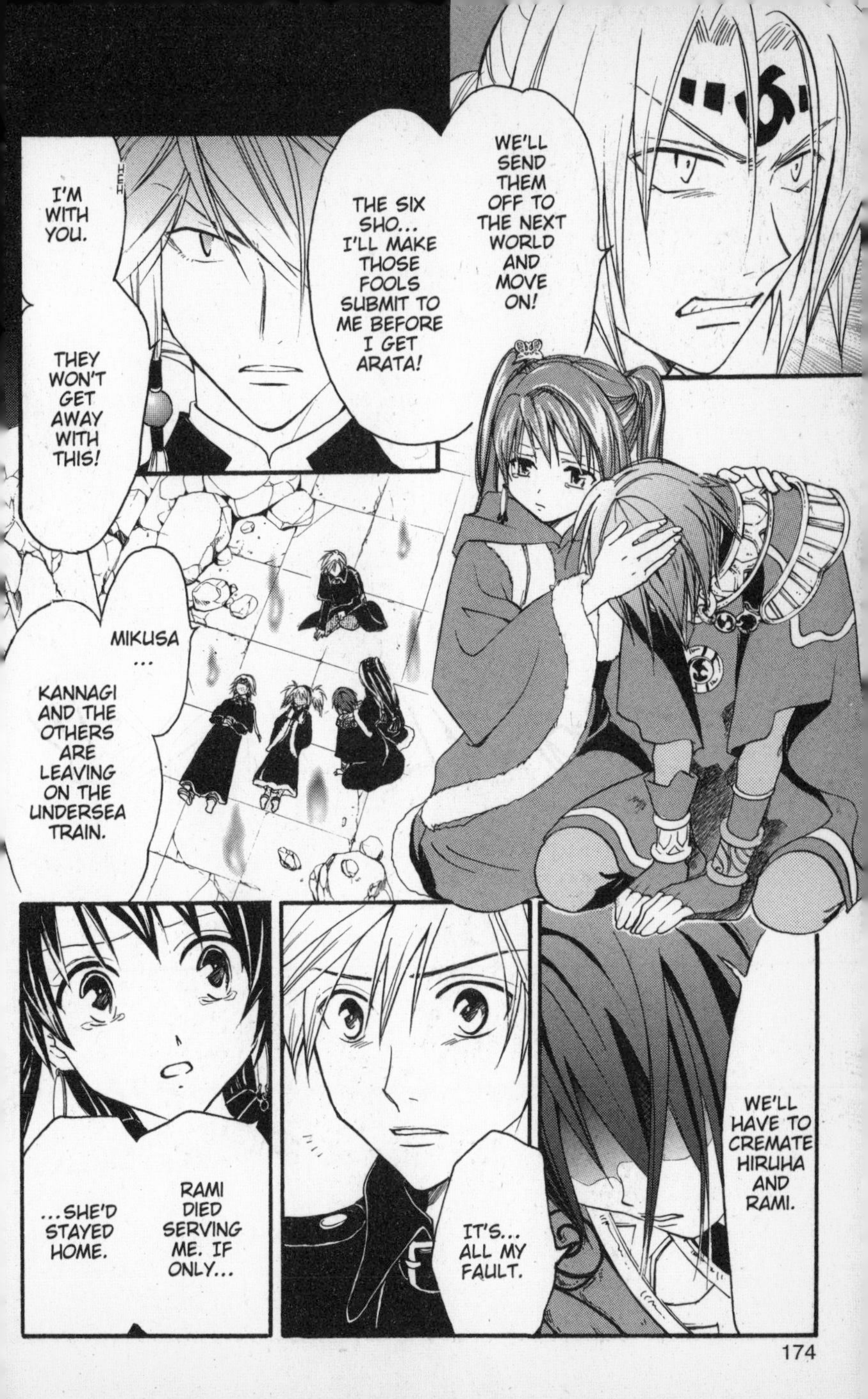
WE'LL SEND THEM OFF TO THE NEXT WORLD AND MOVE ON!
THE SIX SHO... I'LL MAKE THOSE FOOLS SUBMIT TO ME BEFORE I GET ARATA!
HEH
I'M WITH YOU.
THEY WON'T GET AWAY WITH THIS!
MIKUSA...
KANNAGI AND THE OTHERS ARE LEAVING ON THE UNDERSEA TRAIN.
WE'LL HAVE TO CREMATE HIRUHA AND RAMI.
IT'S... ALL MY FAULT.
RAMI DIED SERVING ME. IF ONLY...
...SHE'D STAYED HOME.

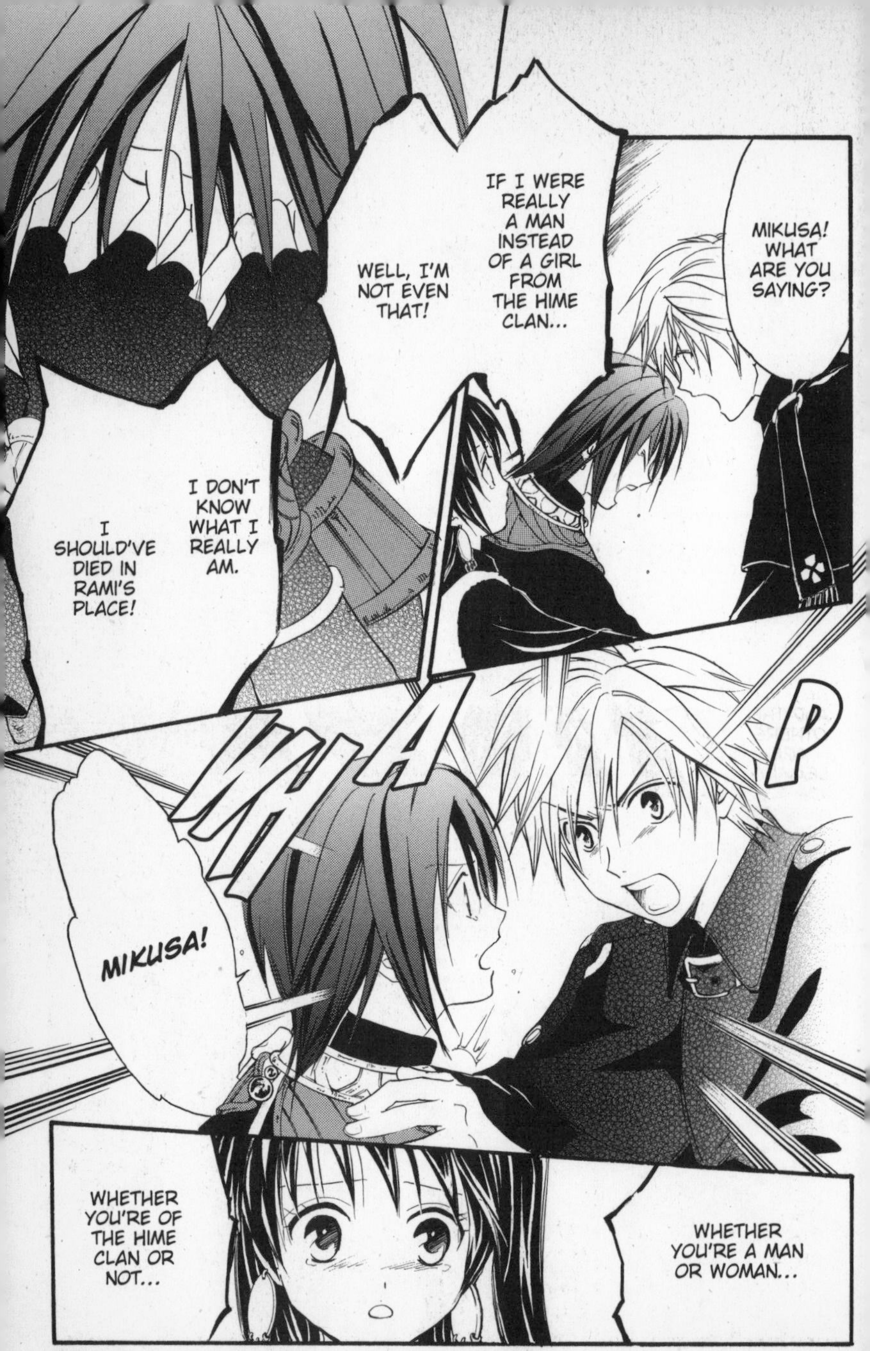
MIKUSA! WHAT ARE YOU SAYING?
IF I WERE REALLY A MAN INSTEAD OF A GIRL FROM THE HIME CLAN...
WELL, I'M NOT EVEN THAT!
I DON'T KNOW WHAT I REALLY AM.
I SHOULD'VE DIED IN RAMI'S PLACE!
WHAP
MIKUSA!
WHETHER YOU'RE A MAN OR WOMAN...
WHETHER YOU'RE OF THE HIME CLAN OR NOT...

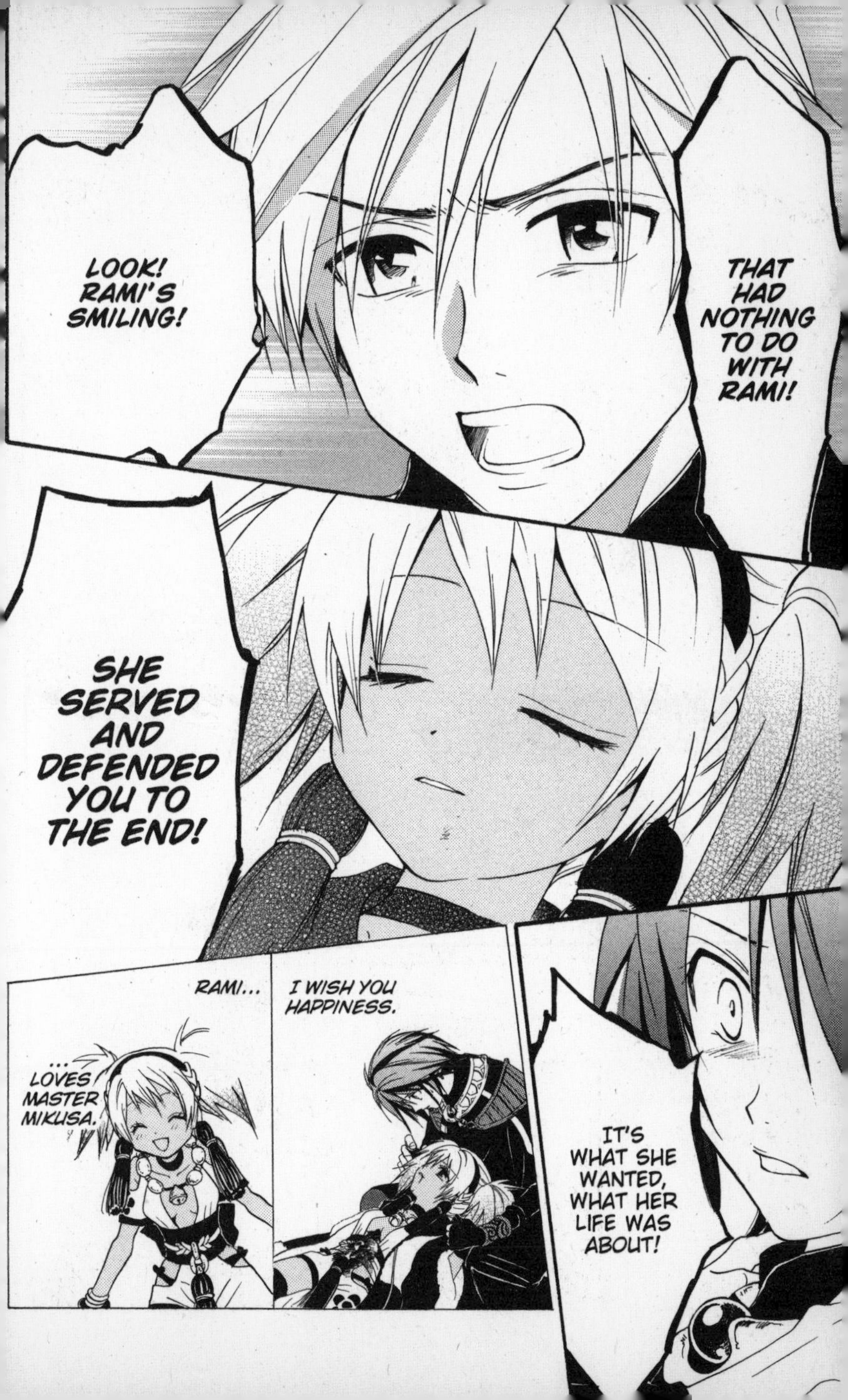
THAT HAD NOTHING TO DO WITH RAMI!
LOOK! RAMI'S SMILING!
SHE SERVED AND DEFENDED YOU TO THE END!
IT'S WHAT SHE WANTED, WHAT HER LIFE WAS ABOUT!
I WISH YOU HAPPINESS.
RAMI...
...LOVES MASTER MIKUSA.

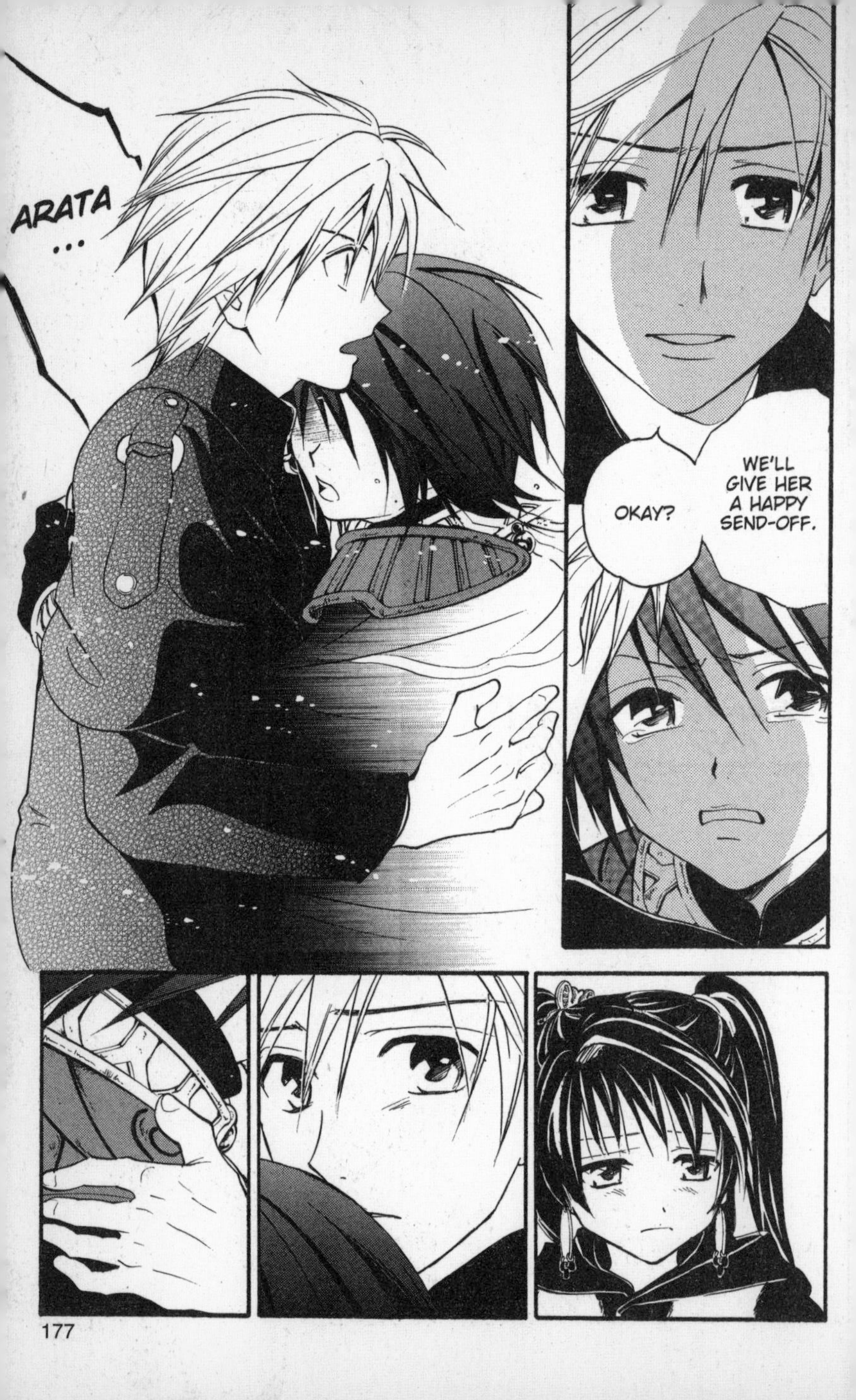
WE'LL GIVE HER A HAPPY SEND-OFF.
OKAY?
ARATA ...

I'M SORRY, MIKUSA, I...

...WASN'T ABLE TO DO ANYTHING FOR YOU.

VRUMB

CHUG CHUG

CHUG

CHUG

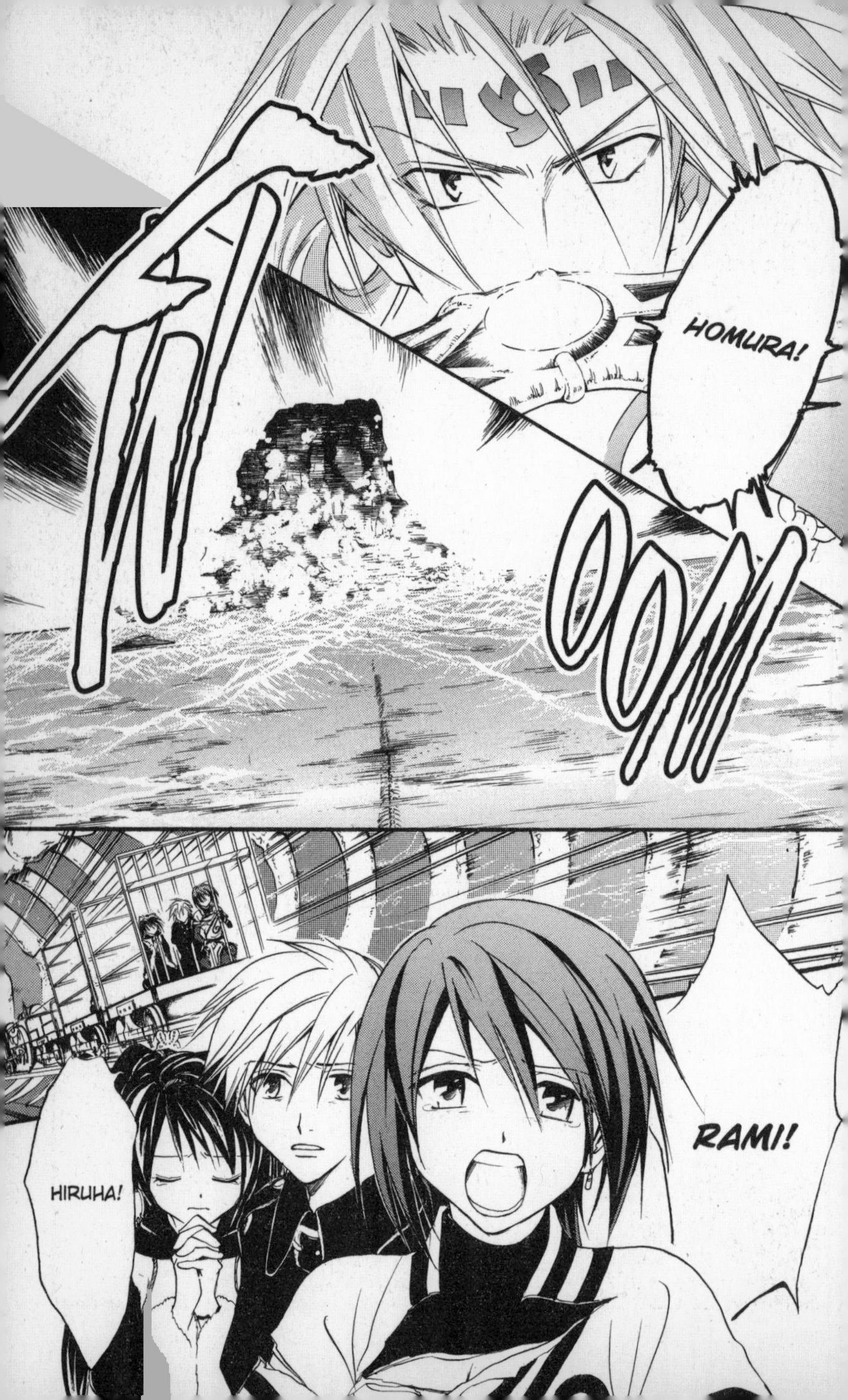
HOMURA!
RAMI!
HIRUHA!

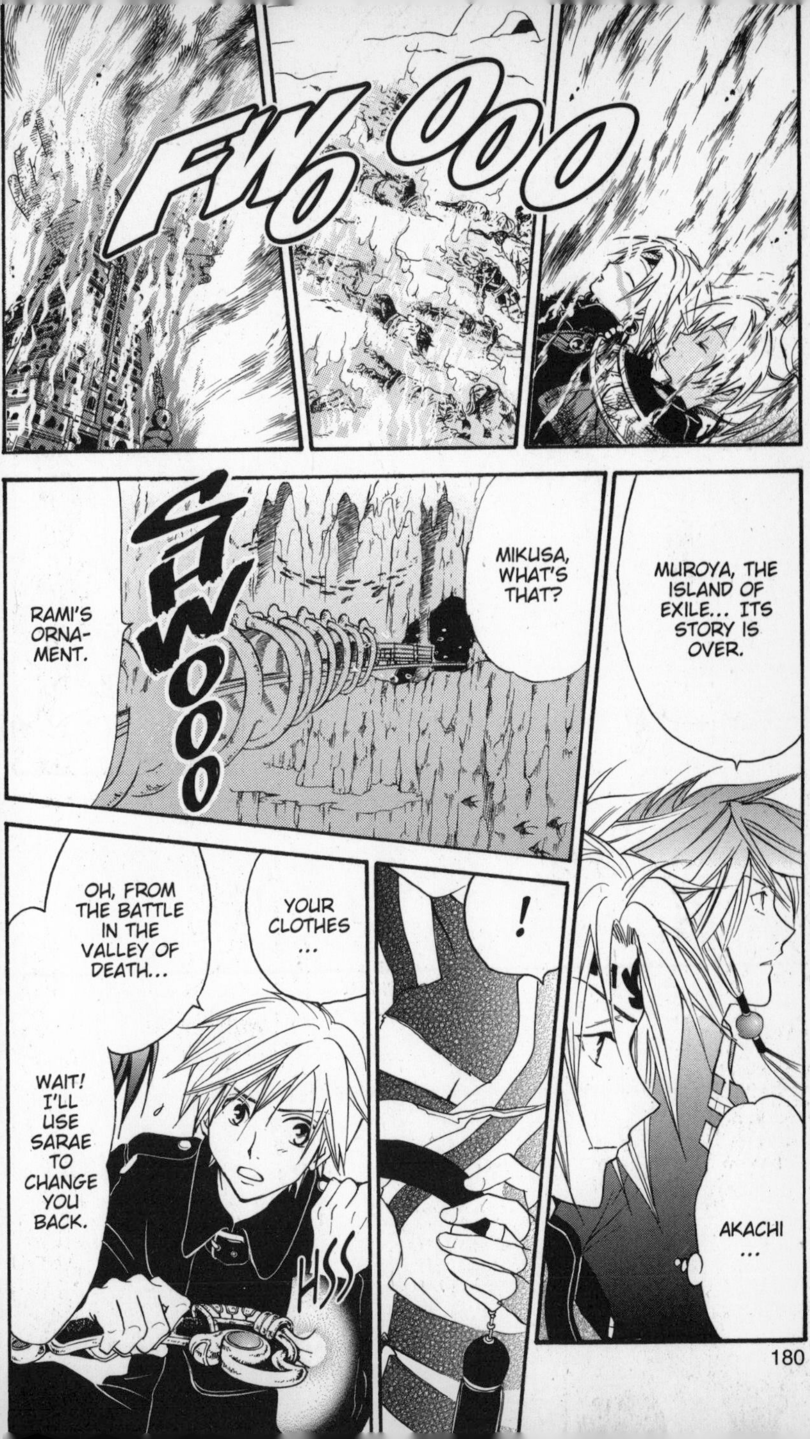
FWOOOO
MUROYA, THE ISLAND OF EXILE... ITS STORY IS OVER.
MIKUSA, WHAT'S THAT?
SWOOO
RAMI'S ORNA-MENT.
AKACHI ...
!
YOUR CLOTHES ...
OH, FROM THE BATTLE IN THE VALLEY OF DEATH...
WAIT! I'LL USE SARAE TO CHANGE YOU BACK.
HSS

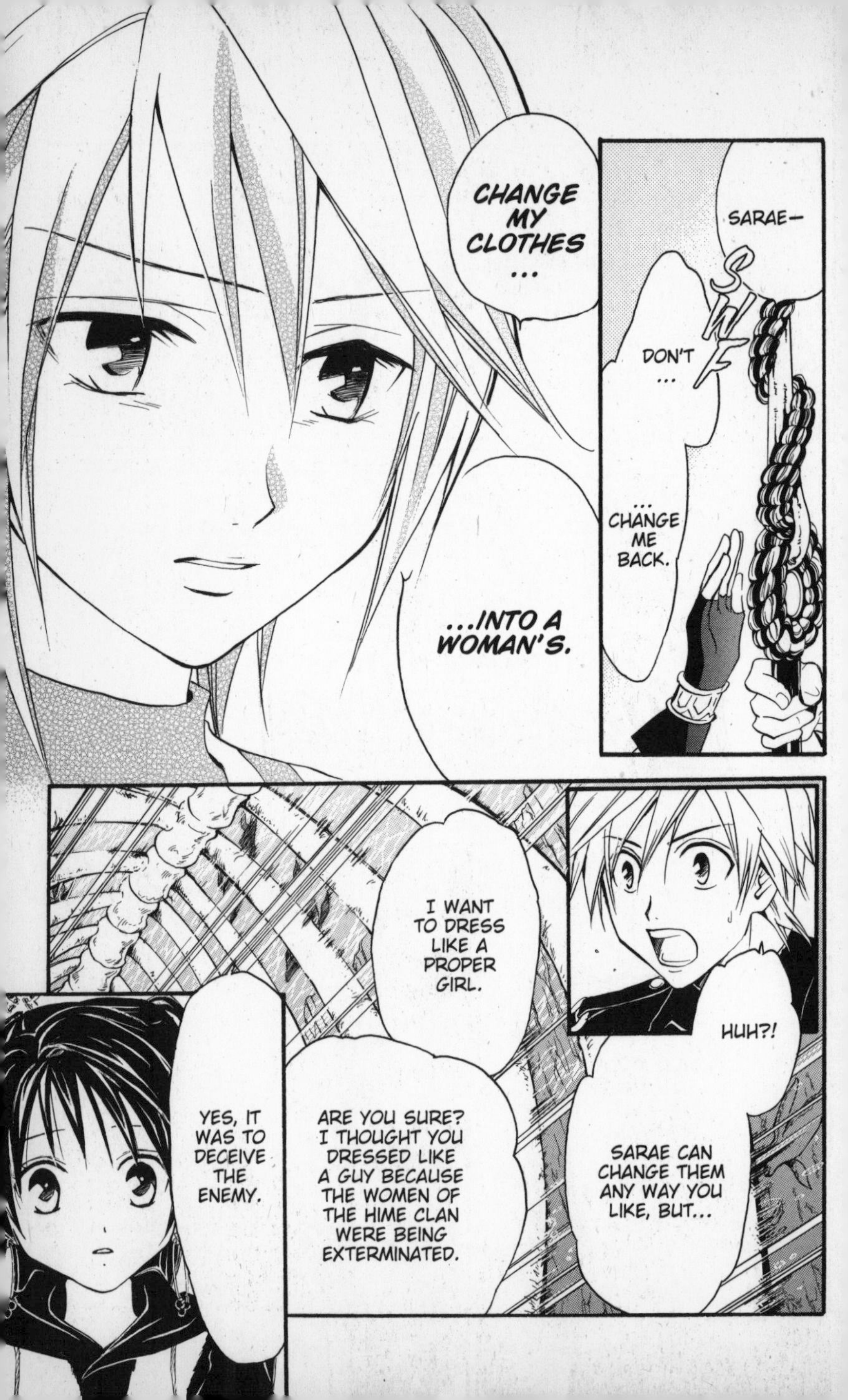
SARAE—
SWF
DON'T ...
... CHANGE ME BACK.
CHANGE MY CLOTHES ...
...INTO A WOMAN'S.
I WANT TO DRESS LIKE A PROPER GIRL.
HUH?!
SARAE CAN CHANGE THEM ANY WAY YOU LIKE, BUT...
ARE YOU SURE? I THOUGHT YOU DRESSED LIKE A GUY BECAUSE THE WOMEN OF THE HIME CLAN WERE BEING EXTERMINATED.
YES, IT WAS TO DECEIVE THE ENEMY.

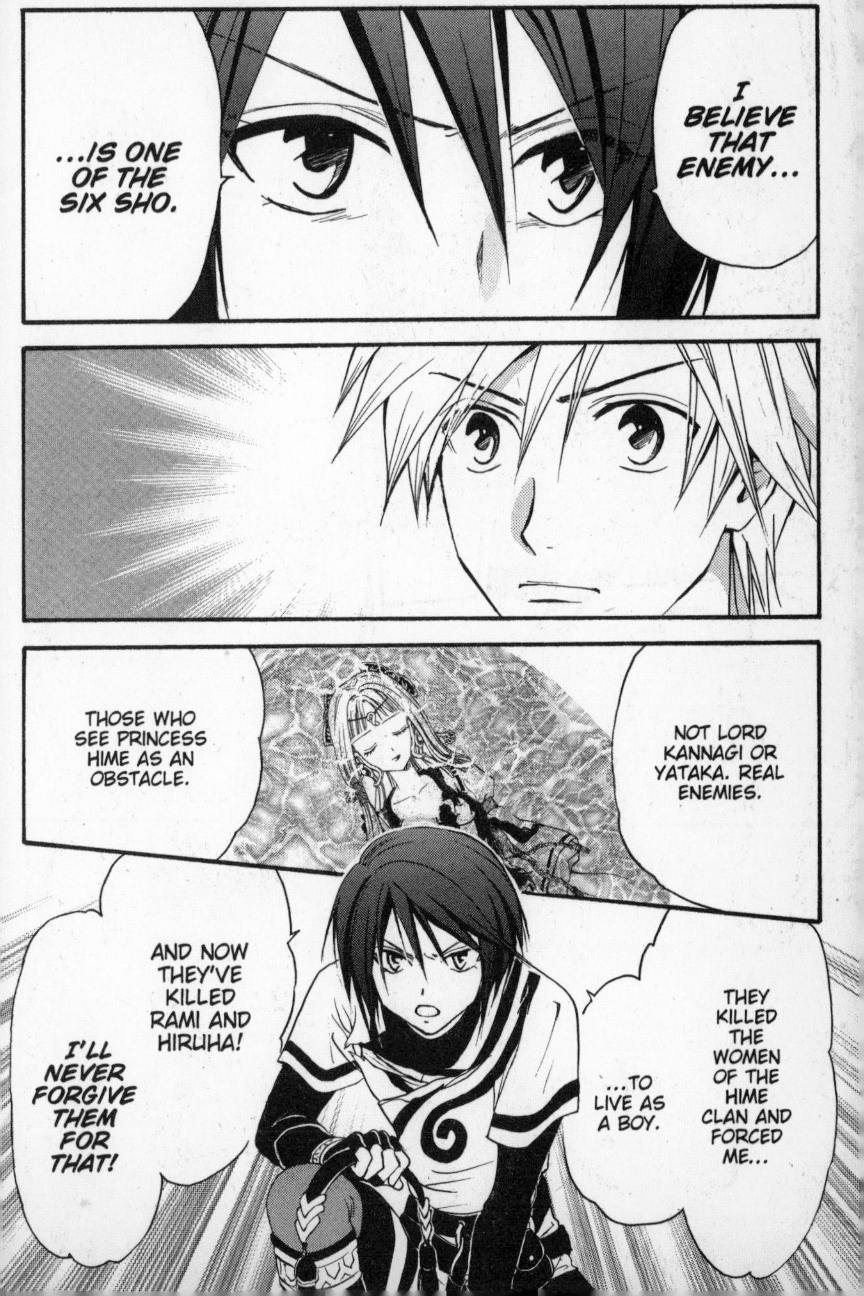
I BELIEVE THAT ENEMY...
...IS ONE OF THE SIX SHO.
NOT LORD KANNAGI OR YATAKA. REAL ENEMIES.
THOSE WHO SEE PRINCESS HIME AS AN OBSTACLE.
THEY KILLED THE WOMEN OF THE HIME CLAN AND FORCED ME...
...TO LIVE AS A BOY.
AND NOW THEY'VE KILLED RAMI AND HIRUHA!
I'LL NEVER FORGIVE THEM FOR THAT!

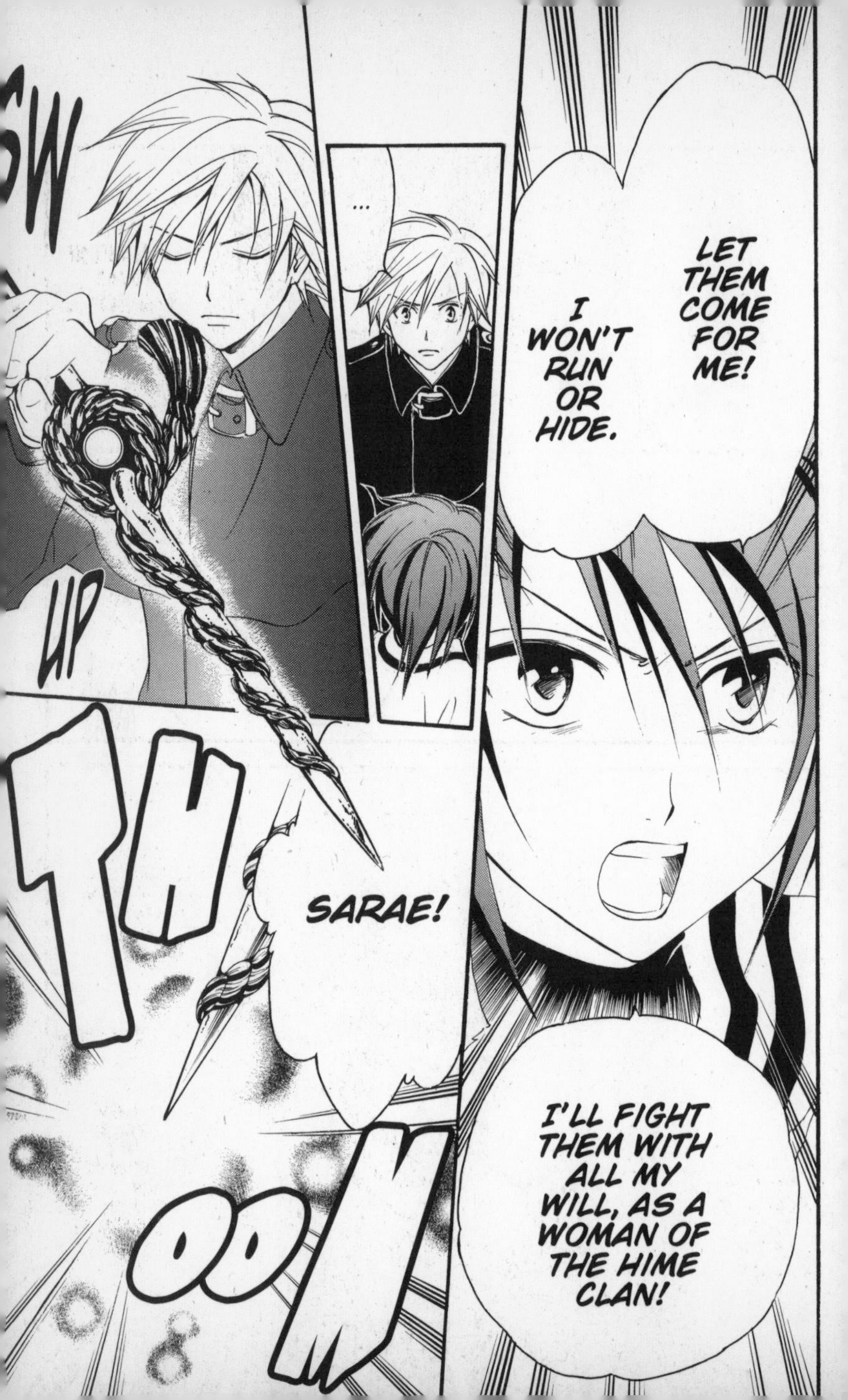
LET THEM COME FOR ME!
I WON'T RUN OR HIDE.
I'LL FIGHT THEM WITH ALL MY WILL, AS A WOMAN OF THE HIME CLAN!
...
SWUP
SARAE!
THOOM

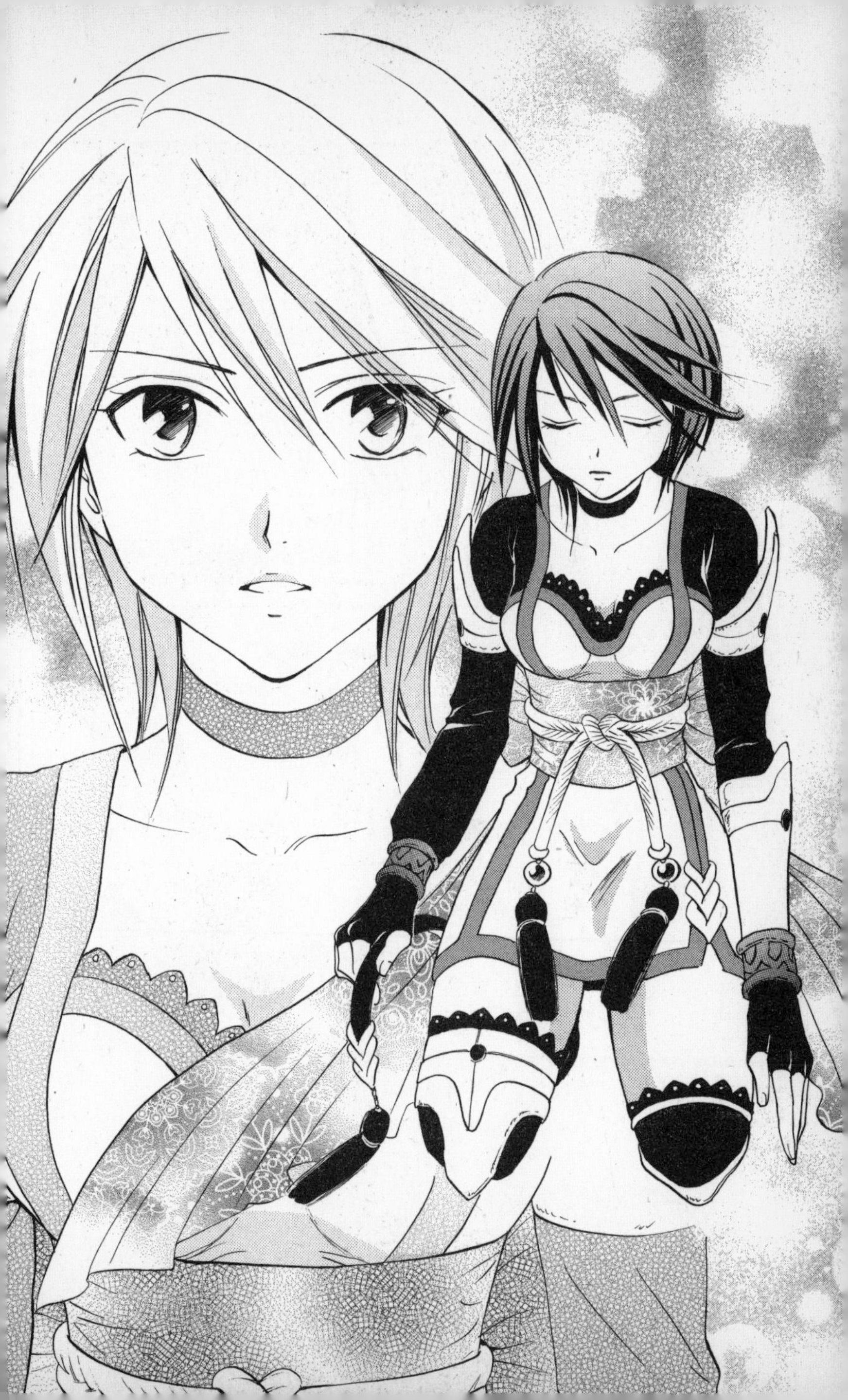

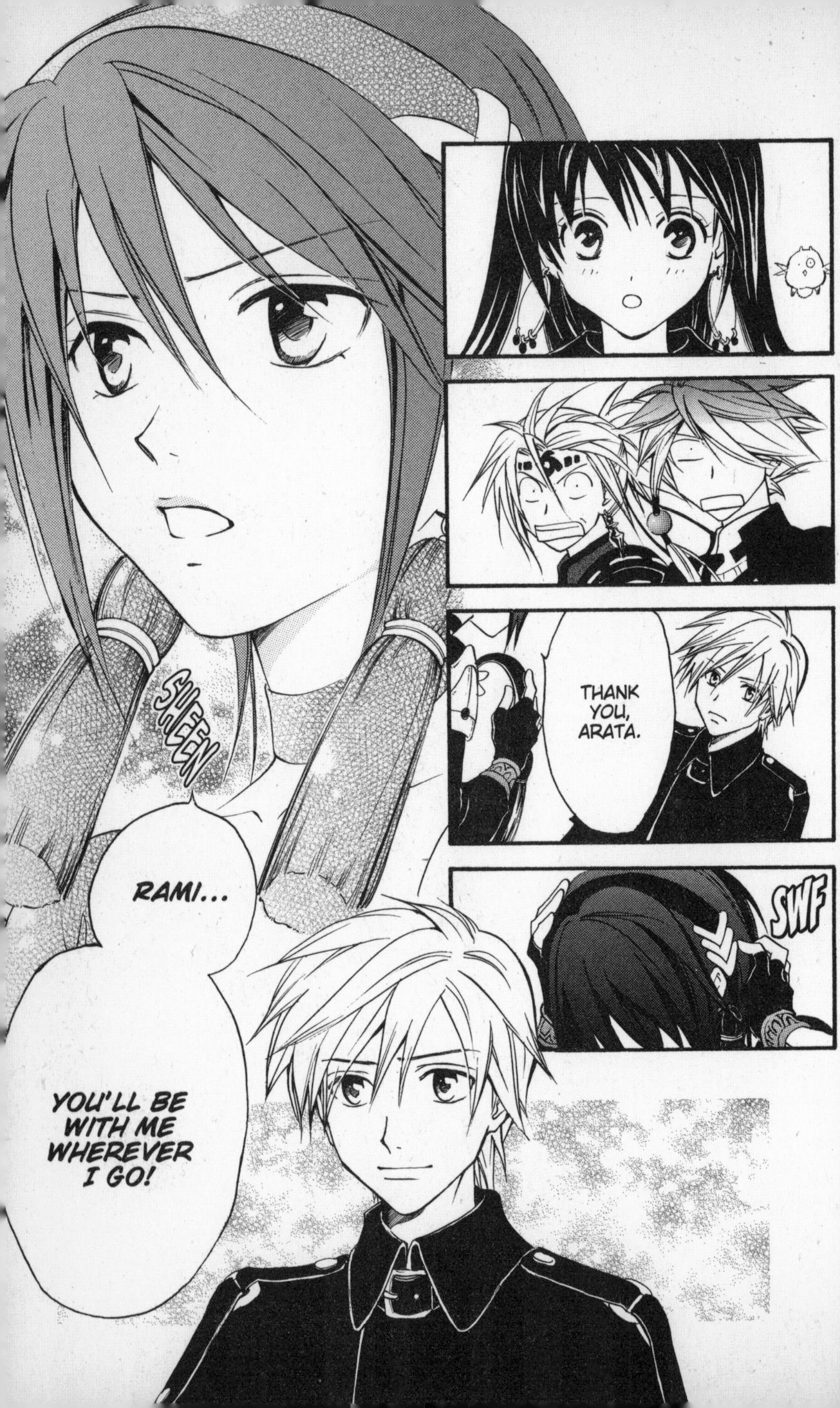
THANK YOU, ARATA.
SWF
SHEEN
RAMI...
YOU'LL BE WITH ME WHEREVER I GO!

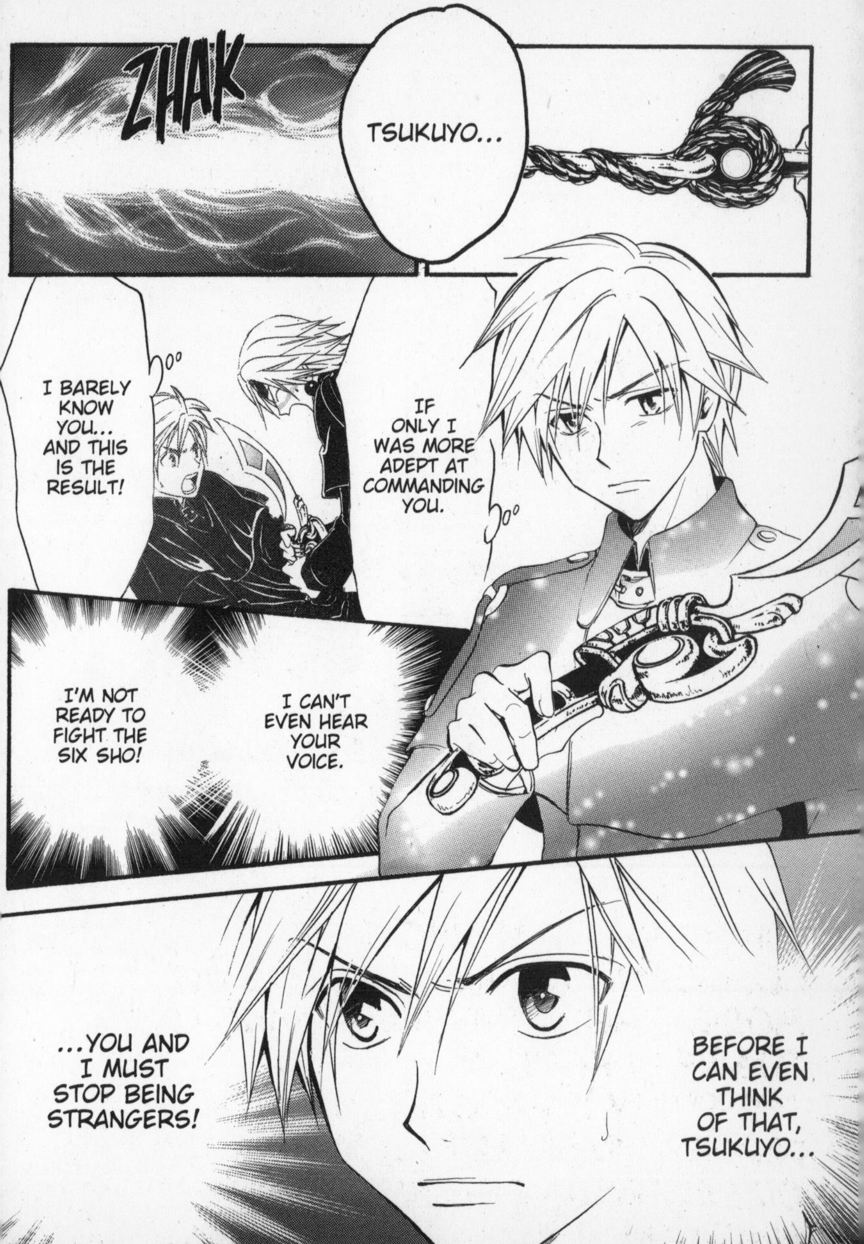
TSUKUYO...
ZHAK
IF ONLY I WAS MORE ADEPT AT COMMANDING YOU.
I BARELY KNOW YOU... AND THIS IS THE RESULT!
I CAN'T EVEN HEAR YOUR VOICE.
I'M NOT READY TO FIGHT THE SIX SHO!
BEFORE I CAN EVEN THINK OF THAT, TSUKUYO...
...YOU AND I MUST STOP BEING STRANGERS!

ARATA: THE LEGEND 14 (THE END)

• MY ASSISTANTS CONTRIBUTED THE FOLLOWING COMMENTS/ILLUSTRATIONS! THANK YOU!

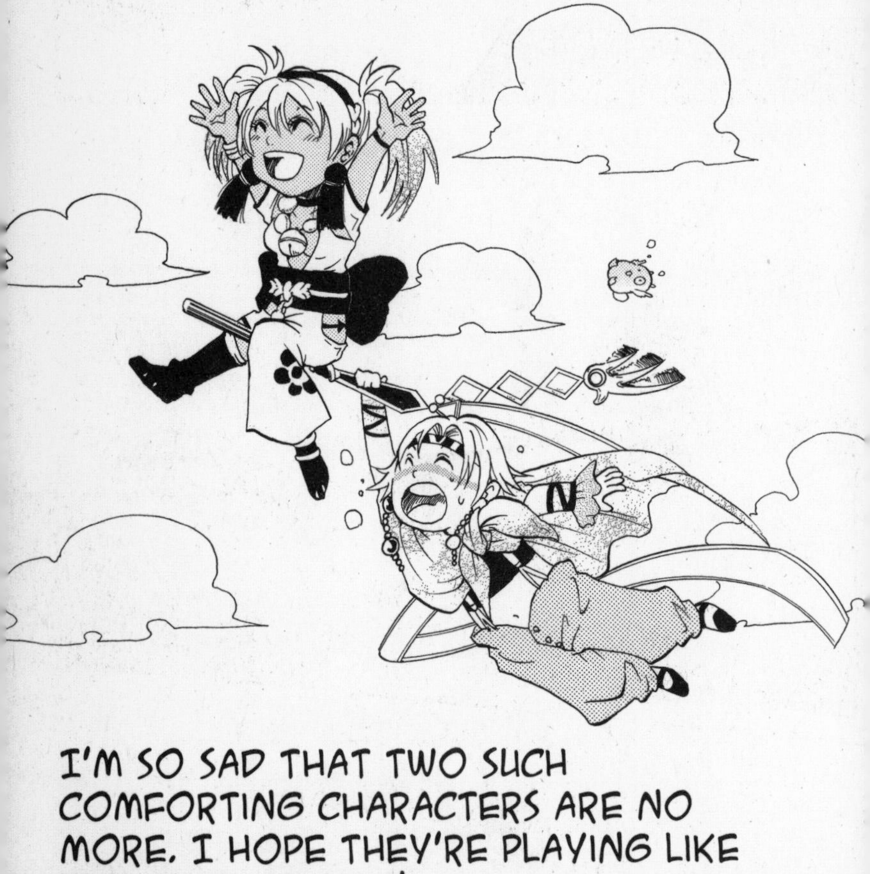

I'M SO SAD THAT TWO SUCH COMFORTING CHARACTERS ARE NO MORE. I HOPE THEY'RE PLAYING LIKE THIS UP IN HEAVEN!
THE STORY IS PROGRESSING AT A FRENETIC PACE! LET'S CONTINUE ON OUR ADVENTURE TOGETHER WITH ARATA!

BY RANYA

CONGRATULATIONS ON THE
COMPLETION OF VOLUME 14!

ON MY FIRST DAY AS AN ASSISTANT, HIRUHA DIED...AND I'D ONLY JUST MET HIM! BOTH RAMI AND HIRUHA HAD AMAZING HEALING POWERS. THEIR PRESENCE WAS SO WARM AND FUZZY. THEY WERE SO CUTE! I HOPE THEY ARE HAPPY IN A NICE, WARM PLACE.

ASSISTANT N

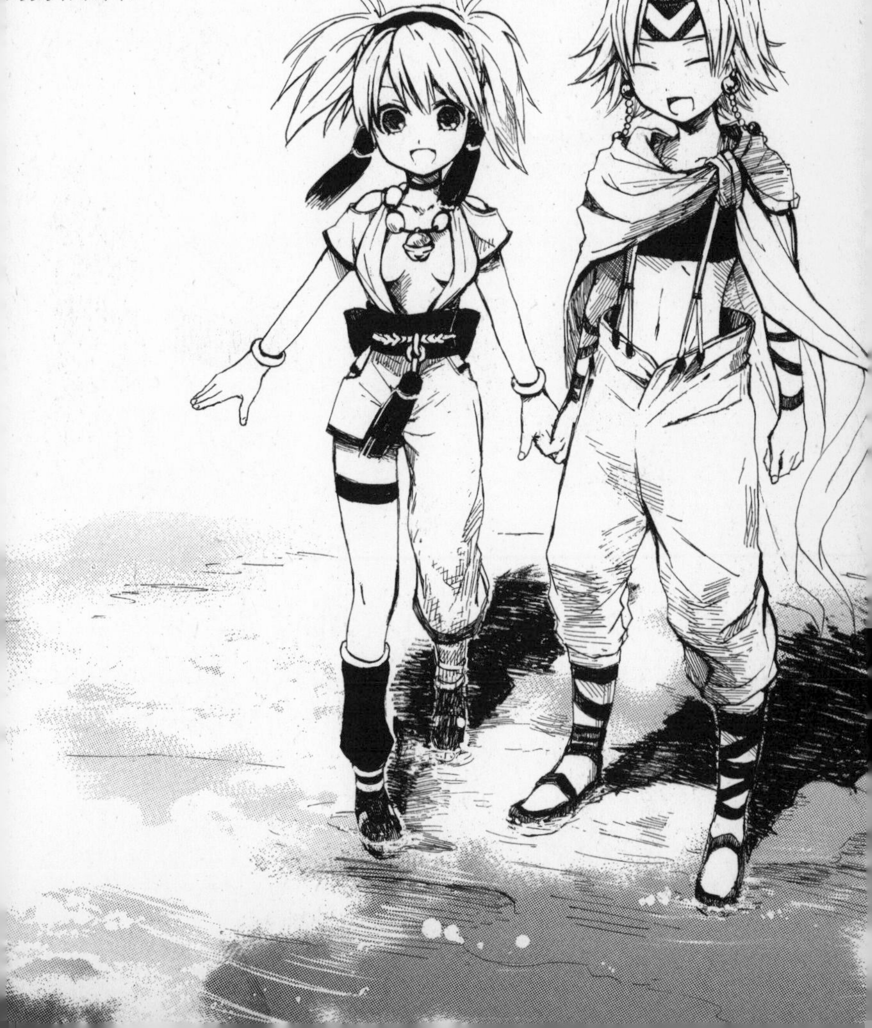

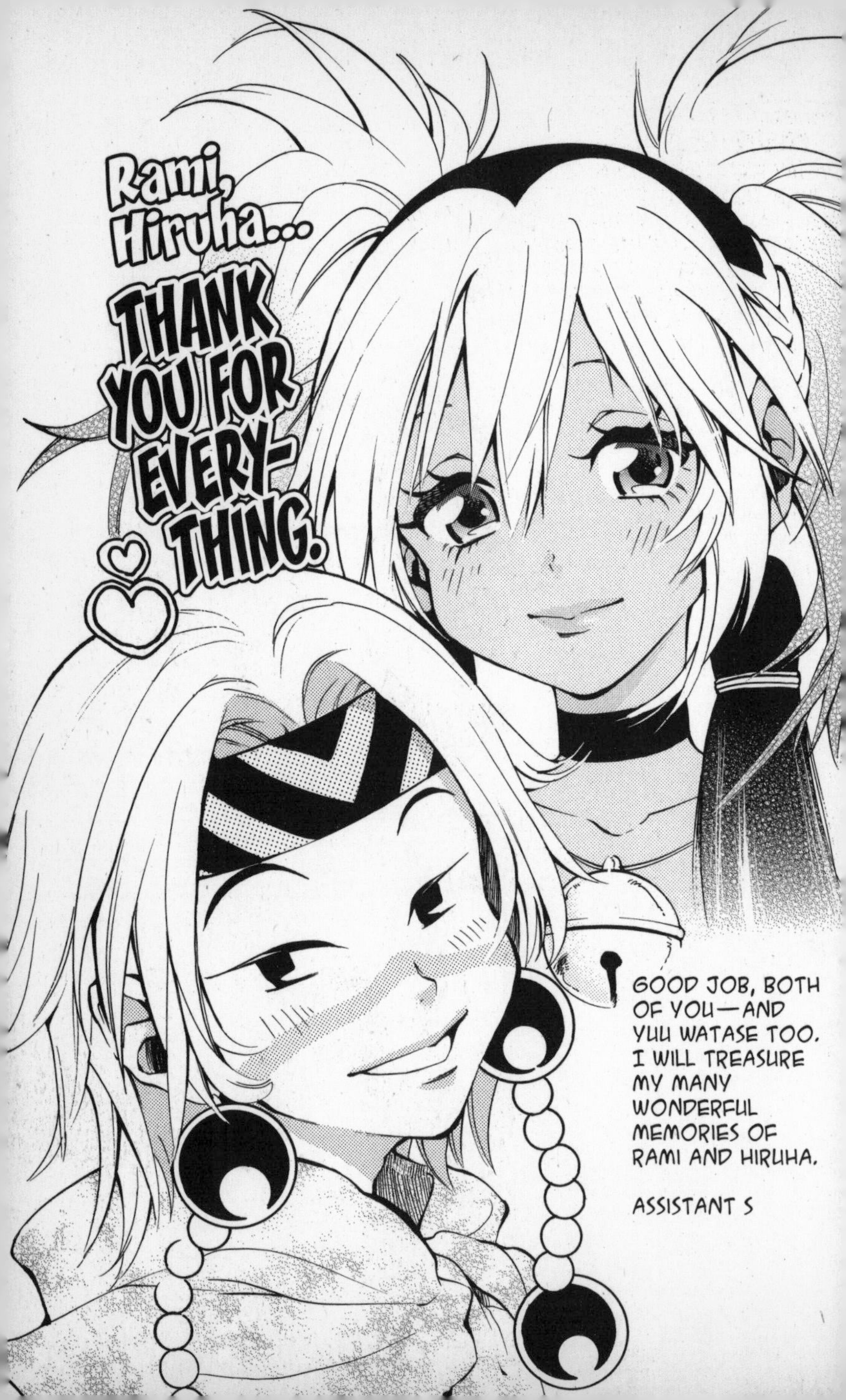
Rami, Hiruha...
THANK YOU FOR EVERY-THING.
GOOD JOB, BOTH OF YOU—AND YUU WATASE TOO. I WILL TREASURE MY MANY WONDERFUL MEMORIES OF RAMI AND HIRUHA.
ASSISTANT S

I recently wrote that I had moved. Well, I've moved again! It's not like a ghost appeared or anything, but...I guess I like to be free as a bird... (?)

Anyway, I'm ready to start anew in body and spirit.

Arata is also undergoing renewal as of this volume. Friends often tell me that there's a connection between reality and what's happening with my characters. Well, I'm done with worrying!

Out of hardship comes joy! It starts now! For Arata, for me, and everyone—don't worry, don't worry!

–Yuu Watase

AUTHOR BIO

Born March 5 in Osaka, Yuu Watase debuted in the *Shôjo Comic* manga anthology in 1989. She won the 43rd Shogakukan Manga Award with *Ceres: Celestial Legend*. One of her most famous works is *Fushigi Yûgi*, a series that has inspired the prequel *Fushigi Yûgi: Genbu Kaiden*. In 2008, *Arata: The Legend* started serialization in *Shonen Sunday*.

ARATA: THE LEGEND

Volume 14

Shonen Sunday Edition

Story and Art by YUU WATASE

ARATAKANGATARI Vol. 14
by Yuu WATASE
© 2009 Yuu WATASE
All rights reserved.
Original Japanese edition published by SHOGAKUKAN.
English translation rights in the United States of America,
Canada, the United Kingdom and Ireland arranged with
SHOGAKUKAN.

English Adaptation: Lance Caselman
Translation: JN Productions
Touch-up Art & Lettering: Rina Mapa
Design: Ronnie Casson
Editor: Gary Leach

Printed in Canada

Published by VIZ Media, LLC
P.O. Box 77010
San Francisco, CA 94107

10 9 8 7 6 5 4 3 2 1
First printing, June 2013

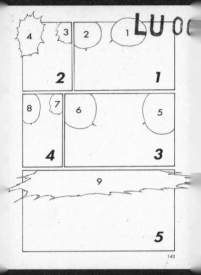

142

← Follow the action this way

HIS IS THE LAST PAC

ta: The Legend has been printed in
inal Japanese format in order to pres
orientation of the original artwork.

se turn it around and begin reading f
t to left. Unlike English, Japanese is read r
eft, so Japanese comics are read in reverse
from the way English comics are typi
. Have fun with it!